Shakespeare's
HAMLET

THE **MANGA EDITION**

Shakespeare's
HAMLET

THE MANGA EDITION

Adam Sexton • Tintin Pantoja

WILEY

Wiley Publishing, Inc.

Published by Wiley Publishing, Inc., Hoboken, New Jersey

Library of Congress Control Number: 2007940615

ISBN: 978-0-470-09757-1

Printed in the United States of America

10 9 8 7 6 5 4 3 2 1

Book design by Elizabeth Brooks
Book production by Wiley Publishing, Inc. Composition Services

CONTENTS

Adam Sexton is the author of *Master Class in Fiction Writing* and the editor of the anthologies *Love Stories, Rap on Rap,* and *Desperately Seeking Madonna.* He has written on art and entertainment for *The New York Times* and *The Village Voice,* and he teaches fiction writing and literature at New York University and critical reading and writing at Parsons School of Design. A graduate of Columbia University and the University of Pennsylvania, he lives in Brooklyn with his wife and son.

Tintin Pantoja is a graphic artist dividing her time between Indonesia and Manila. She graduated from the School of Visual Arts in New York in 2006, having arrived in New York—her first time in America—a month before the World Trade Center attacks in 2001. She is now working on several illustrated projects. Tintin's work can be viewed on her Web site: tintin pantoja.com

Suiting the Action to the Word: Shakespeare and Manga

by Adam Sexton

"Suit the action to the word, the word to the action..."
—*Hamlet* (Act III, Scene 2)

Four hundred years after the writing of William Shakespeare's plays, it is clear that they are timeless. This is due in part to their infinite adaptability. The plays have been translated into dozens of languages and performed all over the world. Famously creative stage productions have included a version of *Julius Caesar* set in Fascist Europe during the 1930s and a so-called "voodoo *Macbeth*." Nor have gender and age proved barriers to casting Shakespeare's characters. The role of Hamlet is occasionally played by a woman—an appropriate reversal, considering that boys acted all the female roles in Shakespeare's day—while the teenaged Romeo and Juliet have been portrayed by couples in their forties and fifties.

It is common knowledge that the plays of Shakespeare transfer especially well to the movie screen. Such has been the case since Thomas Edison made one of the first sound films ever using a scene from *As You Like It*. Recent cinema standouts include *William Shakespeare's Romeo + Juliet*, directed by Baz Luhrmann, and Michael Almereyda's *Hamlet*. Both take place in the present day or near future: Leonardo DiCaprio's Romeo wears a Hawaiian shirt—and Julia Stiles' Ophelia wears a wire, so Claudius and Polonius can eavesdrop on her conversation with Hamlet. Otherwise, these adaptations remain surprisingly faithful to Shakespeare's texts. And both hit the audience as hard as conventional stage productions in which the actors are outfitted with doublets and hose, crossed swords, and what Hamlet calls "a bare bodkin"—his unsheathed dagger (replaced in Almereyda's movie by a gun).

Shakespeare's plays have been set to music as well, in operas and ballets by composers such as Verdi, Tchaikovsky, and Prokofiev. The early comedy *Two Gentlemen of Verona* was adapted for Broadway by the composer of *Hair*, and it won the Tony award for Best Musical the same year that *Grease* was nominated. In the words of theater critic Jan Kott, Shakespeare is indeed "our contemporary."

In short, though some consider the plays of William Shakespeare to be sacrosanct, they have been cut, expanded (it was common in the Victorian era to add songs and even happy endings to the tragedies), and adapted to multiple media, emerging none the worse for wear. Although we cannot be sure of this, it seems likely that the writer, who was a popular artist and a savvy businessman as well as an incomparable poet, would approve.

The graphic novels known as *manga* (Japanese for "whimsical pictures") are a natural medium for Shakespeare's work. Like his tragedies, comedies, histories, and romances, which are thrillingly dynamic if properly staged, manga are of course visual. In fact, a manga is potentially *more* visual than a stage production of one of the plays of Shakespeare. Unbound by the physical realities of the theater, the graphic novel can depict any situation, no matter how fantastical or violent, that its creators are able to pencil, ink, and shade.

Take *Romeo and Juliet*'s famous Queen Mab speech. Even the most creative stage director cannot faithfully present the minuscule fairy described by Mercutio. Manga artists can. The same is true of the drowning of Ophelia in *Hamlet*. It is precisely because these vignettes are unstageable that Shakespeare has his characters describe Queen Mab and the death of Ophelia in such great detail—they must help us imagine them. In its unlimited ability to dramatize, the graphic novel more closely resembles a contemporary film with a colossal special-effects budget than anything produced in the Elizabethan era or since.

At the same time, manga are potentially no less verbal than Shakespeare's spectacularly wordy plays, with this crucial difference: in a production of one of the plays onstage or onscreen, we can hear the words but can't see them. Though Shakespeare is never easy, reading helps. And that is precisely what manga adaptations of the plays allow. Perusing a Shakespeare manga, the reader can linger over speeches, rereading them in part or altogether. Especially in the long and intricate soliloquies typical of Shakespearean tragedy, this allows for an appreciation of the playwright's craft that is difficult if not impossible as those soliloquies move past us during a performance.

Overall, turning the pages of a manga version of one of Shakespeare's plays is something like reading the text of that play while attending a performance, but at one's own pace. Manga is not merely a new medium for the plays of William Shakespeare, but one that is distinctly different from anything to have come before.

A note on authenticity: In order to fit our adaptations into books of less than 200 pages, the writers and editors of *The Manga Editions* have cut words, lines, speeches, even entire scenes from Shakespeare's plays, a practice almost universal among stage and film directors. We have never paraphrased the playwright's language, however, nor have we summarized action. Everything you read in *The Manga Editions* was written by William Shakespeare himself. Finally, footnotes don't interrupt the characters' speeches here, any more than they would in a production of one of Shakespeare's plays onstage or on film.

There is no play better suited to the *manga* approach than *Hamlet*, Shakespeare's tragedy about Hamlet, prince of Denmark, who is instructed by the ghost of his father, King Hamlet, to kill his Uncle Claudius. Since murdering Hamlet's father, Claudius has become king of Denmark himself and has married Hamlet's mother, Queen Gertrude. Prince Hamlet has a girlfriend, Ophelia, who is the daughter of Claudius's most trusted advisor (Polonius) and the sister of Hamlet's rival, Laertes. Hamlet's best friend, Horatio, and two college chums, Rosencrantz and Guildenstern, visit him during the play. Of all these characters, only one survives to the end of the story.

The play is manga-friendly because it is unarguably action-packed, complete with a terrifying ghost, a tussle in an open grave, and a climactic swordfight during which four central characters die violent deaths. At least one character in *Hamlet* goes insane and two characters commit suicide, one of them by accident. There's an inadvertent murder, as well as two accomplished from afar, by trickery. Another murder, achieved by pouring poison into the victim's ear, takes place before the story starts and is reenacted in the course of a play within the play.

At the same time, not one of Shakespeare's plays contains more internal material—thoughts, feelings, hopes, fears and ideas—than *Hamlet*. Hamlet himself delivers five soliloquies throughout the course of the tragedy named for him, and all are masterpieces of poetry and rhetoric, philosophy and wordplay. Though *Shakespeare's Hamlet: The Manga Edition* doesn't explain the soliloquies, it gives us the opportunity to read and reread them in the context of the visually-presented action described above. By means of dynamic new medium of manga, Shakespeare's timeless tragedy is thereby made new—again.

ACT I

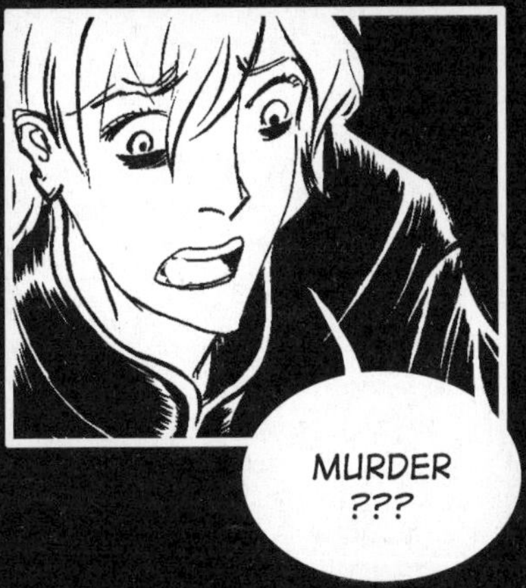
MURDER ???

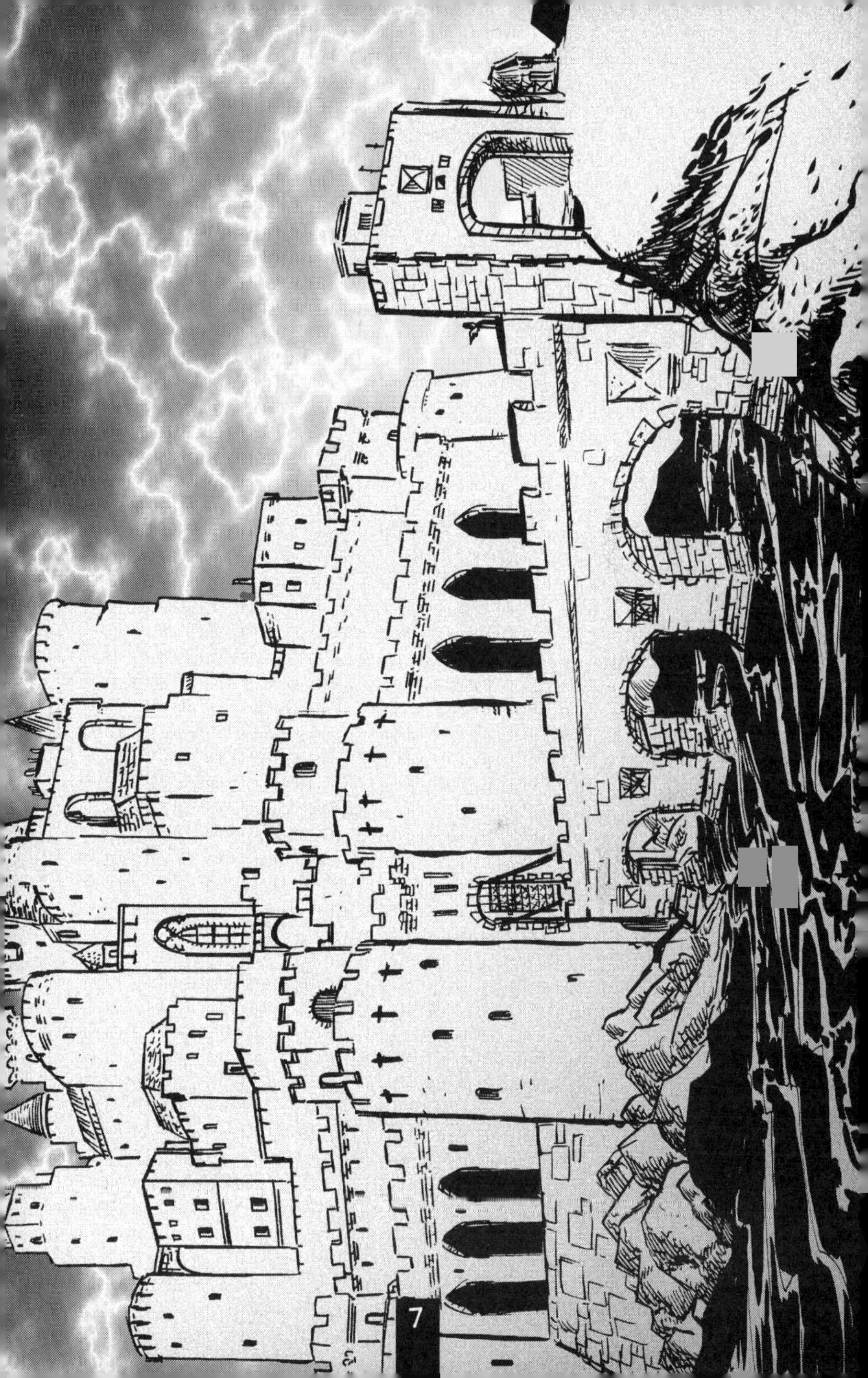

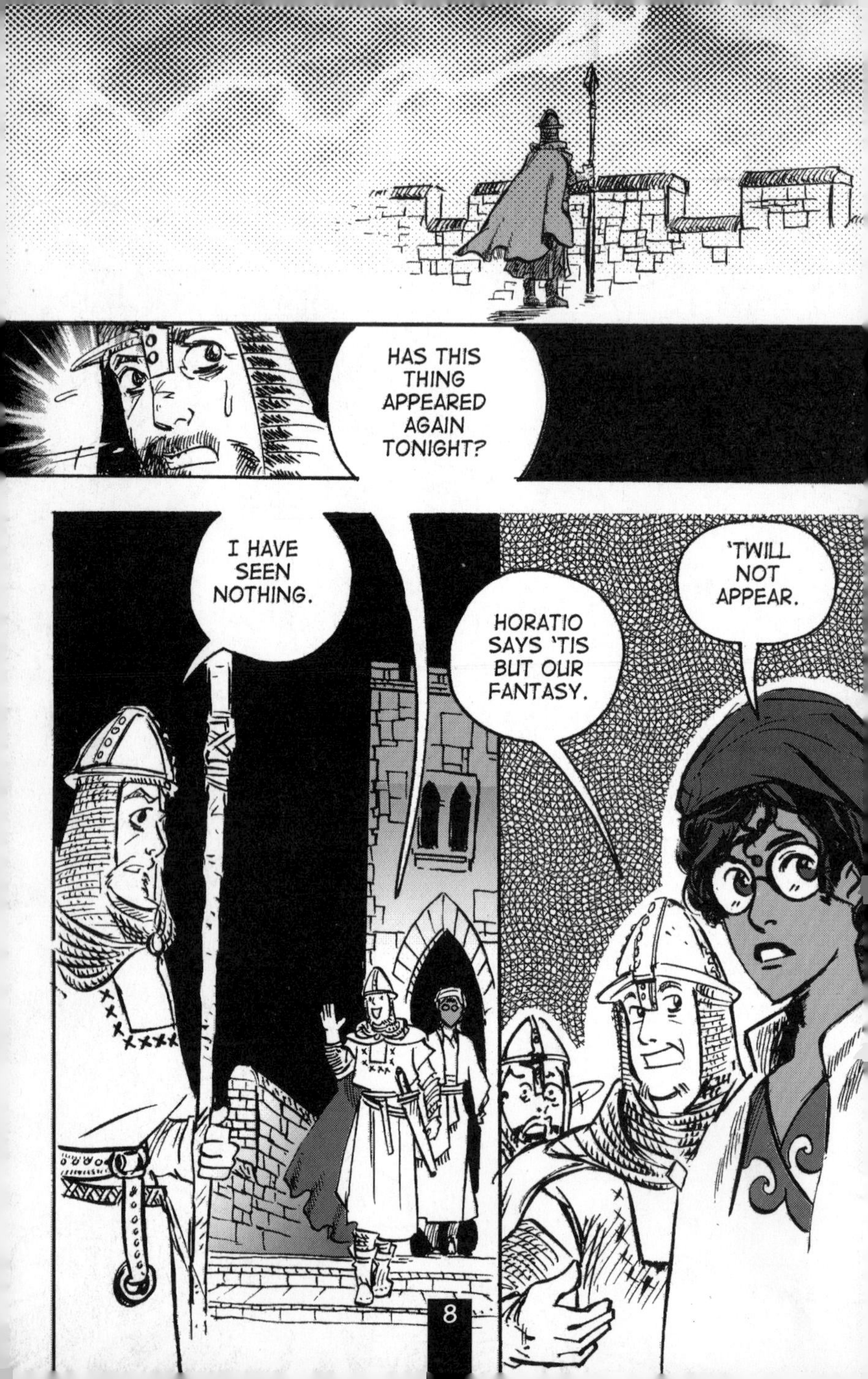
HAS THIS THING APPEARED AGAIN TONIGHT?
I HAVE SEEN NOTHING.
HORATIO SAYS 'TIS BUT OUR FANTASY.
'TWILL NOT APPEAR.

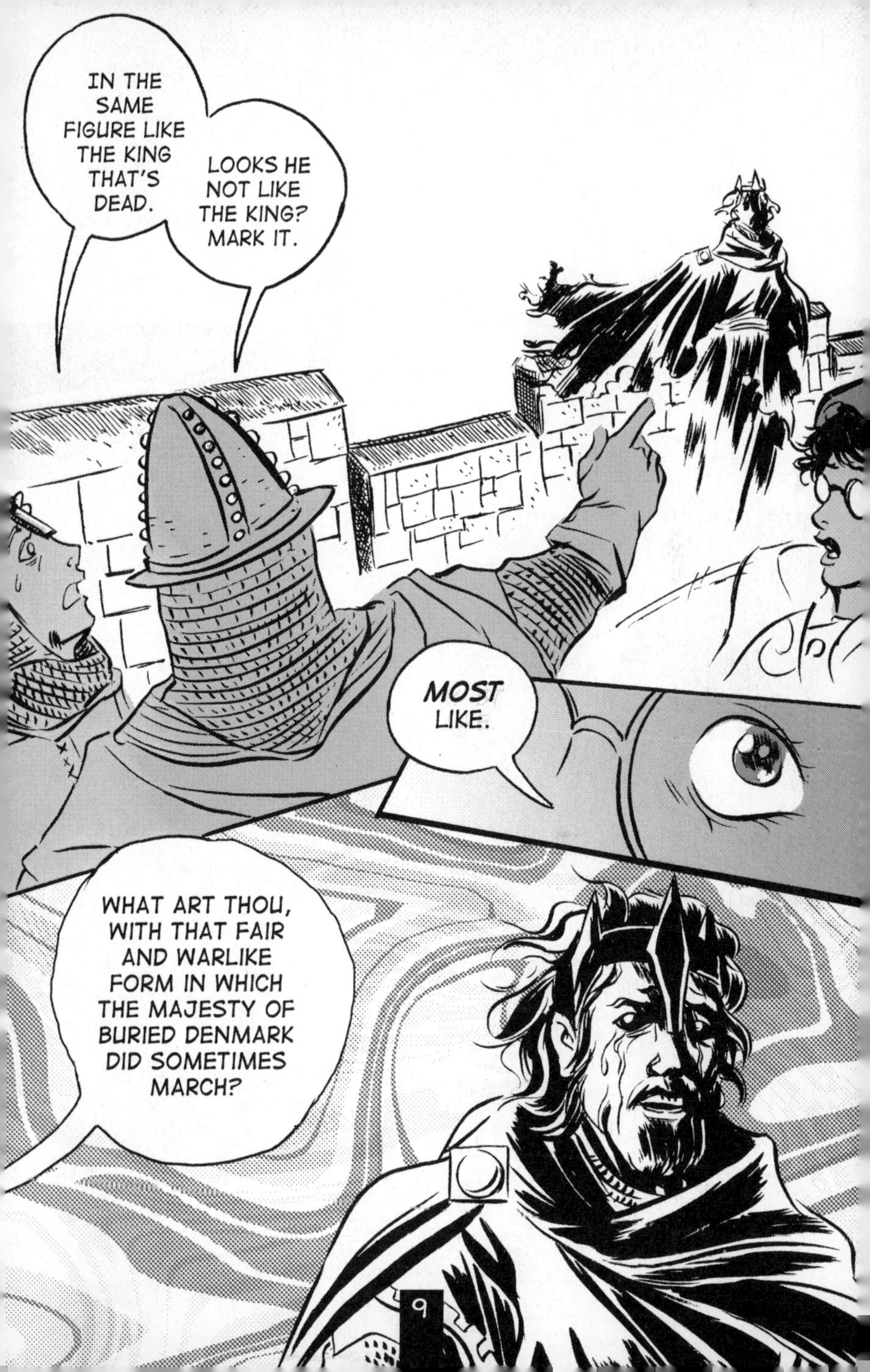

IN THE SAME FIGURE LIKE THE KING THAT'S DEAD.
LOOKS HE NOT LIKE THE KING? MARK IT.
MOST LIKE.
WHAT ART THOU, WITH THAT FAIR AND WARLIKE FORM IN WHICH THE MAJESTY OF BURIED DENMARK DID SOMETIMES MARCH?

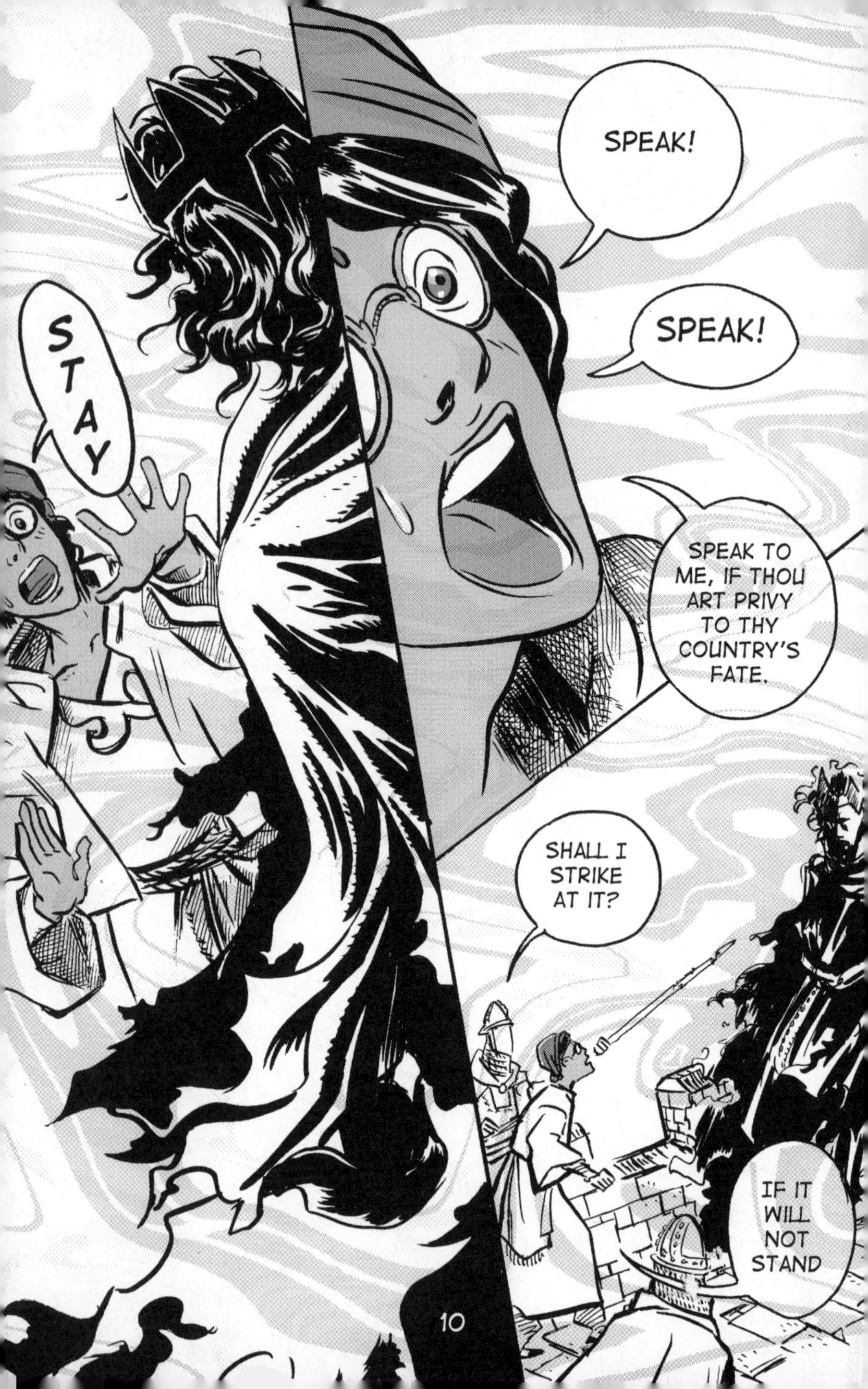
STAY
SPEAK!
SPEAK!
SPEAK TO ME, IF THOU ART PRIVY TO THY COUNTRY'S FATE.
SHALL I STRIKE AT IT?
IF IT WILL NOT STAND

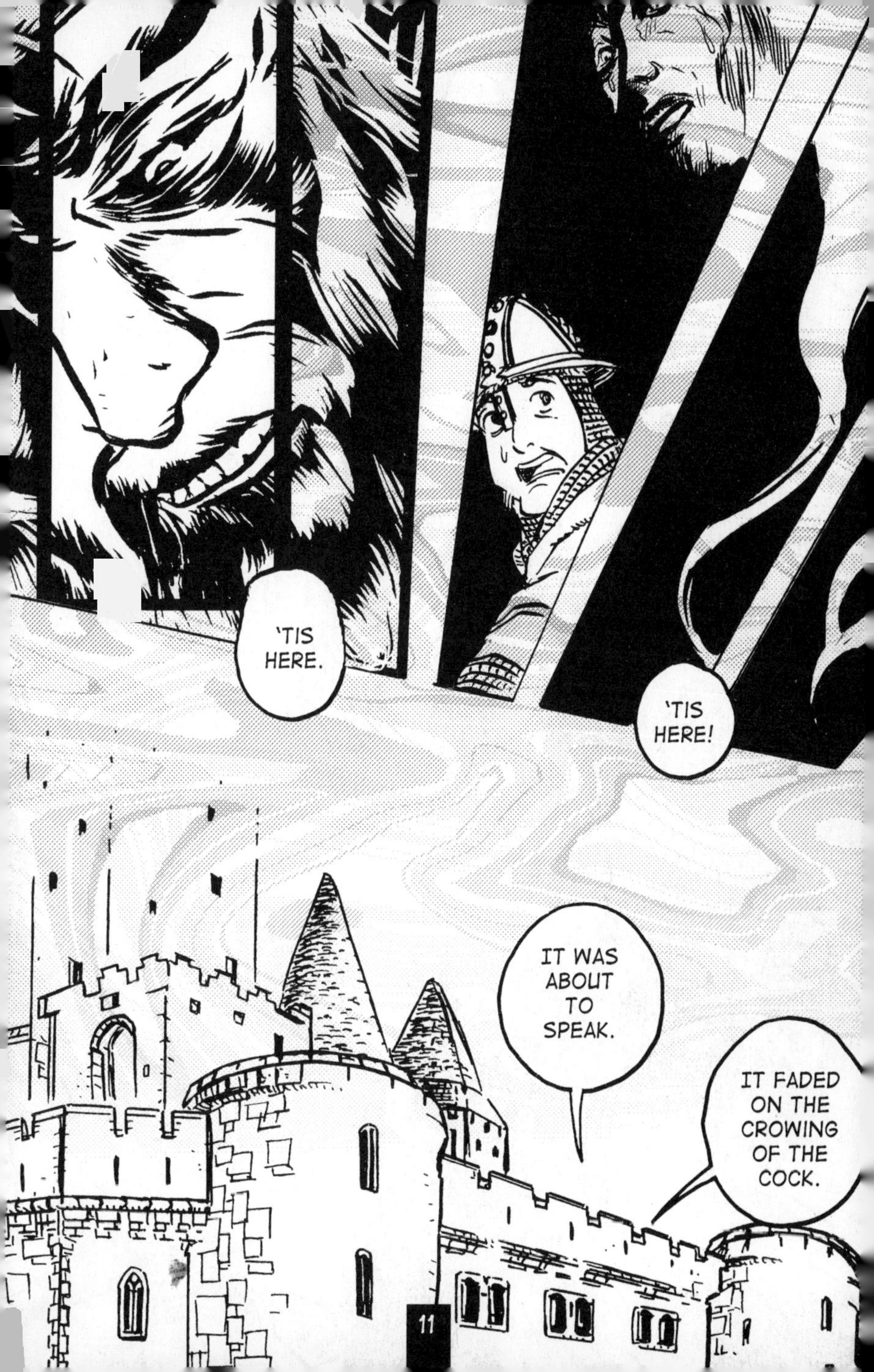
'TIS HERE.
'TIS HERE!
IT WAS ABOUT TO SPEAK.
IT FADED ON THE CROWING OF THE COCK.

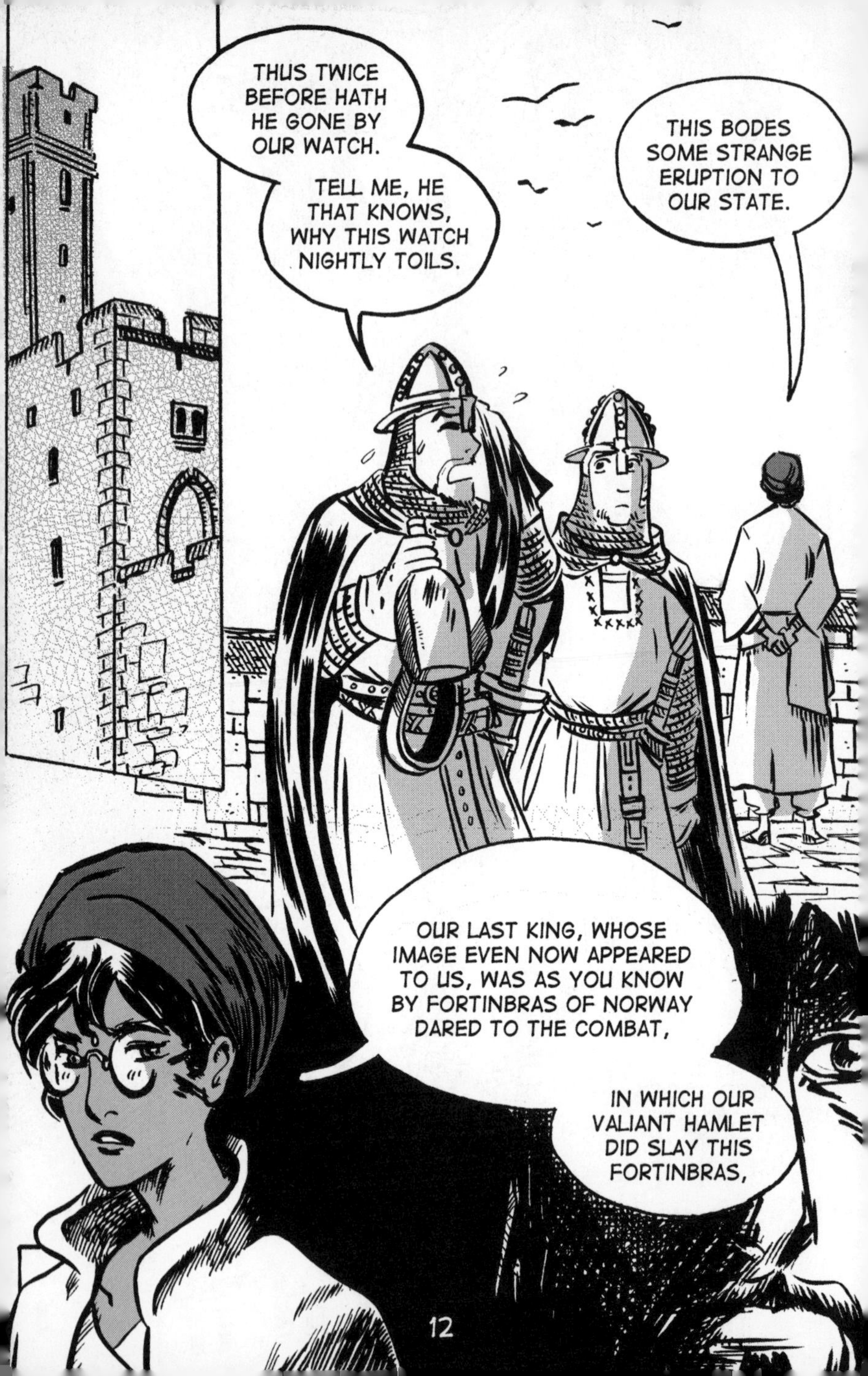
THUS TWICE BEFORE HATH HE GONE BY OUR WATCH.
TELL ME, HE THAT KNOWS, WHY THIS WATCH NIGHTLY TOILS.
THIS BODES SOME STRANGE ERUPTION TO OUR STATE.
OUR LAST KING, WHOSE IMAGE EVEN NOW APPEARED TO US, WAS AS YOU KNOW BY FORTINBRAS OF NORWAY DARED TO THE COMBAT,
IN WHICH OUR VALIANT HAMLET DID SLAY THIS FORTINBRAS,

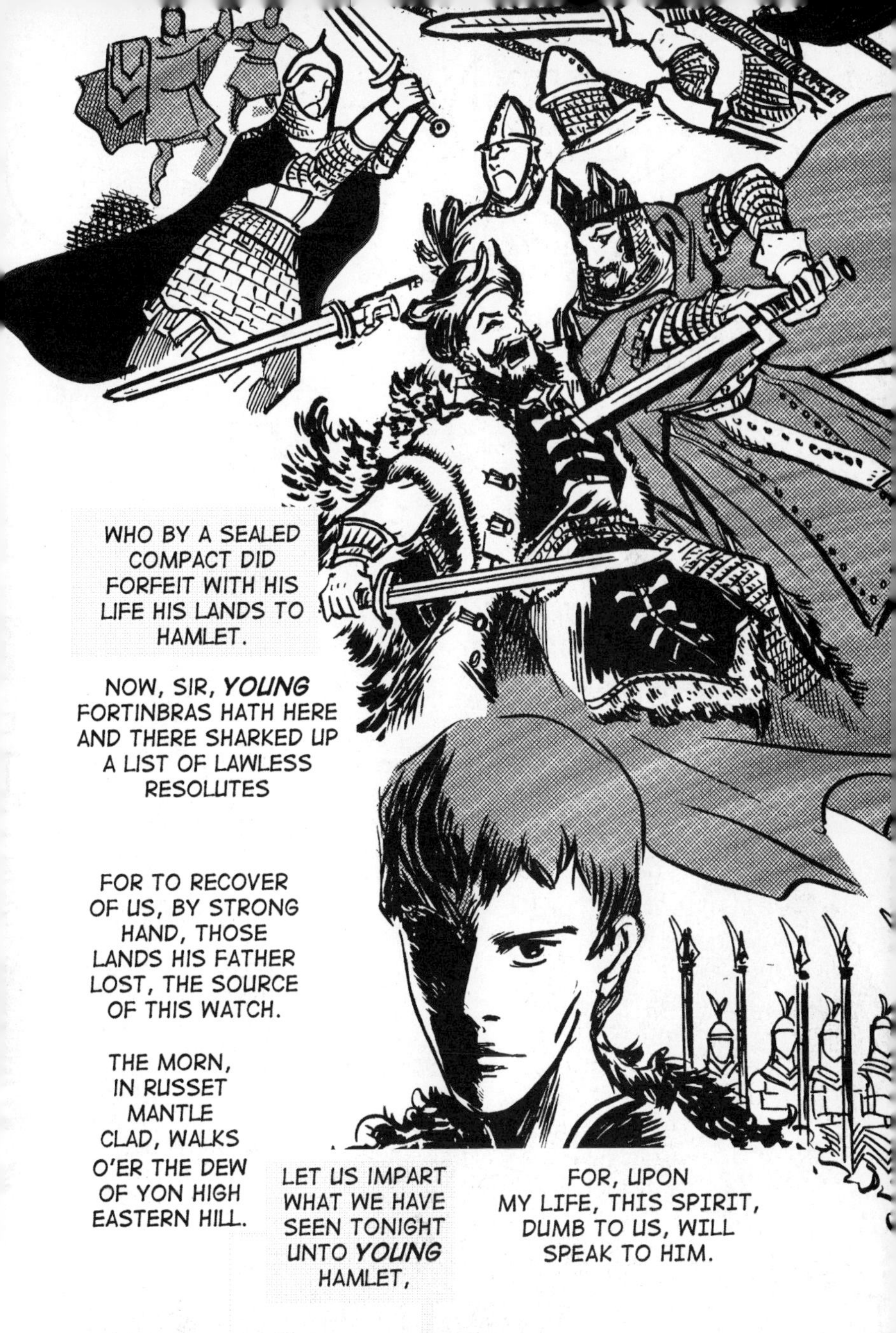
WHO BY A SEALED COMPACT DID FORFEIT WITH HIS LIFE HIS LANDS TO HAMLET.
NOW, SIR, *YOUNG* FORTINBRAS HATH HERE AND THERE SHARKED UP A LIST OF LAWLESS RESOLUTES
FOR TO RECOVER OF US, BY STRONG HAND, THOSE LANDS HIS FATHER LOST, THE SOURCE OF THIS WATCH.
THE MORN, IN RUSSET MANTLE CLAD, WALKS O'ER THE DEW OF YON HIGH EASTERN HILL.
LET US IMPART WHAT WE HAVE SEEN TONIGHT UNTO *YOUNG* HAMLET,
FOR, UPON MY LIFE, THIS SPIRIT, DUMB TO US, WILL SPEAK TO HIM.

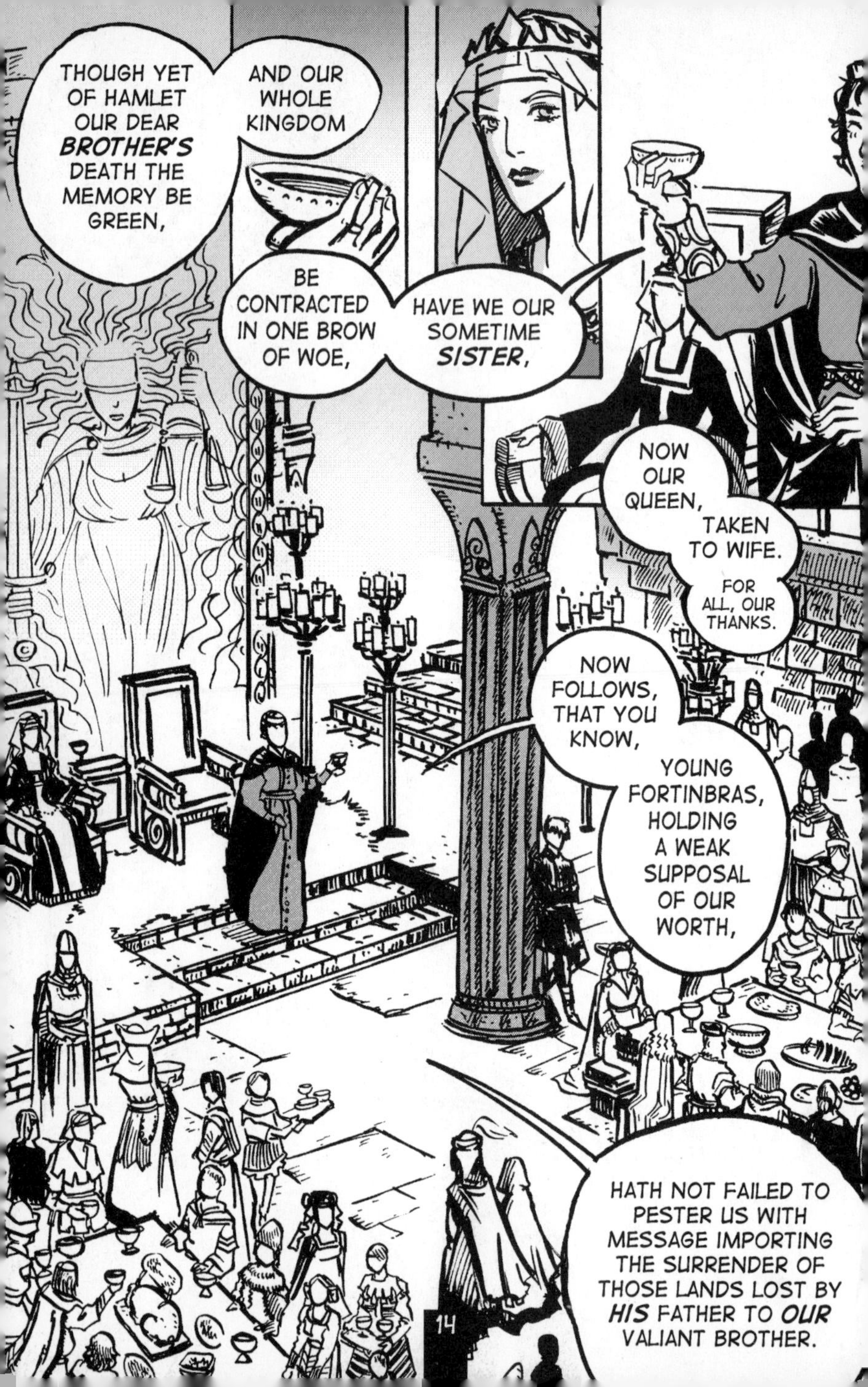
THOUGH YET OF HAMLET OUR DEAR BROTHER'S DEATH THE MEMORY BE GREEN,
AND OUR WHOLE KINGDOM
BE CONTRACTED IN ONE BROW OF WOE,
HAVE WE OUR SOMETIME SISTER,
NOW OUR QUEEN,
TAKEN TO WIFE.
FOR ALL, OUR THANKS.
NOW FOLLOWS, THAT YOU KNOW,
YOUNG FORTINBRAS, HOLDING A WEAK SUPPOSAL OF OUR WORTH,
HATH NOT FAILED TO PESTER US WITH MESSAGE IMPORTING THE SURRENDER OF THOSE LANDS LOST BY HIS FATHER TO OUR VALIANT BROTHER.
14

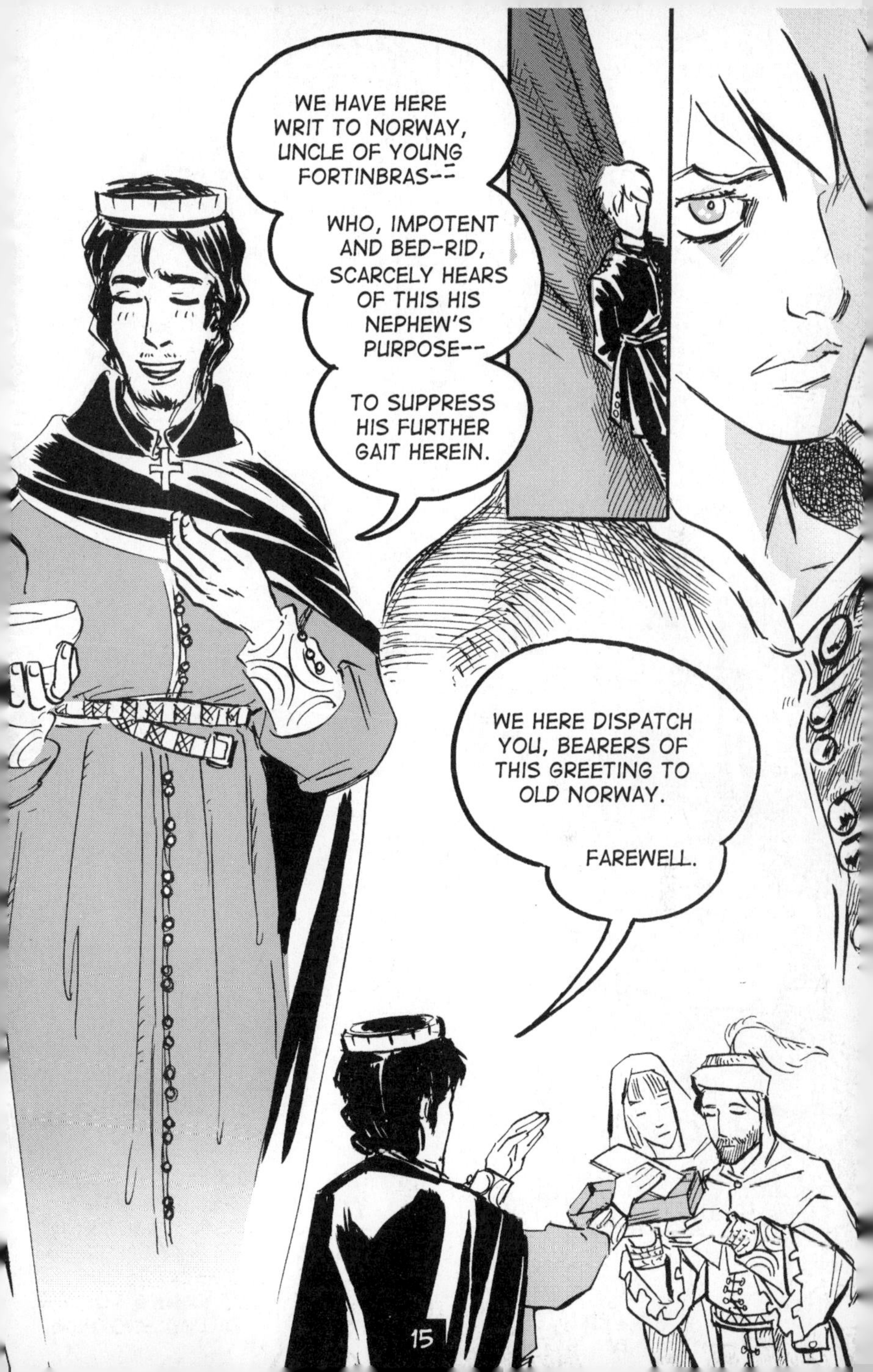
WE HAVE HERE WRIT TO NORWAY, UNCLE OF YOUNG FORTINBRAS--
WHO, IMPOTENT AND BED-RID, SCARCELY HEARS OF THIS HIS NEPHEW'S PURPOSE--
TO SUPPRESS HIS FURTHER GAIT HEREIN.
WE HERE DISPATCH YOU, BEARERS OF THIS GREETING TO OLD NORWAY.
FAREWELL.

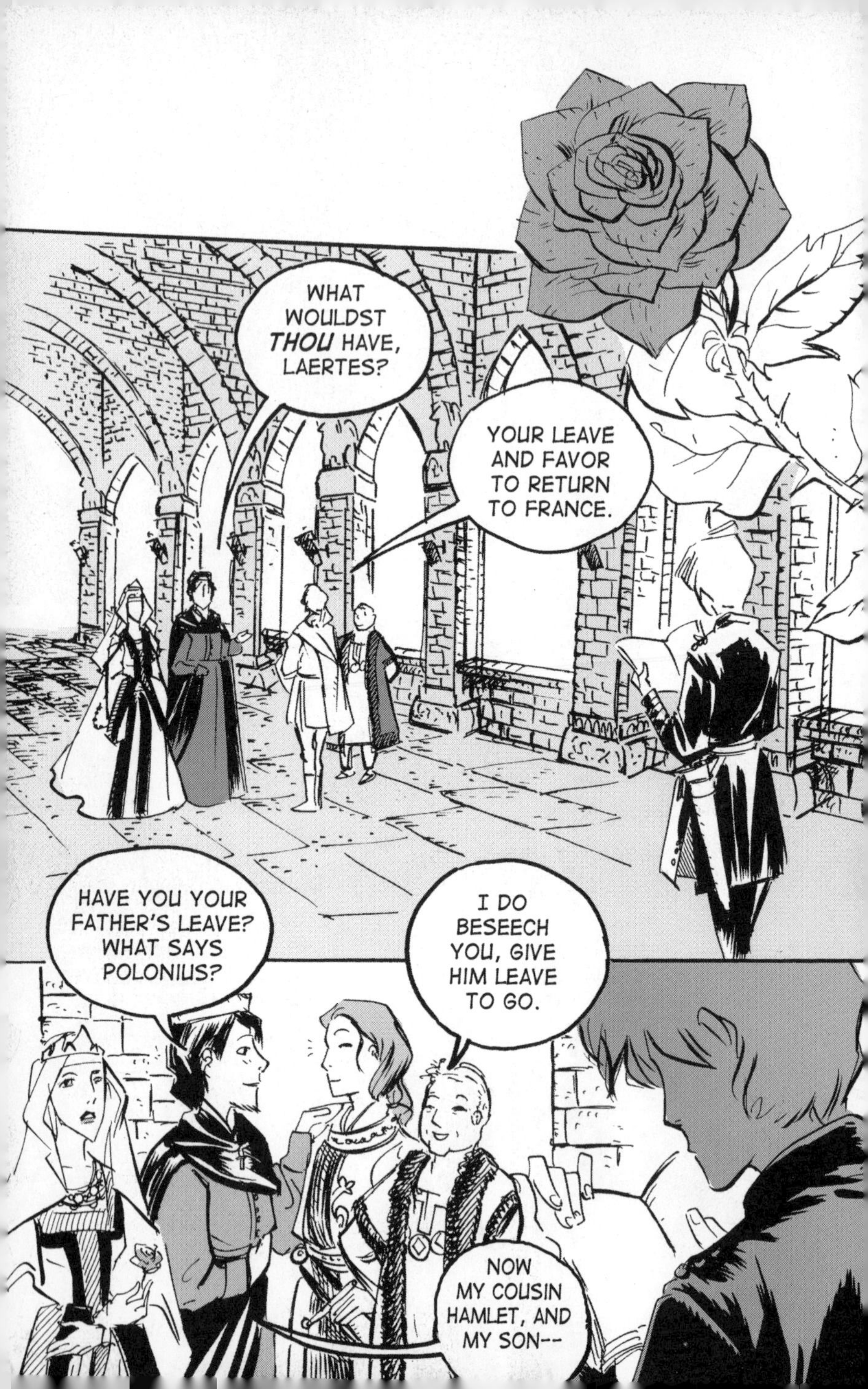
WHAT WOULDST *THOU* HAVE, LAERTES?
YOUR LEAVE AND FAVOR TO RETURN TO FRANCE.
HAVE YOU YOUR FATHER'S LEAVE? WHAT SAYS POLONIUS?
I DO BESEECH YOU, GIVE HIM LEAVE TO GO.
NOW MY COUSIN HAMLET, AND MY SON--

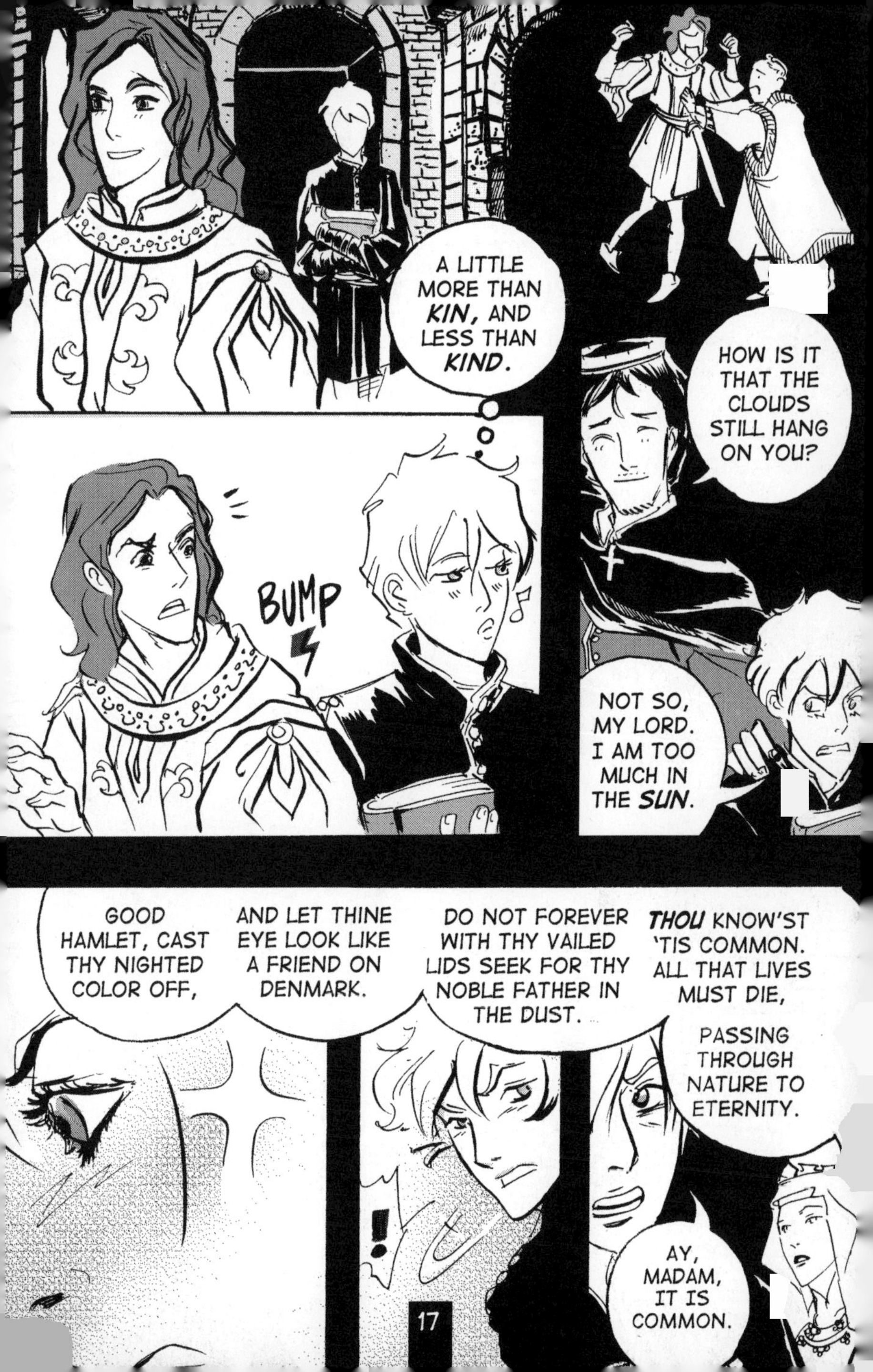
A LITTLE MORE THAN KIN, AND LESS THAN KIND.
BUMP
HOW IS IT THAT THE CLOUDS STILL HANG ON YOU?
NOT SO, MY LORD. I AM TOO MUCH IN THE SUN.
GOOD HAMLET, CAST THY NIGHTED COLOR OFF,
AND LET THINE EYE LOOK LIKE A FRIEND ON DENMARK.
DO NOT FOREVER WITH THY VAILED LIDS SEEK FOR THY NOBLE FATHER IN THE DUST...
THOU KNOW'ST 'TIS COMMON. ALL THAT LIVES MUST DIE,
PASSING THROUGH NATURE TO ETERNITY.
!
AY, MADAM, IT IS COMMON.

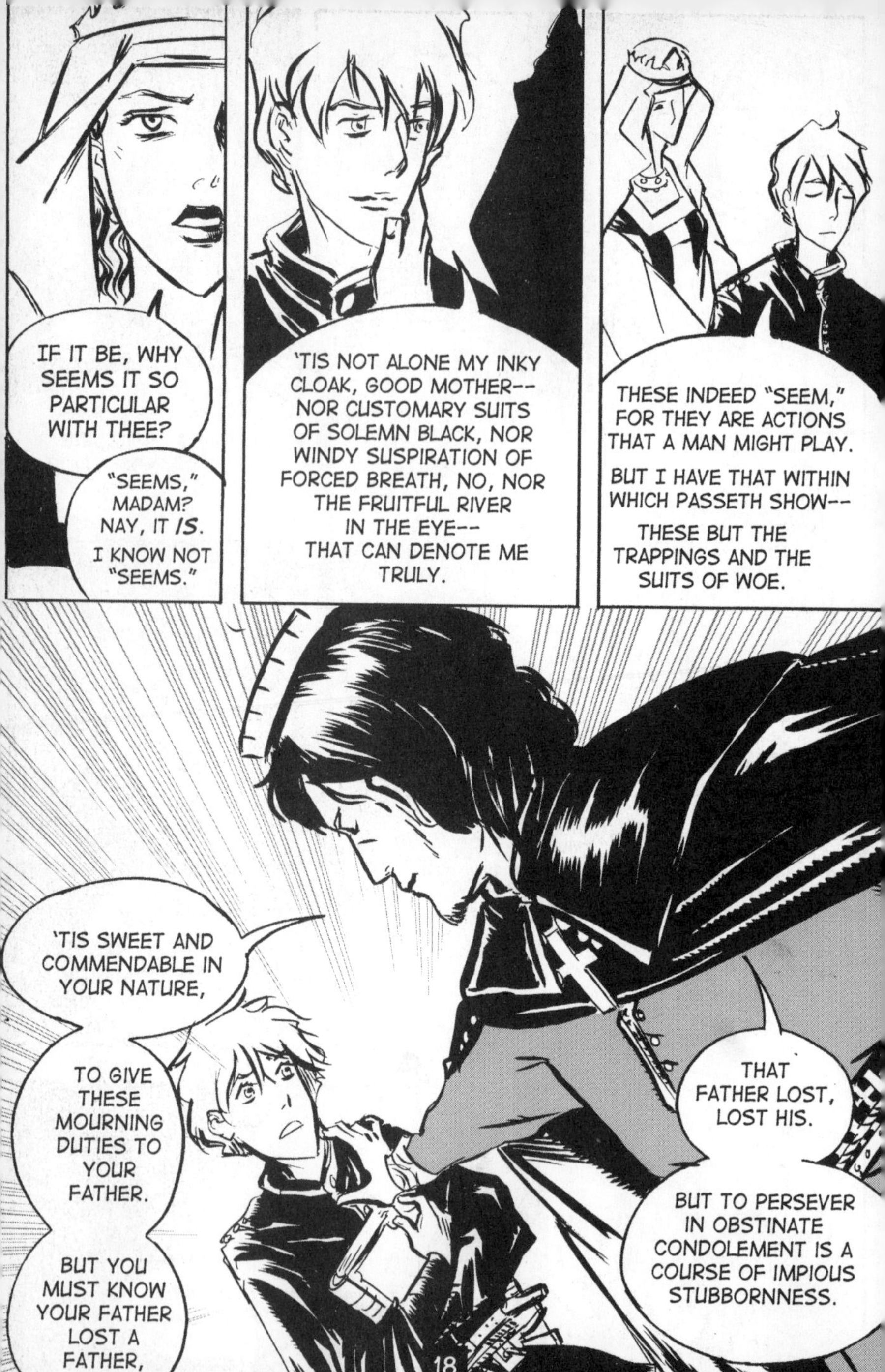
IF IT BE, WHY SEEMS IT SO PARTICULAR WITH THEE?
"SEEMS," MADAM? NAY, IT *IS*.
I KNOW NOT "SEEMS."
'TIS NOT ALONE MY INKY CLOAK, GOOD MOTHER-- NOR CUSTOMARY SUITS OF SOLEMN BLACK, NOR WINDY SUSPIRATION OF FORCED BREATH, NO, NOR THE FRUITFUL RIVER IN THE EYE-- THAT CAN DENOTE ME TRULY.
THESE INDEED "SEEM," FOR THEY ARE ACTIONS THAT A MAN MIGHT PLAY.
BUT I HAVE THAT WITHIN WHICH PASSETH SHOW--
THESE BUT THE TRAPPINGS AND THE SUITS OF WOE.
'TIS SWEET AND COMMENDABLE IN YOUR NATURE,
TO GIVE THESE MOURNING DUTIES TO YOUR FATHER.
BUT YOU MUST KNOW YOUR FATHER LOST A FATHER,
THAT FATHER LOST, LOST HIS.
BUT TO PERSEVER IN OBSTINATE CONDOLEMENT IS A COURSE OF IMPIOUS STUBBORNNESS.

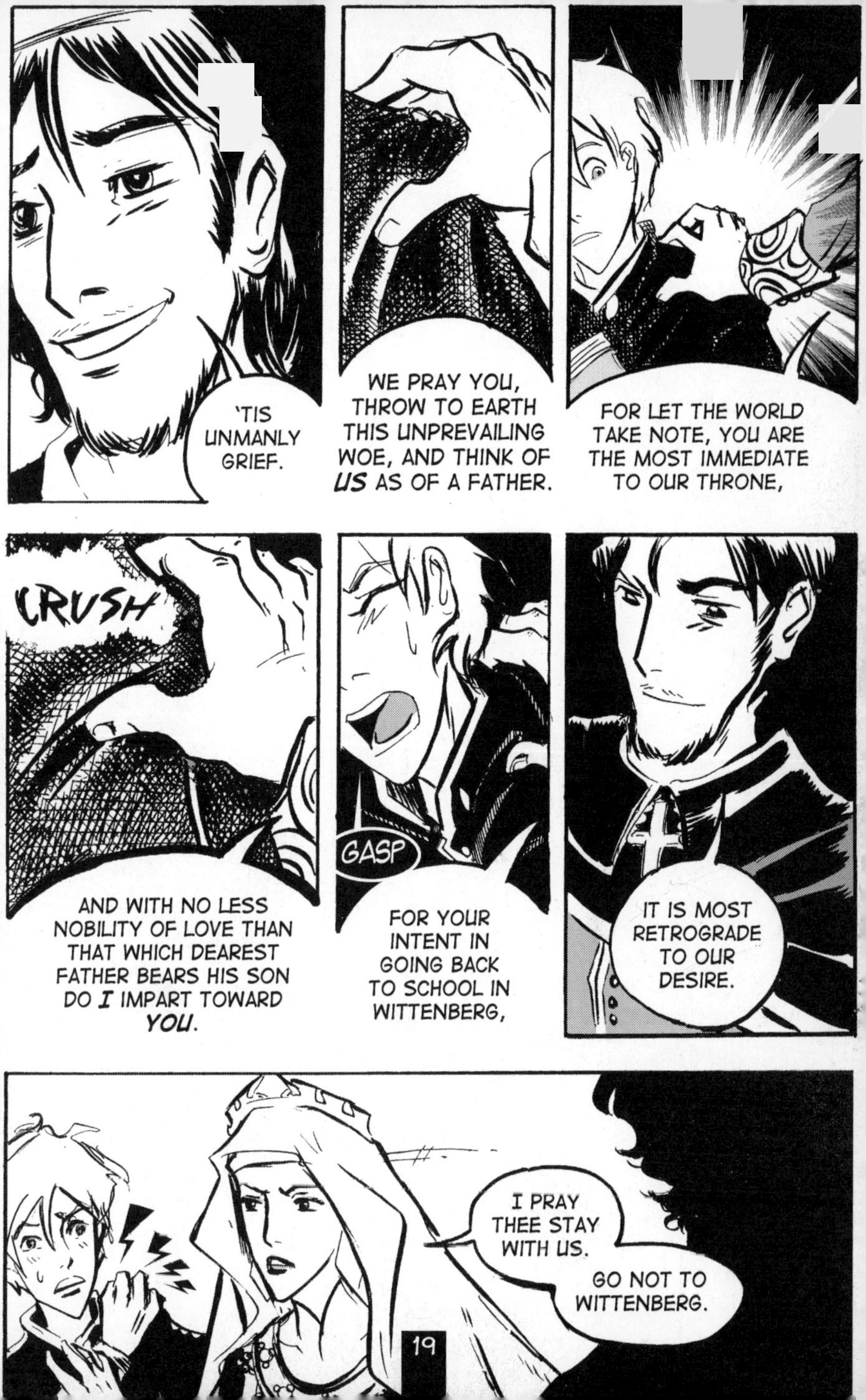
'TIS UNMANLY GRIEF.
WE PRAY YOU, THROW TO EARTH THIS UNPREVAILING WOE, AND THINK OF *US* AS OF A FATHER.
FOR LET THE WORLD TAKE NOTE, YOU ARE THE MOST IMMEDIATE TO OUR THRONE,
CRUSH
AND WITH NO LESS NOBILITY OF LOVE THAN THAT WHICH DEAREST FATHER BEARS HIS SON DO *I* IMPART TOWARD *YOU*.
GASP
FOR YOUR INTENT IN GOING BACK TO SCHOOL IN WITTENBERG,
IT IS MOST RETROGRADE TO OUR DESIRE.
I PRAY THEE STAY WITH US.
GO NOT TO WITTENBERG.

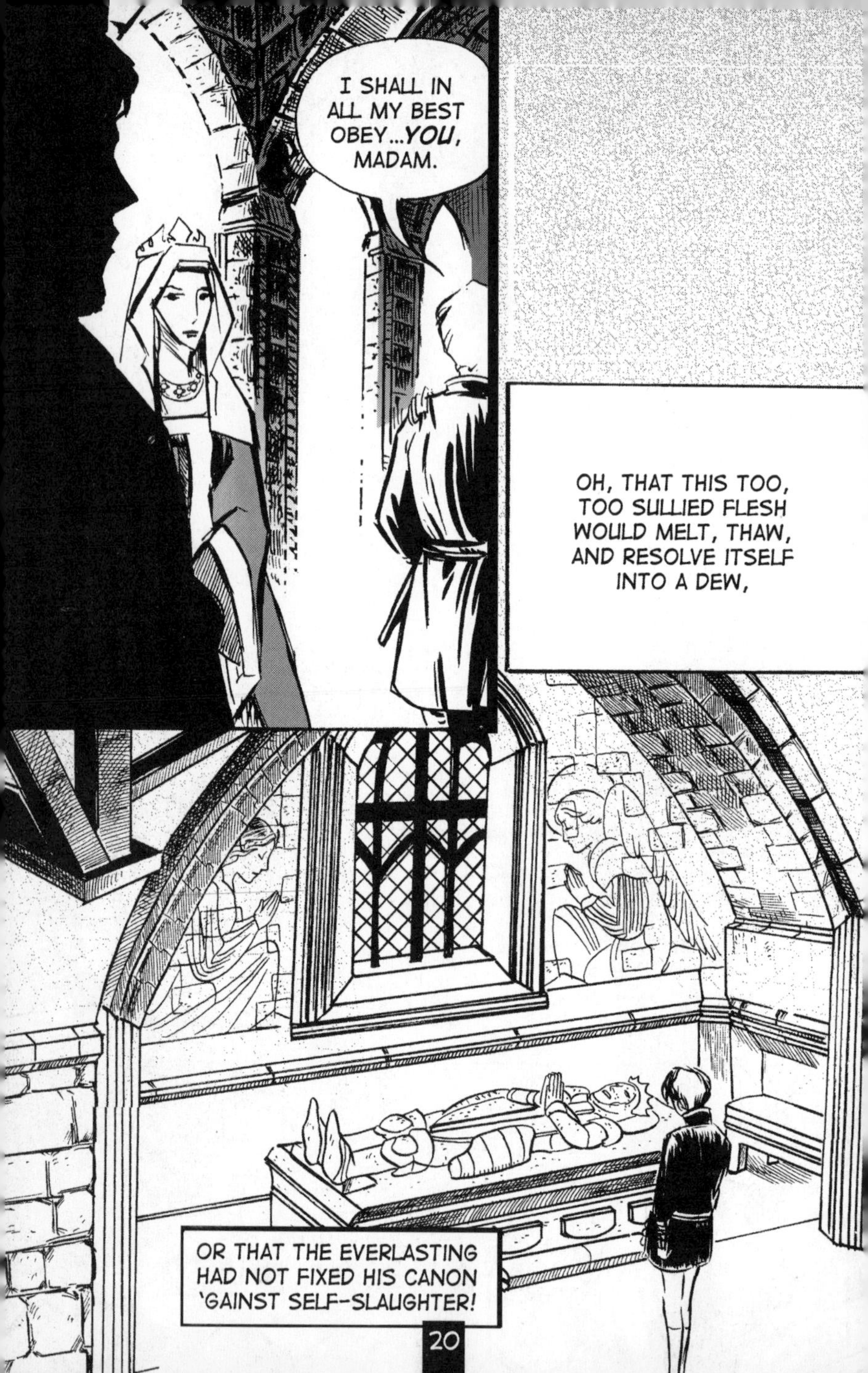
I SHALL IN ALL MY BEST OBEY...*YOU*, MADAM.
OH, THAT THIS TOO, TOO SULLIED FLESH WOULD MELT, THAW, AND RESOLVE ITSELF INTO A DEW,
OR THAT THE EVERLASTING HAD NOT FIXED HIS CANON 'GAINST SELF-SLAUGHTER!

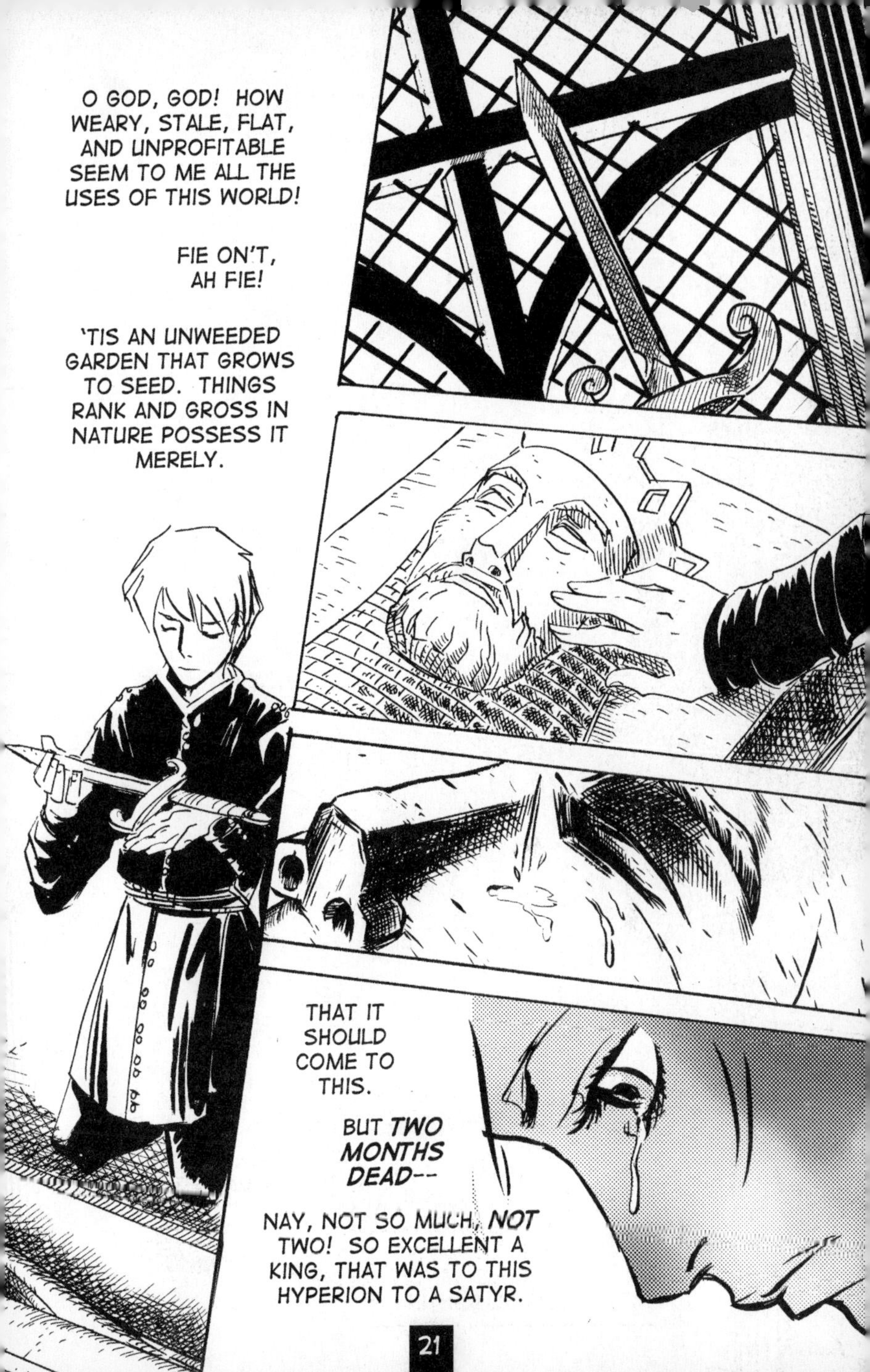

O GOD, GOD! HOW WEARY, STALE, FLAT, AND UNPROFITABLE SEEM TO ME ALL THE USES OF THIS WORLD!
FIE ON'T, AH FIE!
'TIS AN UNWEEDED GARDEN THAT GROWS TO SEED. THINGS RANK AND GROSS IN NATURE POSSESS IT MERELY.
THAT IT SHOULD COME TO THIS.
BUT *TWO MONTHS DEAD*--
NAY, NOT SO MUCH, *NOT* TWO! SO EXCELLENT A KING, THAT WAS TO THIS HYPERION TO A SATYR.

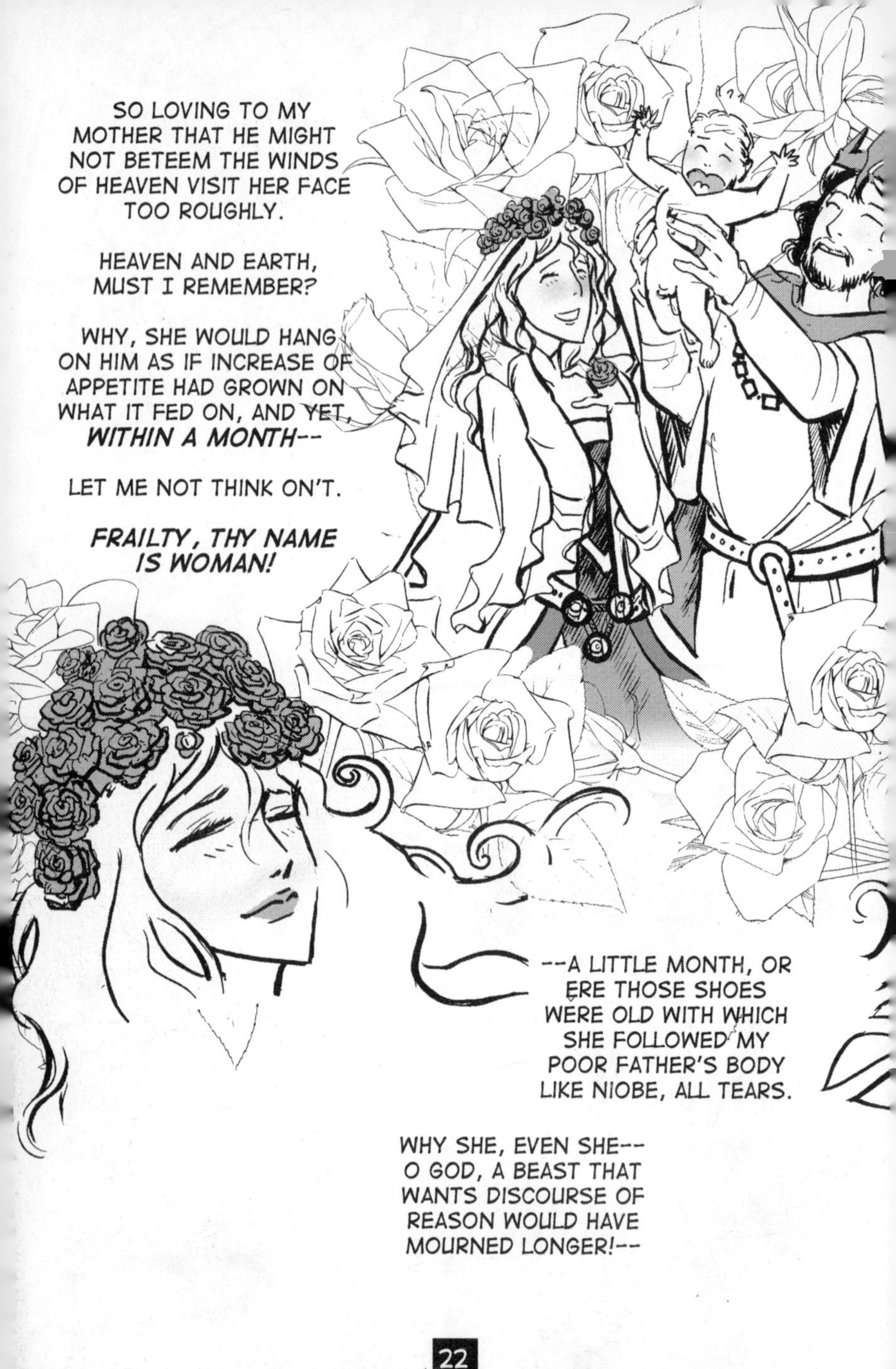
SO LOVING TO MY MOTHER THAT HE MIGHT NOT BETEEM THE WINDS OF HEAVEN VISIT HER FACE TOO ROUGHLY.
HEAVEN AND EARTH, MUST I REMEMBER?
WHY, SHE WOULD HANG ON HIM AS IF INCREASE OF APPETITE HAD GROWN ON WHAT IT FED ON, AND YET, *WITHIN A MONTH*--
LET ME NOT THINK ON'T.
FRAILTY, THY NAME IS WOMAN!
--A LITTLE MONTH, OR ERE THOSE SHOES WERE OLD WITH WHICH SHE FOLLOWED MY POOR FATHER'S BODY LIKE NIOBE, ALL TEARS.
WHY SHE, EVEN SHE-- O GOD, A BEAST THAT WANTS DISCOURSE OF REASON WOULD HAVE MOURNED LONGER!--

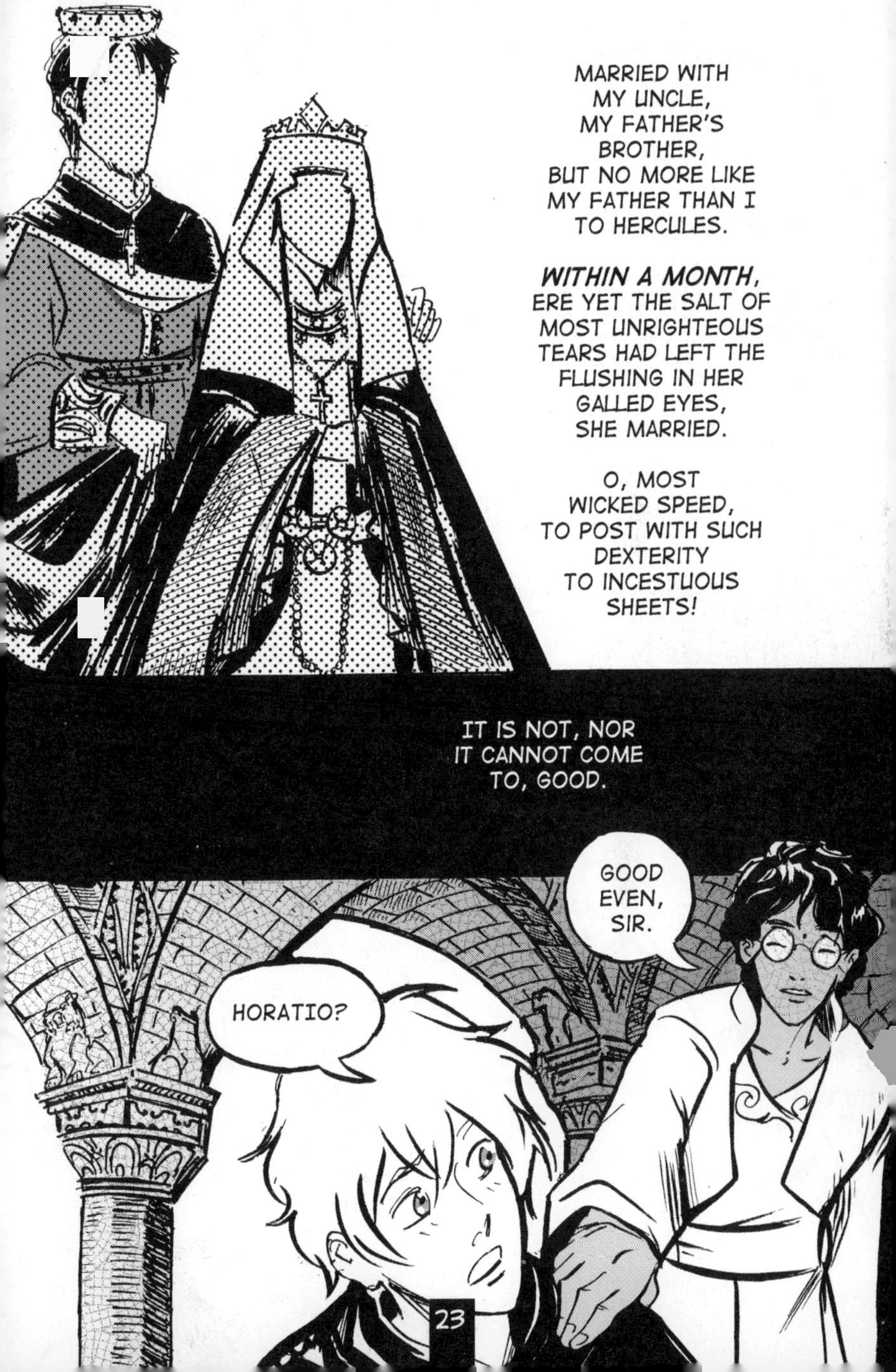
MARRIED WITH MY UNCLE, MY FATHER'S BROTHER, BUT NO MORE LIKE MY FATHER THAN I TO HERCULES.
WITHIN A MONTH, ERE YET THE SALT OF MOST UNRIGHTEOUS TEARS HAD LEFT THE FLUSHING IN HER GALLED EYES, SHE MARRIED.
O, MOST WICKED SPEED, TO POST WITH SUCH DEXTERITY TO INCESTUOUS SHEETS!
IT IS NOT, NOR IT CANNOT COME TO, GOOD.
HORATIO?
GOOD EVEN, SIR.

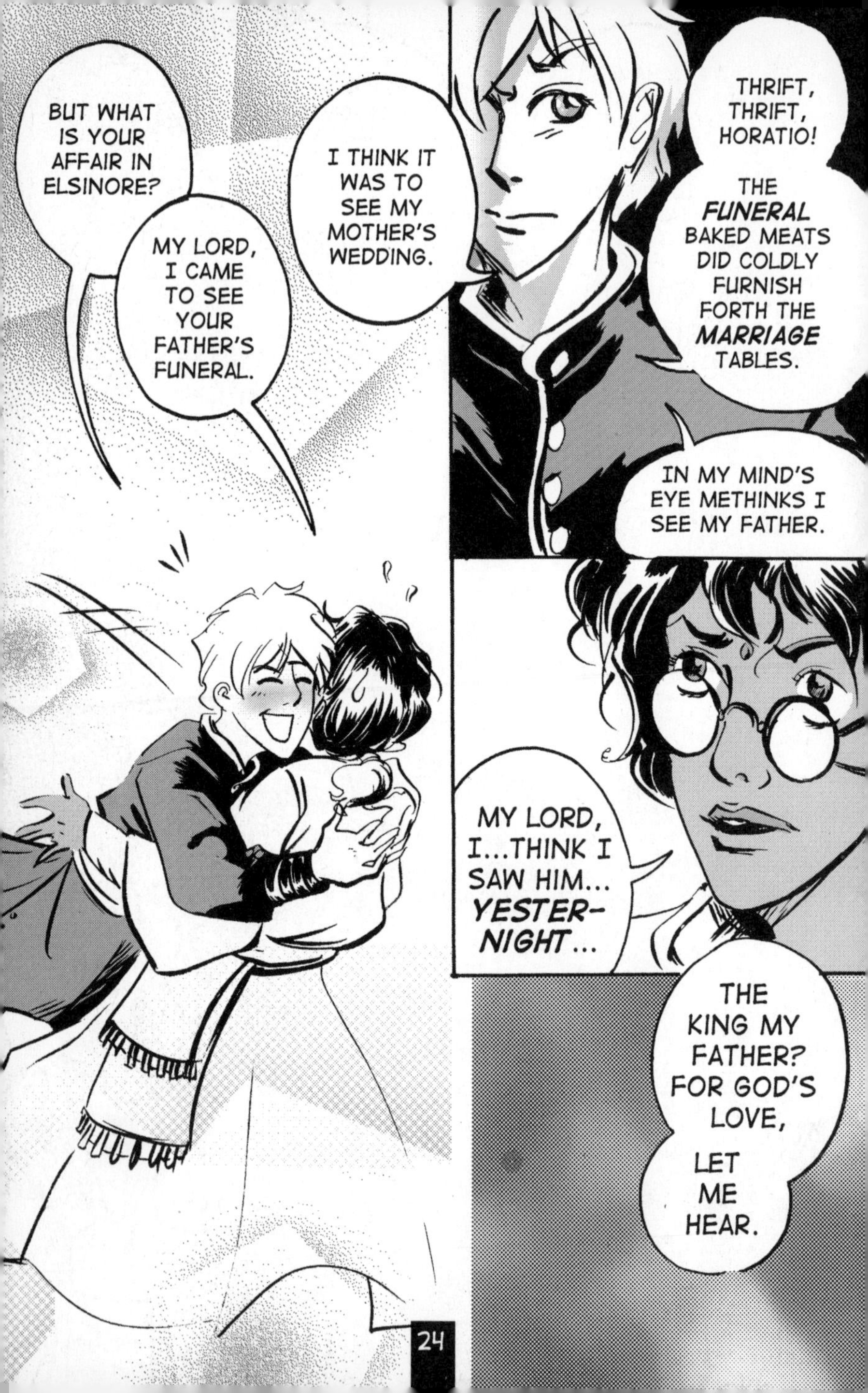
BUT WHAT IS YOUR AFFAIR IN ELSINORE?
MY LORD, I CAME TO SEE YOUR FATHER'S FUNERAL.
I THINK IT WAS TO SEE MY MOTHER'S WEDDING.
THRIFT, THRIFT, HORATIO!
THE *FUNERAL* BAKED MEATS DID COLDLY FURNISH FORTH THE *MARRIAGE* TABLES.
IN MY MIND'S EYE METHINKS I SEE MY FATHER.
MY LORD, I...THINK I SAW HIM... ***YESTER-NIGHT***...
THE KING MY FATHER? FOR GOD'S LOVE,
LET ME HEAR.

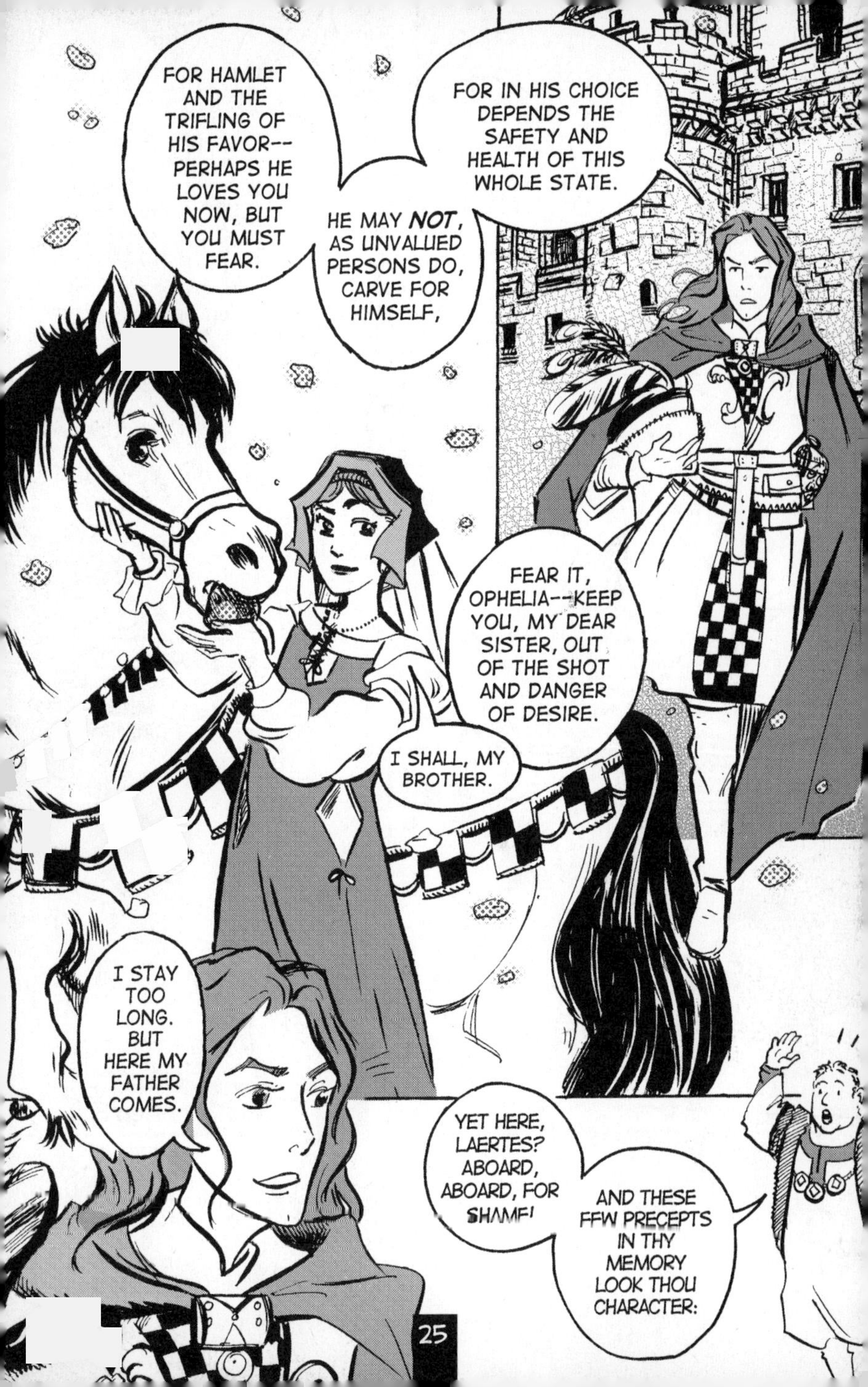
FOR HAMLET AND THE TRIFLING OF HIS FAVOR--PERHAPS HE LOVES YOU NOW, BUT YOU MUST FEAR.
HE MAY NOT, AS UNVALUED PERSONS DO, CARVE FOR HIMSELF,
FOR IN HIS CHOICE DEPENDS THE SAFETY AND HEALTH OF THIS WHOLE STATE.
FEAR IT, OPHELIA--KEEP YOU, MY DEAR SISTER, OUT OF THE SHOT AND DANGER OF DESIRE.
I SHALL, MY BROTHER.
I STAY TOO LONG. BUT HERE MY FATHER COMES.
YET HERE, LAERTES? ABOARD, ABOARD, FOR SHAME!
AND THESE FEW PRECEPTS IN THY MEMORY LOOK THOU CHARACTER:

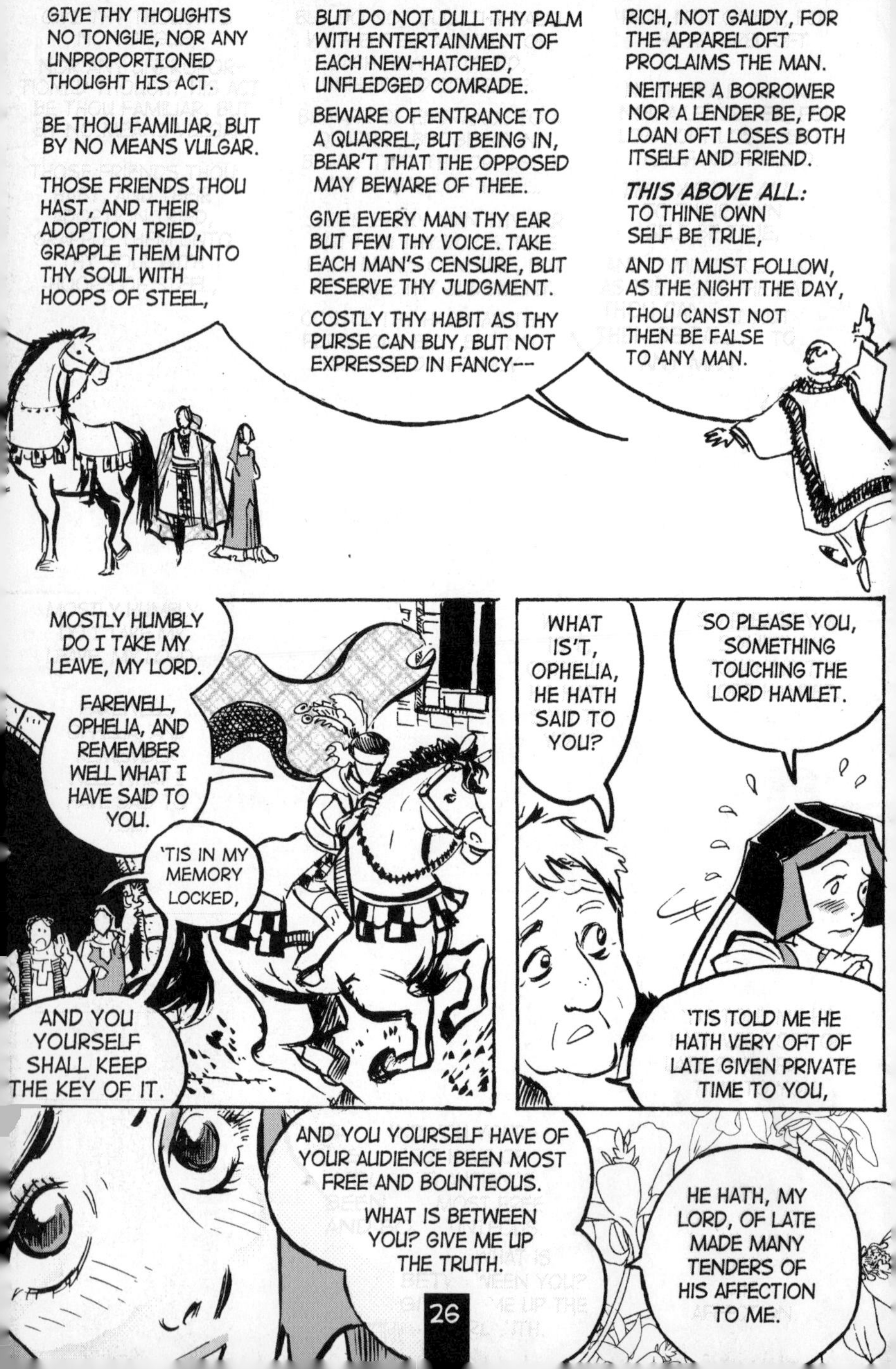

GIVE THY THOUGHTS NO TONGUE, NOR ANY UNPROPORTIONED THOUGHT HIS ACT.
BE THOU FAMILIAR, BUT BY NO MEANS VULGAR.
THOSE FRIENDS THOU HAST, AND THEIR ADOPTION TRIED, GRAPPLE THEM UNTO THY SOUL WITH HOOPS OF STEEL,
BUT DO NOT DULL THY PALM WITH ENTERTAINMENT OF EACH NEW-HATCHED, UNFLEDGED COMRADE.
BEWARE OF ENTRANCE TO A QUARREL, BUT BEING IN, BEAR'T THAT THE OPPOSED MAY BEWARE OF THEE.
GIVE EVERY MAN THY EAR BUT FEW THY VOICE. TAKE EACH MAN'S CENSURE, BUT RESERVE THY JUDGMENT.
COSTLY THY HABIT AS THY PURSE CAN BUY, BUT NOT EXPRESSED IN FANCY--
RICH, NOT GAUDY, FOR THE APPAREL OFT PROCLAIMS THE MAN.
NEITHER A BORROWER NOR A LENDER BE, FOR LOAN OFT LOSES BOTH ITSELF AND FRIEND.
THIS ABOVE ALL: TO THINE OWN SELF BE TRUE,
AND IT MUST FOLLOW, AS THE NIGHT THE DAY,
THOU CANST NOT THEN BE FALSE TO ANY MAN.
MOSTLY HUMBLY DO I TAKE MY LEAVE, MY LORD.
FAREWELL, OPHELIA, AND REMEMBER WELL WHAT I HAVE SAID TO YOU.
'TIS IN MY MEMORY LOCKED,
AND YOU YOURSELF SHALL KEEP THE KEY OF IT.
WHAT IS'T, OPHELIA, HE HATH SAID TO YOU?
SO PLEASE YOU, SOMETHING TOUCHING THE LORD HAMLET.
'TIS TOLD ME HE HATH VERY OFT OF LATE GIVEN PRIVATE TIME TO YOU,
AND YOU YOURSELF HAVE OF YOUR AUDIENCE BEEN MOST FREE AND BOUNTEOUS.
WHAT IS BETWEEN YOU? GIVE ME UP THE TRUTH.
HE HATH, MY LORD, OF LATE MADE MANY TENDERS OF HIS AFFECTION TO ME.

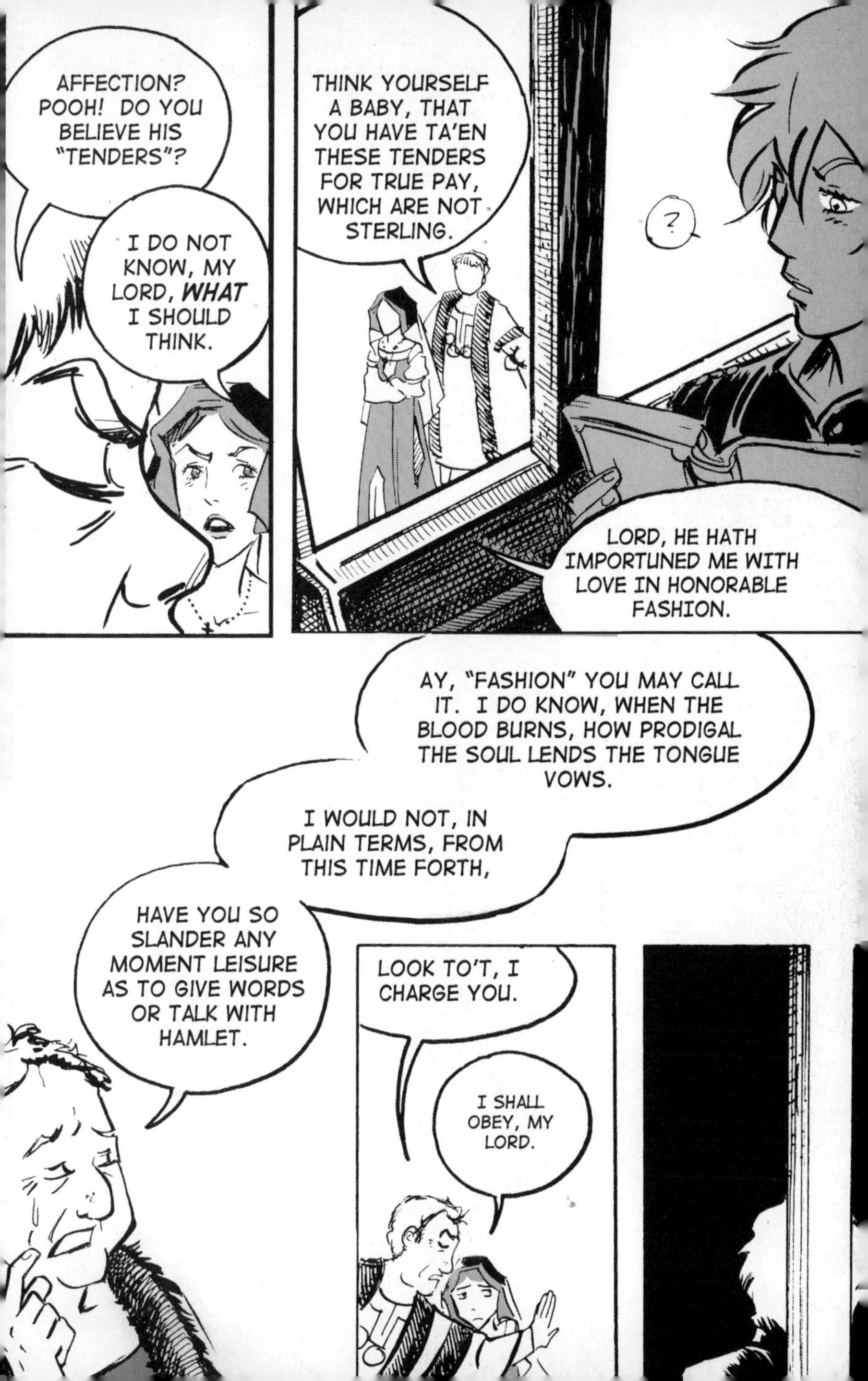
AFFECTION? POOH! DO YOU BELIEVE HIS "TENDERS"?
I DO NOT KNOW, MY LORD, *WHAT* I SHOULD THINK.
THINK YOURSELF A BABY, THAT YOU HAVE TA'EN THESE TENDERS FOR TRUE PAY, WHICH ARE NOT STERLING.
?
LORD, HE HATH IMPORTUNED ME WITH LOVE IN HONORABLE FASHION.
AY, "FASHION" YOU MAY CALL IT. I DO KNOW, WHEN THE BLOOD BURNS, HOW PRODIGAL THE SOUL LENDS THE TONGUE VOWS.
I WOULD NOT, IN PLAIN TERMS, FROM THIS TIME FORTH,
HAVE YOU SO SLANDER ANY MOMENT LEISURE AS TO GIVE WORDS OR TALK WITH HAMLET.
LOOK TO'T, I CHARGE YOU.
I SHALL OBEY, MY LORD.

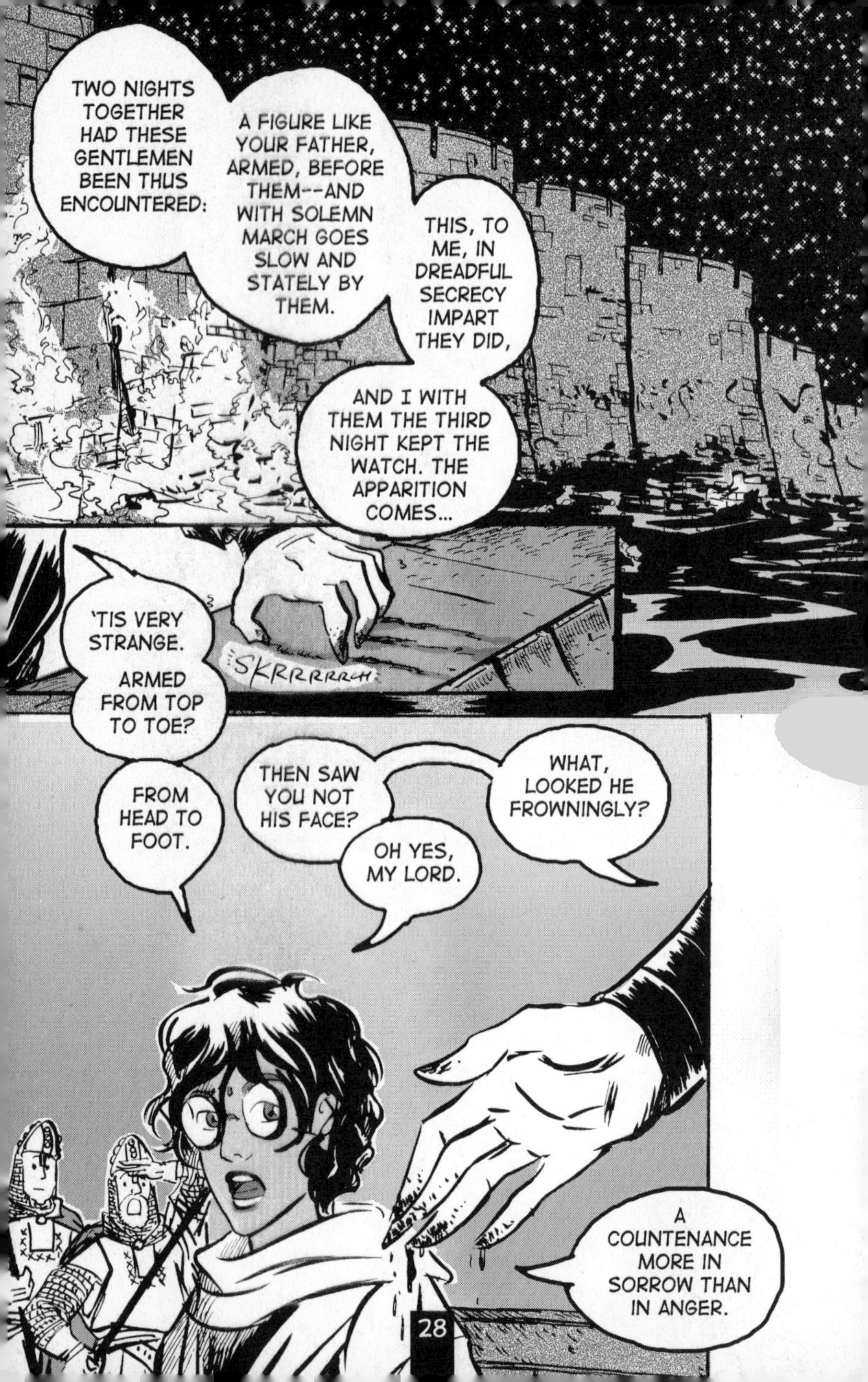
TWO NIGHTS TOGETHER HAD THESE GENTLEMEN BEEN THUS ENCOUNTERED:
A FIGURE LIKE YOUR FATHER, ARMED, BEFORE THEM--AND WITH SOLEMN MARCH GOES SLOW AND STATELY BY THEM.
THIS, TO ME, IN DREADFUL SECRECY IMPART THEY DID,
AND I WITH THEM THE THIRD NIGHT KEPT THE WATCH. THE APPARITION COMES...
'TIS VERY STRANGE.
SKRRRRRCH
ARMED FROM TOP TO TOE?
FROM HEAD TO FOOT.
THEN SAW YOU NOT HIS FACE?
OH YES, MY LORD.
WHAT, LOOKED HE FROWNINGLY?
A COUNTENANCE MORE IN SORROW THAN IN ANGER.

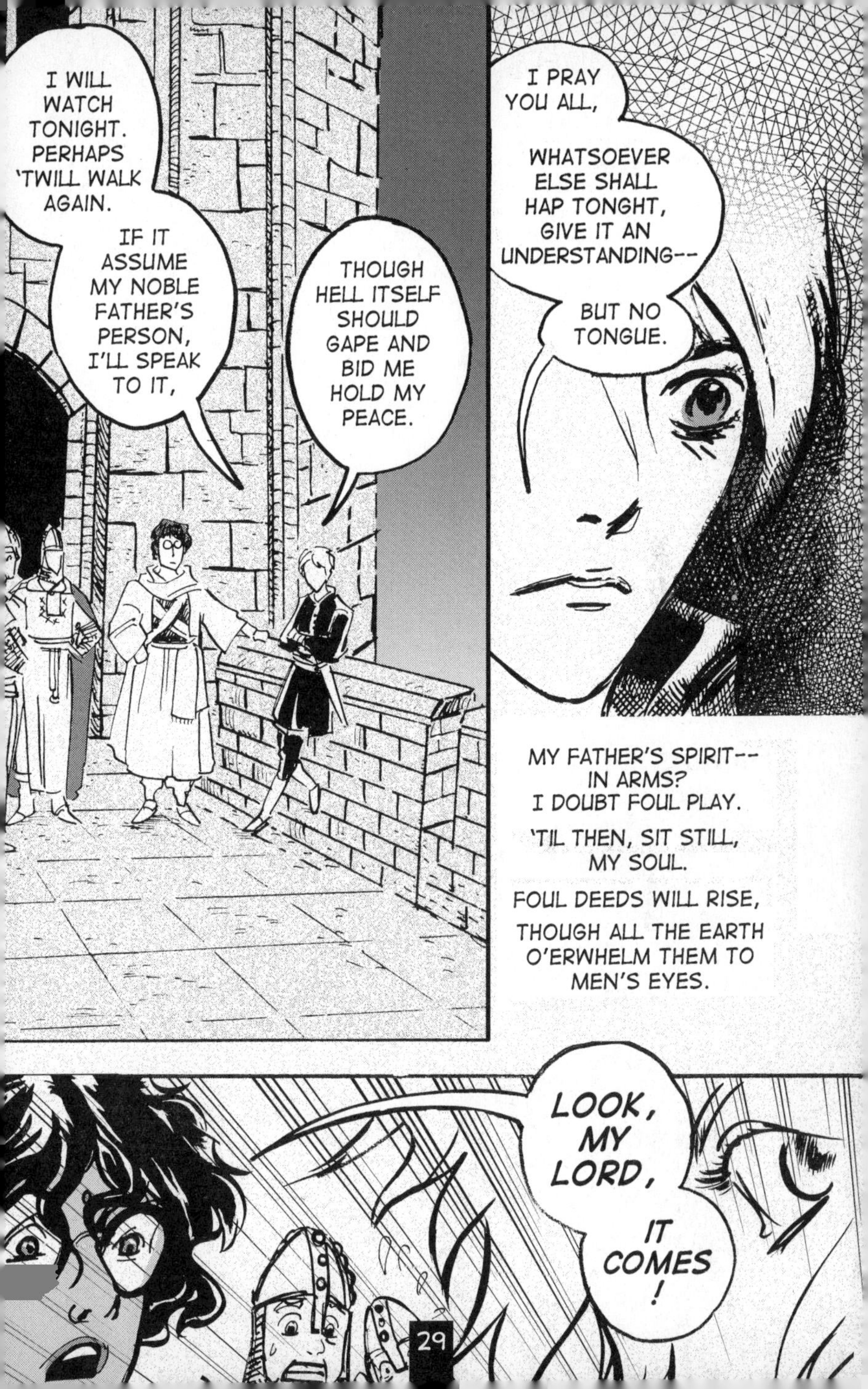
I WILL WATCH TONIGHT. PERHAPS 'TWILL WALK AGAIN.
IF IT ASSUME MY NOBLE FATHER'S PERSON, I'LL SPEAK TO IT,
THOUGH HELL ITSELF SHOULD GAPE AND BID ME HOLD MY PEACE.
I PRAY YOU ALL,
WHATSOEVER ELSE SHALL HAP TONGHT, GIVE IT AN UNDERSTANDING--
BUT NO TONGUE.
MY FATHER'S SPIRIT-- IN ARMS? I DOUBT FOUL PLAY.
'TIL THEN, SIT STILL, MY SOUL.
FOUL DEEDS WILL RISE,
THOUGH ALL THE EARTH O'ERWHELM THEM TO MEN'S EYES.
LOOK, MY LORD,
IT COMES!

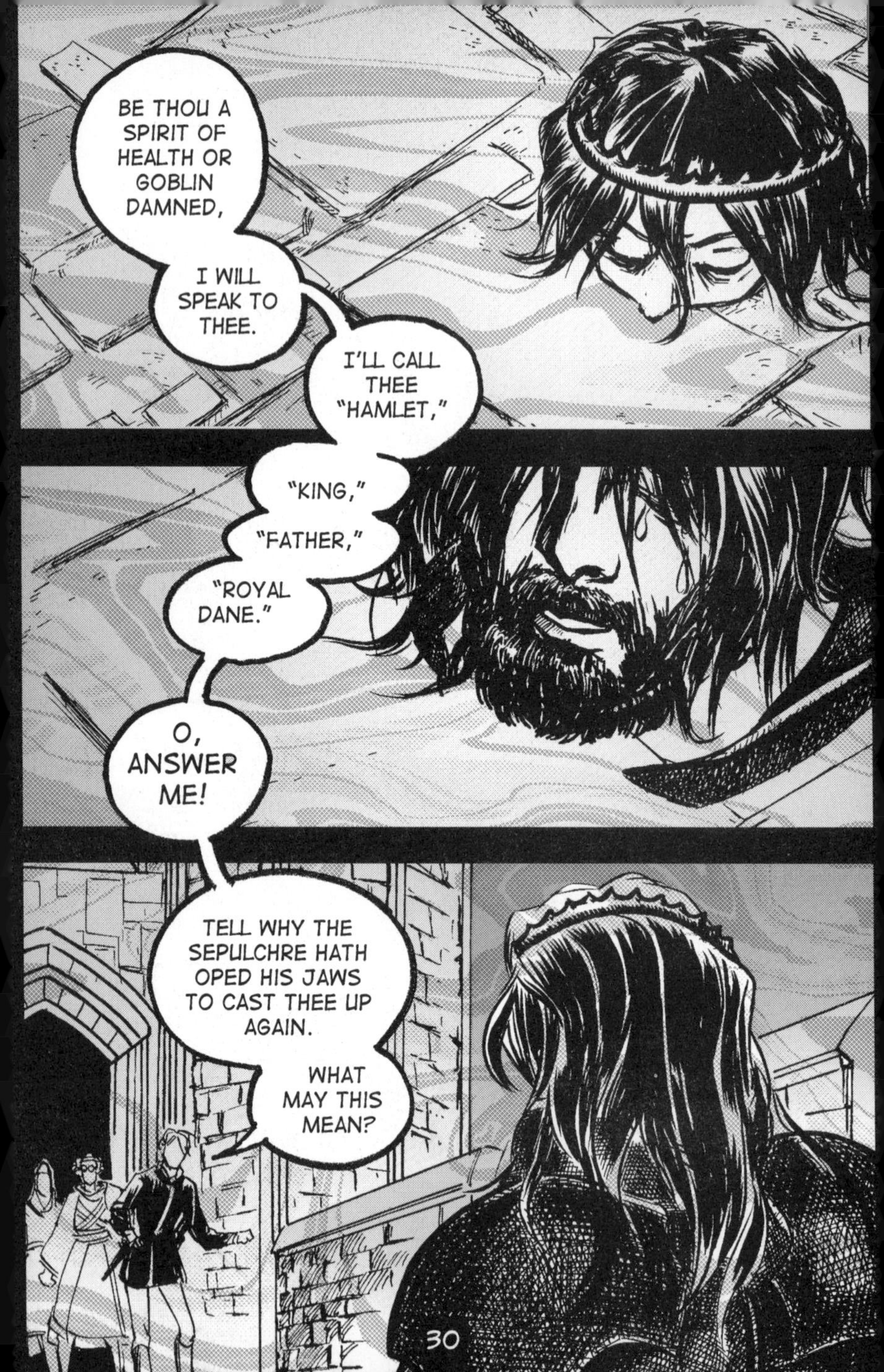
BE THOU A SPIRIT OF HEALTH OR GOBLIN DAMNED,
I WILL SPEAK TO THEE.
I'LL CALL THEE "HAMLET,"
"KING,"
"FATHER,"
"ROYAL DANE."
O, ANSWER ME!
TELL WHY THE SEPULCHRE HATH OPED HIS JAWS TO CAST THEE UP AGAIN.
WHAT MAY THIS MEAN?

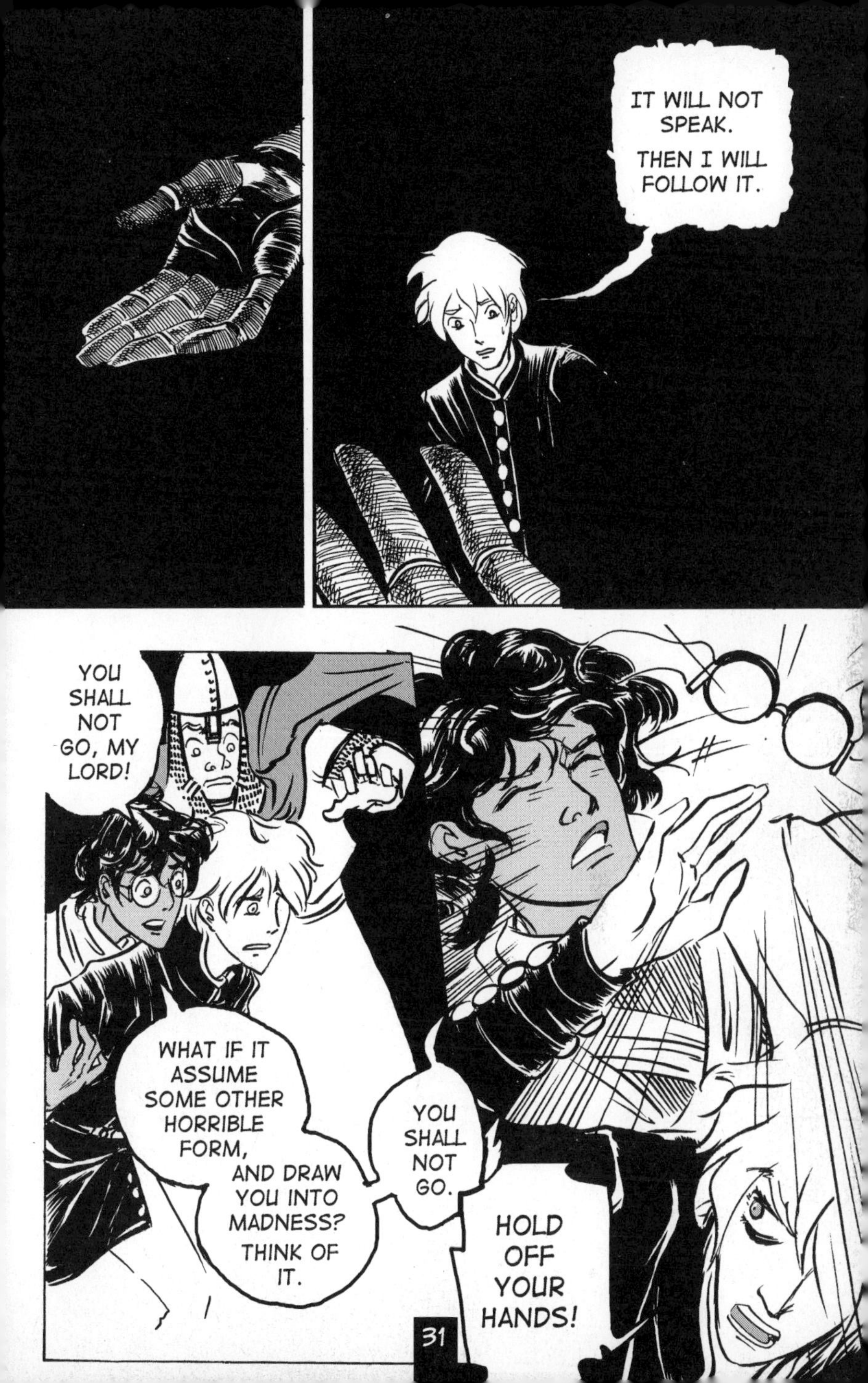
IT WILL NOT SPEAK.
THEN I WILL FOLLOW IT.
YOU SHALL NOT GO, MY LORD!
WHAT IF IT ASSUME SOME OTHER HORRIBLE FORM,
AND DRAW YOU INTO MADNESS?
THINK OF IT.
YOU SHALL NOT GO.
HOLD OFF YOUR HANDS!

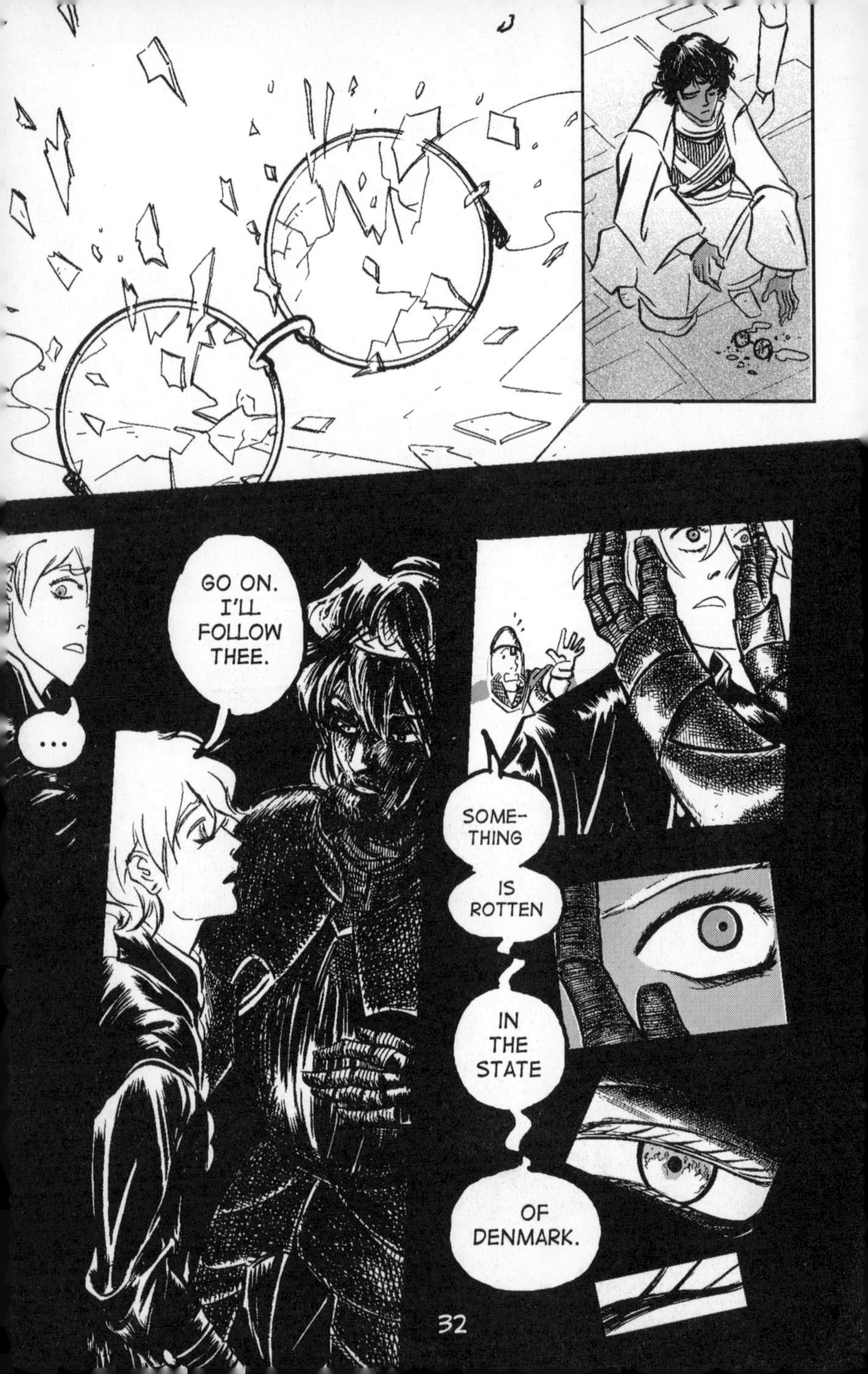
...
GO ON. I'LL FOLLOW THEE.
SOME-THING IS ROTTEN IN THE STATE OF DENMARK.

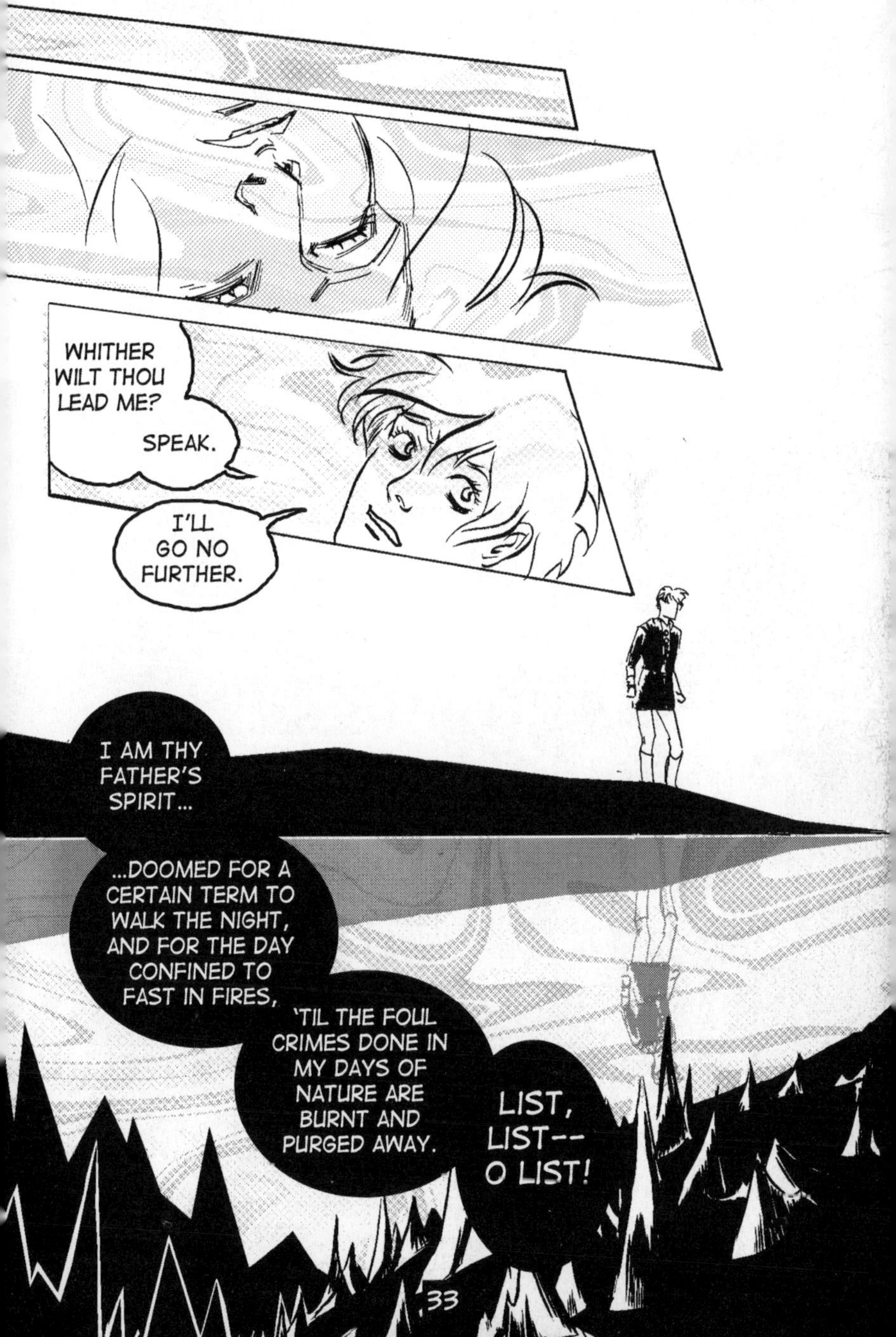
WHITHER WILT THOU LEAD ME?
SPEAK.
I'LL GO NO FURTHER.
I AM THY FATHER'S SPIRIT...
...DOOMED FOR A CERTAIN TERM TO WALK THE NIGHT, AND FOR THE DAY CONFINED TO FAST IN FIRES,
'TIL THE FOUL CRIMES DONE IN MY DAYS OF NATURE ARE BURNT AND PURGED AWAY.
LIST, LIST-- O LIST!

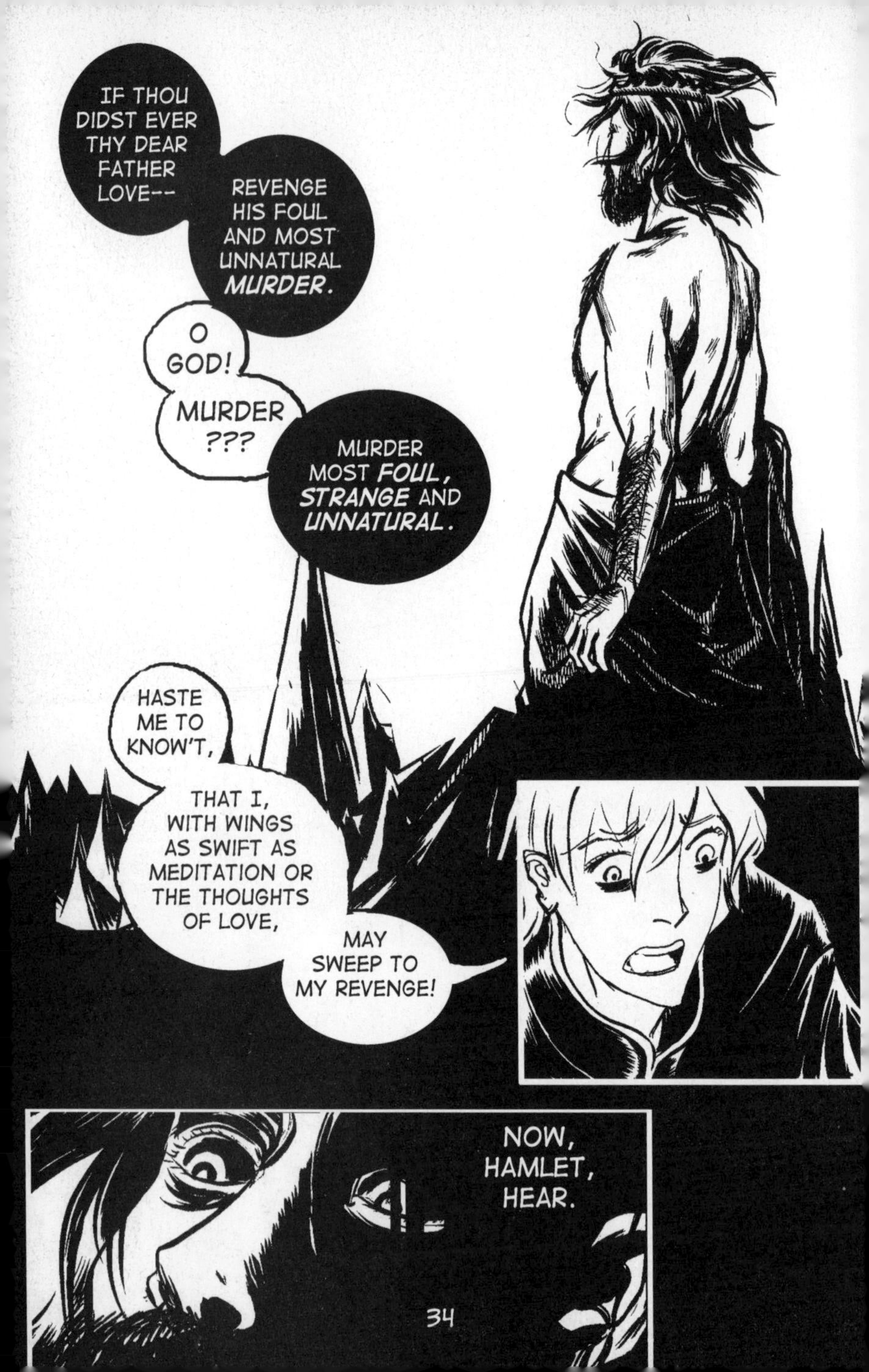
IF THOU DIDST EVER THY DEAR FATHER LOVE--
REVENGE HIS FOUL AND MOST UNNATURAL MURDER.
O GOD!
MURDER ???
MURDER MOST FOUL, STRANGE AND UNNATURAL.
HASTE ME TO KNOW'T,
THAT I, WITH WINGS AS SWIFT AS MEDITATION OR THE THOUGHTS OF LOVE,
MAY SWEEP TO MY REVENGE!
NOW, HAMLET, HEAR.

'TIS GIVEN OUT THAT, SLEEPING IN MY ORCHARD, A SERPENT STUNG ME.
BUT, THOU NOBLE YOUTH, THE SERPENT THAT DID STING THY FATHER'S LIFE NOW WEARS HIS FATHER'S CROWN.
MINE UNCLE ???
AY, THAT *INCESTUOUS* BEAST WON TO HIS SHAMEFUL *LUST* THE WILL OF MY MOST SEEMING-VIRTUOUS QUEEN.
BUT SOFT! METHINKS I SCENT THE MORNING AIR. BRIEF LET ME BE...
SLEEPING WITHIN MY ORCHARD, MY CUSTOM ALWAYS OF THE AFTERNOON...

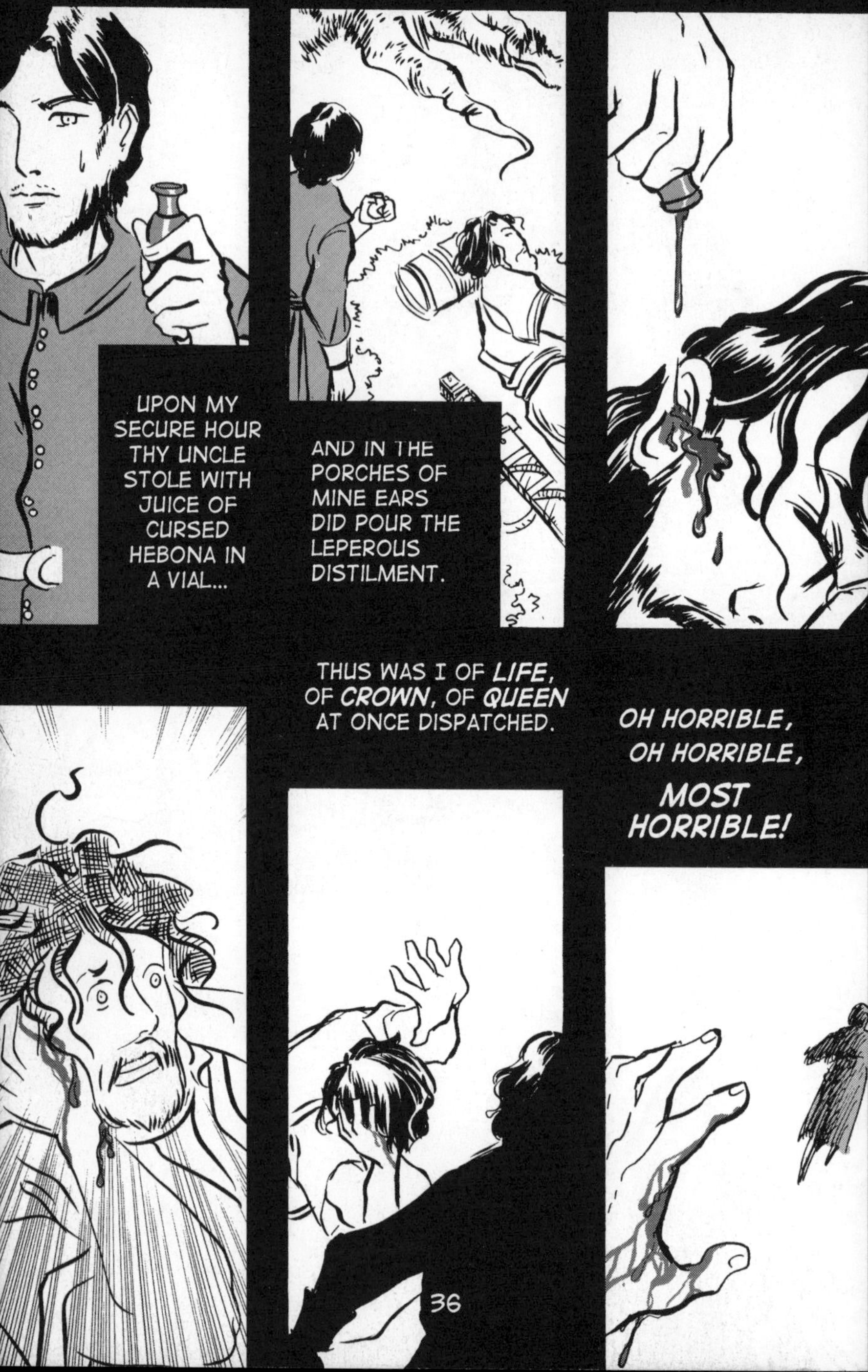
UPON MY SECURE HOUR THY UNCLE STOLE WITH JUICE OF CURSED HEBONA IN A VIAL...
AND IN THE PORCHES OF MINE EARS DID POUR THE LEPEROUS DISTILMENT.
THUS WAS I OF *LIFE*, OF *CROWN*, OF *QUEEN* AT ONCE DISPATCHED.
OH HORRIBLE, OH HORRIBLE, MOST HORRIBLE!

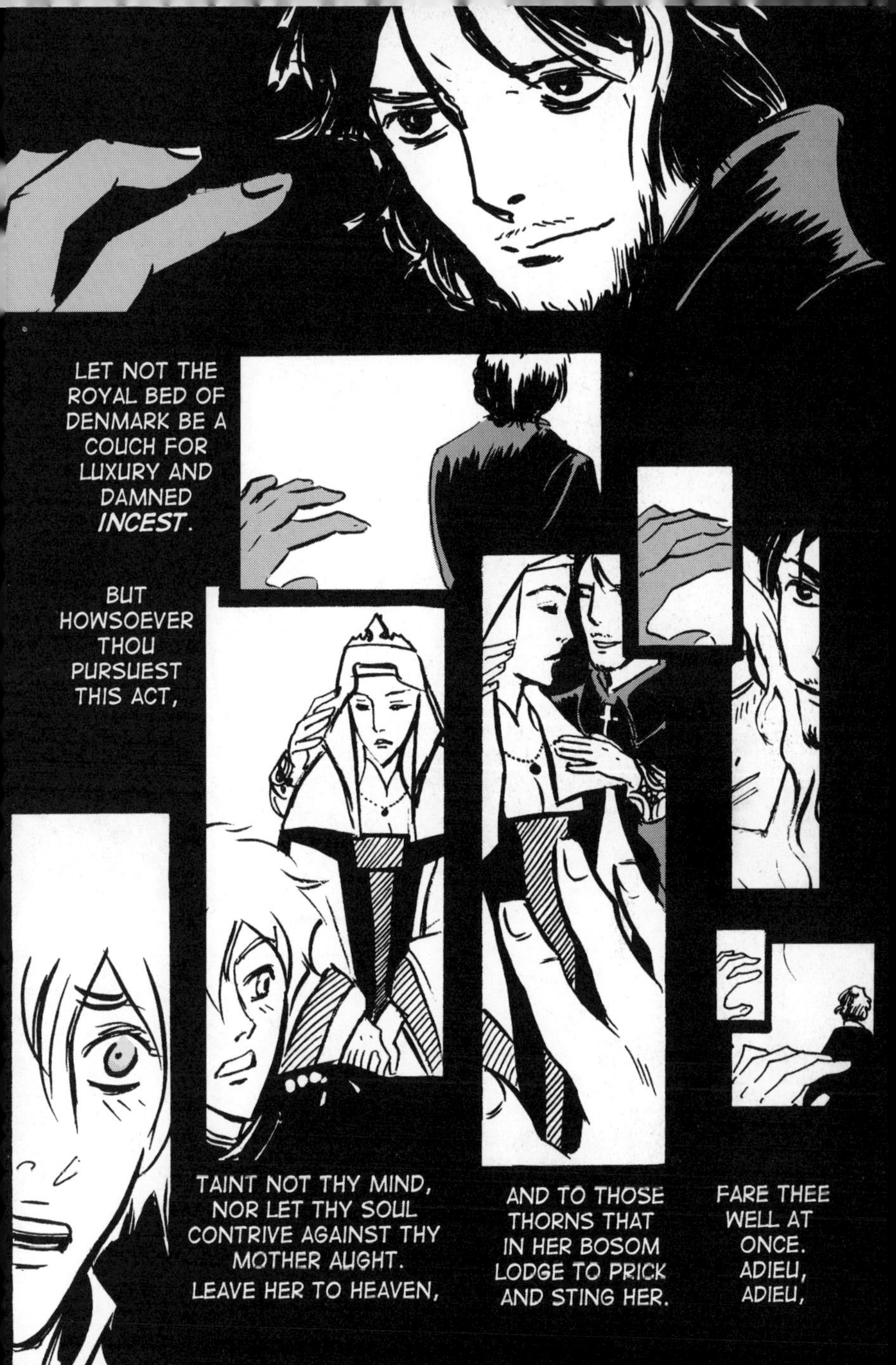
LET NOT THE ROYAL BED OF DENMARK BE A COUCH FOR LUXURY AND DAMNED *INCEST*.
BUT HOWSOEVER THOU PURSUEST THIS ACT,
TAINT NOT THY MIND, NOR LET THY SOUL CONTRIVE AGAINST THY MOTHER AUGHT.
LEAVE HER TO HEAVEN,
AND TO THOSE THORNS THAT IN HER BOSOM LODGE TO PRICK AND STING HER.
FARE THEE WELL AT ONCE.
ADIEU, ADIEU,

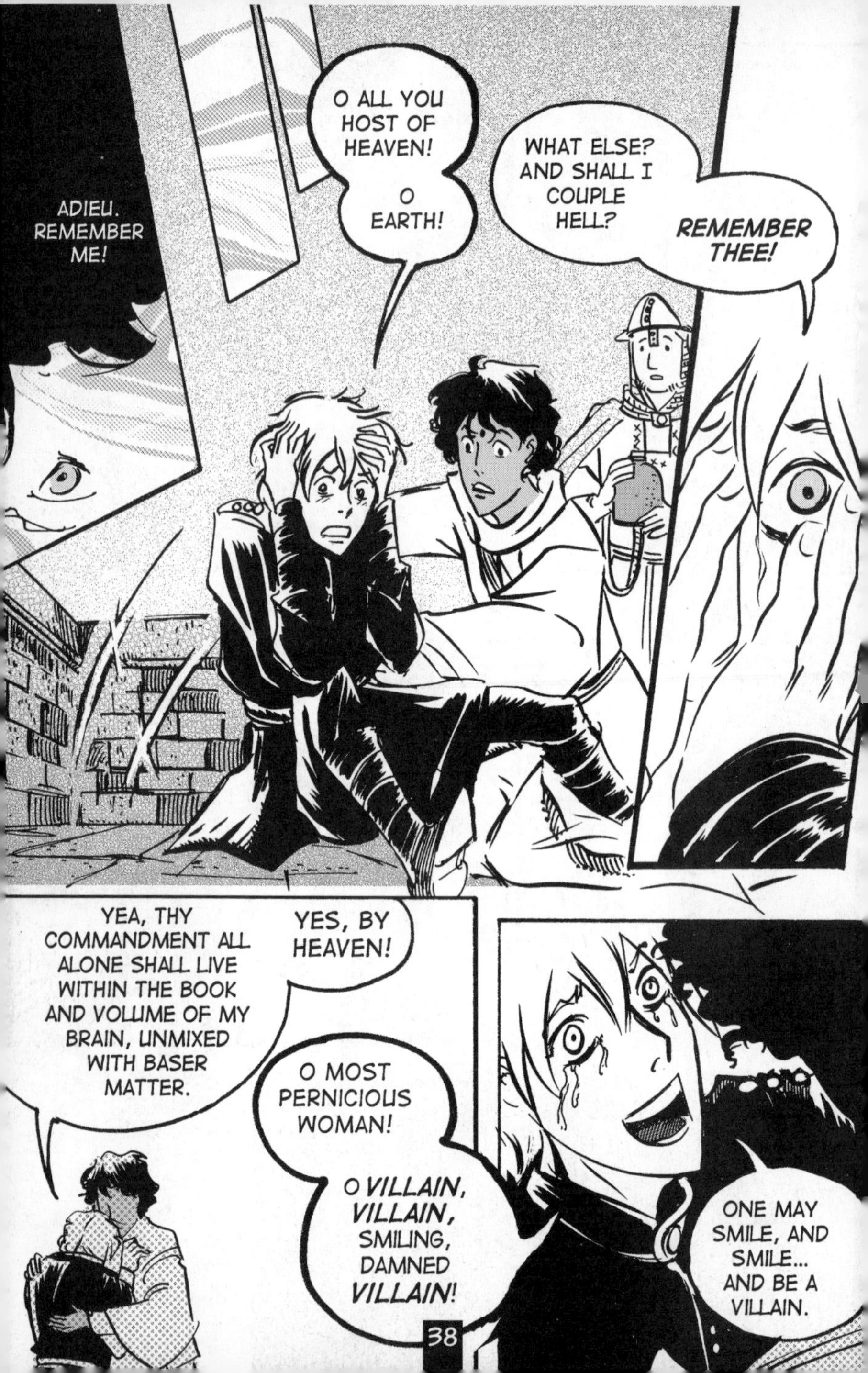
ADIEU. REMEMBER ME!
O ALL YOU HOST OF HEAVEN!
O EARTH!
WHAT ELSE? AND SHALL I COUPLE HELL?
REMEMBER THEE!
YEA, THY COMMANDMENT ALL ALONE SHALL LIVE WITHIN THE BOOK AND VOLUME OF MY BRAIN, UNMIXED WITH BASER MATTER.
YES, BY HEAVEN!
O MOST PERNICIOUS WOMAN!
O VILLAIN, VILLAIN, SMILING, DAMNED VILLAIN!
ONE MAY SMILE, AND SMILE... AND BE A VILLAIN.

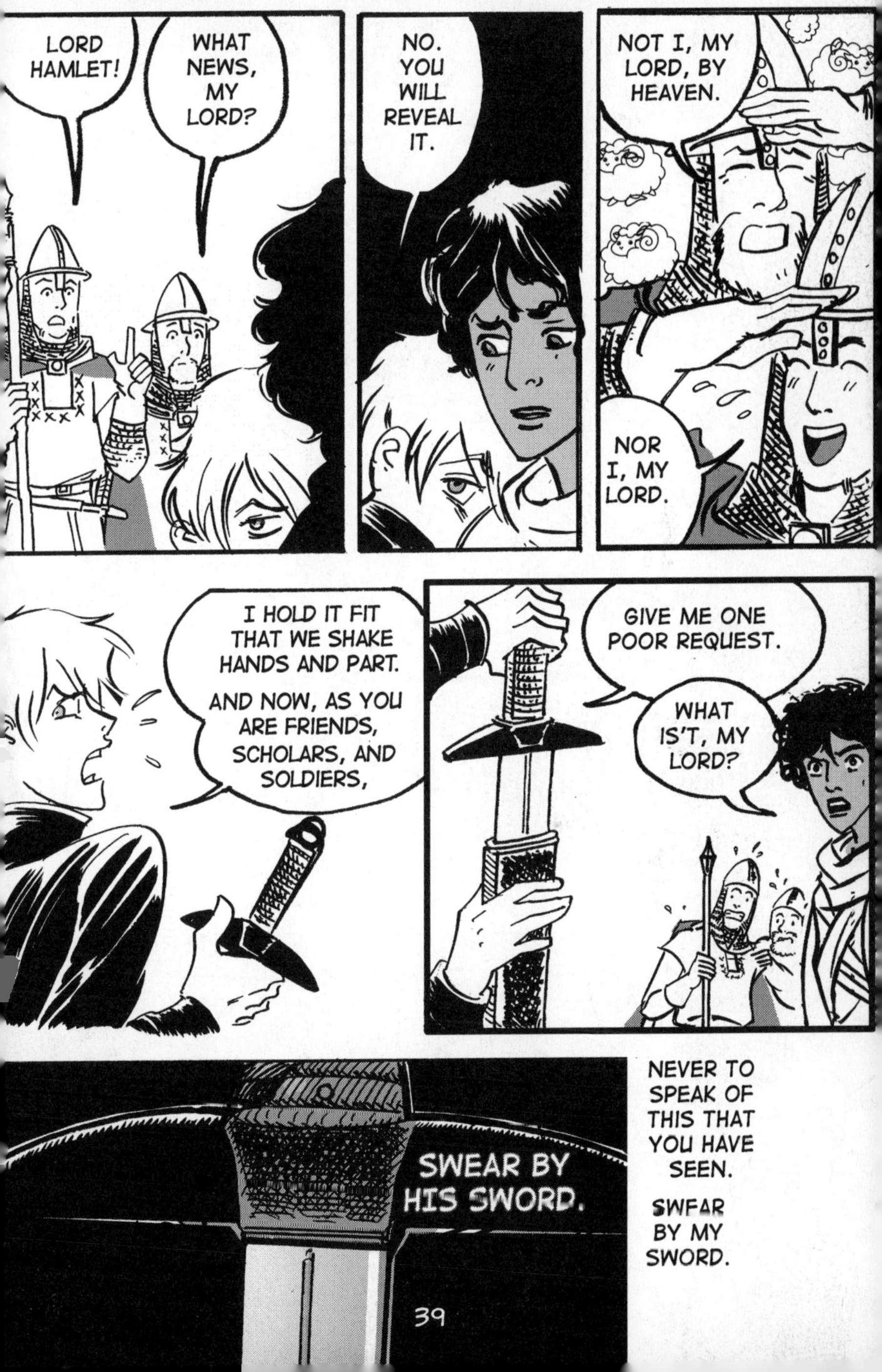
LORD HAMLET!
WHAT NEWS, MY LORD?
NO. YOU WILL REVEAL IT.
NOT I, MY LORD, BY HEAVEN.
NOR I, MY LORD.
I HOLD IT FIT THAT WE SHAKE HANDS AND PART.
AND NOW, AS YOU ARE FRIENDS, SCHOLARS, AND SOLDIERS,
GIVE ME ONE POOR REQUEST.
WHAT IS'T, MY LORD?
SWEAR BY HIS SWORD.
NEVER TO SPEAK OF THIS THAT YOU HAVE SEEN.
SWEAR BY MY SWORD.

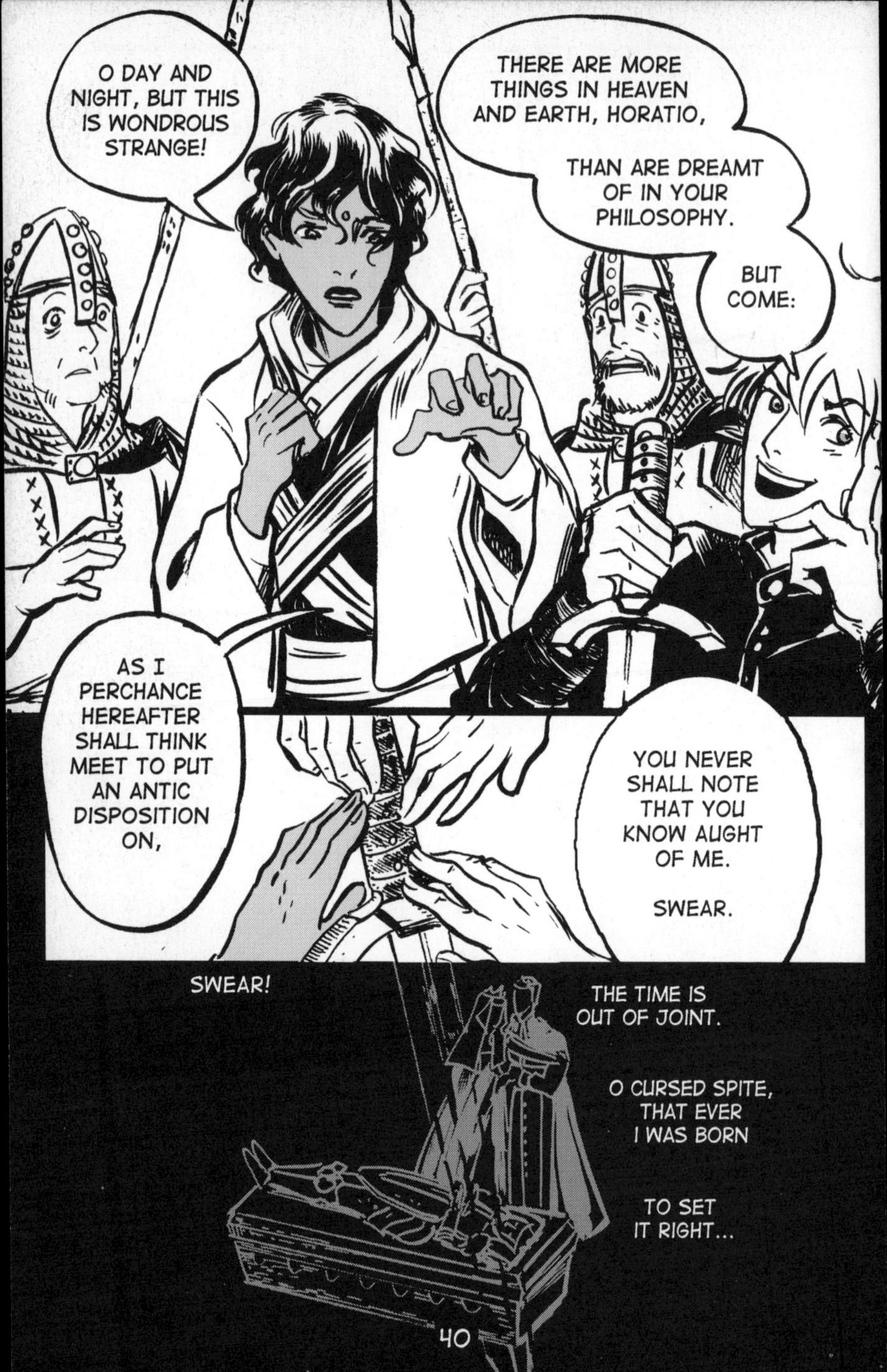
O DAY AND NIGHT, BUT THIS IS WONDROUS STRANGE!
THERE ARE MORE THINGS IN HEAVEN AND EARTH, HORATIO,
THAN ARE DREAMT OF IN YOUR PHILOSOPHY.
BUT COME:
AS I PERCHANCE HEREAFTER SHALL THINK MEET TO PUT AN ANTIC DISPOSITION ON,
YOU NEVER SHALL NOTE THAT YOU KNOW AUGHT OF ME.
SWEAR.
SWEAR!
THE TIME IS OUT OF JOINT.
O CURSED SPITE, THAT EVER I WAS BORN
TO SET IT RIGHT...

Aᴄᴛ II

I'LL HAVE GROUNDS MORE RELATIVE THAN THIS.

THE **PLAY'S** THE THING WHEREIN I'LL CATCH THE CONSCIENCE OF THE KING.

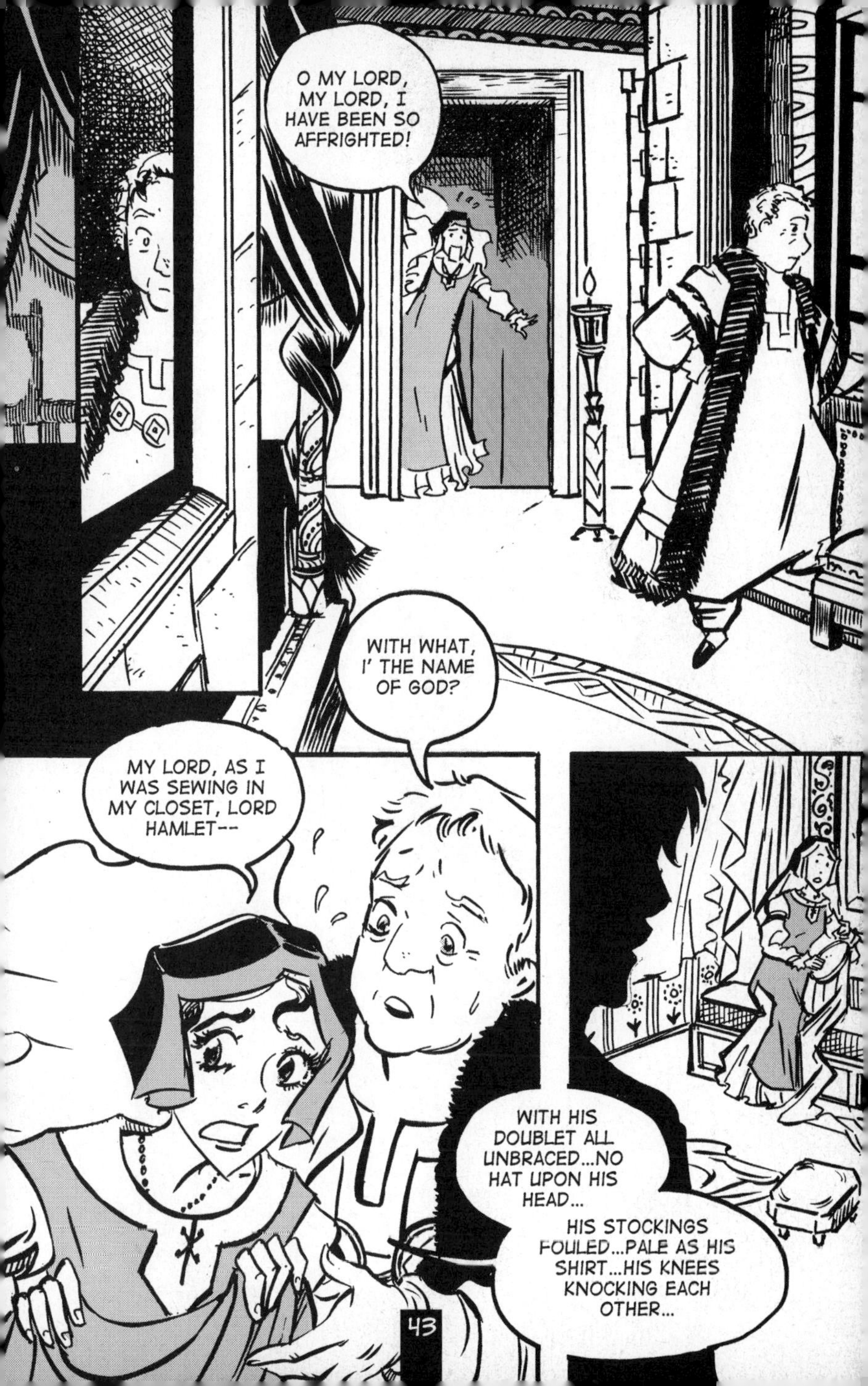
O MY LORD, MY LORD, I HAVE BEEN SO AFFRIGHTED!
WITH WHAT, I' THE NAME OF GOD?
MY LORD, AS I WAS SEWING IN MY CLOSET, LORD HAMLET--
WITH HIS DOUBLET ALL UNBRACED...NO HAT UPON HIS HEAD...
HIS STOCKINGS FOULED...PALE AS HIS SHIRT...HIS KNEES KNOCKING EACH OTHER...

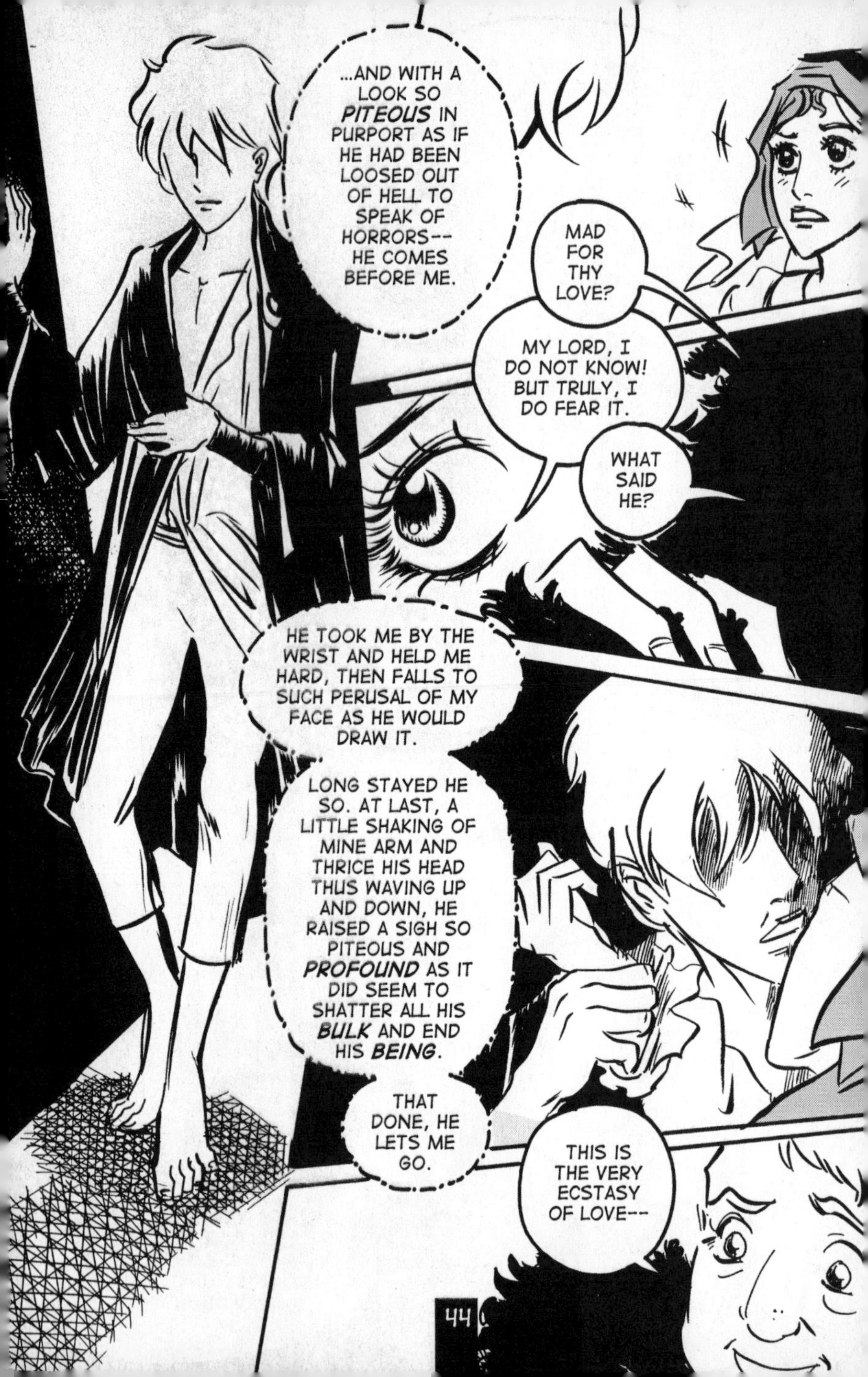
...AND WITH A LOOK SO *PITEOUS* IN PURPORT AS IF HE HAD BEEN LOOSED OUT OF HELL TO SPEAK OF HORRORS-- HE COMES BEFORE ME.
MAD FOR THY LOVE?
MY LORD, I DO NOT KNOW! BUT TRULY, I DO FEAR IT.
WHAT SAID HE?
HE TOOK ME BY THE WRIST AND HELD ME HARD, THEN FALLS TO SUCH PERUSAL OF MY FACE AS HE WOULD DRAW IT.
LONG STAYED HE SO. AT LAST, A LITTLE SHAKING OF MINE ARM AND THRICE HIS HEAD THUS WAVING UP AND DOWN, HE RAISED A SIGH SO PITEOUS AND *PROFOUND* AS IT DID SEEM TO SHATTER ALL HIS *BULK* AND END HIS *BEING*.
THAT DONE, HE LETS ME GO.
THIS IS THE VERY ECSTASY OF LOVE--

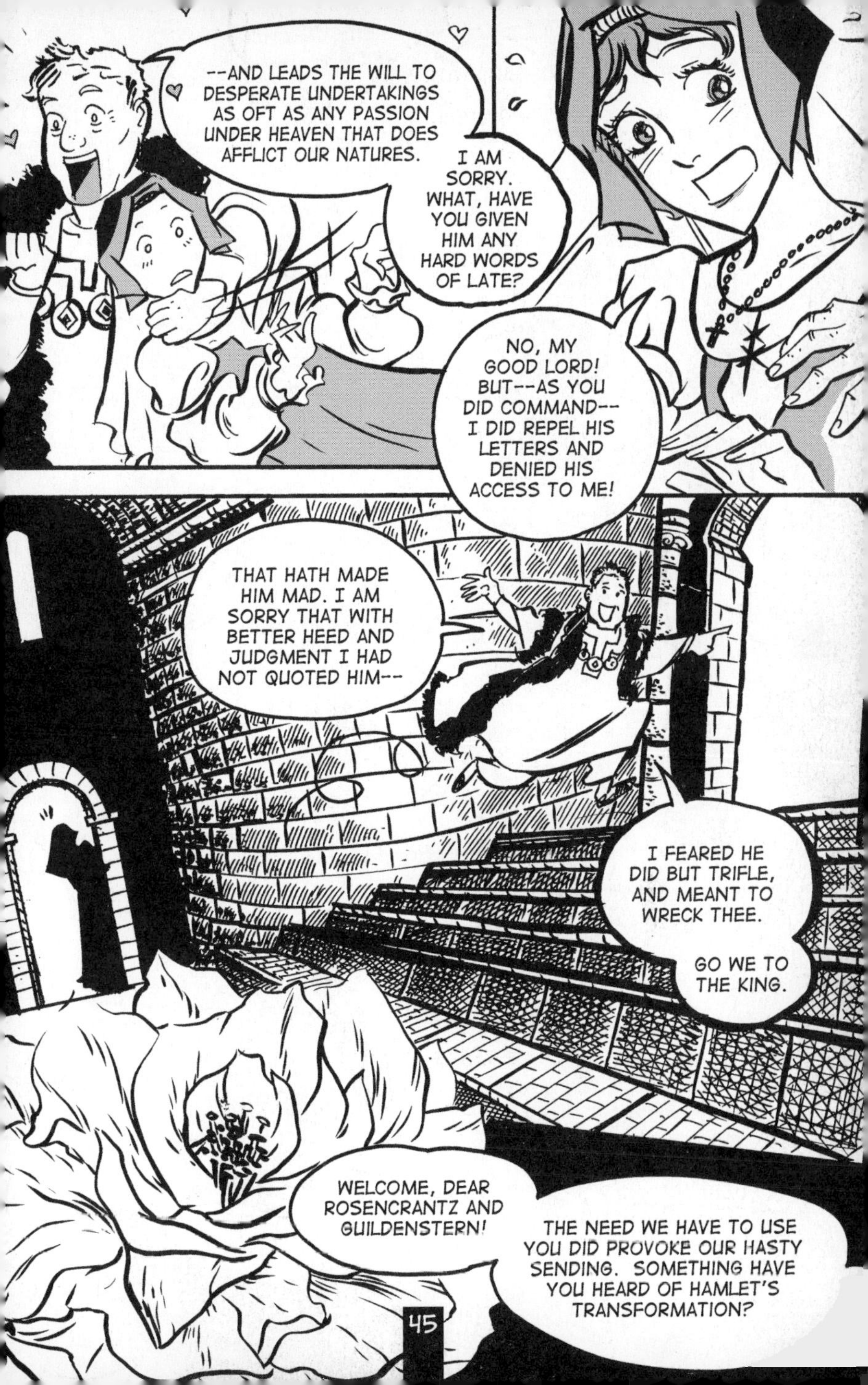
--AND LEADS THE WILL TO DESPERATE UNDERTAKINGS AS OFT AS ANY PASSION UNDER HEAVEN THAT DOES AFFLICT OUR NATURES.
I AM SORRY. WHAT, HAVE YOU GIVEN HIM ANY HARD WORDS OF LATE?
NO, MY GOOD LORD! BUT--AS YOU DID COMMAND--I DID REPEL HIS LETTERS AND DENIED HIS ACCESS TO ME!
THAT HATH MADE HIM MAD. I AM SORRY THAT WITH BETTER HEED AND JUDGMENT I HAD NOT QUOTED HIM--
I FEARED HE DID BUT TRIFLE, AND MEANT TO WRECK THEE.
GO WE TO THE KING.
WELCOME, DEAR ROSENCRANTZ AND GUILDENSTERN!
THE NEED WE HAVE TO USE YOU DID PROVOKE OUR HASTY SENDING. SOMETHING HAVE YOU HEARD OF HAMLET'S TRANSFORMATION?

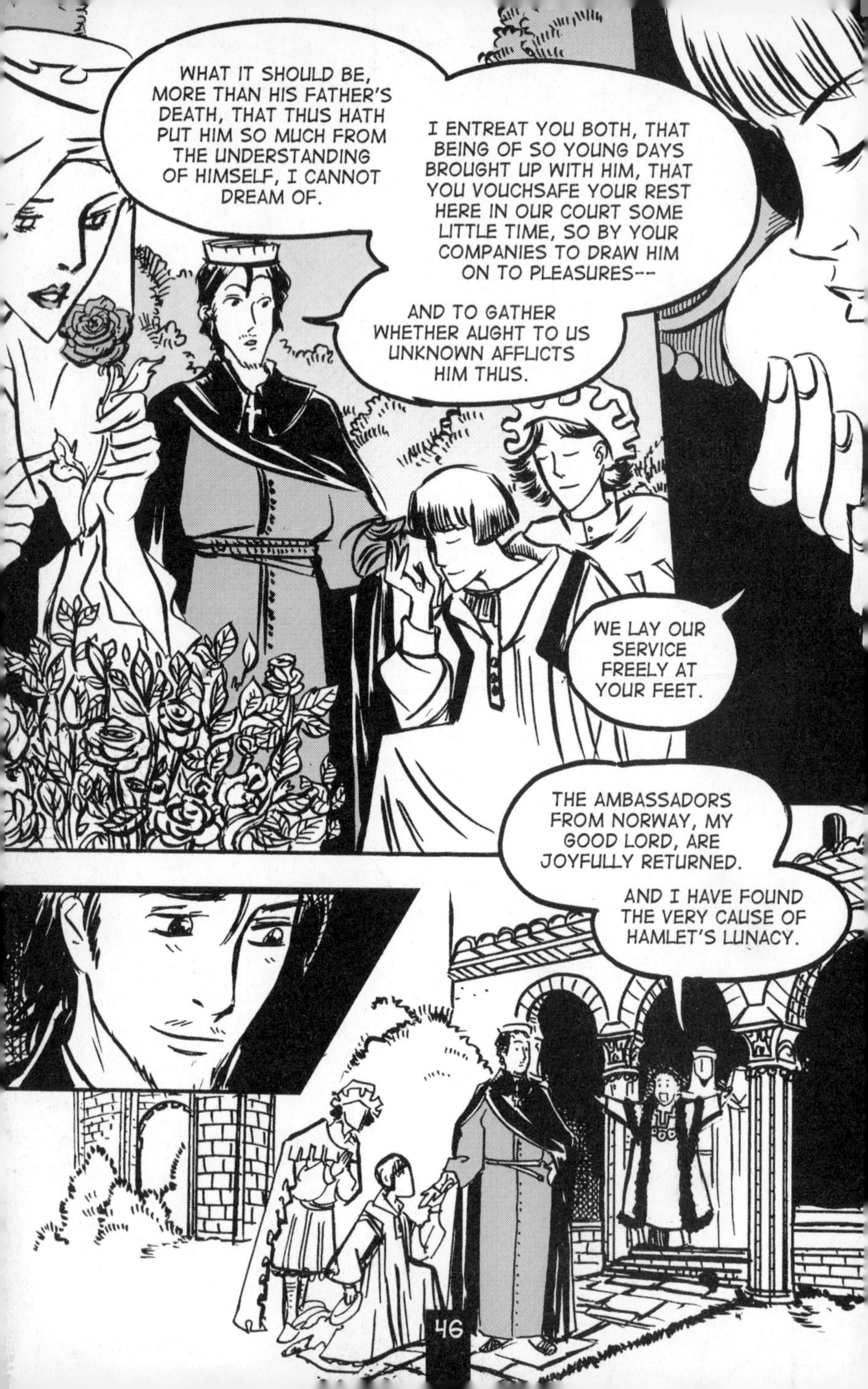
WHAT IT SHOULD BE, MORE THAN HIS FATHER'S DEATH, THAT THUS HATH PUT HIM SO MUCH FROM THE UNDERSTANDING OF HIMSELF, I CANNOT DREAM OF.
I ENTREAT YOU BOTH, THAT BEING OF SO YOUNG DAYS BROUGHT UP WITH HIM, THAT YOU VOUCHSAFE YOUR REST HERE IN OUR COURT SOME LITTLE TIME, SO BY YOUR COMPANIES TO DRAW HIM ON TO PLEASURES--
AND TO GATHER WHETHER AUGHT TO US UNKNOWN AFFLICTS HIM THUS.
WE LAY OUR SERVICE FREELY AT YOUR FEET.
THE AMBASSADORS FROM NORWAY, MY GOOD LORD, ARE JOYFULLY RETURNED.
AND I HAVE FOUND THE VERY CAUSE OF HAMLET'S LUNACY.

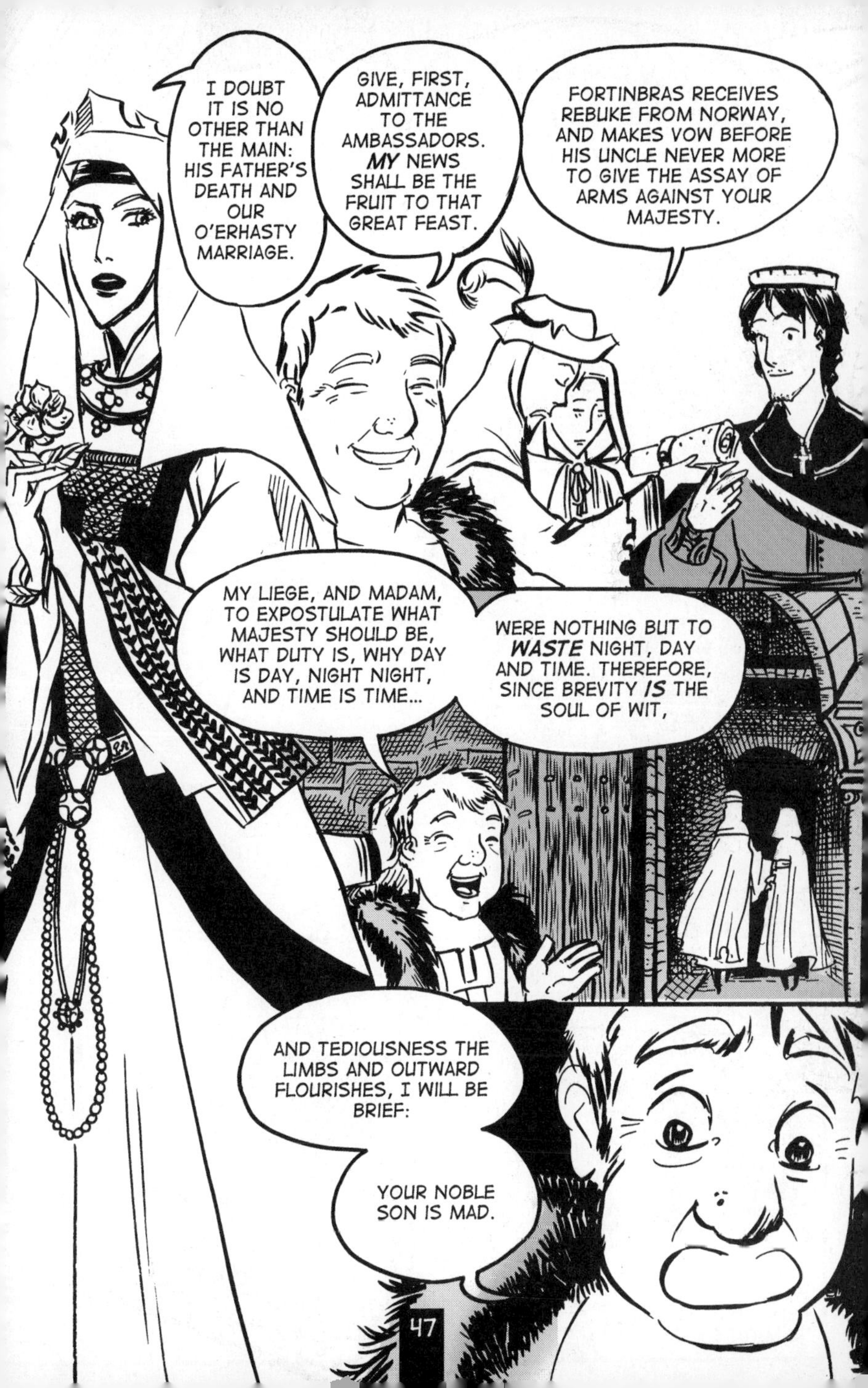
I DOUBT IT IS NO OTHER THAN THE MAIN: HIS FATHER'S DEATH AND OUR O'ERHASTY MARRIAGE.
GIVE, FIRST, ADMITTANCE TO THE AMBASSADORS. *MY* NEWS SHALL BE THE FRUIT TO THAT GREAT FEAST.
FORTINBRAS RECEIVES REBUKE FROM NORWAY, AND MAKES VOW BEFORE HIS UNCLE NEVER MORE TO GIVE THE ASSAY OF ARMS AGAINST YOUR MAJESTY.
MY LIEGE, AND MADAM, TO EXPOSTULATE WHAT MAJESTY SHOULD BE, WHAT DUTY IS, WHY DAY IS DAY, NIGHT NIGHT, AND TIME IS TIME...
WERE NOTHING BUT TO *WASTE* NIGHT, DAY AND TIME. THEREFORE, SINCE BREVITY *IS* THE SOUL OF WIT,
AND TEDIOUSNESS THE LIMBS AND OUTWARD FLOURISHES, I WILL BE BRIEF:
YOUR NOBLE SON IS MAD.

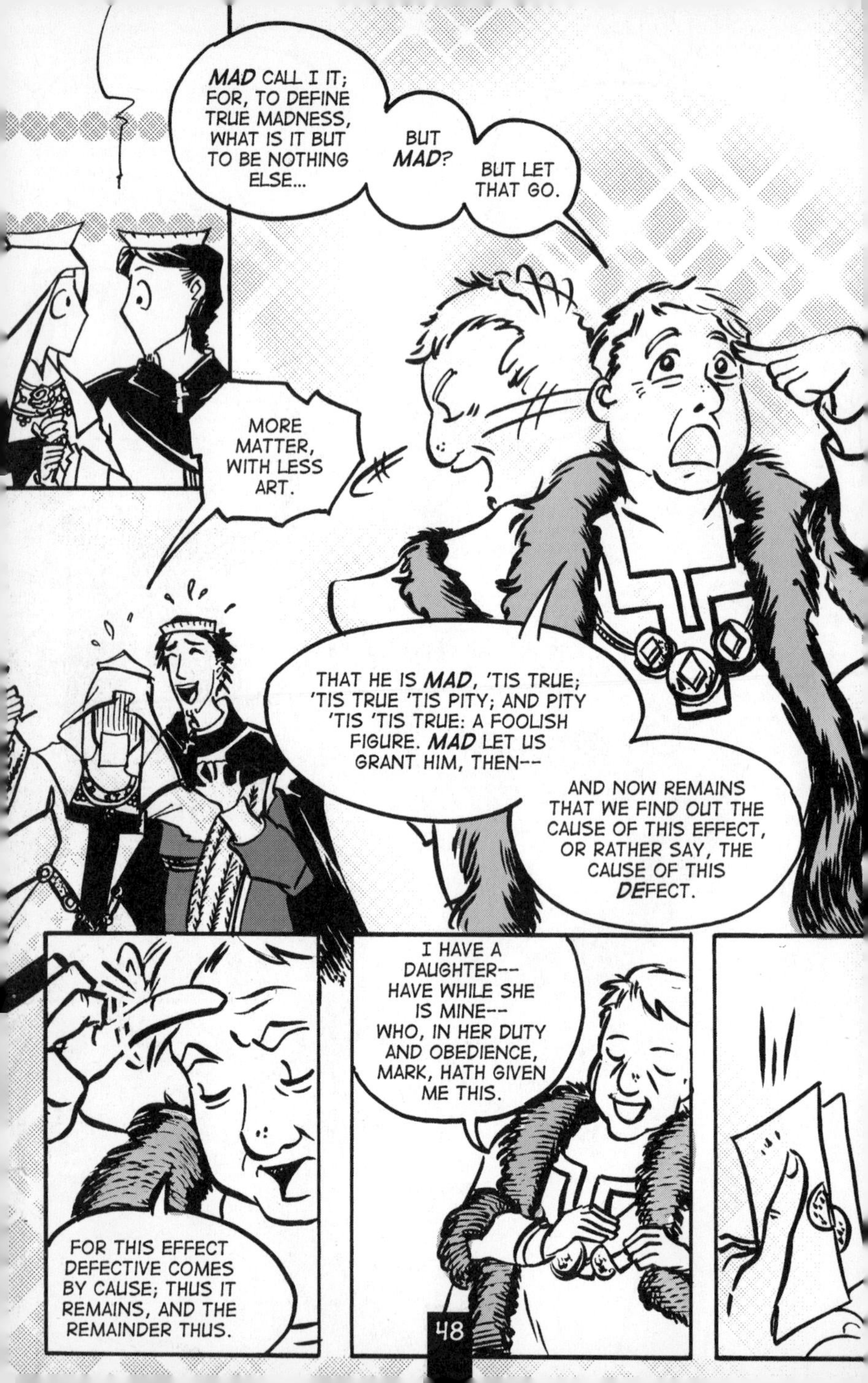
MAD CALL I IT; FOR, TO DEFINE TRUE MADNESS, WHAT IS IT BUT TO BE NOTHING ELSE...
BUT MAD?
BUT LET THAT GO.
MORE MATTER, WITH LESS ART.
THAT HE IS MAD, 'TIS TRUE; 'TIS TRUE 'TIS PITY; AND PITY 'TIS 'TIS TRUE: A FOOLISH FIGURE. MAD LET US GRANT HIM, THEN--
AND NOW REMAINS THAT WE FIND OUT THE CAUSE OF THIS EFFECT, OR RATHER SAY, THE CAUSE OF THIS DEFECT.
FOR THIS EFFECT DEFECTIVE COMES BY CAUSE; THUS IT REMAINS, AND THE REMAINDER THUS.
I HAVE A DAUGHTER-- HAVE WHILE SHE IS MINE-- WHO, IN HER DUTY AND OBEDIENCE, MARK, HATH GIVEN ME THIS.

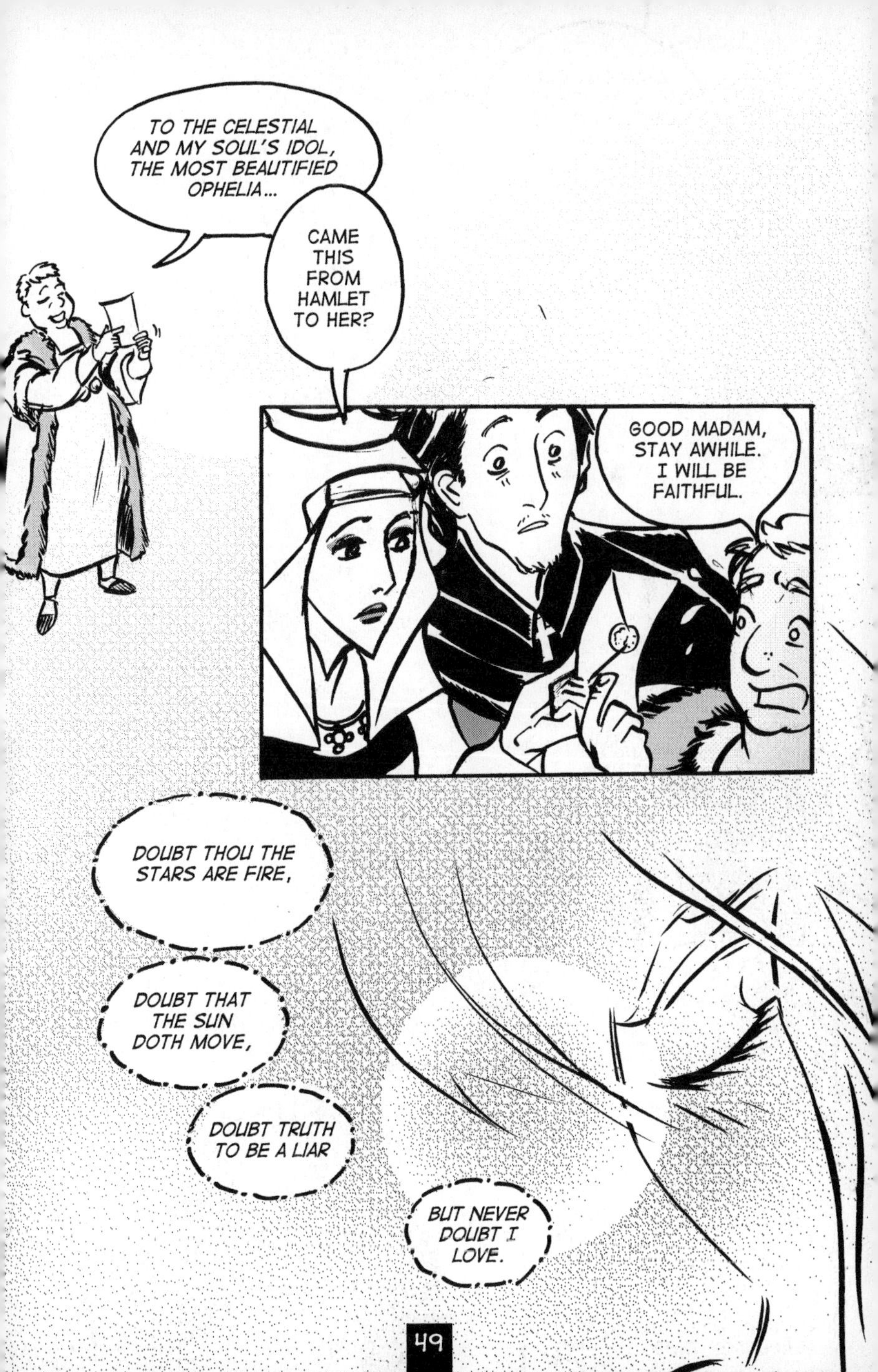
TO THE CELESTIAL AND MY SOUL'S IDOL, THE MOST BEAUTIFIED OPHELIA...
CAME THIS FROM HAMLET TO HER?
GOOD MADAM, STAY AWHILE. I WILL BE FAITHFUL.
DOUBT THOU THE STARS ARE FIRE,
DOUBT THAT THE SUN DOTH MOVE,
DOUBT TRUTH TO BE A LIAR
BUT NEVER DOUBT I LOVE.

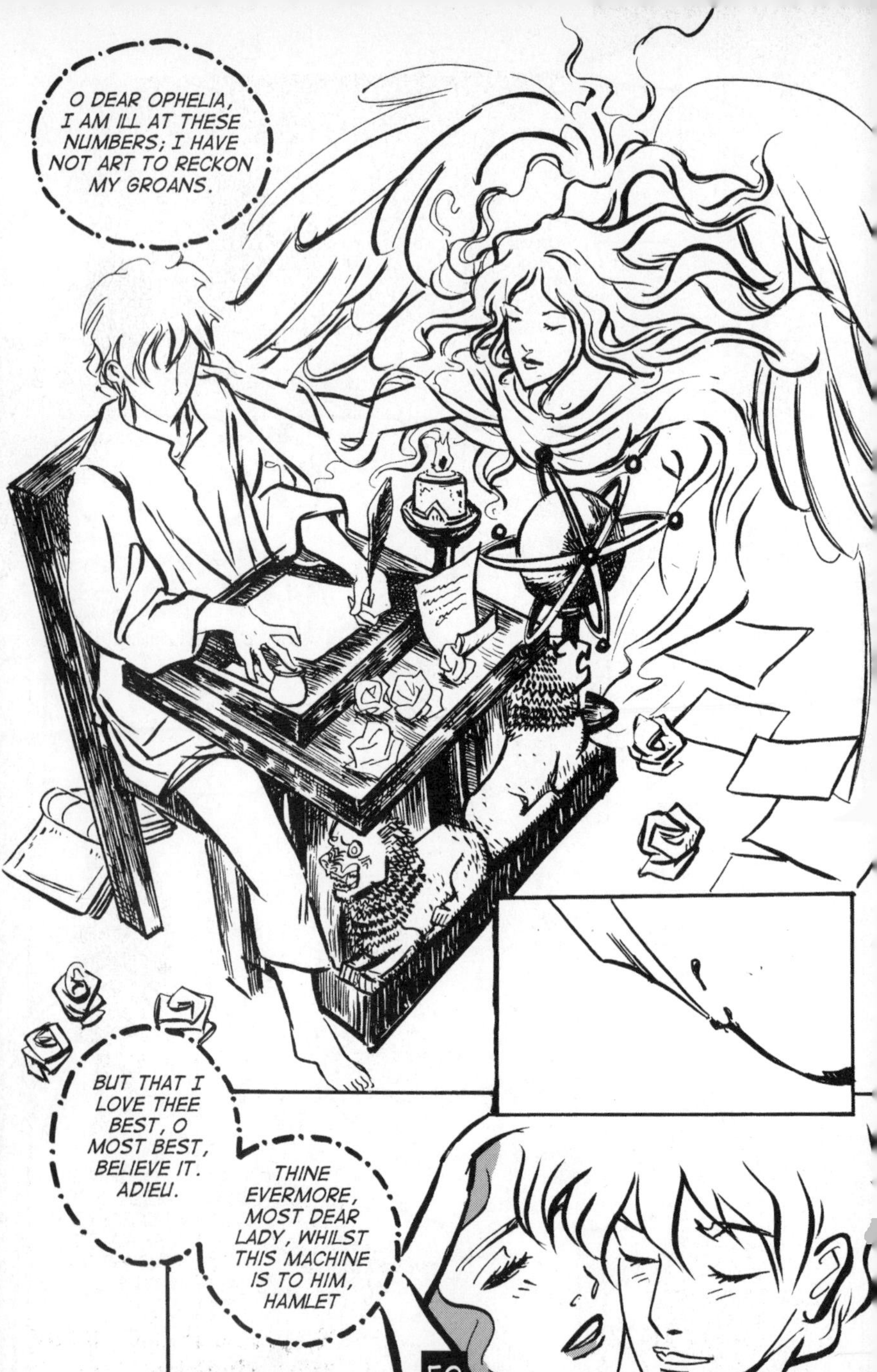
O DEAR OPHELIA, I AM ILL AT THESE NUMBERS; I HAVE NOT ART TO RECKON MY GROANS.
BUT THAT I LOVE THEE BEST, O MOST BEST, BELIEVE IT. ADIEU.
THINE EVERMORE, MOST DEAR LADY, WHILST THIS MACHINE IS TO HIM, HAMLET

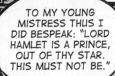

TO MY YOUNG MISTRESS THUS I DID BESPEAK: "LORD HAMLET IS A PRINCE, OUT OF THY STAR. THIS MUST NOT BE."

AND THEN I PRECEPTS GAVE HER: THAT SHE SHOULD LOCK HERSELF FROM HIS RESORT, ADMIT NO MESSENGERS, RECEIVE NO TOKENS. WHICH DONE, SHE TOOK THE FRUITS OF MY ADVICE;

AND HE, REPELLED (A SHORT TALE TO MAKE) FELL INTO A *SADNESS*, THEN INTO A *FAST*, THENCE TO A *WATCH*, THENCE INTO A *WEAKNESS*, THENCE TO A *LIGHTNESS*-- AND, BY THIS DECLENSION,

INTO THE *MADNESS* WHEREIN NOW HE RAVES AND WE ALL MOURN FOR.

51

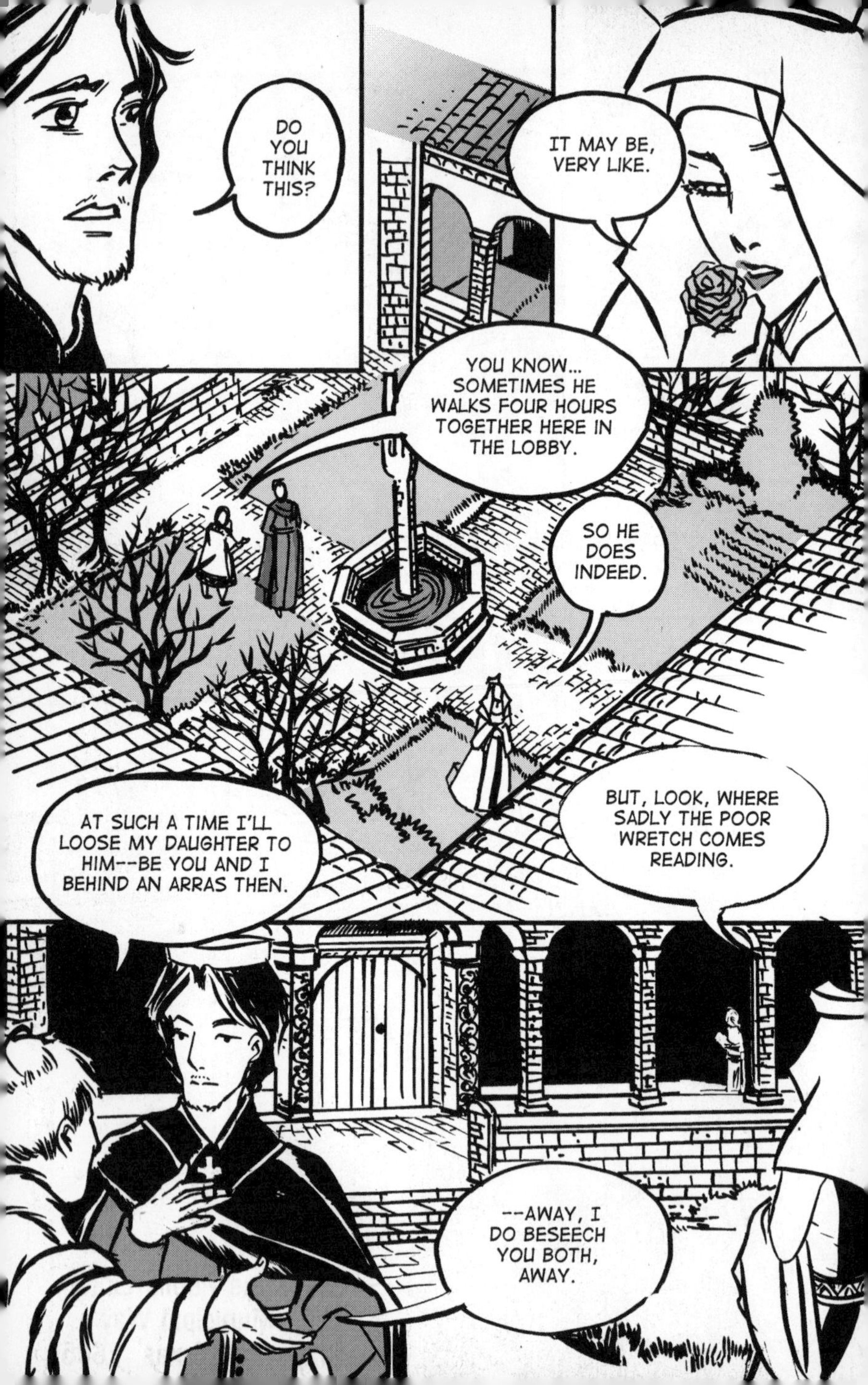
DO YOU THINK THIS?
IT MAY BE, VERY LIKE.
YOU KNOW... SOMETIMES HE WALKS FOUR HOURS TOGETHER HERE IN THE LOBBY.
SO HE DOES INDEED.
AT SUCH A TIME I'LL LOOSE MY DAUGHTER TO HIM--BE YOU AND I BEHIND AN ARRAS THEN.
BUT, LOOK, WHERE SADLY THE POOR WRETCH COMES READING.
--AWAY, I DO BESEECH YOU BOTH, AWAY.

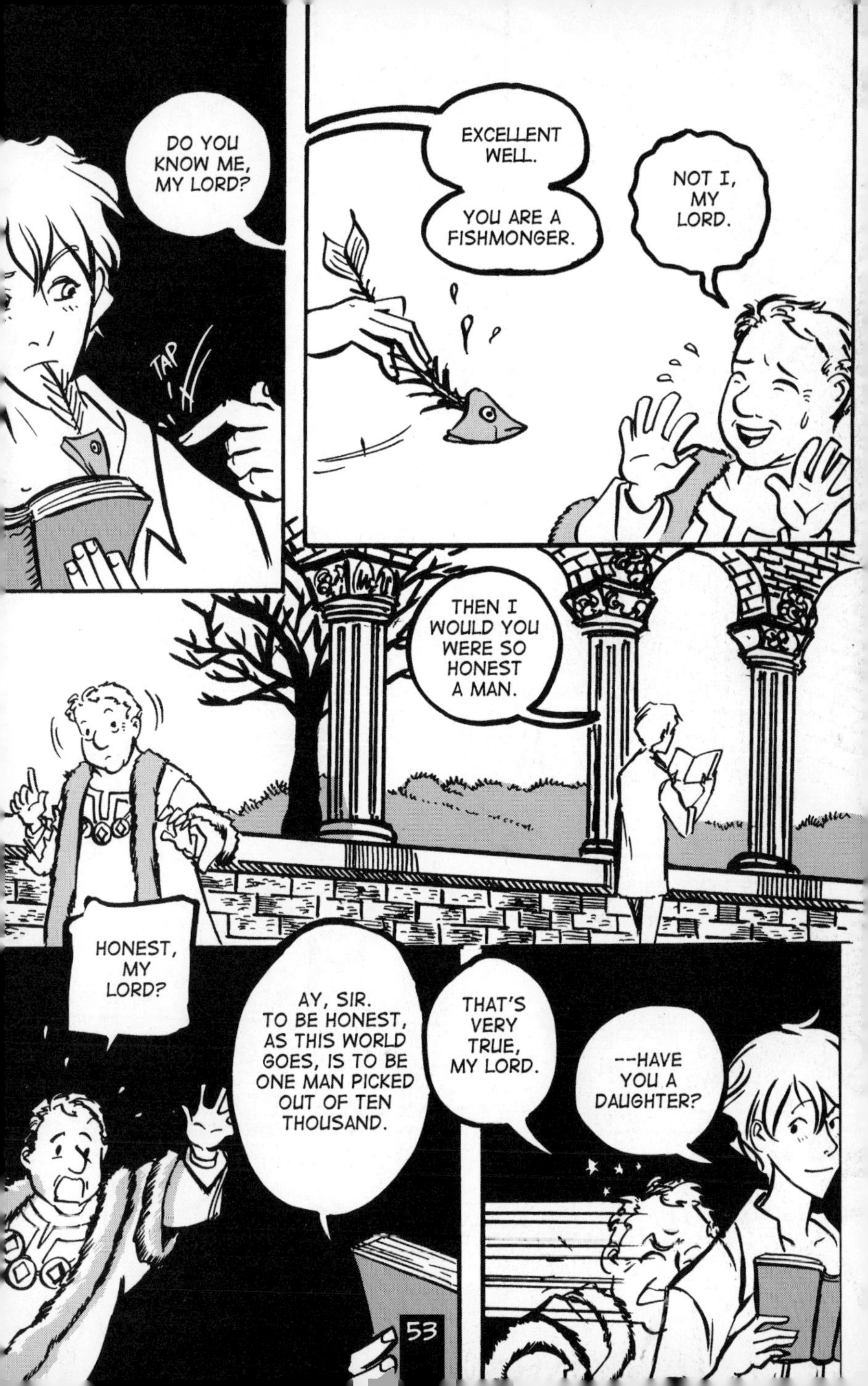
DO YOU KNOW ME, MY LORD?
EXCELLENT WELL.
YOU ARE A FISHMONGER.
TAP
NOT I, MY LORD.
THEN I WOULD YOU WERE SO HONEST A MAN.
HONEST, MY LORD?
AY, SIR. TO BE HONEST, AS THIS WORLD GOES, IS TO BE ONE MAN PICKED OUT OF TEN THOUSAND.
THAT'S VERY TRUE, MY LORD.
--HAVE YOU A DAUGHTER?

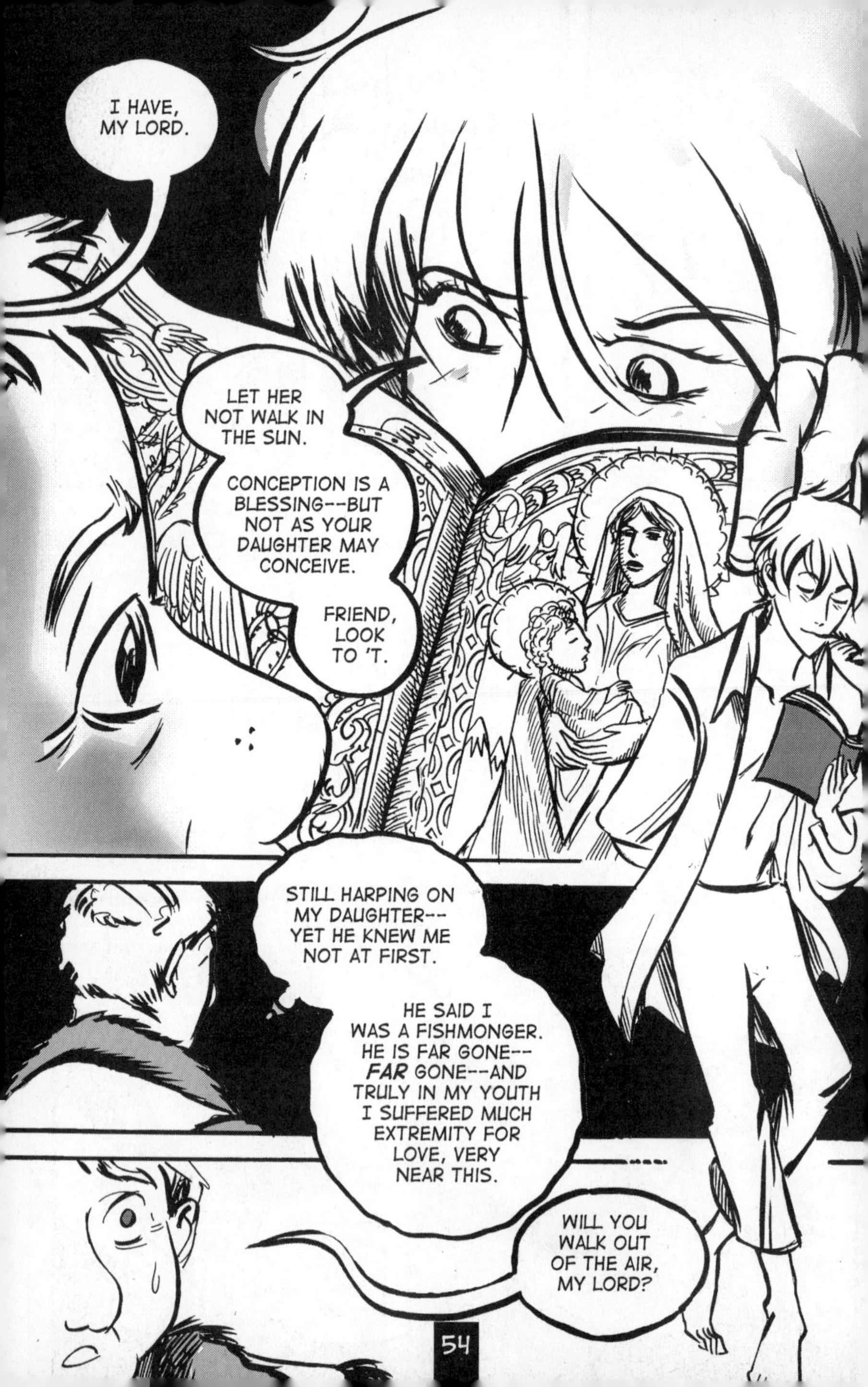
I HAVE, MY LORD.
LET HER NOT WALK IN THE SUN.
CONCEPTION IS A BLESSING--BUT NOT AS YOUR DAUGHTER MAY CONCEIVE.
FRIEND, LOOK TO 'T.
STILL HARPING ON MY DAUGHTER-- YET HE KNEW ME NOT AT FIRST.
HE SAID I WAS A FISHMONGER. HE IS FAR GONE-- *FAR* GONE--AND TRULY IN MY YOUTH I SUFFERED MUCH EXTREMITY FOR LOVE, VERY NEAR THIS.
WILL YOU WALK OUT OF THE AIR, MY LORD?

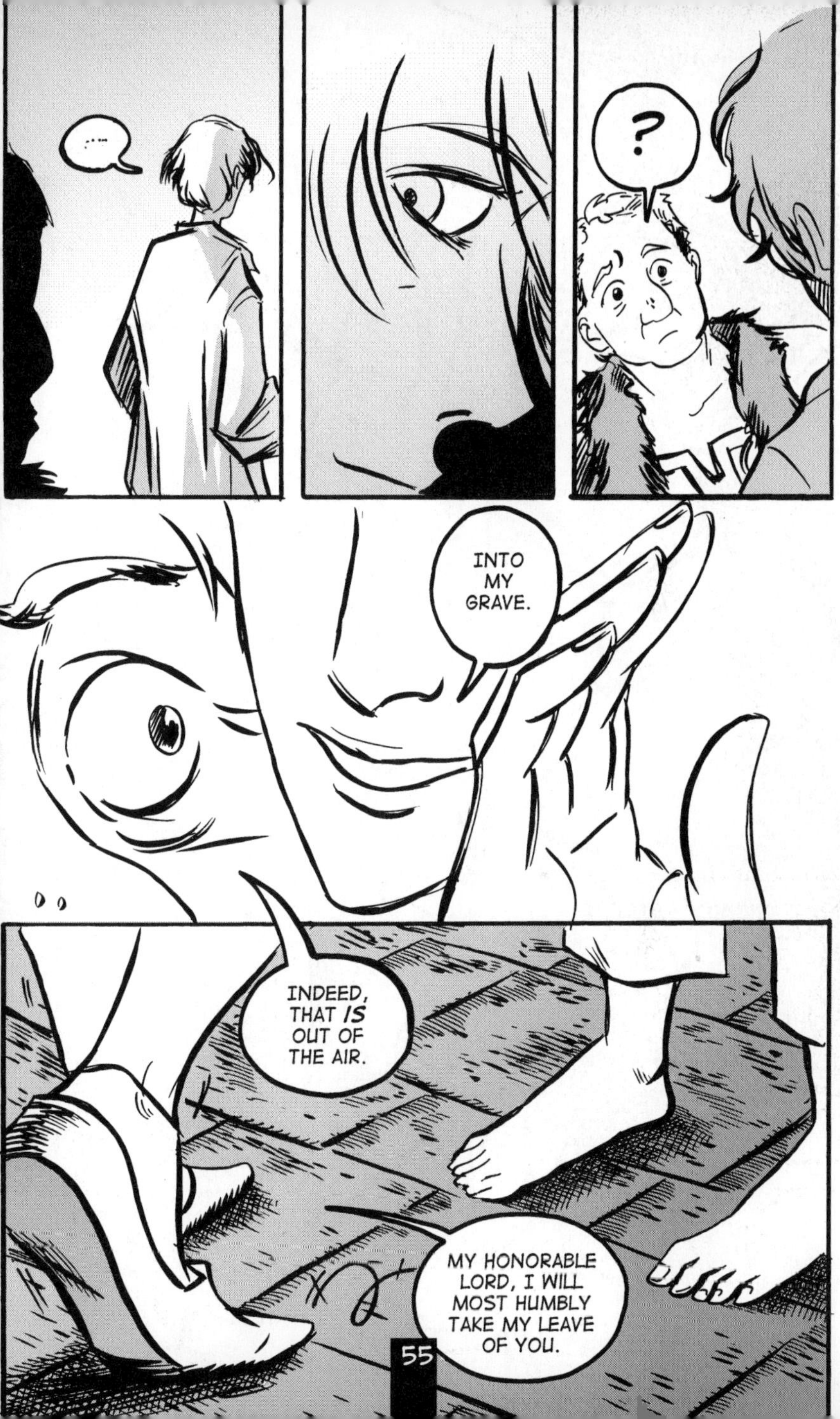
...
?
INTO MY GRAVE.
INDEED, THAT *IS* OUT OF THE AIR.
MY HONORABLE LORD, I WILL MOST HUMBLY TAKE MY LEAVE OF YOU.

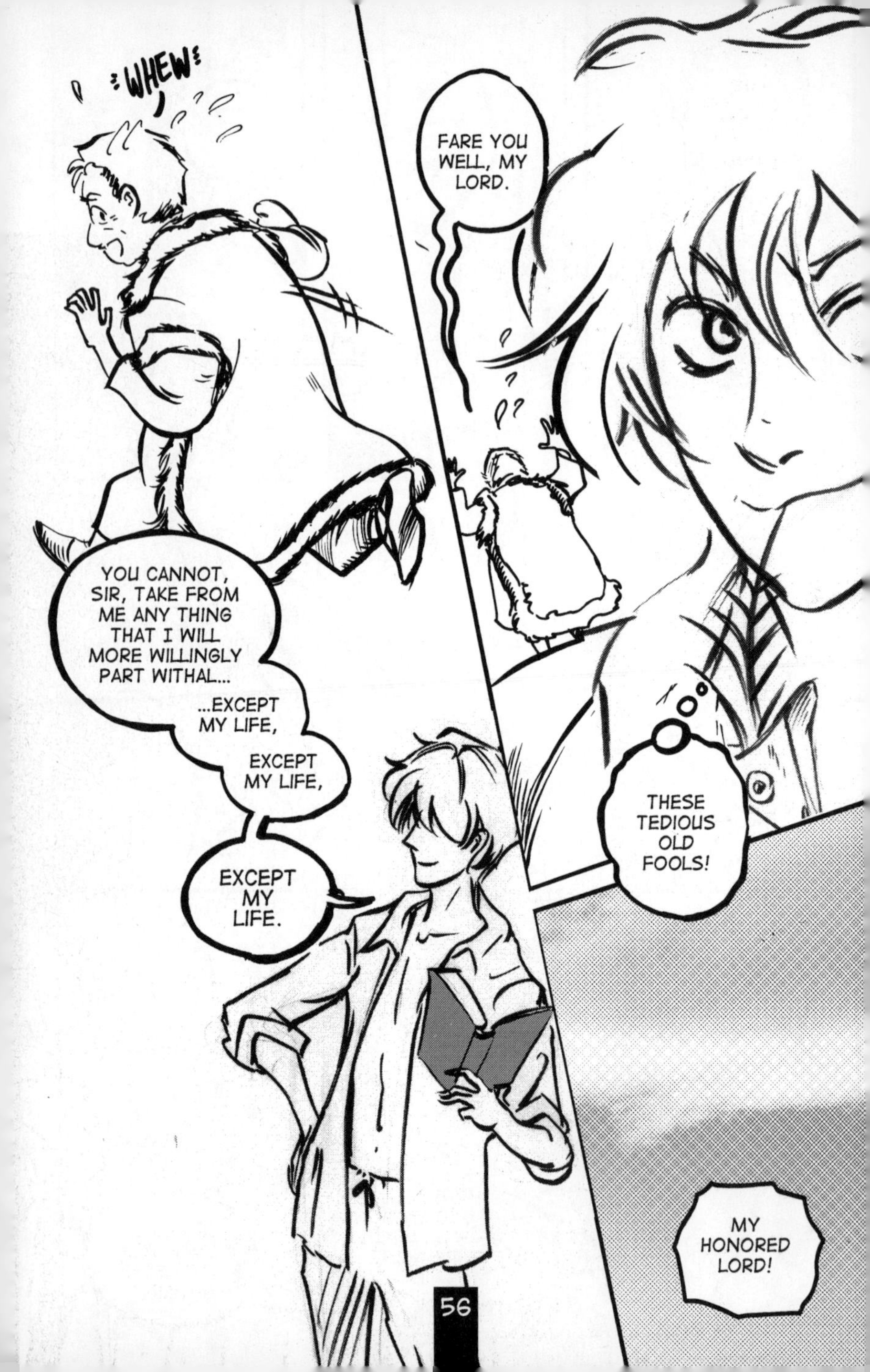
WHEW
YOU CANNOT, SIR, TAKE FROM ME ANY THING THAT I WILL MORE WILLINGLY PART WITHAL...
...EXCEPT MY LIFE,
EXCEPT MY LIFE,
EXCEPT MY LIFE.
FARE YOU WELL, MY LORD.
THESE TEDIOUS OLD FOOLS!
MY HONORED LORD!

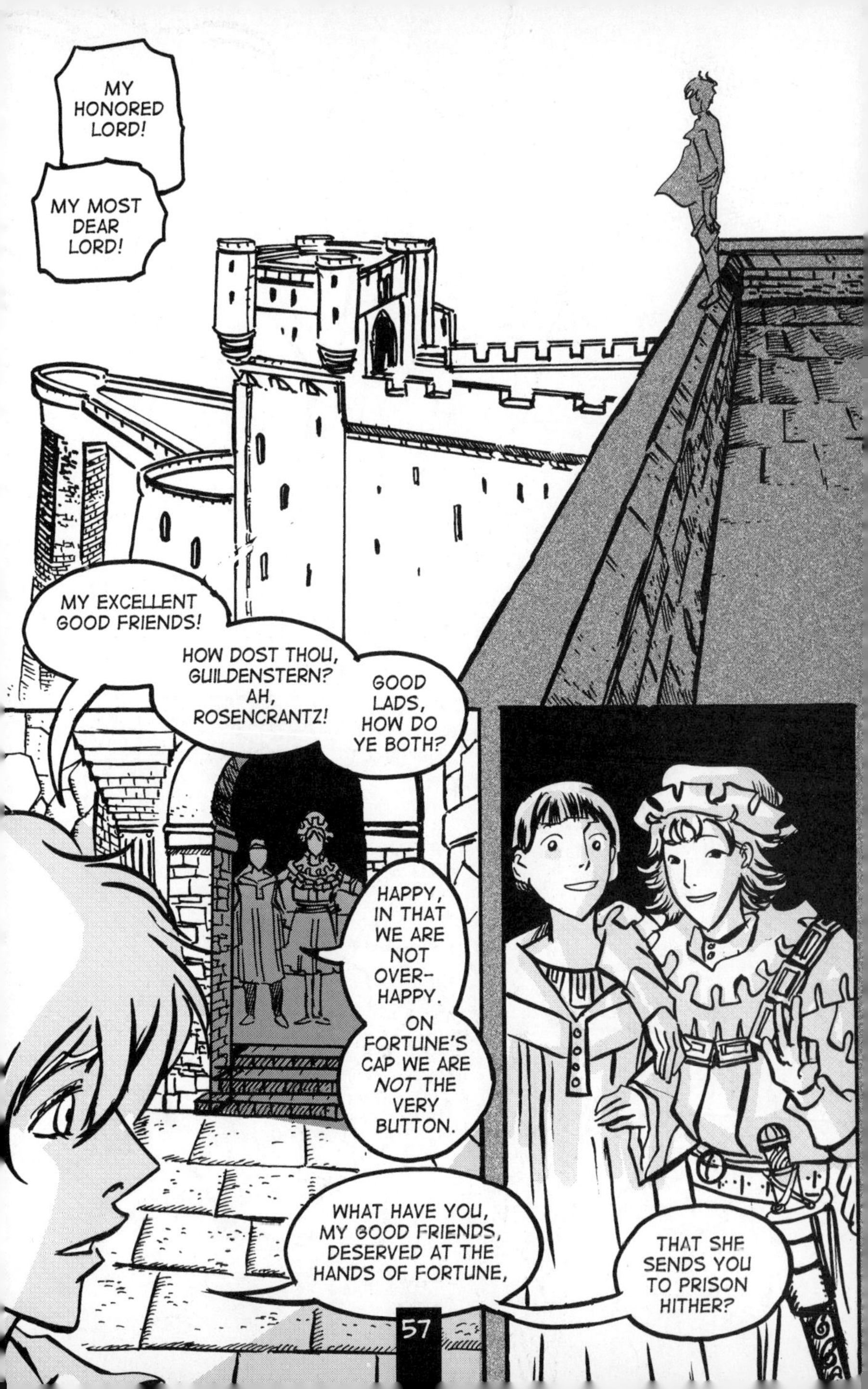
MY HONORED LORD!
MY MOST DEAR LORD!
MY EXCELLENT GOOD FRIENDS!
HOW DOST THOU, GUILDENSTERN? AH, ROSENCRANTZ!
GOOD LADS, HOW DO YE BOTH?
HAPPY, IN THAT WE ARE NOT OVER-HAPPY.
ON FORTUNE'S CAP WE ARE *NOT* THE VERY BUTTON.
WHAT HAVE YOU, MY GOOD FRIENDS, DESERVED AT THE HANDS OF FORTUNE,
THAT SHE SENDS YOU TO PRISON HITHER?

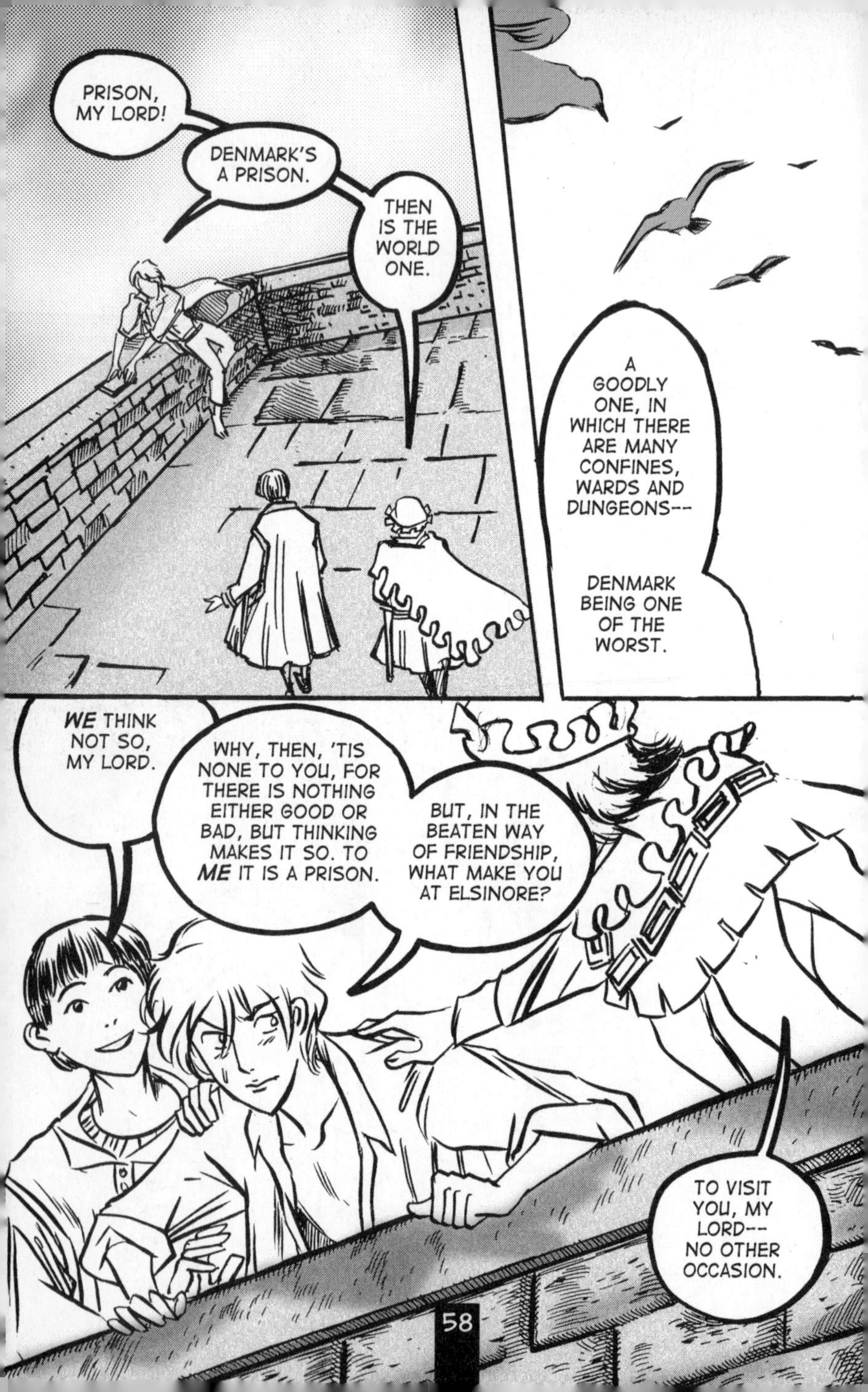
PRISON, MY LORD!
DENMARK'S A PRISON.
THEN IS THE WORLD ONE.
A GOODLY ONE, IN WHICH THERE ARE MANY CONFINES, WARDS AND DUNGEONS--
DENMARK BEING ONE OF THE WORST.
WE THINK NOT SO, MY LORD.
WHY, THEN, 'TIS NONE TO YOU, FOR THERE IS NOTHING EITHER GOOD OR BAD, BUT THINKING MAKES IT SO. TO *ME* IT IS A PRISON.
BUT, IN THE BEATEN WAY OF FRIENDSHIP, WHAT MAKE YOU AT ELSINORE?
TO VISIT YOU, MY LORD-- NO OTHER OCCASION.

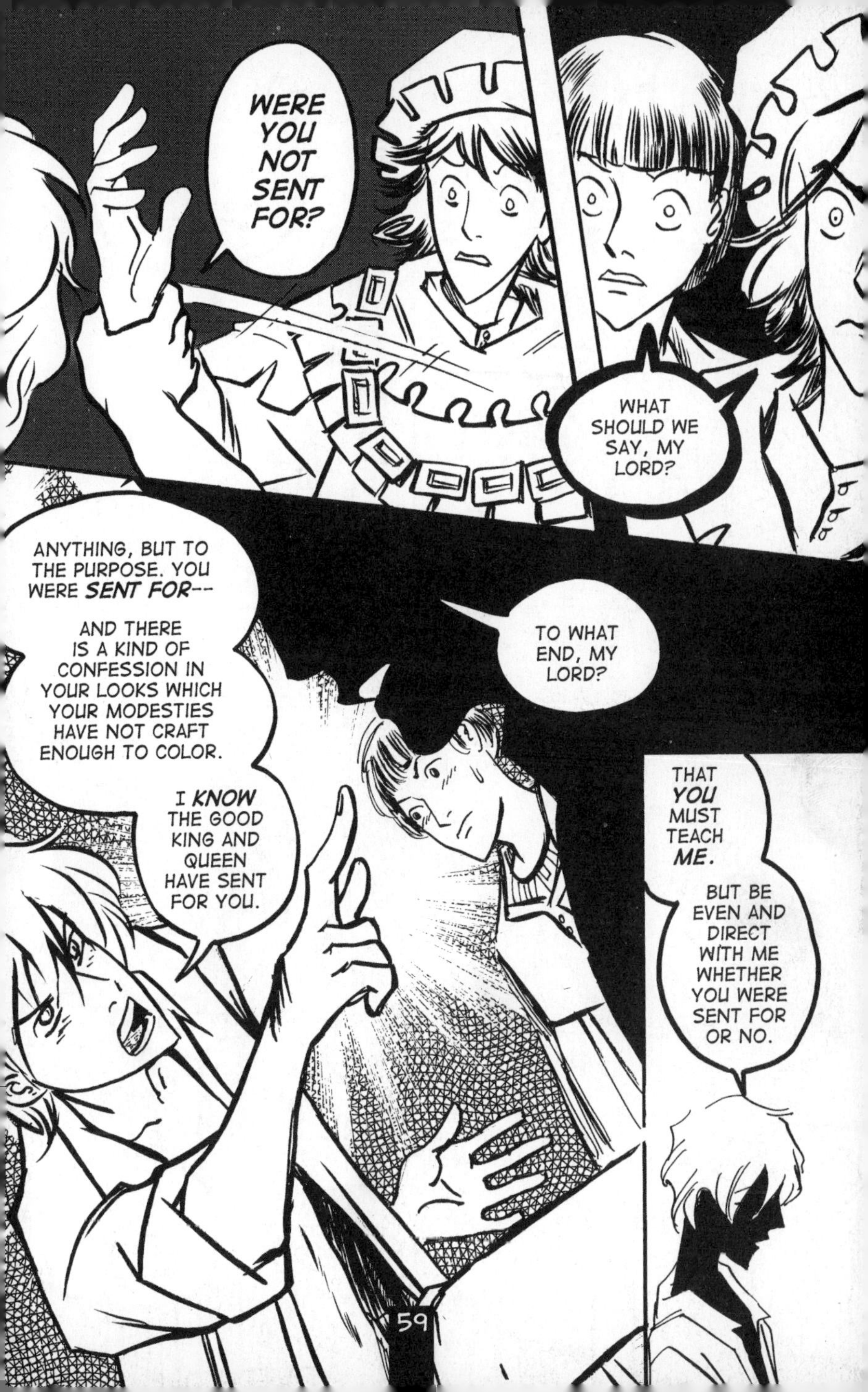
WERE YOU NOT SENT FOR?
WHAT SHOULD WE SAY, MY LORD?
ANYTHING, BUT TO THE PURPOSE. YOU WERE SENT FOR--
AND THERE IS A KIND OF CONFESSION IN YOUR LOOKS WHICH YOUR MODESTIES HAVE NOT CRAFT ENOUGH TO COLOR.
I KNOW THE GOOD KING AND QUEEN HAVE SENT FOR YOU.
TO WHAT END, MY LORD?
THAT YOU MUST TEACH ME.
BUT BE EVEN AND DIRECT WITH ME WHETHER YOU WERE SENT FOR OR NO.

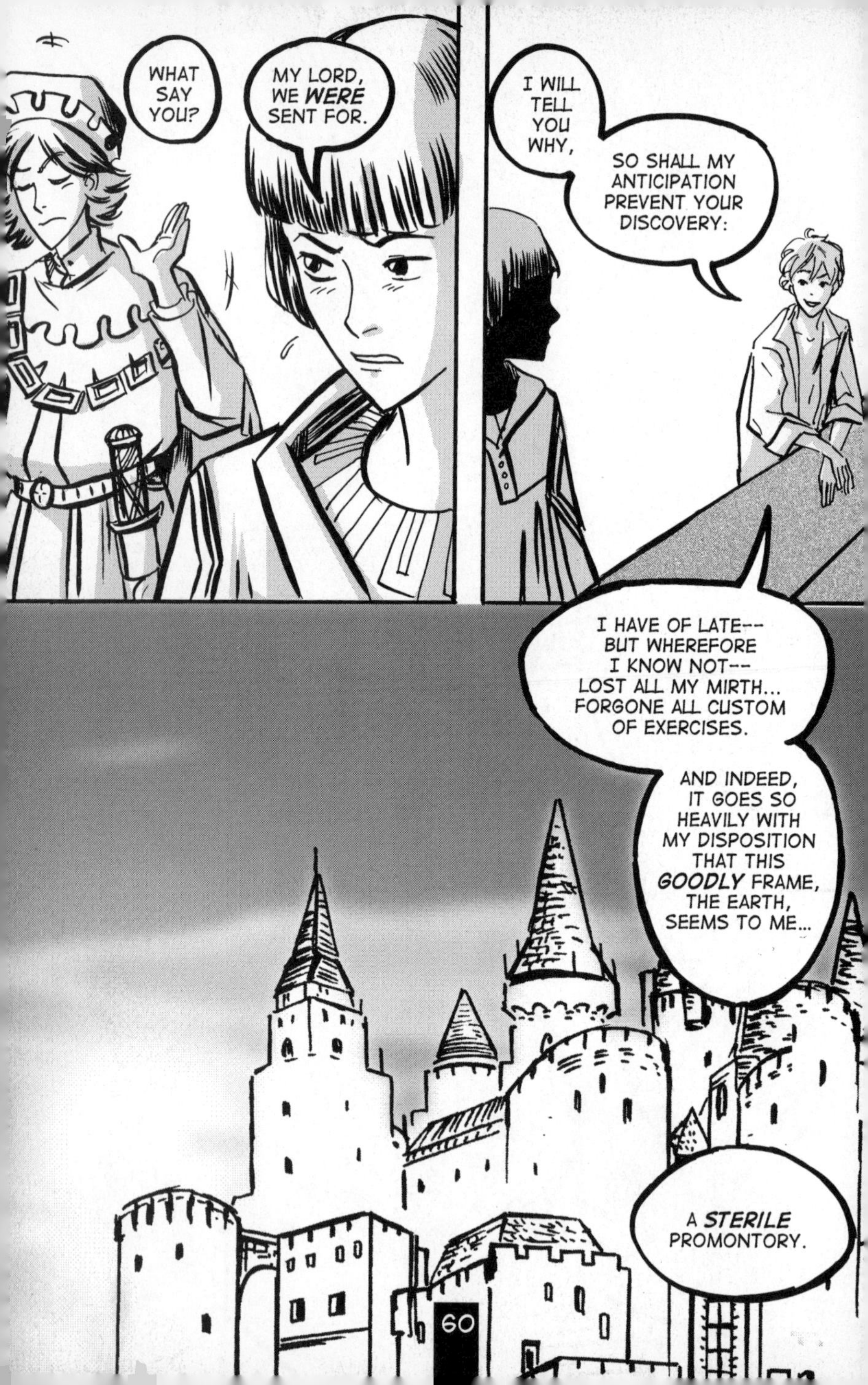
WHAT SAY YOU?
MY LORD, WE *WERE* SENT FOR.
I WILL TELL YOU WHY,
SO SHALL MY ANTICIPATION PREVENT YOUR DISCOVERY:
I HAVE OF LATE-- BUT WHEREFORE I KNOW NOT-- LOST ALL MY MIRTH... FORGONE ALL CUSTOM OF EXERCISES.
AND INDEED, IT GOES SO HEAVILY WITH MY DISPOSITION THAT THIS *GOODLY* FRAME, THE EARTH, SEEMS TO ME...
A *STERILE* PROMONTORY.

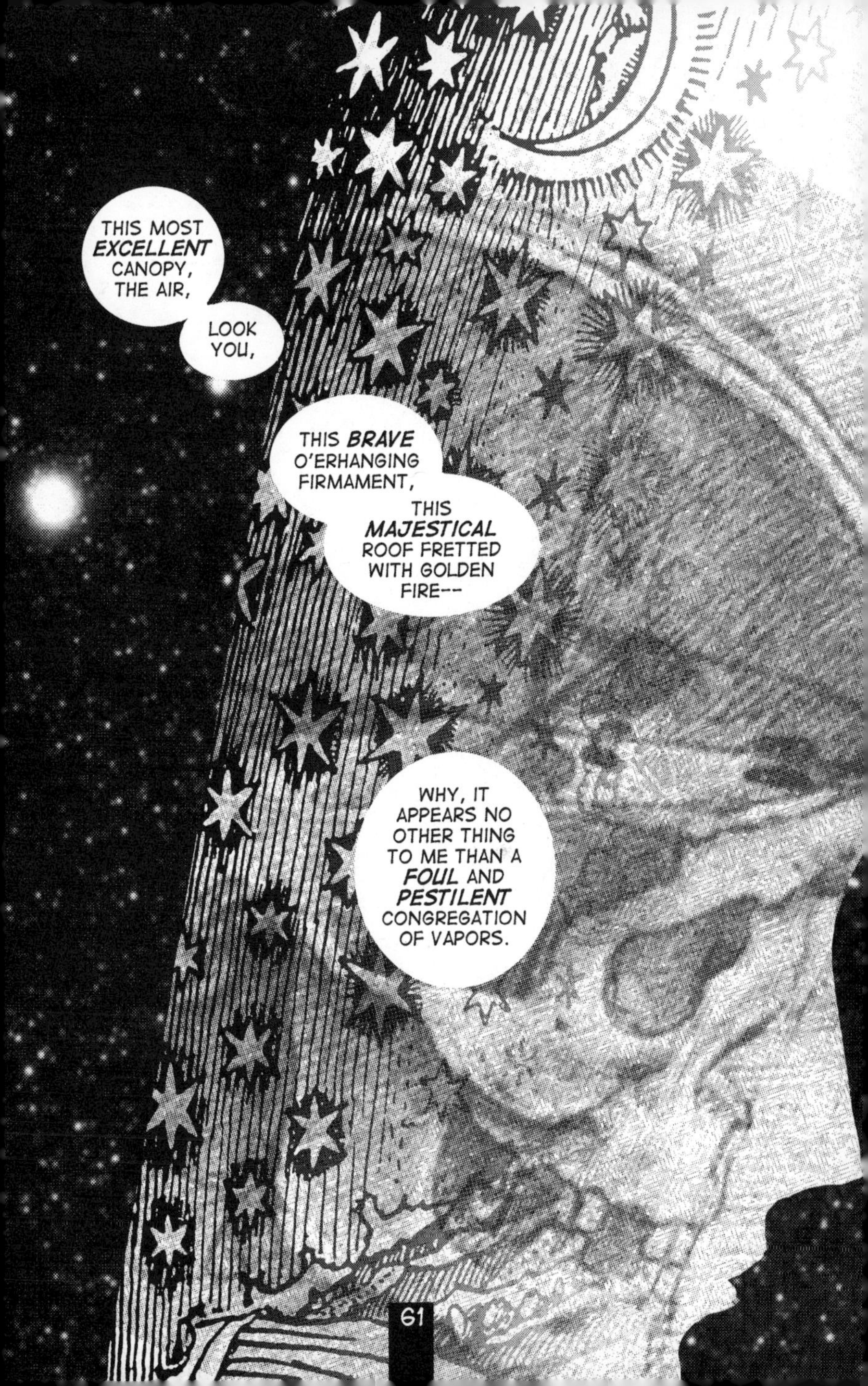
THIS MOST *EXCELLENT* CANOPY, THE AIR,
LOOK YOU,
THIS *BRAVE* O'ERHANGING FIRMAMENT,
THIS *MAJESTICAL* ROOF FRETTED WITH GOLDEN FIRE--
WHY, IT APPEARS NO OTHER THING TO ME THAN A *FOUL* AND *PESTILENT* CONGREGATION OF VAPORS.

WHAT A PIECE OF WORK IS A MAN!
HOW NOBLE IN REASON, HOW INFINITE IN FACULTY!
IN FORM AND MOVING HOW EXPRESS AND ADMIRABLE! IN ACTION, HOW LIKE AN ANGEL--
IN APPREHENSION, HOW LIKE A GOD!
THE BEAUTY OF THE WORLD! THE PARAGON OF ANIMALS!
AND YET, TO ME, WHAT IS THIS QUINTESSENCE OF DUST?
MAN DELIGHTS NOT ME--

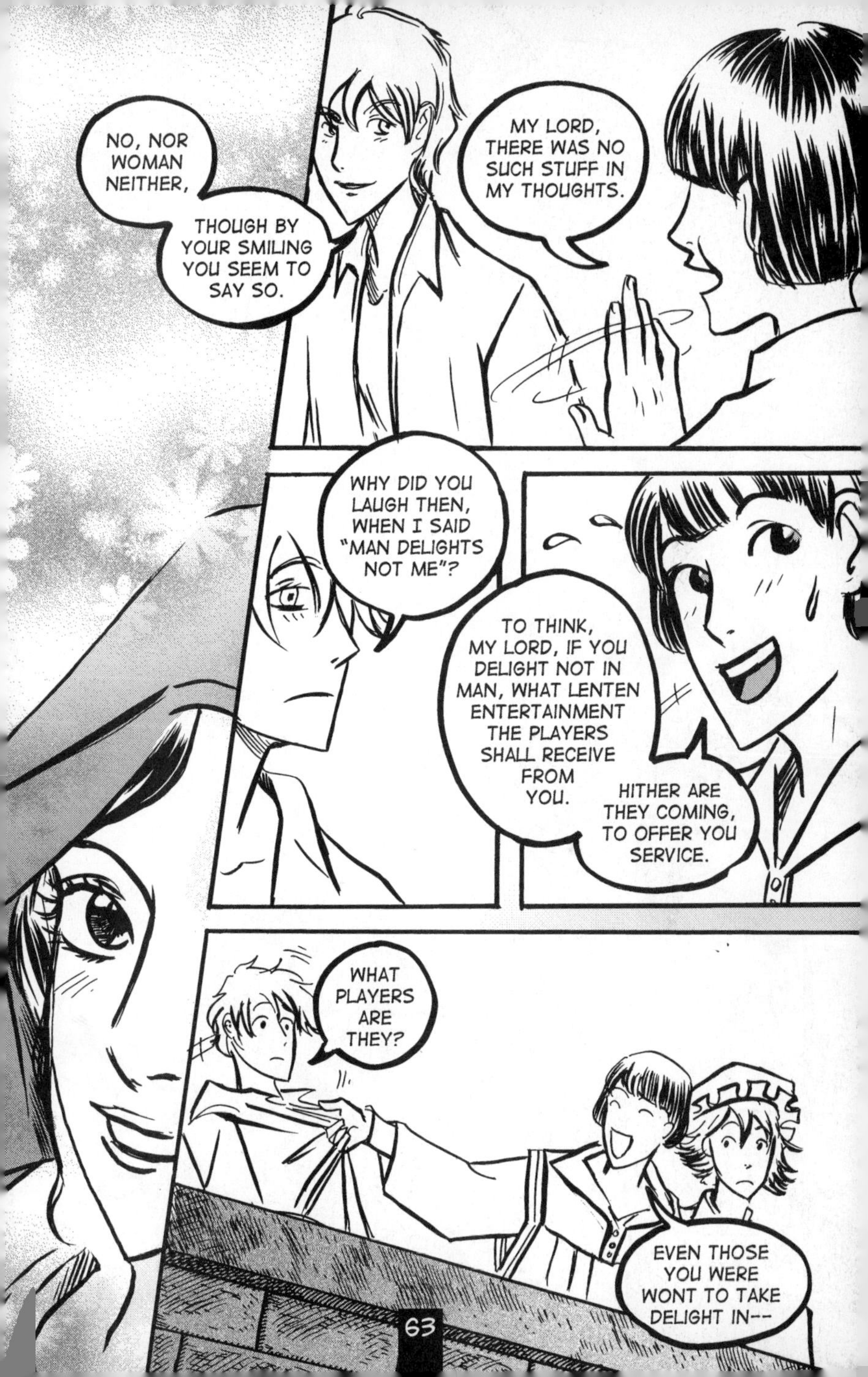

NO, NOR WOMAN NEITHER,
THOUGH BY YOUR SMILING YOU SEEM TO SAY SO.
MY LORD, THERE WAS NO SUCH STUFF IN MY THOUGHTS.
WHY DID YOU LAUGH THEN, WHEN I SAID "MAN DELIGHTS NOT ME"?
TO THINK, MY LORD, IF YOU DELIGHT NOT IN MAN, WHAT LENTEN ENTERTAINMENT THE PLAYERS SHALL RECEIVE FROM YOU.
HITHER ARE THEY COMING, TO OFFER YOU SERVICE.
WHAT PLAYERS ARE THEY?
EVEN THOSE YOU WERE WONT TO TAKE DELIGHT IN--

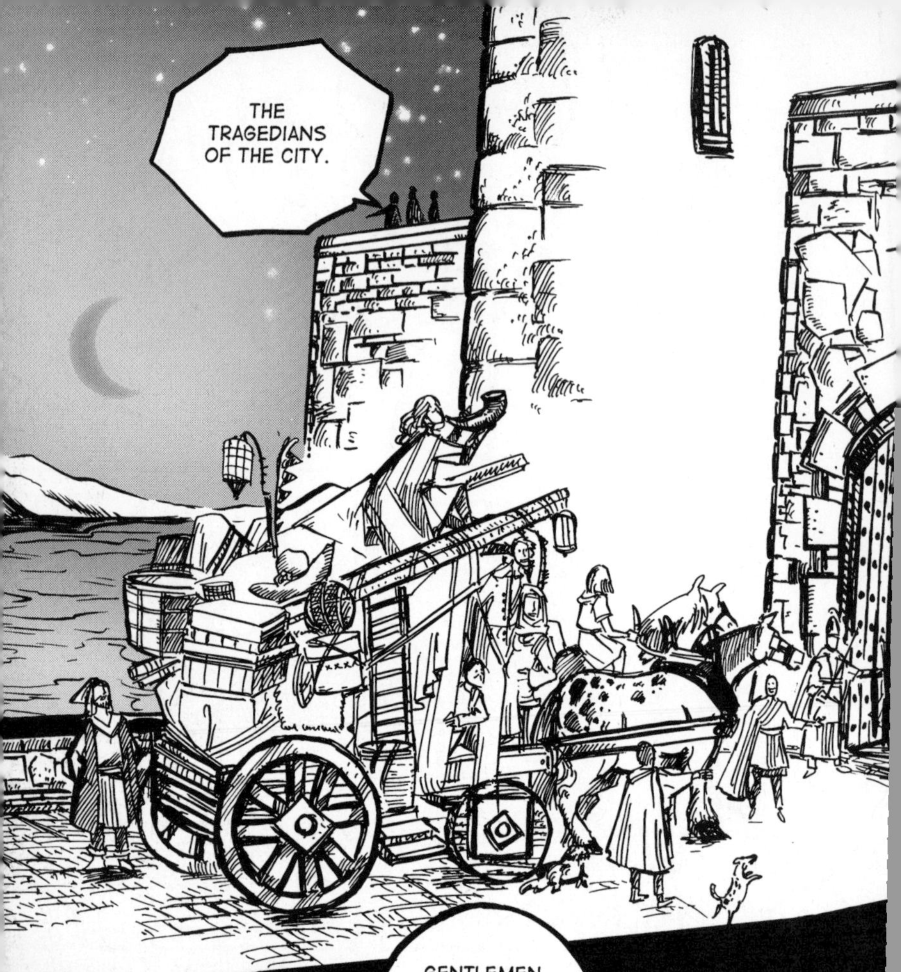
THE TRAGEDIANS OF THE CITY.

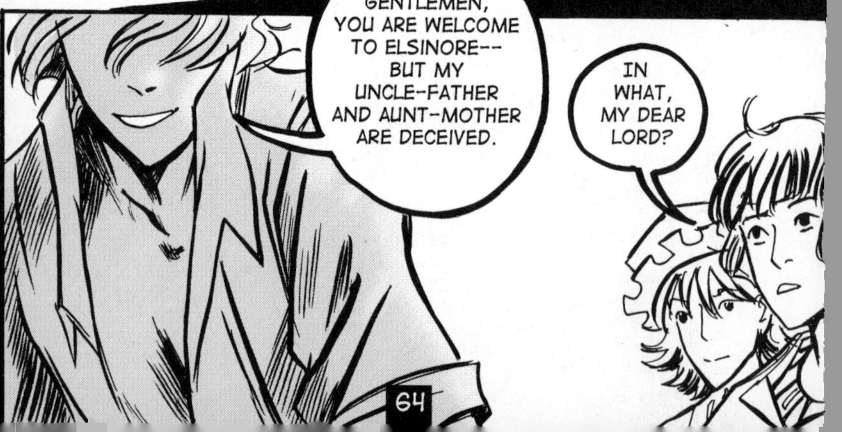
GENTLEMEN, YOU ARE WELCOME TO ELSINORE-- BUT MY UNCLE-FATHER AND AUNT-MOTHER ARE DECEIVED.
IN WHAT, MY DEAR LORD?

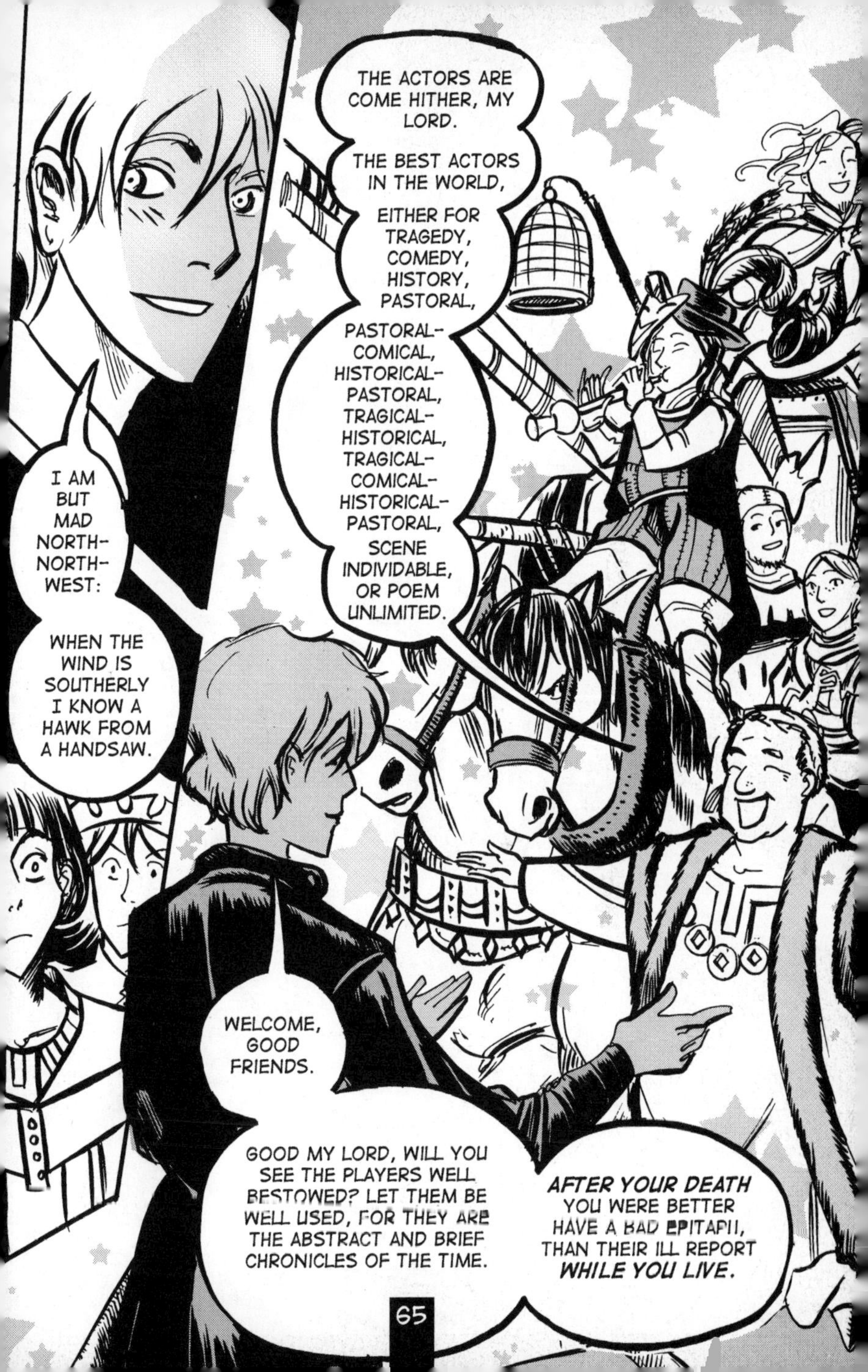
I AM BUT MAD NORTH-NORTH-WEST:
WHEN THE WIND IS SOUTHERLY I KNOW A HAWK FROM A HANDSAW.
THE ACTORS ARE COME HITHER, MY LORD.
THE BEST ACTORS IN THE WORLD,
EITHER FOR TRAGEDY, COMEDY, HISTORY, PASTORAL,
PASTORAL-COMICAL, HISTORICAL-PASTORAL, TRAGICAL-HISTORICAL, TRAGICAL-COMICAL-HISTORICAL-PASTORAL, SCENE INDIVIDABLE, OR POEM UNLIMITED.
WELCOME, GOOD FRIENDS.
GOOD MY LORD, WILL YOU SEE THE PLAYERS WELL BESTOWED? LET THEM BE WELL USED, FOR THEY ARE THE ABSTRACT AND BRIEF CHRONICLES OF THE TIME.
AFTER YOUR DEATH YOU WERE BETTER HAVE A BAD EPITAPH, THAN THEIR ILL REPORT *WHILE YOU LIVE*.

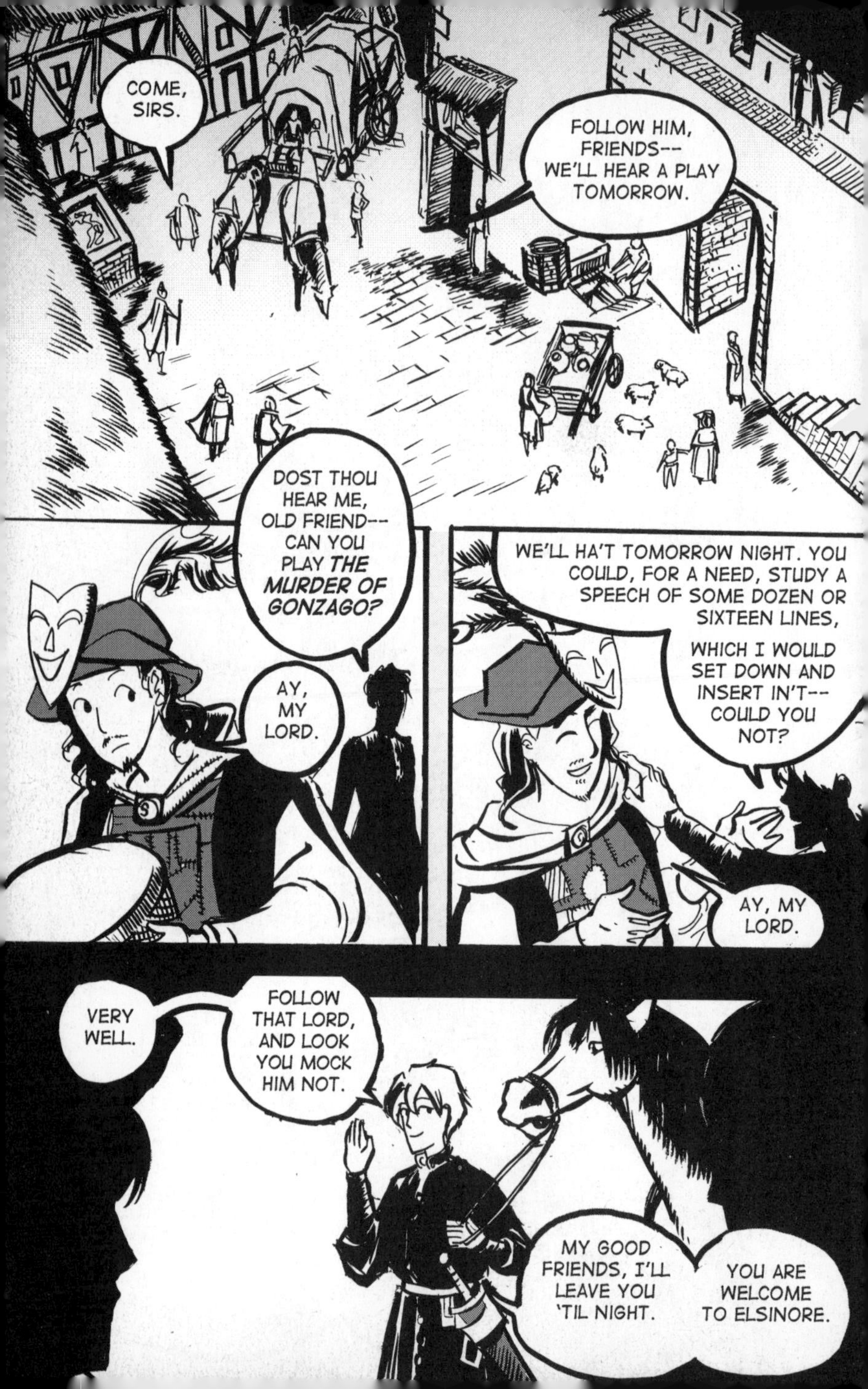
COME, SIRS.
FOLLOW HIM, FRIENDS-- WE'LL HEAR A PLAY TOMORROW.
DOST THOU HEAR ME, OLD FRIEND-- CAN YOU PLAY *THE MURDER OF GONZAGO?*
AY, MY LORD.
WE'LL HA'T TOMORROW NIGHT. YOU COULD, FOR A NEED, STUDY A SPEECH OF SOME DOZEN OR SIXTEEN LINES,
WHICH I WOULD SET DOWN AND INSERT IN'T-- COULD YOU NOT?
AY, MY LORD.
VERY WELL.
FOLLOW THAT LORD, AND LOOK YOU MOCK HIM NOT.
MY GOOD FRIENDS, I'LL LEAVE YOU 'TIL NIGHT.
YOU ARE WELCOME TO ELSINORE.

OHHHHH,
WHAT A ROGUE AND PEASANT SLAVE AM I!
AM I A COWARD?
WHO CALLS ME VILLAIN?
BREAKS MY PATE ACROSS? PLUCKS OFF MY BEARD, AND BLOWS IT IN MY FACE? TWEAKS ME BY THE NOSE? GIVES ME THE LIE I' THE THROAT, AS DEEP AS TO THE LUNGS?
WHO DOES ME THIS?
HA!
'SWOUNDS, I SHOULD TAKE IT, FOR IT CANNOT BE BUT I AM PIGEON-LIVERED AND LACK GALL TO MAKE OPPRESSION BITTER, OR ERE THIS I SHOULD HA' FATTED ALL THE REGION KITES WITH THIS SLAVE'S OFFAL:

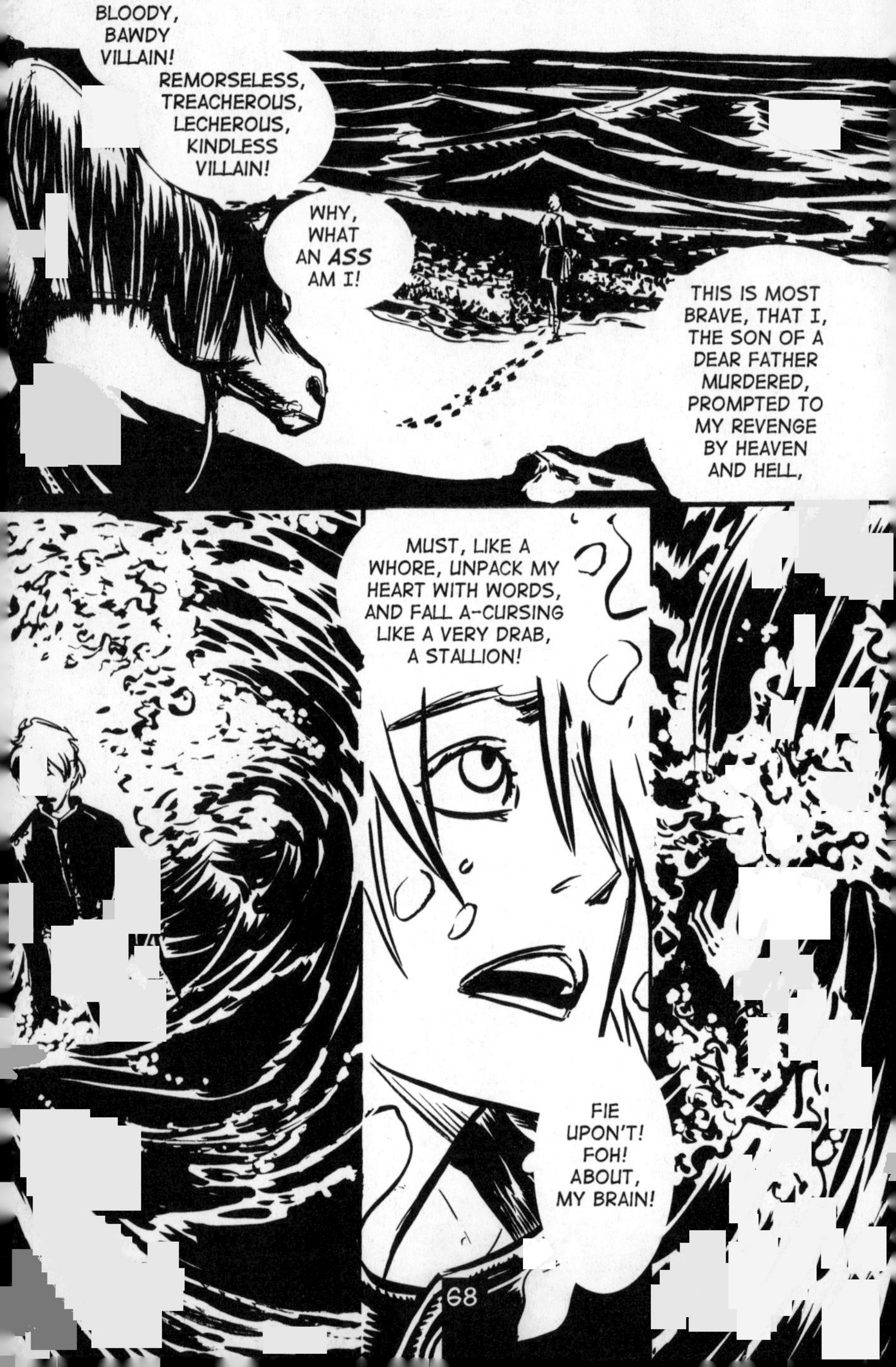
BLOODY, BAWDY VILLAIN!
REMORSELESS, TREACHEROUS, LECHEROUS, KINDLESS VILLAIN!
WHY, WHAT AN *ASS* AM I!
THIS IS MOST BRAVE, THAT I, THE SON OF A DEAR FATHER MURDERED, PROMPTED TO MY REVENGE BY HEAVEN AND HELL,
MUST, LIKE A WHORE, UNPACK MY HEART WITH WORDS, AND FALL A-CURSING LIKE A VERY DRAB, A STALLION!
FIE UPON'T! FOH! ABOUT, MY BRAIN!

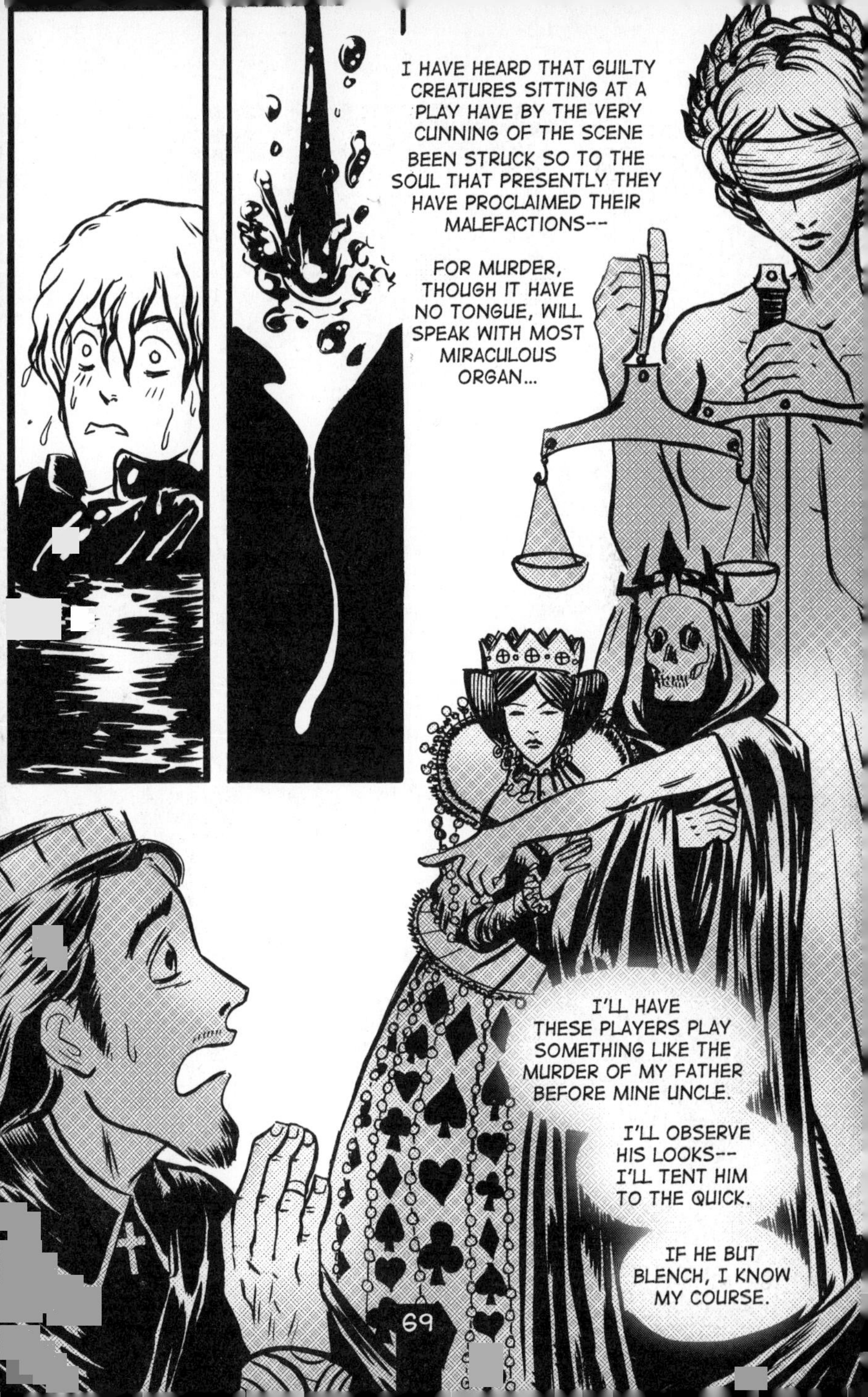
I HAVE HEARD THAT GUILTY CREATURES SITTING AT A PLAY HAVE BY THE VERY CUNNING OF THE SCENE
BEEN STRUCK SO TO THE SOUL THAT PRESENTLY THEY HAVE PROCLAIMED THEIR MALEFACTIONS--
FOR MURDER, THOUGH IT HAVE NO TONGUE, WILL SPEAK WITH MOST MIRACULOUS ORGAN...
I'LL HAVE THESE PLAYERS PLAY SOMETHING LIKE THE MURDER OF MY FATHER BEFORE MINE UNCLE.
I'LL OBSERVE HIS LOOKS-- I'LL TENT HIM TO THE QUICK.
IF HE BUT BLENCH, I KNOW MY COURSE.

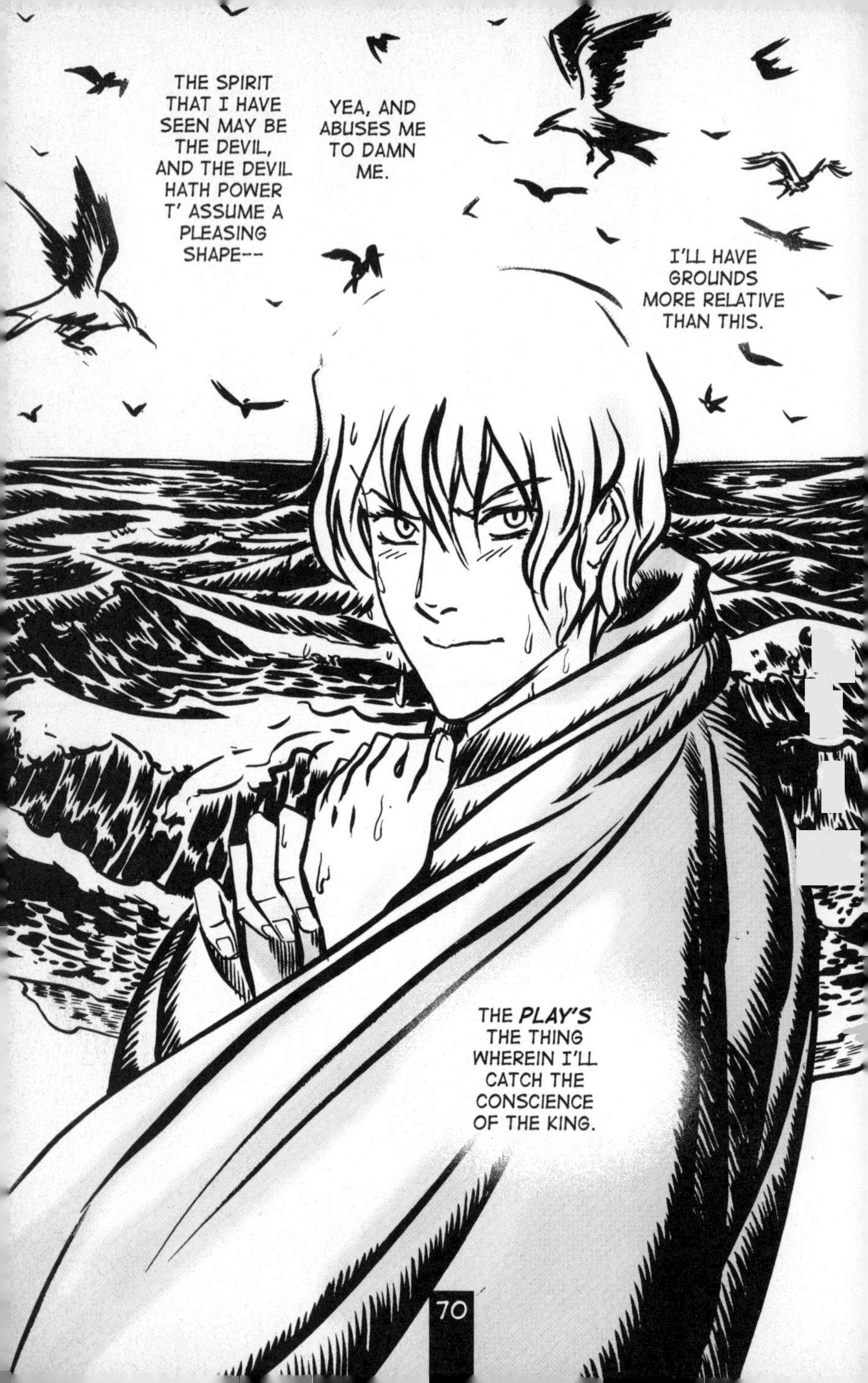
THE SPIRIT THAT I HAVE SEEN MAY BE THE DEVIL, AND THE DEVIL HATH POWER T' ASSUME A PLEASING SHAPE--
YEA, AND ABUSES ME TO DAMN ME.
I'LL HAVE GROUNDS MORE RELATIVE THAN THIS.
THE *PLAY'S* THE THING WHEREIN I'LL CATCH THE CONSCIENCE OF THE KING.

ACT III

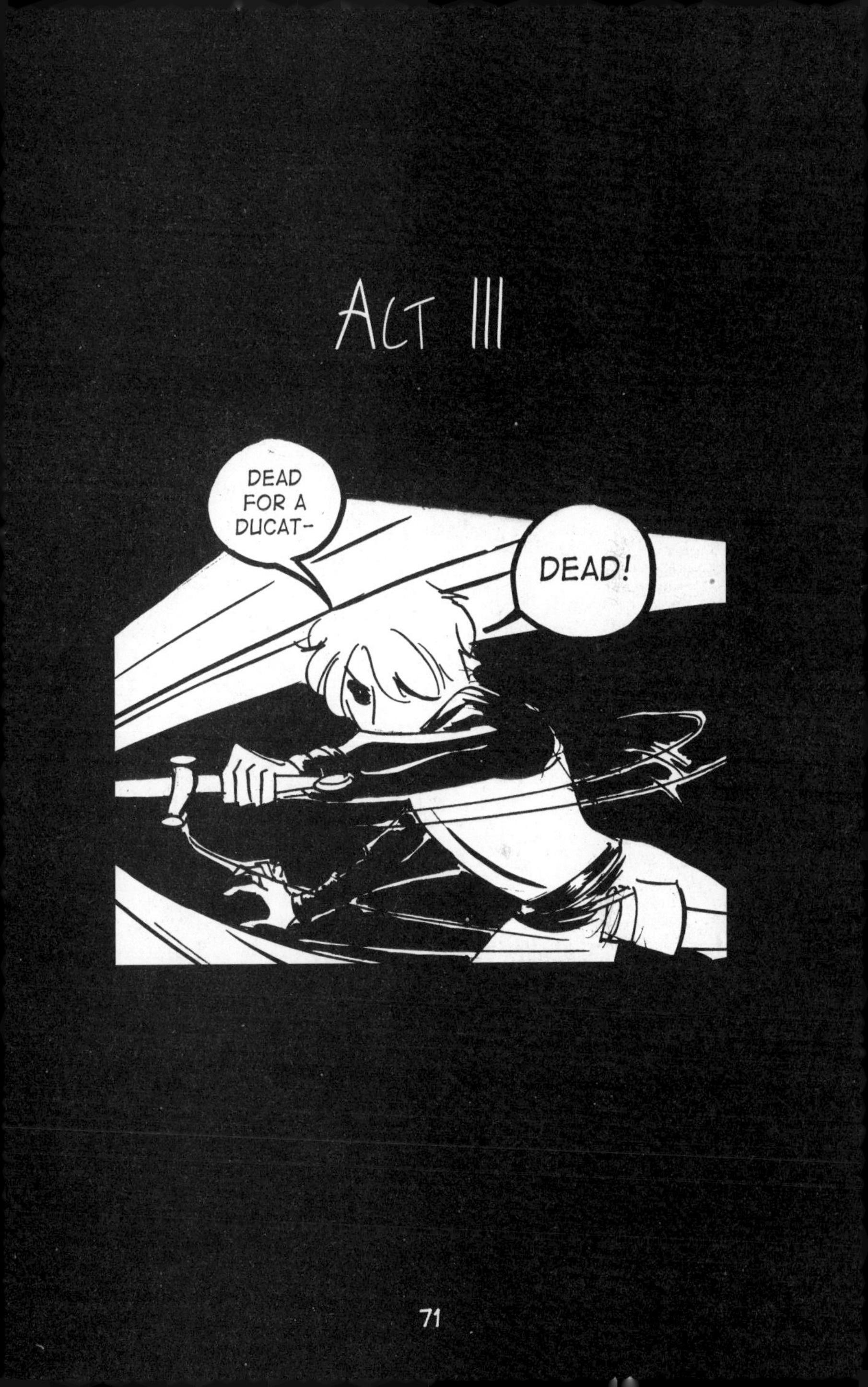
DEAD FOR A DUCAT-
DEAD!

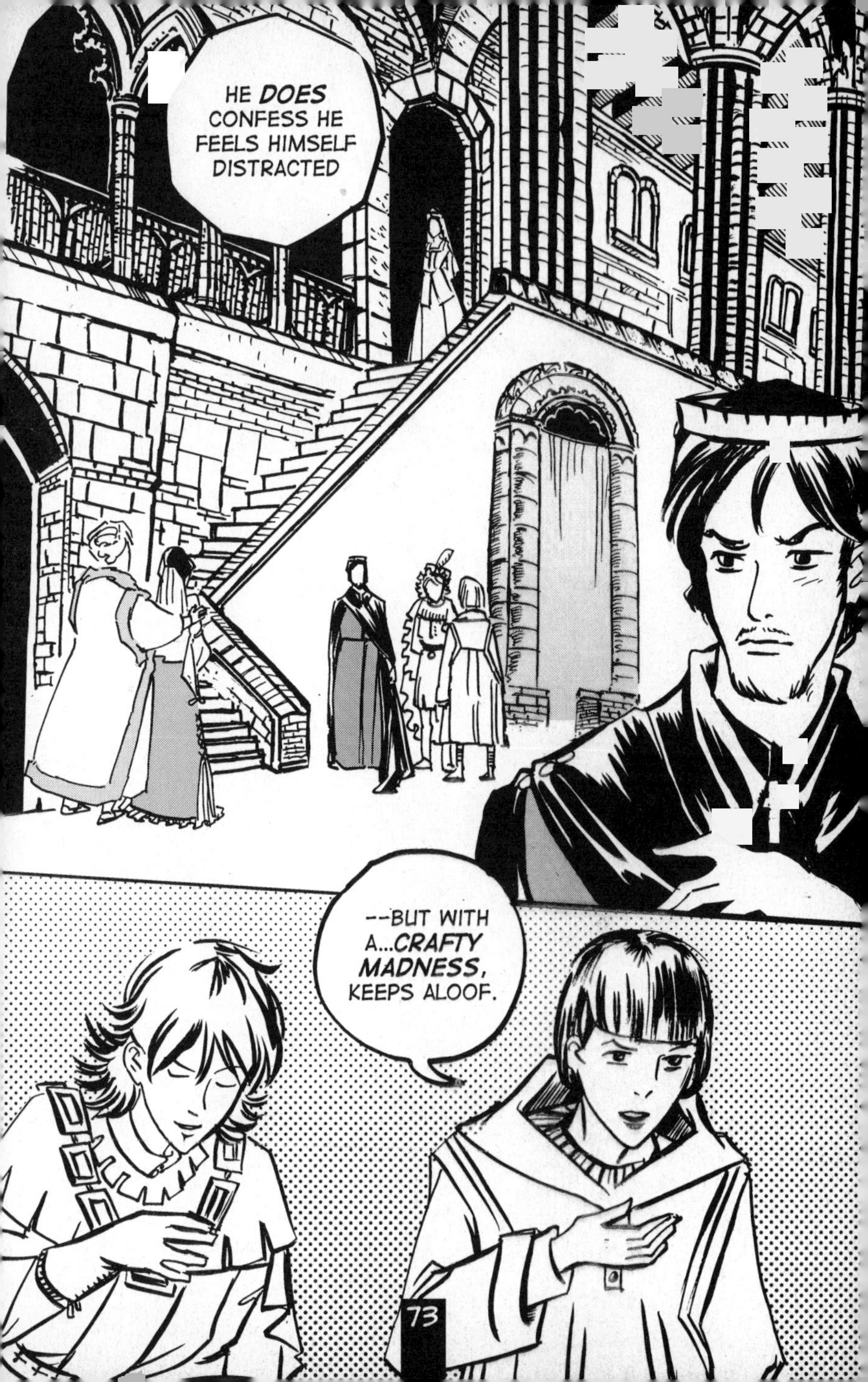
HE DOES CONFESS HE FEELS HIMSELF DISTRACTED
--BUT WITH A...CRAFTY MADNESS, KEEPS ALOOF.

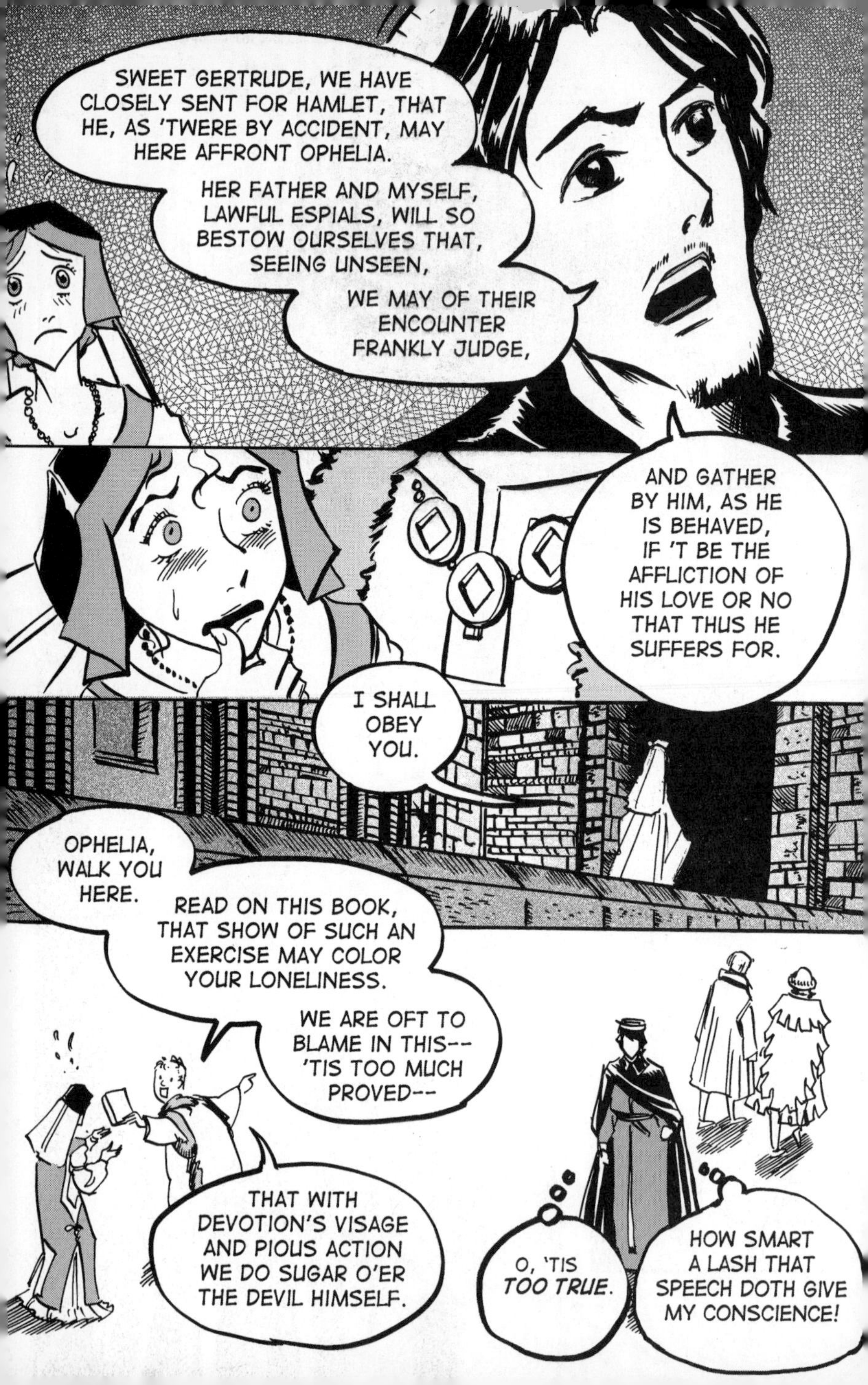
SWEET GERTRUDE, WE HAVE CLOSELY SENT FOR HAMLET, THAT HE, AS 'TWERE BY ACCIDENT, MAY HERE AFFRONT OPHELIA.
HER FATHER AND MYSELF, LAWFUL ESPIALS, WILL SO BESTOW OURSELVES THAT, SEEING UNSEEN,
WE MAY OF THEIR ENCOUNTER FRANKLY JUDGE,
AND GATHER BY HIM, AS HE IS BEHAVED, IF 'T BE THE AFFLICTION OF HIS LOVE OR NO THAT THUS HE SUFFERS FOR.
I SHALL OBEY YOU.
OPHELIA, WALK YOU HERE.
READ ON THIS BOOK, THAT SHOW OF SUCH AN EXERCISE MAY COLOR YOUR LONELINESS.
WE ARE OFT TO BLAME IN THIS-- 'TIS TOO MUCH PROVED--
THAT WITH DEVOTION'S VISAGE AND PIOUS ACTION WE DO SUGAR O'ER THE DEVIL HIMSELF.
O, 'TIS *TOO TRUE*.
HOW SMART A LASH THAT SPEECH DOTH GIVE MY CONSCIENCE!

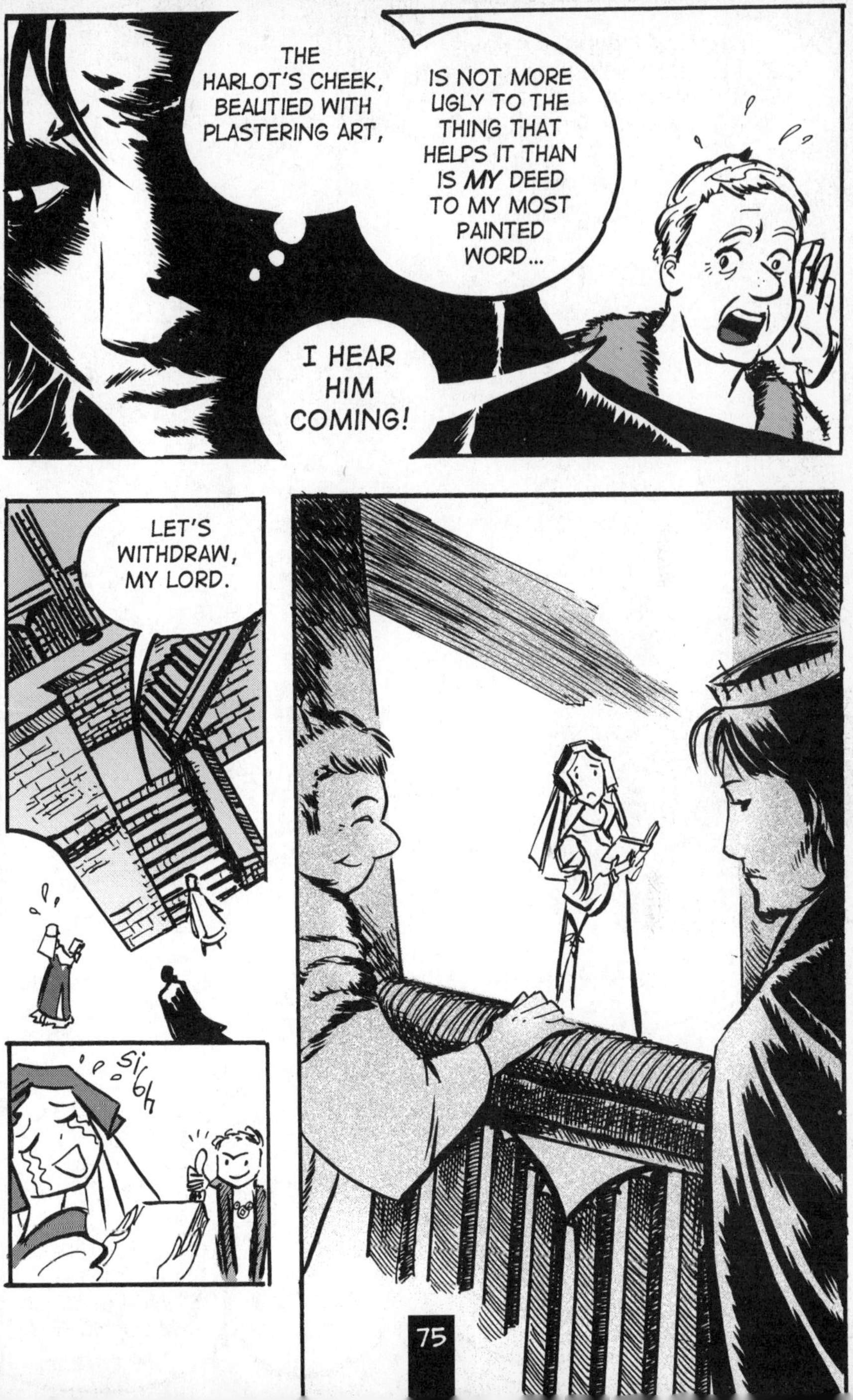
THE HARLOT'S CHEEK, BEAUTIED WITH PLASTERING ART,
IS NOT MORE UGLY TO THE THING THAT HELPS IT THAN IS *MY* DEED TO MY MOST PAINTED WORD...
I HEAR HIM COMING!
LET'S WITHDRAW, MY LORD.
sigh

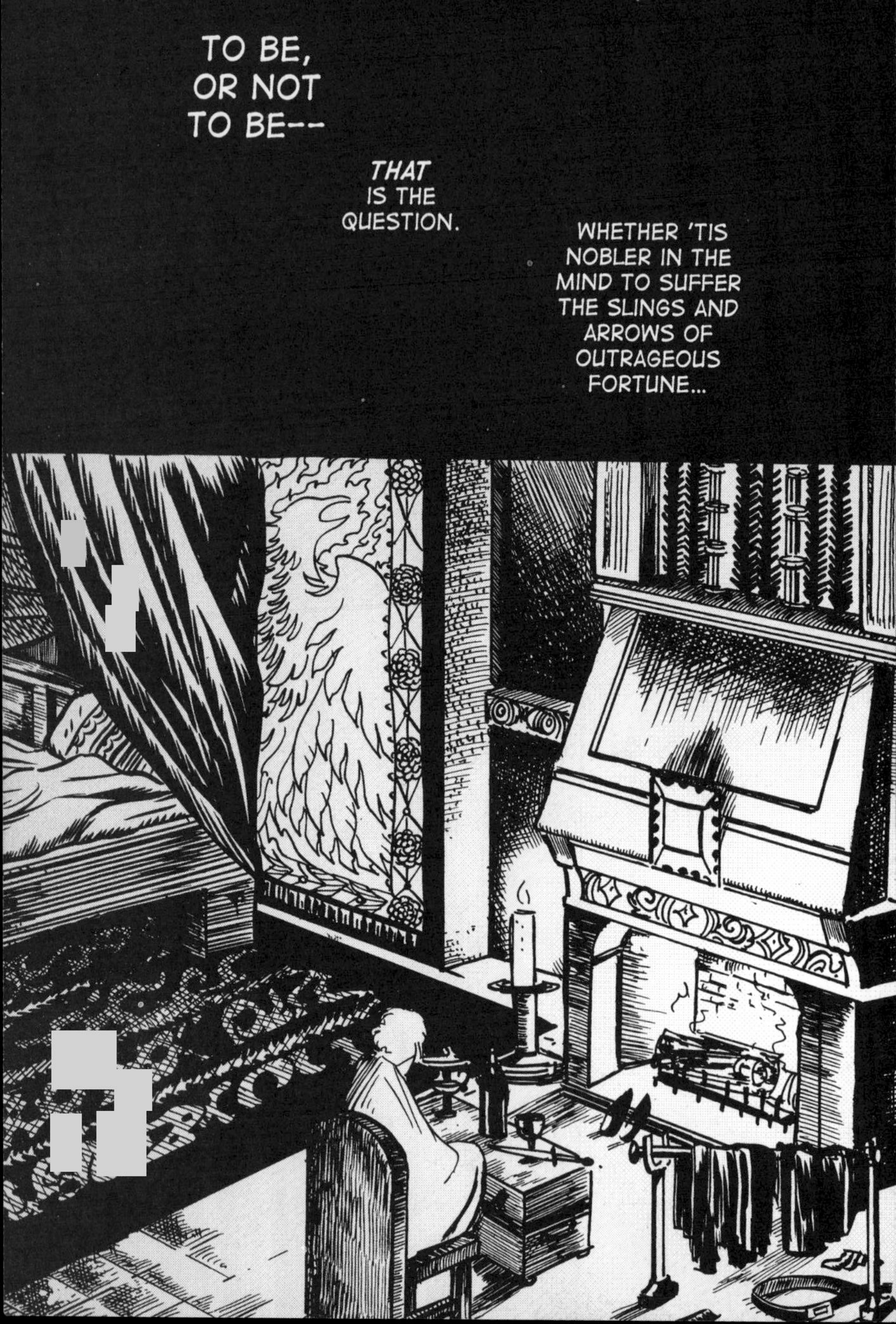
TO BE, OR NOT TO BE--
THAT IS THE QUESTION.
WHETHER 'TIS NOBLER IN THE MIND TO SUFFER THE SLINGS AND ARROWS OF OUTRAGEOUS FORTUNE...

OR TO TAKE ARMS AGAINST A SEA OF TROUBLES,
AND BY OPPOSING, END THEM.
TO DIE, TO SLEEP NO MORE,
AND BY A *SLEEP* TO SAY WE END THE HEARTACHE AND THE THOUSAND NATURAL SHOCKS THAT FLESH IS HEIR TO:
'TIS A CONSUMMATION DEVOUTLY TO BE WISHED.
TO DIE, TO SLEEP;
TO SLEEP, PERCHANCE TO DREAM...

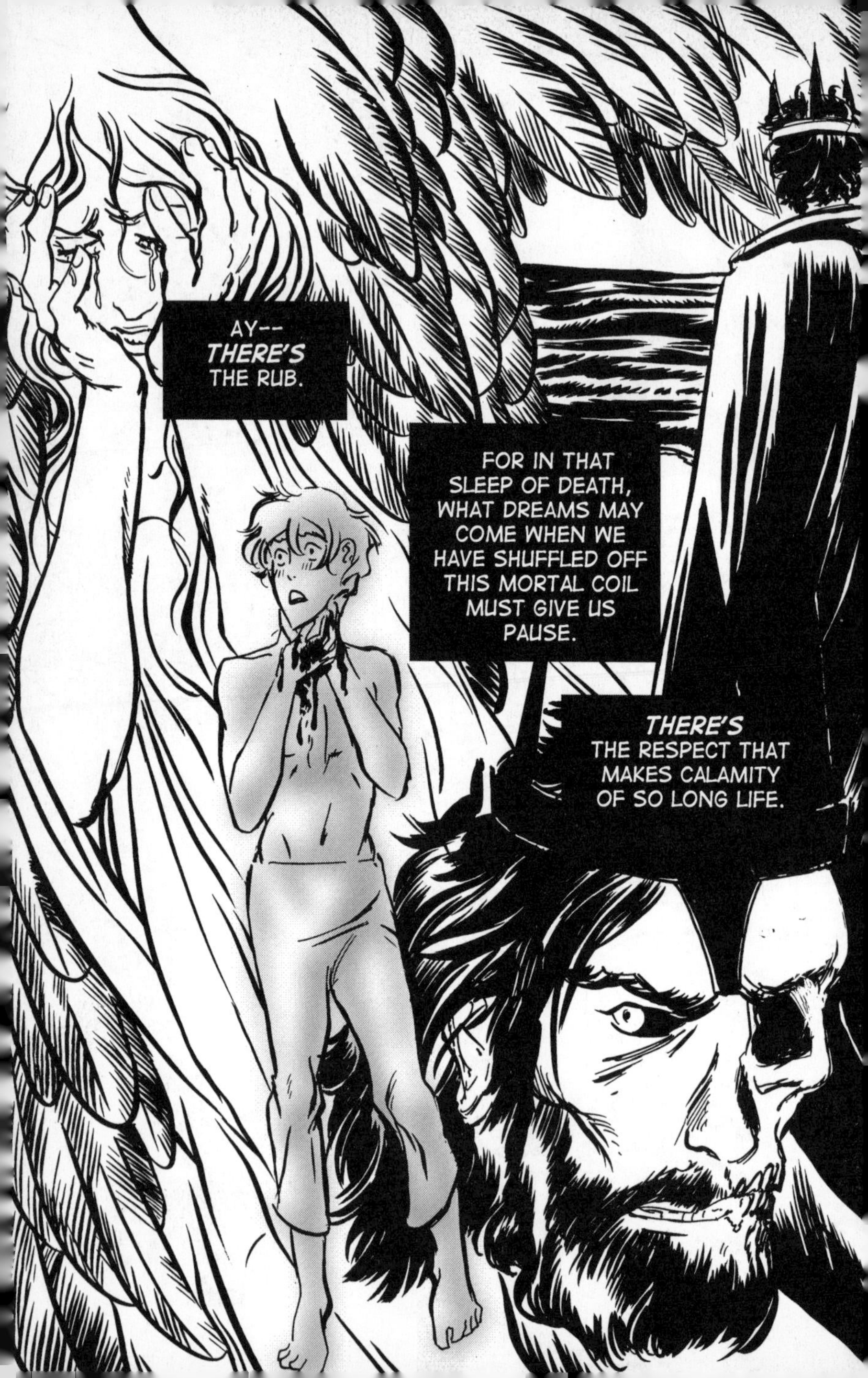
AY-- *THERE'S* THE RUB.
FOR IN THAT SLEEP OF DEATH, WHAT DREAMS MAY COME WHEN WE HAVE SHUFFLED OFF THIS MORTAL COIL MUST GIVE US PAUSE.
THERE'S THE RESPECT THAT MAKES CALAMITY OF SO LONG LIFE.

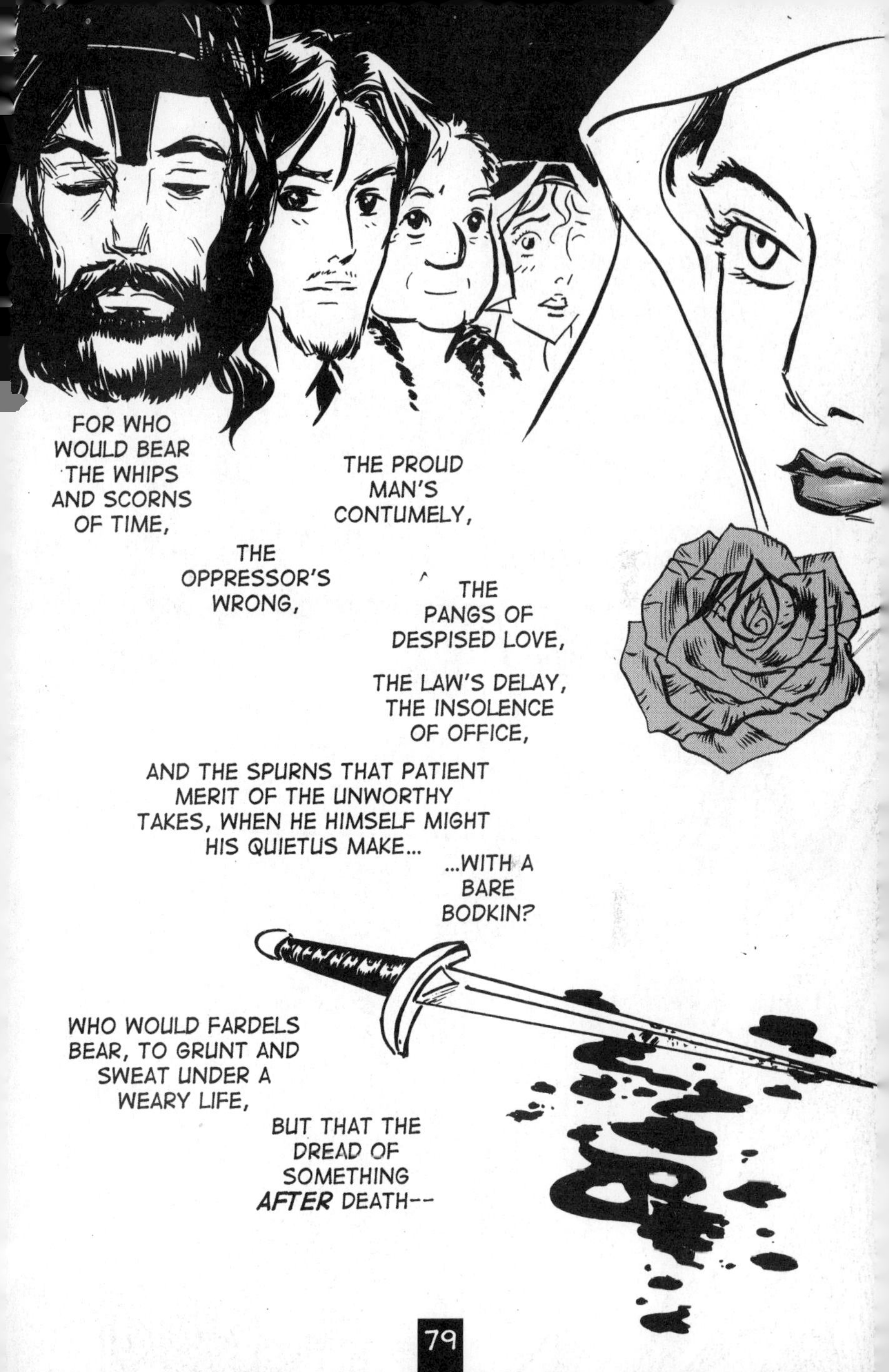
FOR WHO WOULD BEAR THE WHIPS AND SCORNS OF TIME,
THE PROUD MAN'S CONTUMELY,
THE OPPRESSOR'S WRONG,
THE PANGS OF DESPISED LOVE,
THE LAW'S DELAY, THE INSOLENCE OF OFFICE,
AND THE SPURNS THAT PATIENT MERIT OF THE UNWORTHY TAKES, WHEN HE HIMSELF MIGHT HIS QUIETUS MAKE...
...WITH A BARE BODKIN?
WHO WOULD FARDELS BEAR, TO GRUNT AND SWEAT UNDER A WEARY LIFE,
BUT THAT THE DREAD OF SOMETHING *AFTER* DEATH--

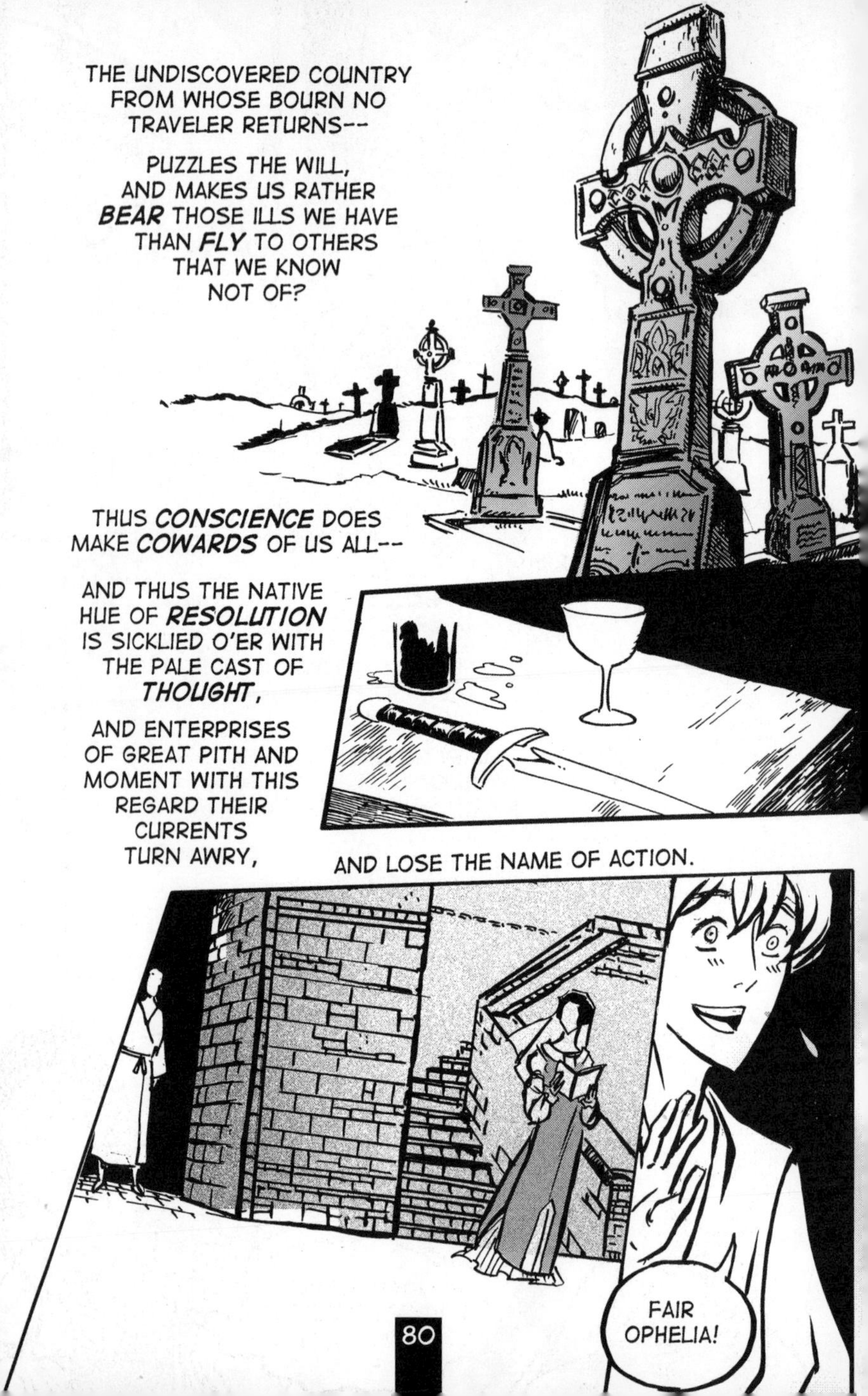

THE UNDISCOVERED COUNTRY FROM WHOSE BOURN NO TRAVELER RETURNS--
PUZZLES THE WILL, AND MAKES US RATHER **BEAR** THOSE ILLS WE HAVE THAN **FLY** TO OTHERS THAT WE KNOW NOT OF?
THUS **CONSCIENCE** DOES MAKE **COWARDS** OF US ALL--
AND THUS THE NATIVE HUE OF **RESOLUTION** IS SICKLIED O'ER WITH THE PALE CAST OF **THOUGHT**,
AND ENTERPRISES OF GREAT PITH AND MOMENT WITH THIS REGARD THEIR CURRENTS TURN AWRY,
AND LOSE THE NAME OF ACTION.
FAIR OPHELIA!

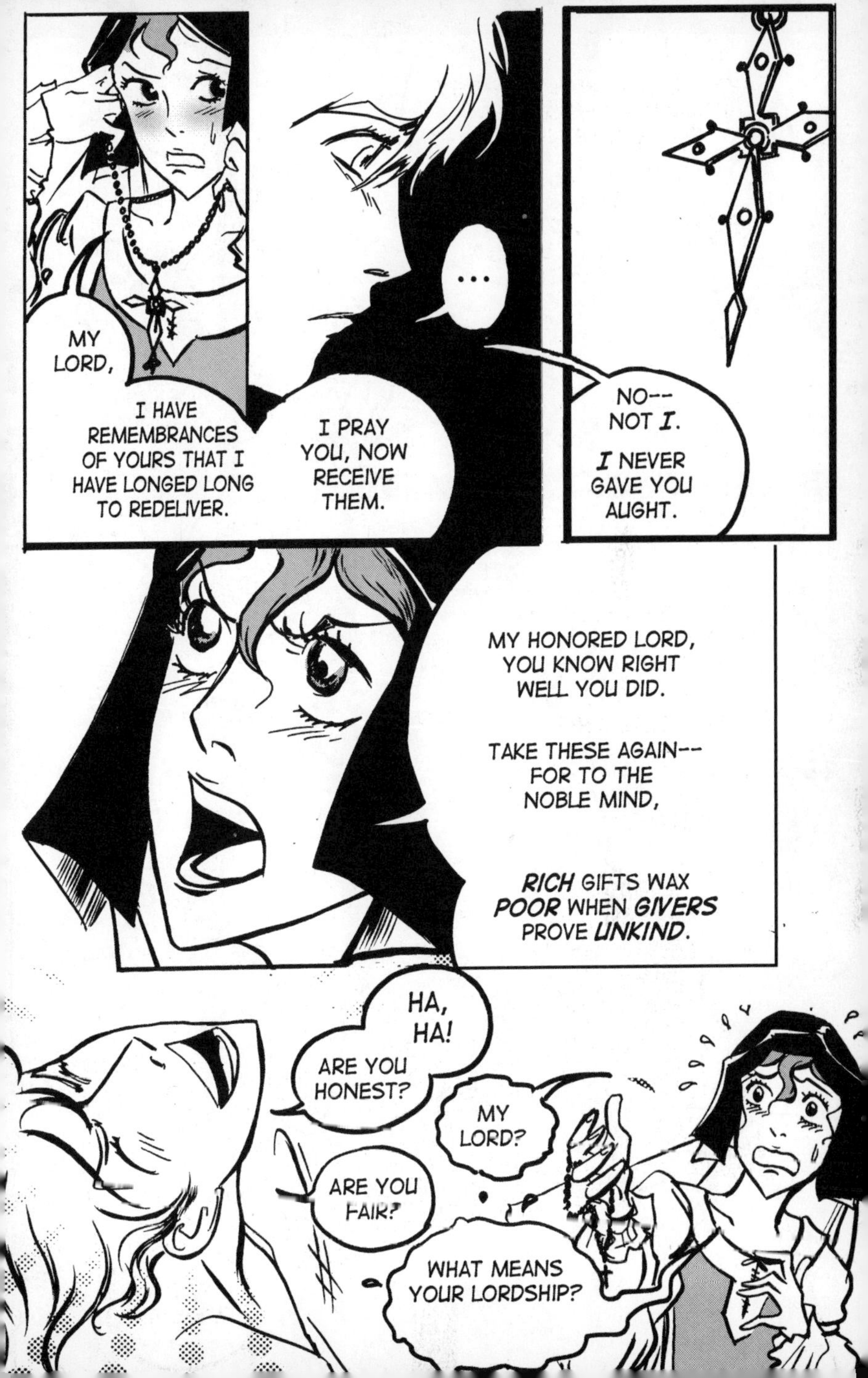
MY LORD,
I HAVE REMEMBRANCES OF YOURS THAT I HAVE LONGED LONG TO REDELIVER.
I PRAY YOU, NOW RECEIVE THEM.
...
NO-- NOT *I*.
I NEVER GAVE YOU AUGHT.
MY HONORED LORD, YOU KNOW RIGHT WELL YOU DID.
TAKE THESE AGAIN-- FOR TO THE NOBLE MIND,
RICH GIFTS WAX ***POOR*** WHEN ***GIVERS*** PROVE ***UNKIND***.
HA, HA!
ARE YOU HONEST?
MY LORD?
ARE YOU FAIR?
WHAT MEANS YOUR LORDSHIP?

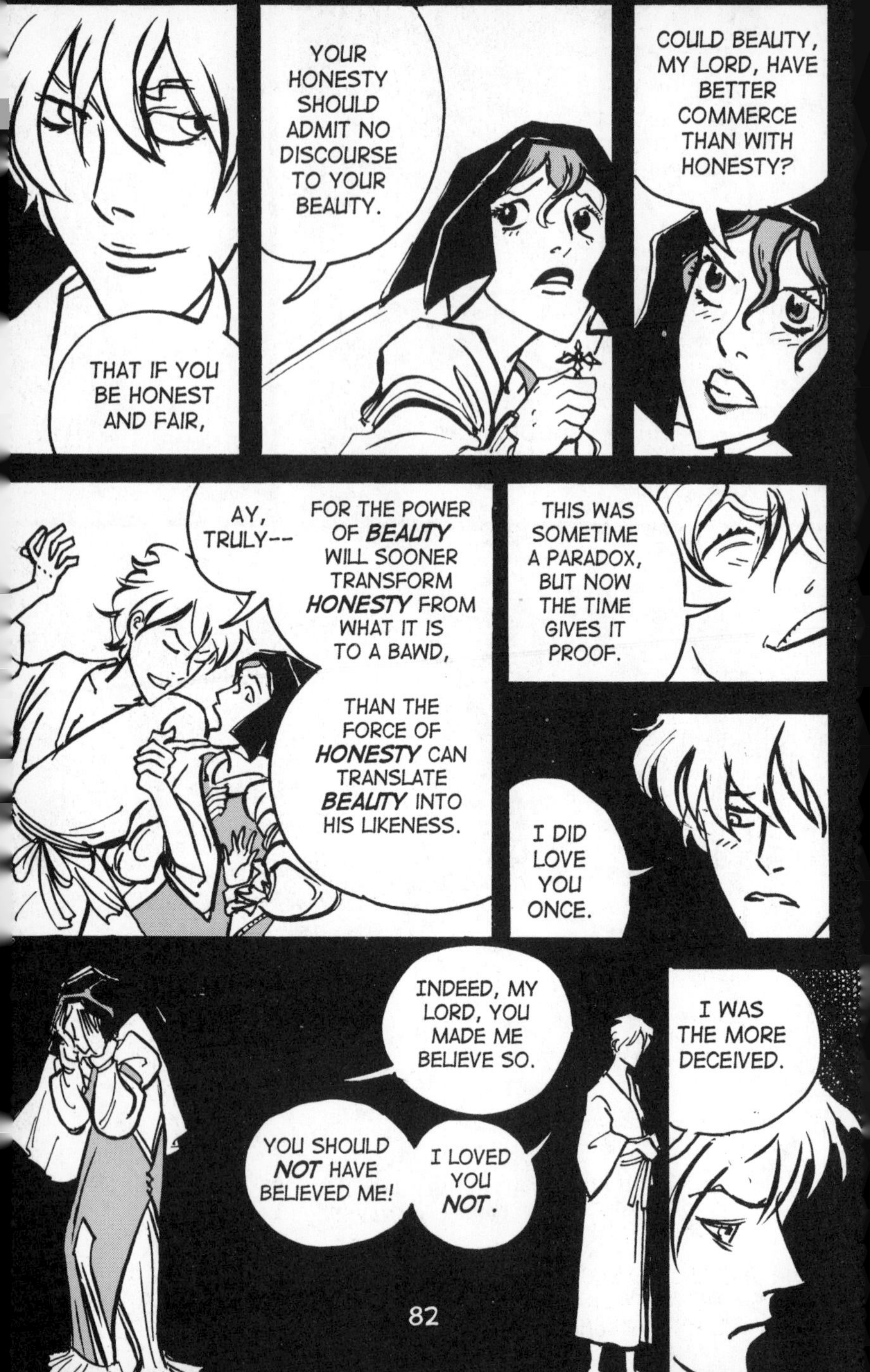
THAT IF YOU BE HONEST AND FAIR,
YOUR HONESTY SHOULD ADMIT NO DISCOURSE TO YOUR BEAUTY.
COULD BEAUTY, MY LORD, HAVE BETTER COMMERCE THAN WITH HONESTY?
AY, TRULY--
FOR THE POWER OF *BEAUTY* WILL SOONER TRANSFORM *HONESTY* FROM WHAT IT IS TO A BAWD,
THAN THE FORCE OF *HONESTY* CAN TRANSLATE *BEAUTY* INTO HIS LIKENESS.
THIS WAS SOMETIME A PARADOX, BUT NOW THE TIME GIVES IT PROOF.
I DID LOVE YOU ONCE.
INDEED, MY LORD, YOU MADE ME BELIEVE SO.
YOU SHOULD *NOT* HAVE BELIEVED ME!
I LOVED YOU *NOT*.
I WAS THE MORE DECEIVED.

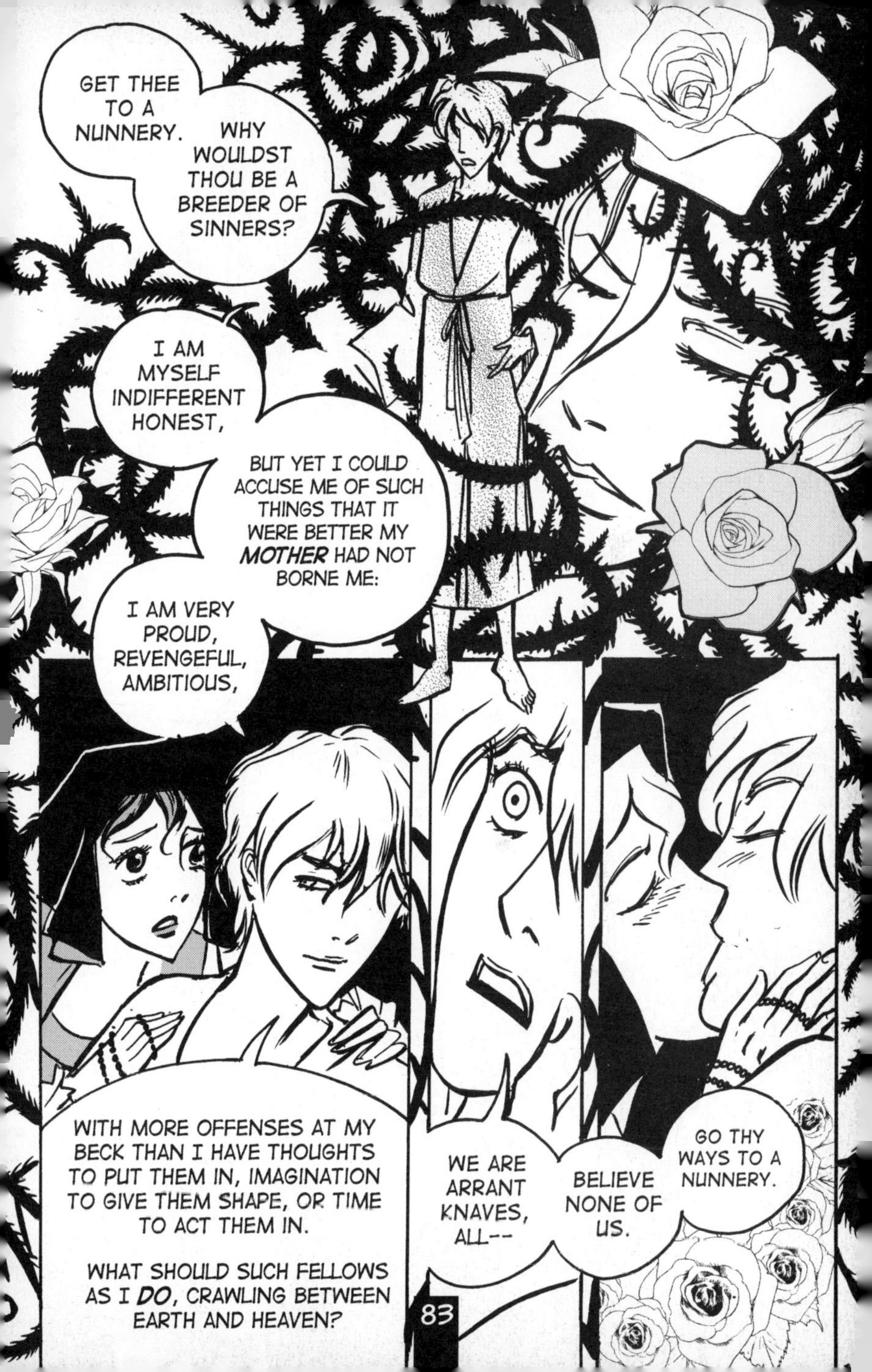
GET THEE TO A NUNNERY.
WHY WOULDST THOU BE A BREEDER OF SINNERS?
I AM MYSELF INDIFFERENT HONEST,
BUT YET I COULD ACCUSE ME OF SUCH THINGS THAT IT WERE BETTER MY *MOTHER* HAD NOT BORNE ME:
I AM VERY PROUD, REVENGEFUL, AMBITIOUS,
WITH MORE OFFENSES AT MY BECK THAN I HAVE THOUGHTS TO PUT THEM IN, IMAGINATION TO GIVE THEM SHAPE, OR TIME TO ACT THEM IN.
WHAT SHOULD SUCH FELLOWS AS I *DO*, CRAWLING BETWEEN EARTH AND HEAVEN?
WE ARE ARRANT KNAVES, ALL--
BELIEVE NONE OF US.
GO THY WAYS TO A NUNNERY.

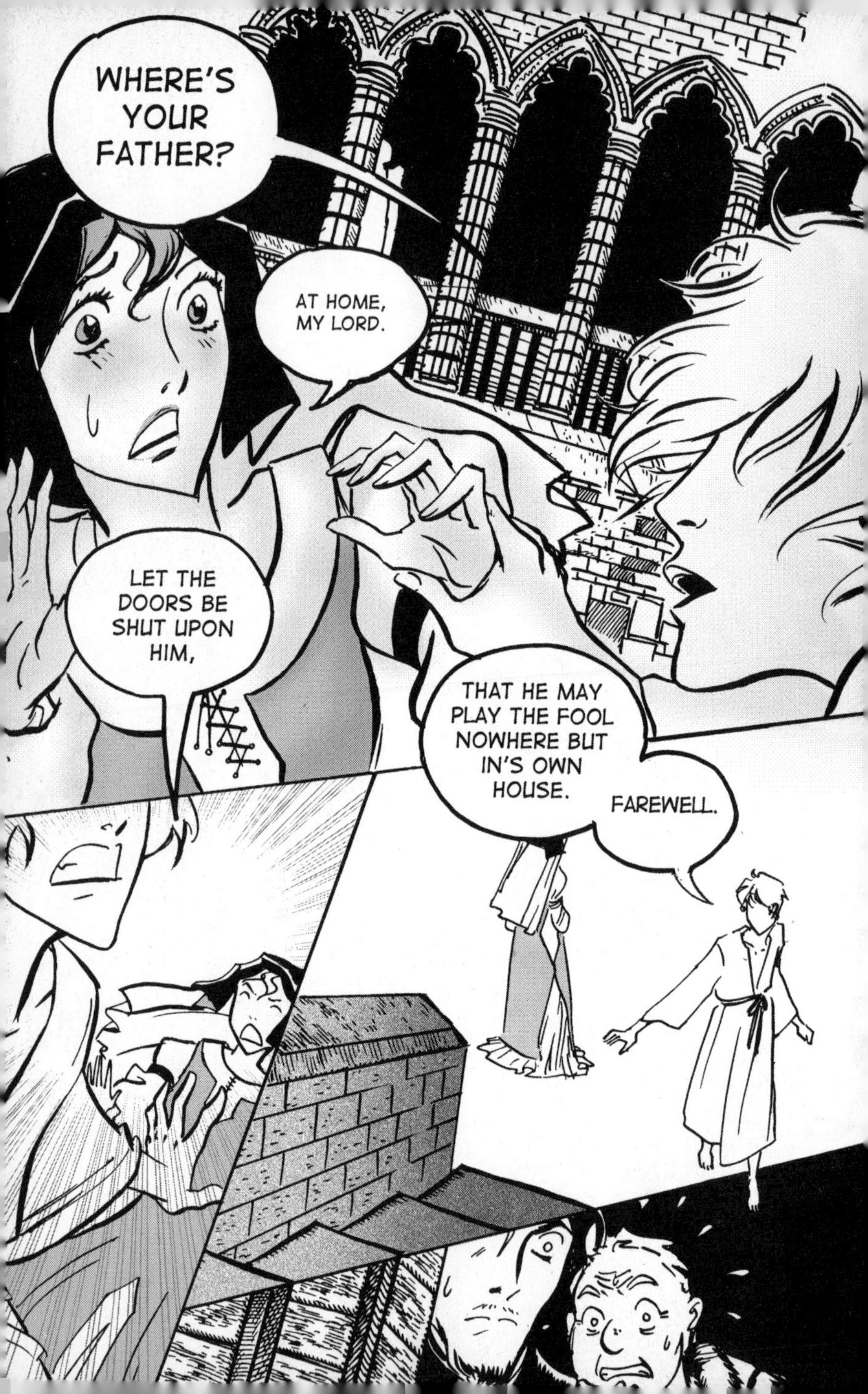
WHERE'S YOUR FATHER?
AT HOME, MY LORD.
LET THE DOORS BE SHUT UPON HIM,
THAT HE MAY PLAY THE FOOL NOWHERE BUT IN'S OWN HOUSE.
FAREWELL.

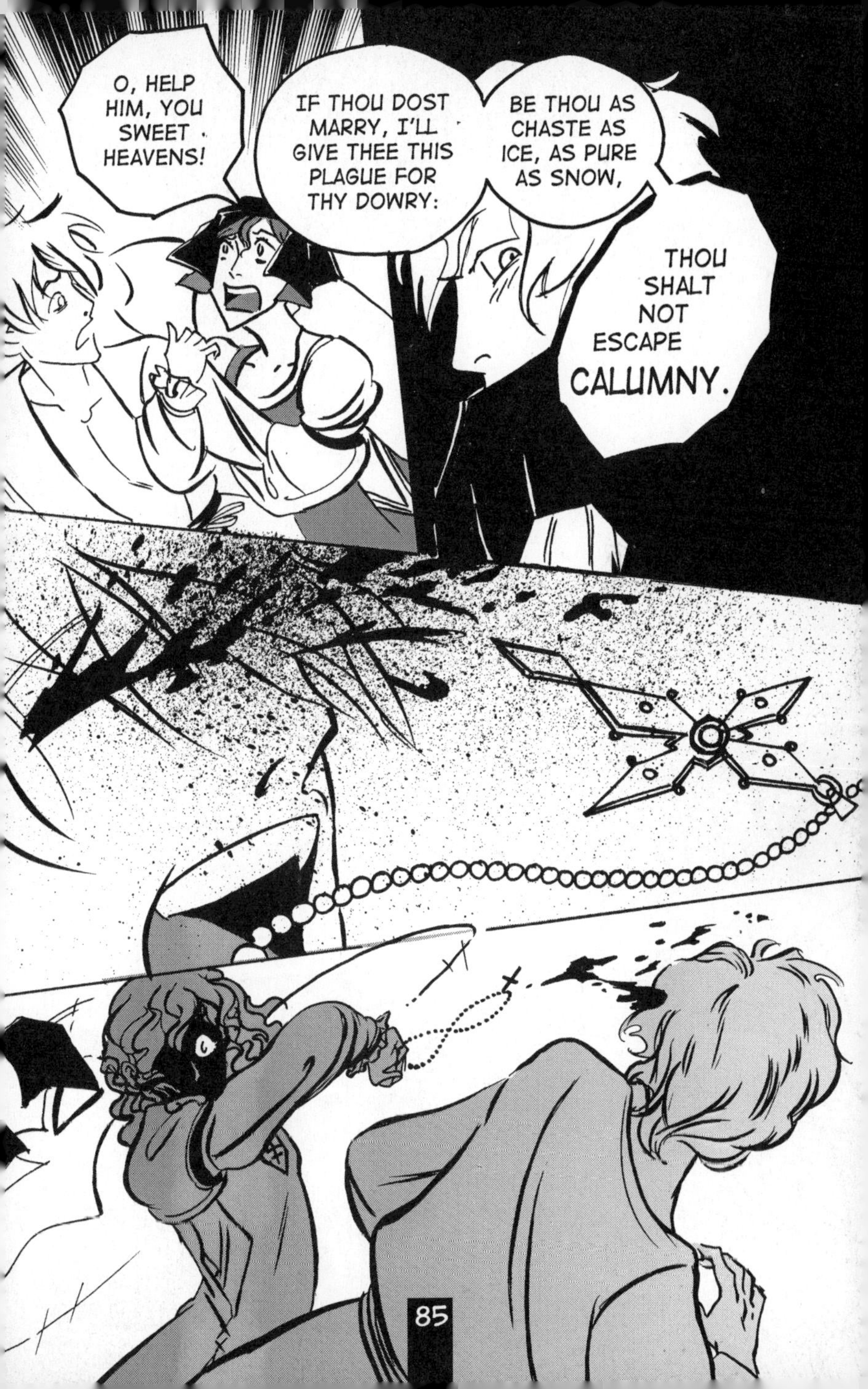
O, HELP HIM, YOU SWEET HEAVENS!
IF THOU DOST MARRY, I'LL GIVE THEE THIS PLAGUE FOR THY DOWRY:
BE THOU AS CHASTE AS ICE, AS PURE AS SNOW,
THOU SHALT NOT ESCAPE CALUMNY.

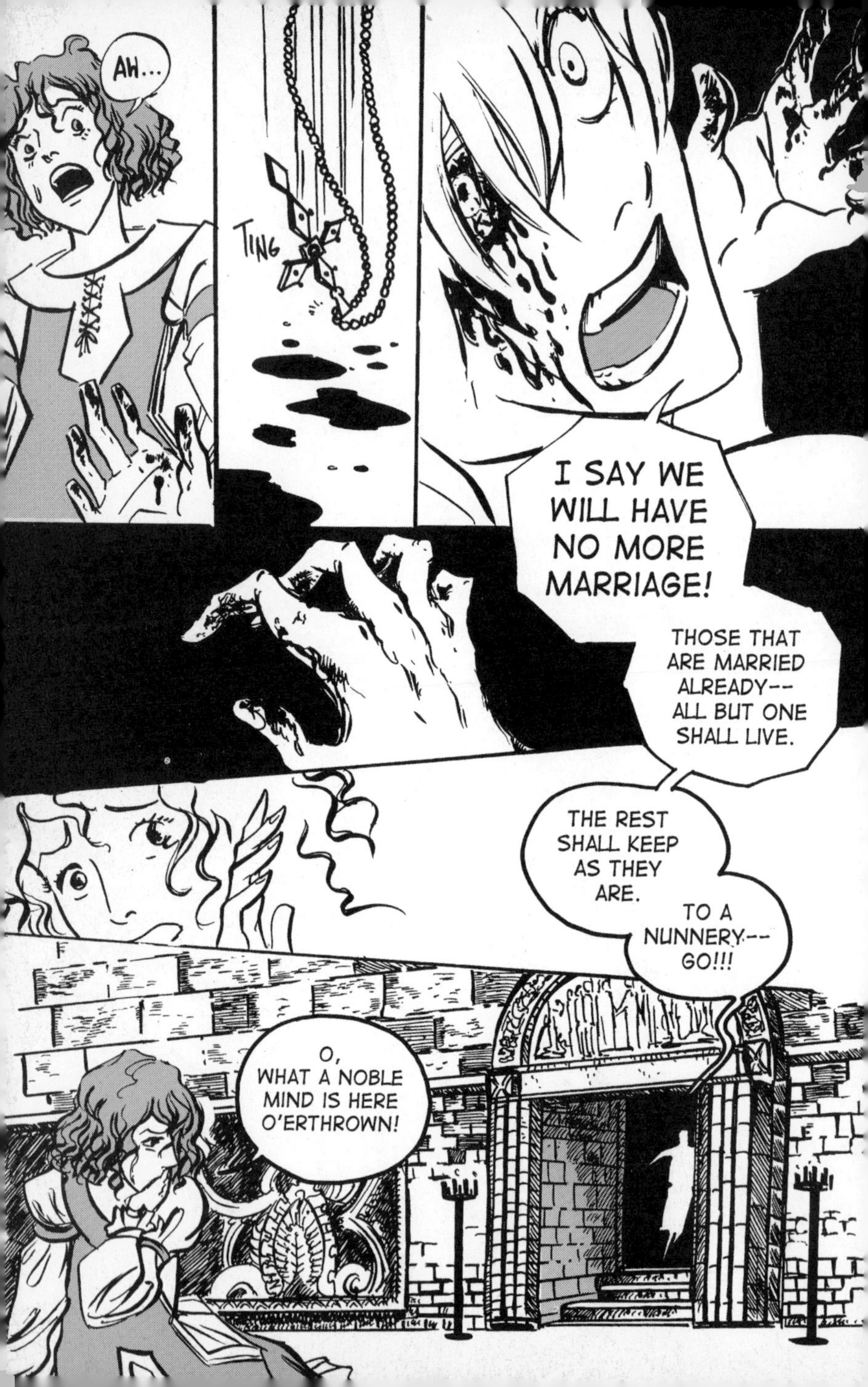
AH...
TING
I SAY WE WILL HAVE NO MORE MARRIAGE!
THOSE THAT ARE MARRIED ALREADY-- ALL BUT ONE SHALL LIVE.
THE REST SHALL KEEP AS THEY ARE.
TO A NUNNERY-- GO!!!
O, WHAT A NOBLE MIND IS HERE O'ERTHROWN!

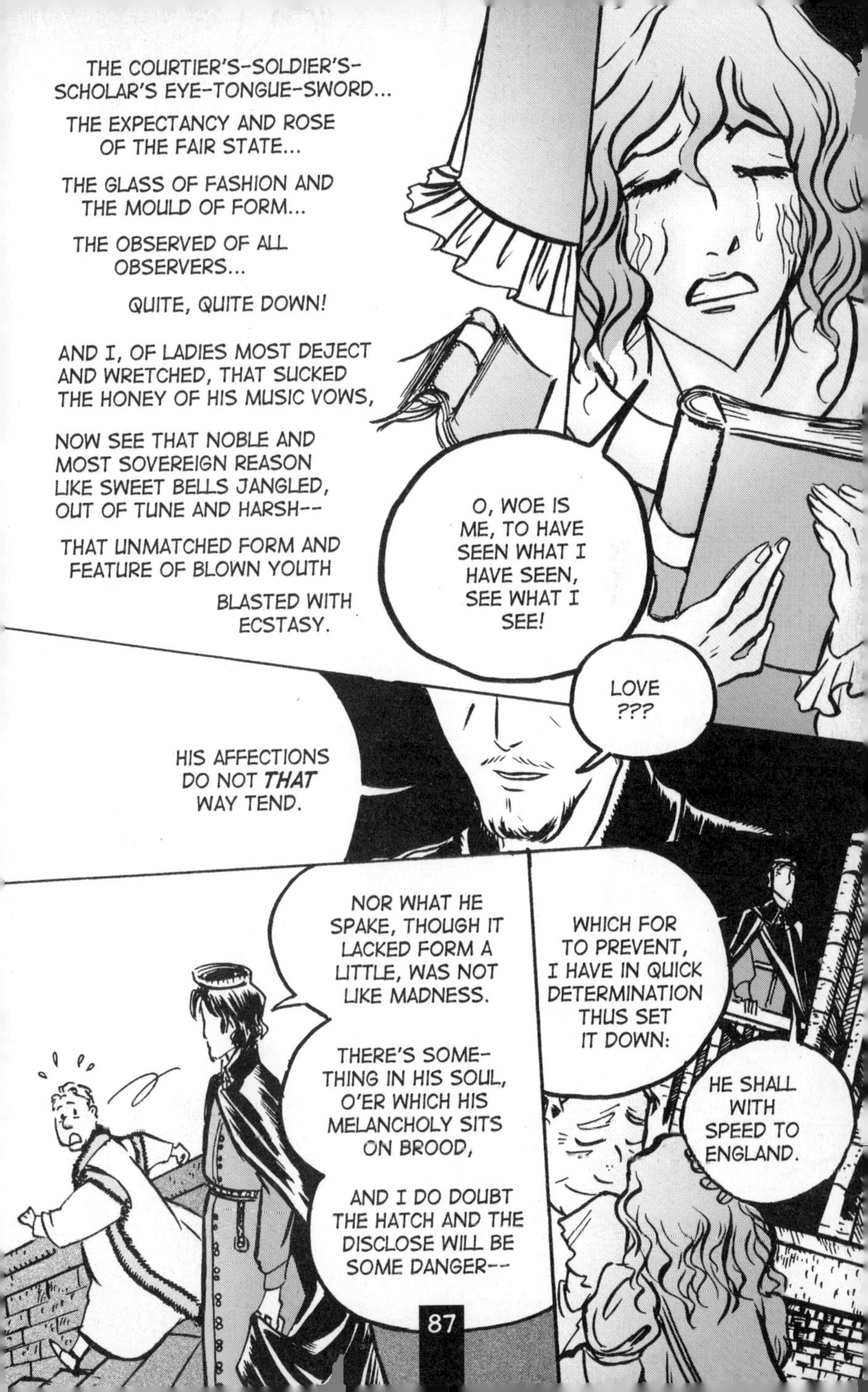
THE COURTIER'S-SOLDIER'S-SCHOLAR'S EYE-TONGUE-SWORD...
THE EXPECTANCY AND ROSE OF THE FAIR STATE...
THE GLASS OF FASHION AND THE MOULD OF FORM...
THE OBSERVED OF ALL OBSERVERS...
QUITE, QUITE DOWN!
AND I, OF LADIES MOST DEJECT AND WRETCHED, THAT SUCKED THE HONEY OF HIS MUSIC VOWS,
NOW SEE THAT NOBLE AND MOST SOVEREIGN REASON LIKE SWEET BELLS JANGLED, OUT OF TUNE AND HARSH--
THAT UNMATCHED FORM AND FEATURE OF BLOWN YOUTH
BLASTED WITH ECSTASY.
O, WOE IS ME, TO HAVE SEEN WHAT I HAVE SEEN, SEE WHAT I SEE!
LOVE ???
HIS AFFECTIONS DO NOT *THAT* WAY TEND.
NOR WHAT HE SPAKE, THOUGH IT LACKED FORM A LITTLE, WAS NOT LIKE MADNESS.
THERE'S SOME-THING IN HIS SOUL, O'ER WHICH HIS MELANCHOLY SITS ON BROOD,
AND I DO DOUBT THE HATCH AND THE DISCLOSE WILL BE SOME DANGER--
WHICH FOR TO PREVENT, I HAVE IN QUICK DETERMINATION THUS SET IT DOWN:
HE SHALL WITH SPEED TO ENGLAND.

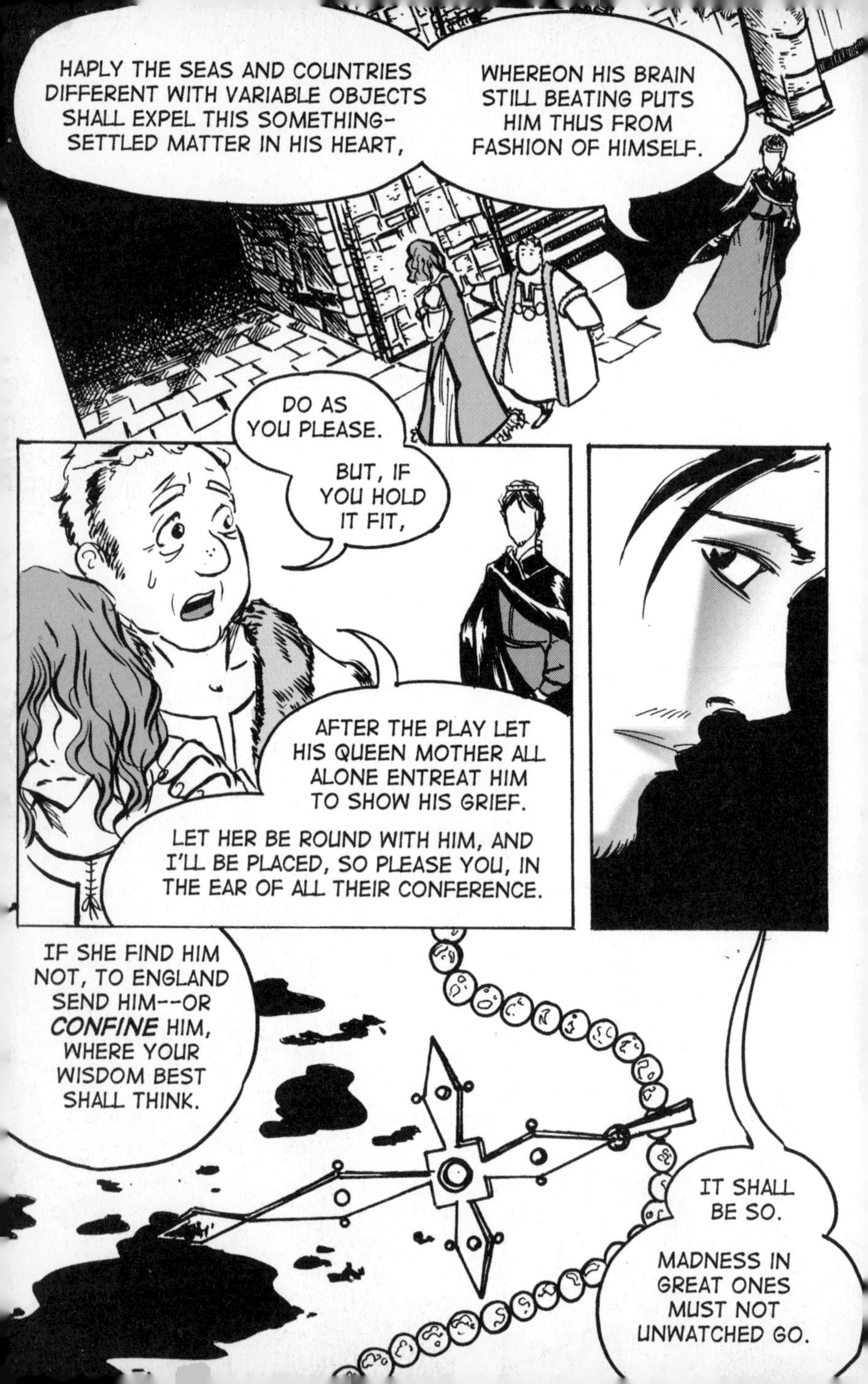
HAPLY THE SEAS AND COUNTRIES DIFFERENT WITH VARIABLE OBJECTS SHALL EXPEL THIS SOMETHING-SETTLED MATTER IN HIS HEART,
WHEREON HIS BRAIN STILL BEATING PUTS HIM THUS FROM FASHION OF HIMSELF.
DO AS YOU PLEASE.
BUT, IF YOU HOLD IT FIT,
AFTER THE PLAY LET HIS QUEEN MOTHER ALL ALONE ENTREAT HIM TO SHOW HIS GRIEF.
LET HER BE ROUND WITH HIM, AND I'LL BE PLACED, SO PLEASE YOU, IN THE EAR OF ALL THEIR CONFERENCE.
IF SHE FIND HIM NOT, TO ENGLAND SEND HIM--OR *CONFINE* HIM, WHERE YOUR WISDOM BEST SHALL THINK.
IT SHALL BE SO.
MADNESS IN GREAT ONES MUST NOT UNWATCHED GO.

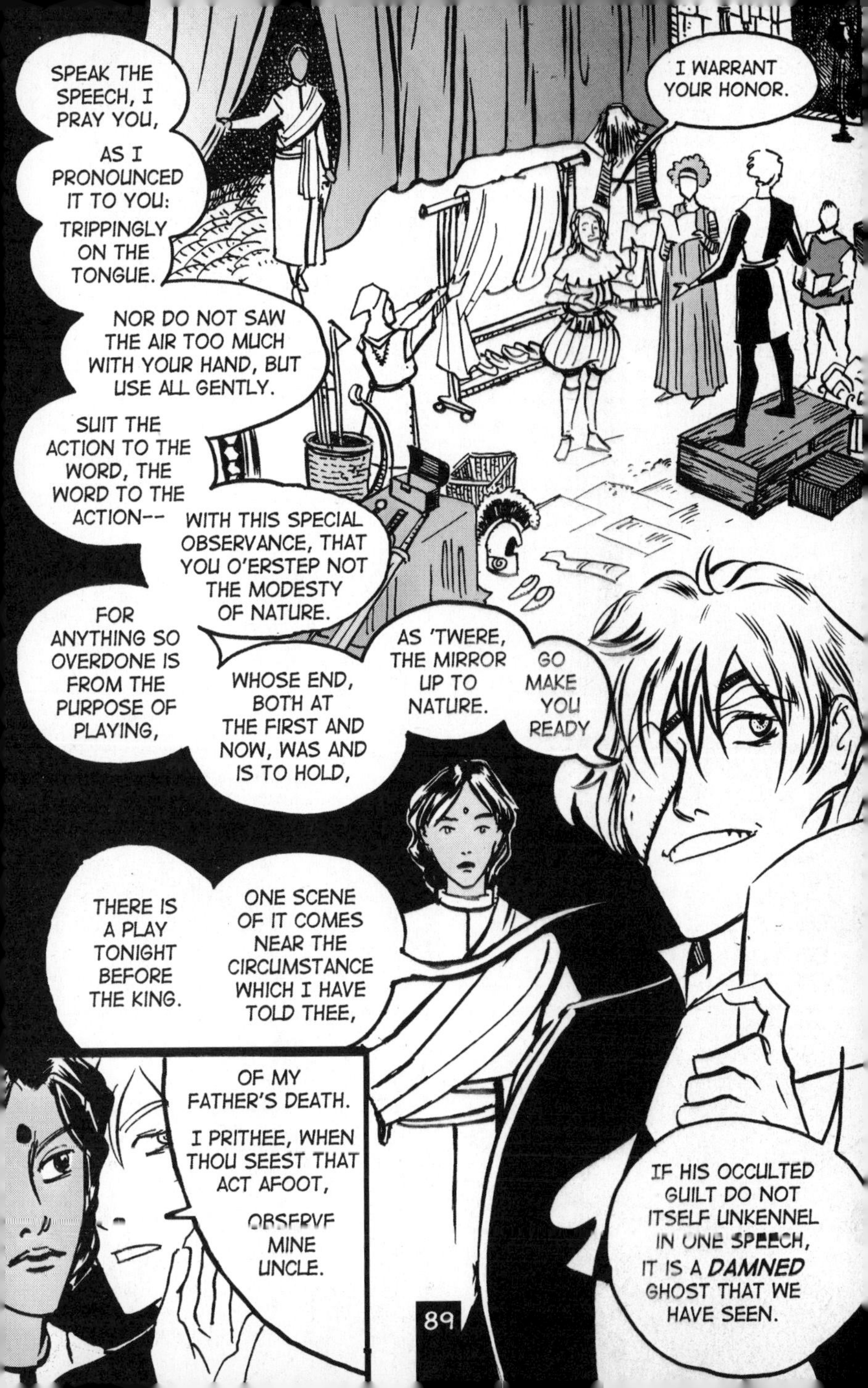
SPEAK THE SPEECH, I PRAY YOU,
AS I PRONOUNCED IT TO YOU:
TRIPPINGLY ON THE TONGUE.
I WARRANT YOUR HONOR.
NOR DO NOT SAW THE AIR TOO MUCH WITH YOUR HAND, BUT USE ALL GENTLY.
SUIT THE ACTION TO THE WORD, THE WORD TO THE ACTION--
WITH THIS SPECIAL OBSERVANCE, THAT YOU O'ERSTEP NOT THE MODESTY OF NATURE.
FOR ANYTHING SO OVERDONE IS FROM THE PURPOSE OF PLAYING,
WHOSE END, BOTH AT THE FIRST AND NOW, WAS AND IS TO HOLD,
AS 'TWERE, THE MIRROR UP TO NATURE.
GO MAKE YOU READY
THERE IS A PLAY TONIGHT BEFORE THE KING.
ONE SCENE OF IT COMES NEAR THE CIRCUMSTANCE WHICH I HAVE TOLD THEE,
OF MY FATHER'S DEATH.
I PRITHEE, WHEN THOU SEEST THAT ACT AFOOT,
OBSERVE MINE UNCLE.
IF HIS OCCULTED GUILT DO NOT ITSELF UNKENNEL IN ONE SPEECH,
IT IS A *DAMNED* GHOST THAT WE HAVE SEEN.

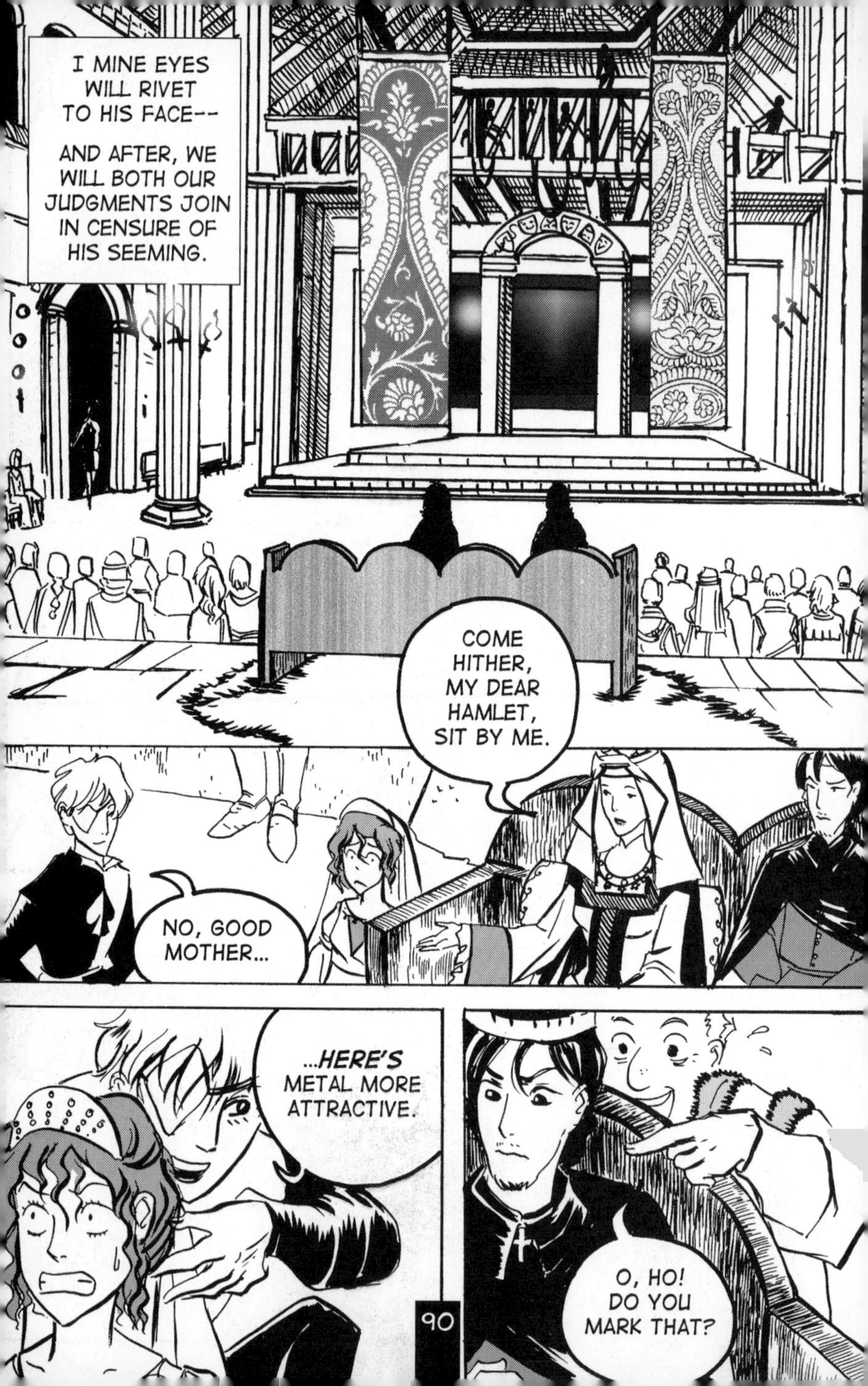
I MINE EYES WILL RIVET TO HIS FACE--
AND AFTER, WE WILL BOTH OUR JUDGMENTS JOIN IN CENSURE OF HIS SEEMING.
COME HITHER, MY DEAR HAMLET, SIT BY ME.
NO, GOOD MOTHER...
...HERE'S METAL MORE ATTRACTIVE.
O, HO! DO YOU MARK THAT?

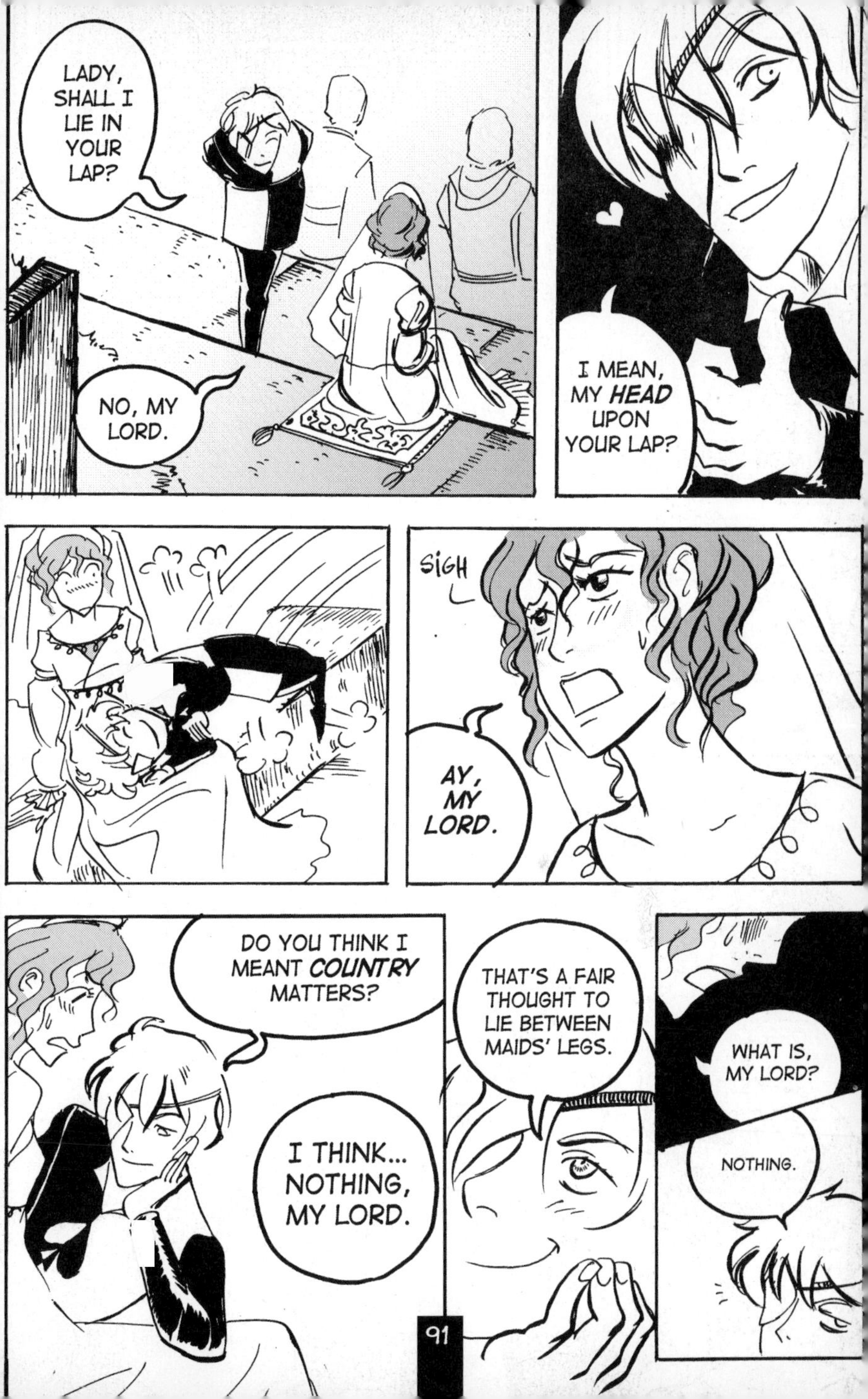
LADY, SHALL I LIE IN YOUR LAP?
NO, MY LORD.
I MEAN, MY *HEAD* UPON YOUR LAP?
SIGH
AY, MY LORD.
DO YOU THINK I MEANT *COUNTRY* MATTERS?
I THINK... NOTHING, MY LORD.
THAT'S A FAIR THOUGHT TO LIE BETWEEN MAIDS' LEGS.
WHAT IS, MY LORD?
NOTHING.

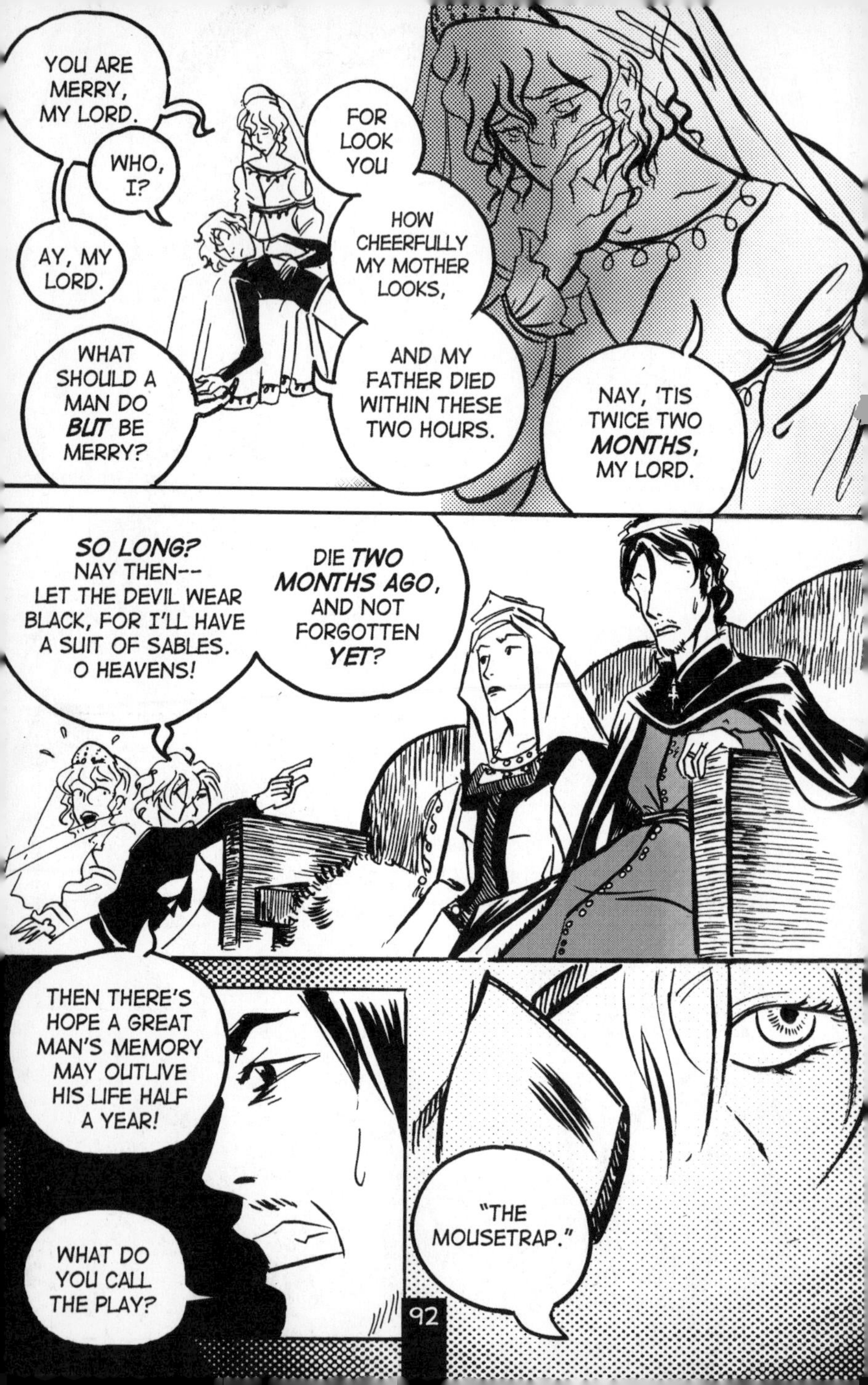
YOU ARE MERRY, MY LORD.
WHO, I?
AY, MY LORD.
FOR LOOK YOU
WHAT SHOULD A MAN DO *BUT* BE MERRY?
HOW CHEERFULLY MY MOTHER LOOKS,
AND MY FATHER DIED WITHIN THESE TWO HOURS.
NAY, 'TIS TWICE TWO *MONTHS,* MY LORD.
SO LONG? NAY THEN-- LET THE DEVIL WEAR BLACK, FOR I'LL HAVE A SUIT OF SABLES. O HEAVENS!
DIE *TWO MONTHS AGO,* AND NOT FORGOTTEN *YET*?
THEN THERE'S HOPE A GREAT MAN'S MEMORY MAY OUTLIVE HIS LIFE HALF A YEAR!
WHAT DO YOU CALL THE PLAY?
"THE MOUSETRAP."

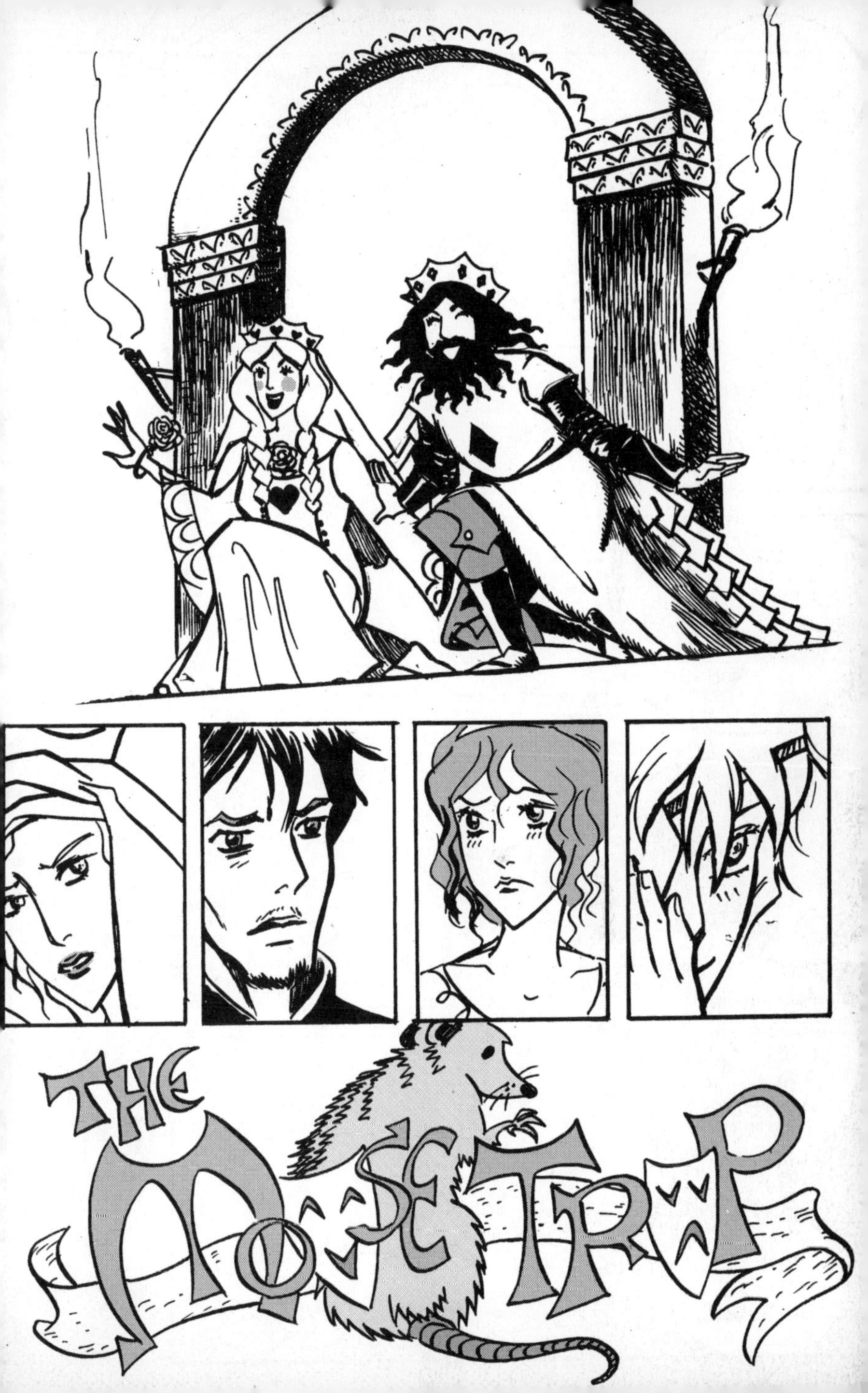
THE MOUSETRAP

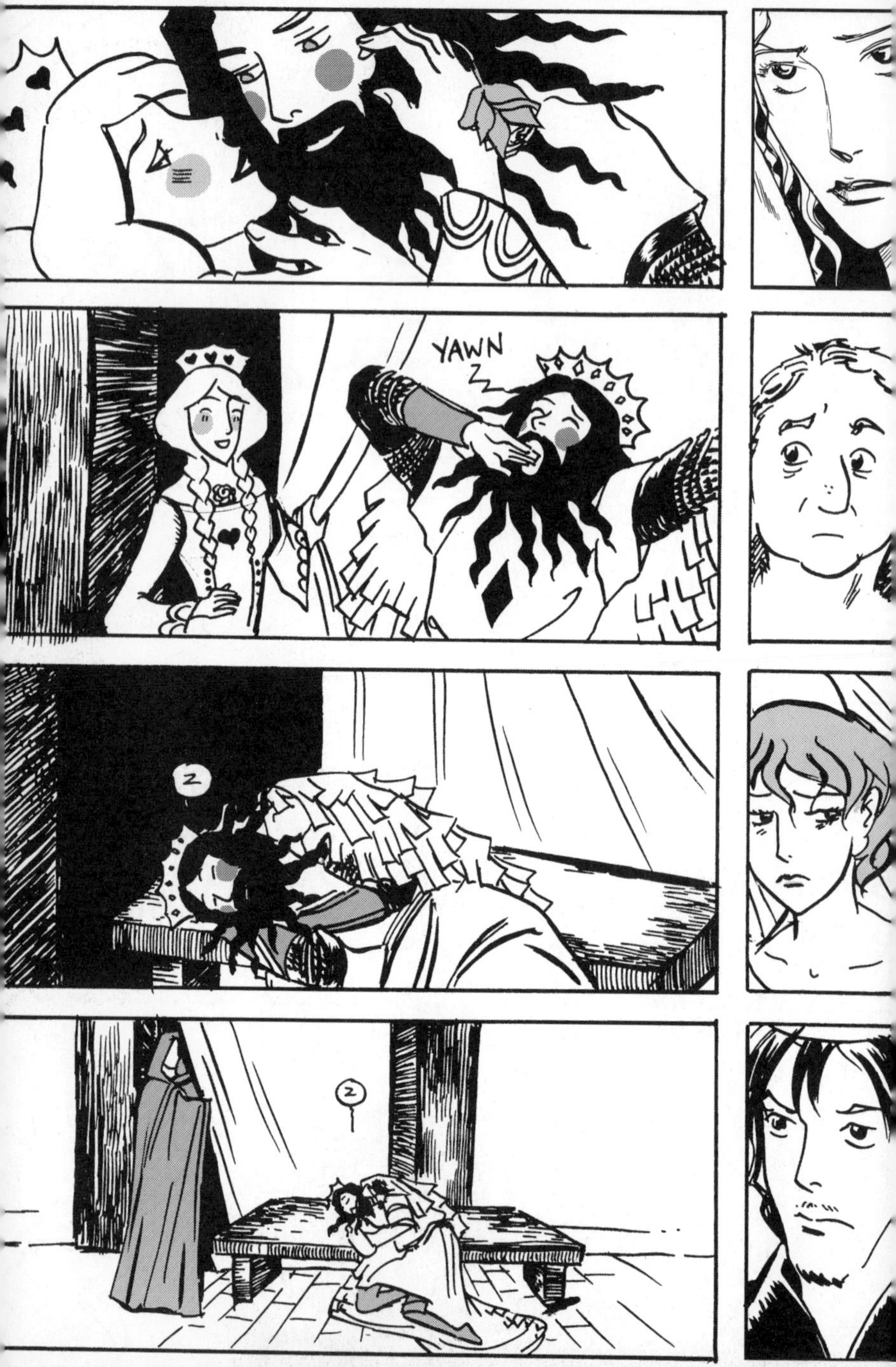
YAWN
Z
Z
Z

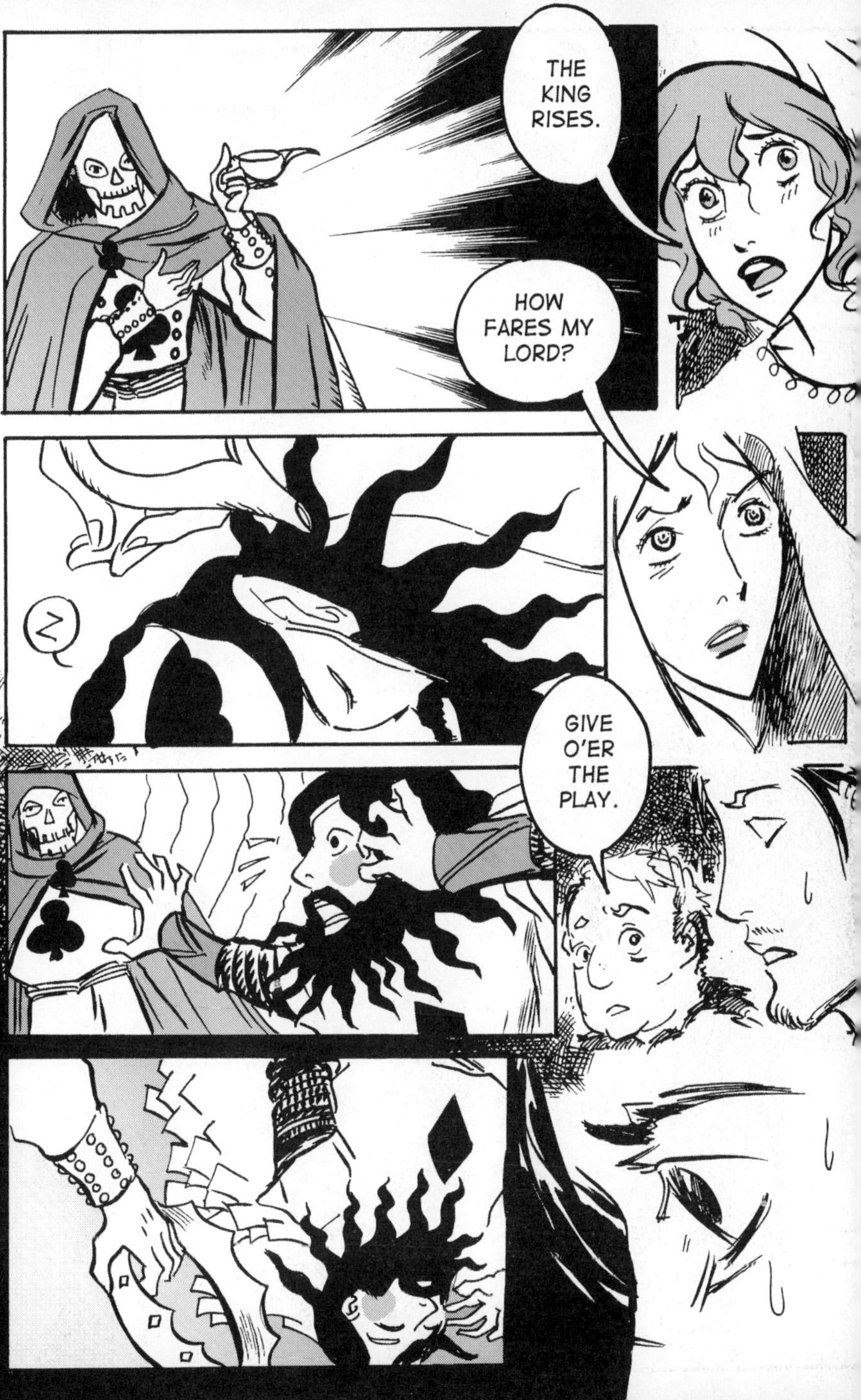
THE KING RISES.
HOW FARES MY LORD?
Z
GIVE O'ER THE PLAY.

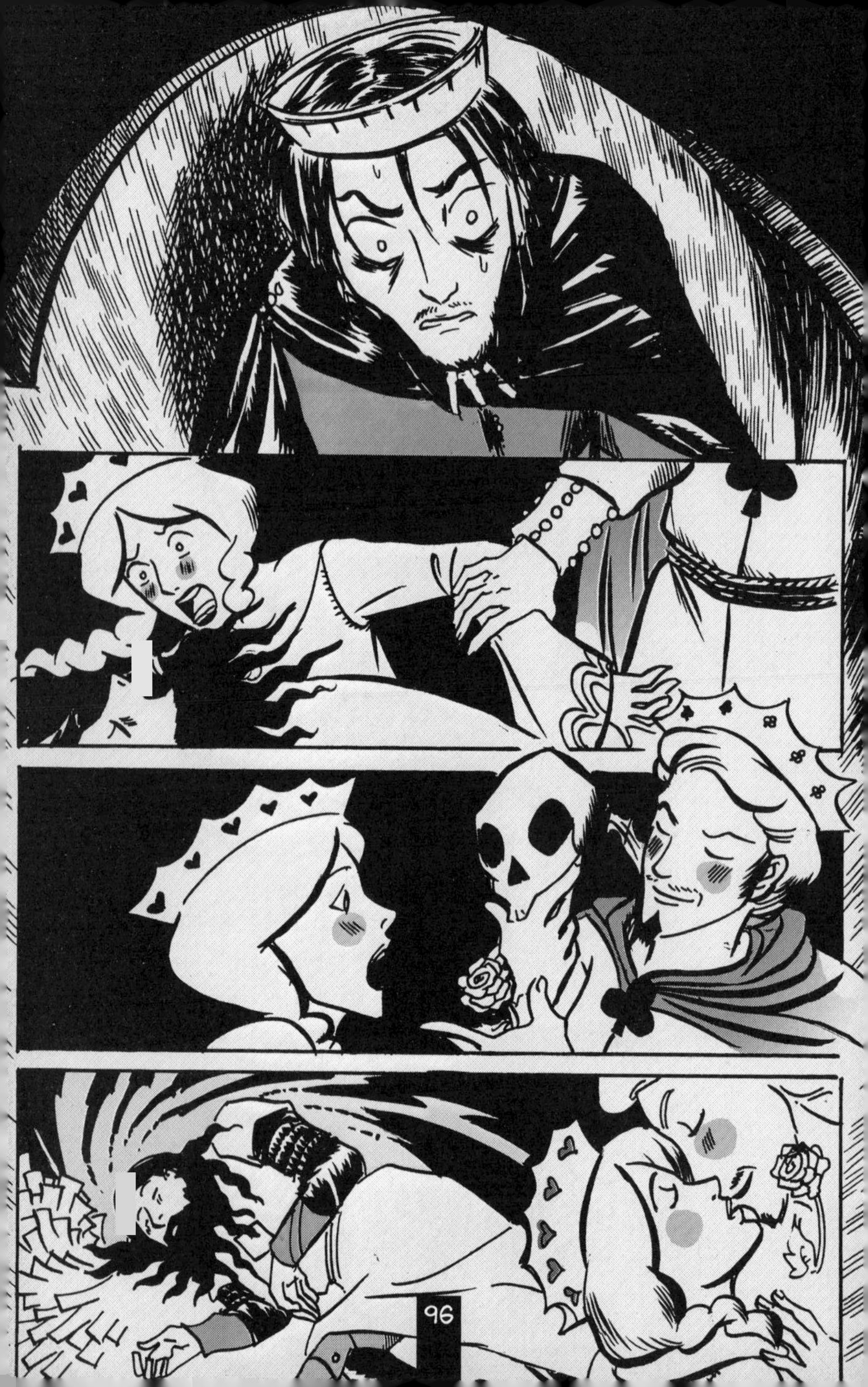

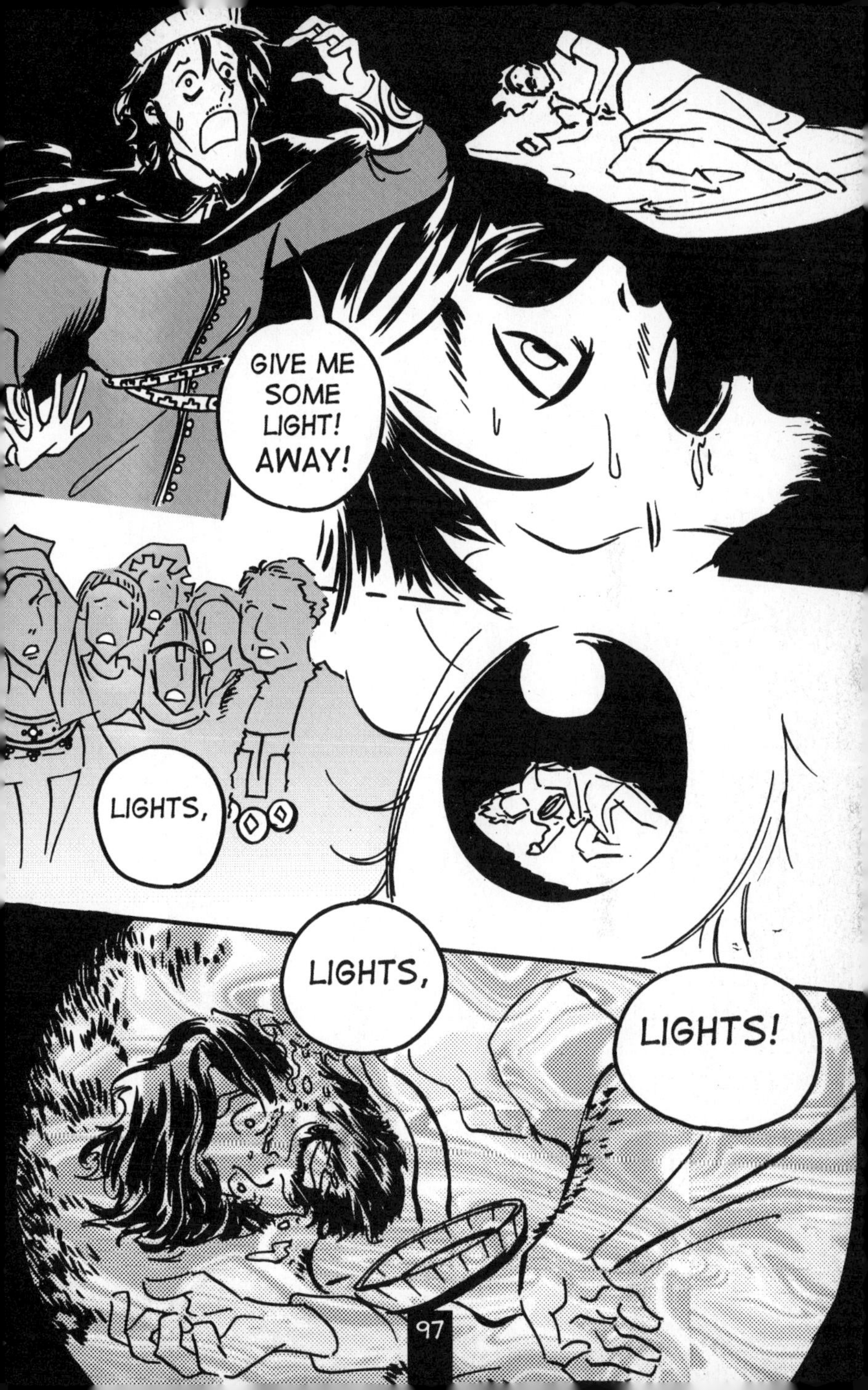
GIVE ME SOME LIGHT! AWAY!
LIGHTS,
LIGHTS,
LIGHTS!

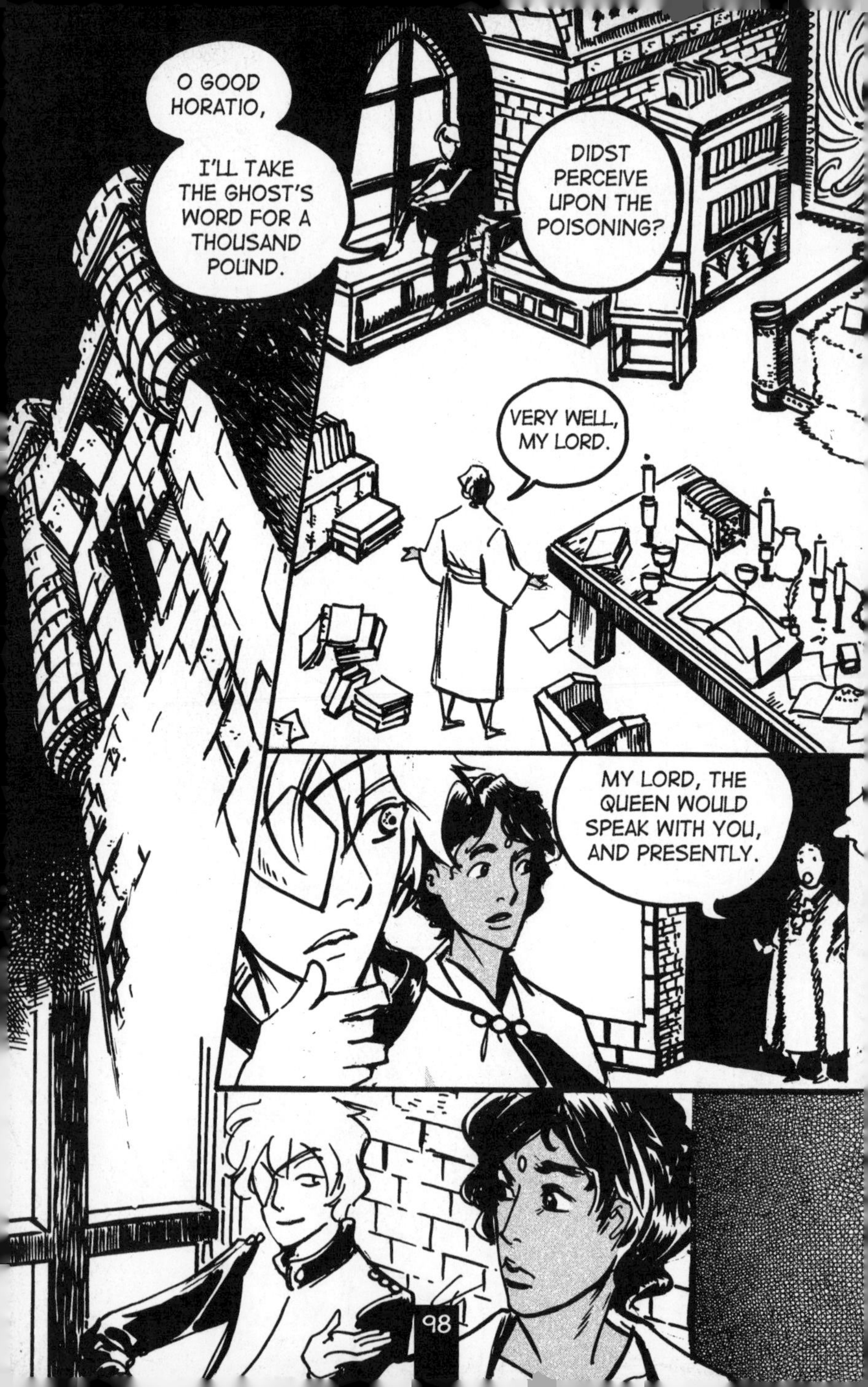
O GOOD HORATIO,
I'LL TAKE THE GHOST'S WORD FOR A THOUSAND POUND.
DIDST PERCEIVE UPON THE POISONING?
VERY WELL, MY LORD.
MY LORD, THE QUEEN WOULD SPEAK WITH YOU, AND PRESENTLY.

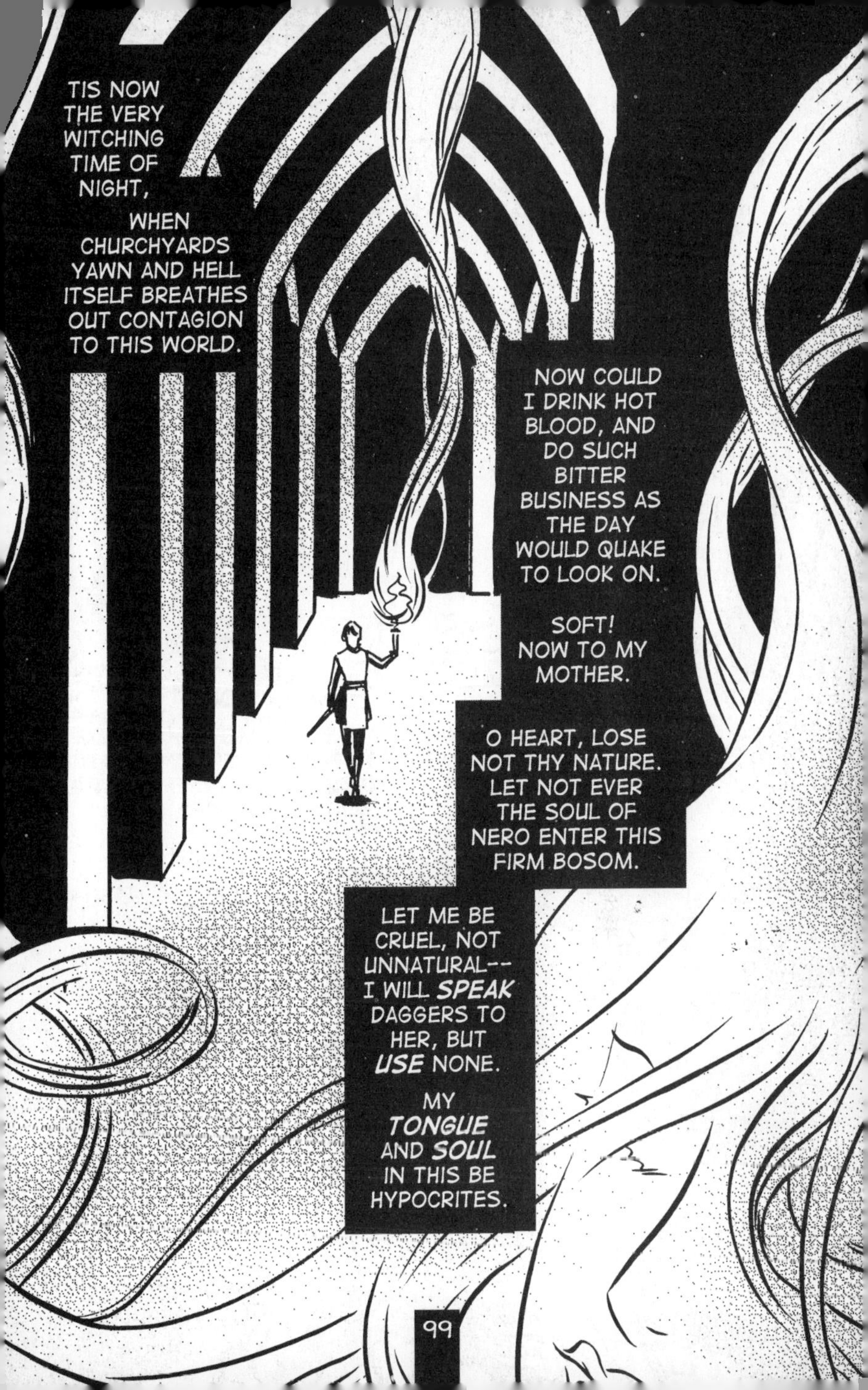
TIS NOW THE VERY WITCHING TIME OF NIGHT,
WHEN CHURCHYARDS YAWN AND HELL ITSELF BREATHES OUT CONTAGION TO THIS WORLD.
NOW COULD I DRINK HOT BLOOD, AND DO SUCH BITTER BUSINESS AS THE DAY WOULD QUAKE TO LOOK ON.
SOFT! NOW TO MY MOTHER.
O HEART, LOSE NOT THY NATURE. LET NOT EVER THE SOUL OF NERO ENTER THIS FIRM BOSOM.
LET ME BE CRUEL, NOT UNNATURAL-- I WILL *SPEAK* DAGGERS TO HER, BUT *USE* NONE.
MY *TONGUE* AND *SOUL* IN THIS BE HYPOCRITES.

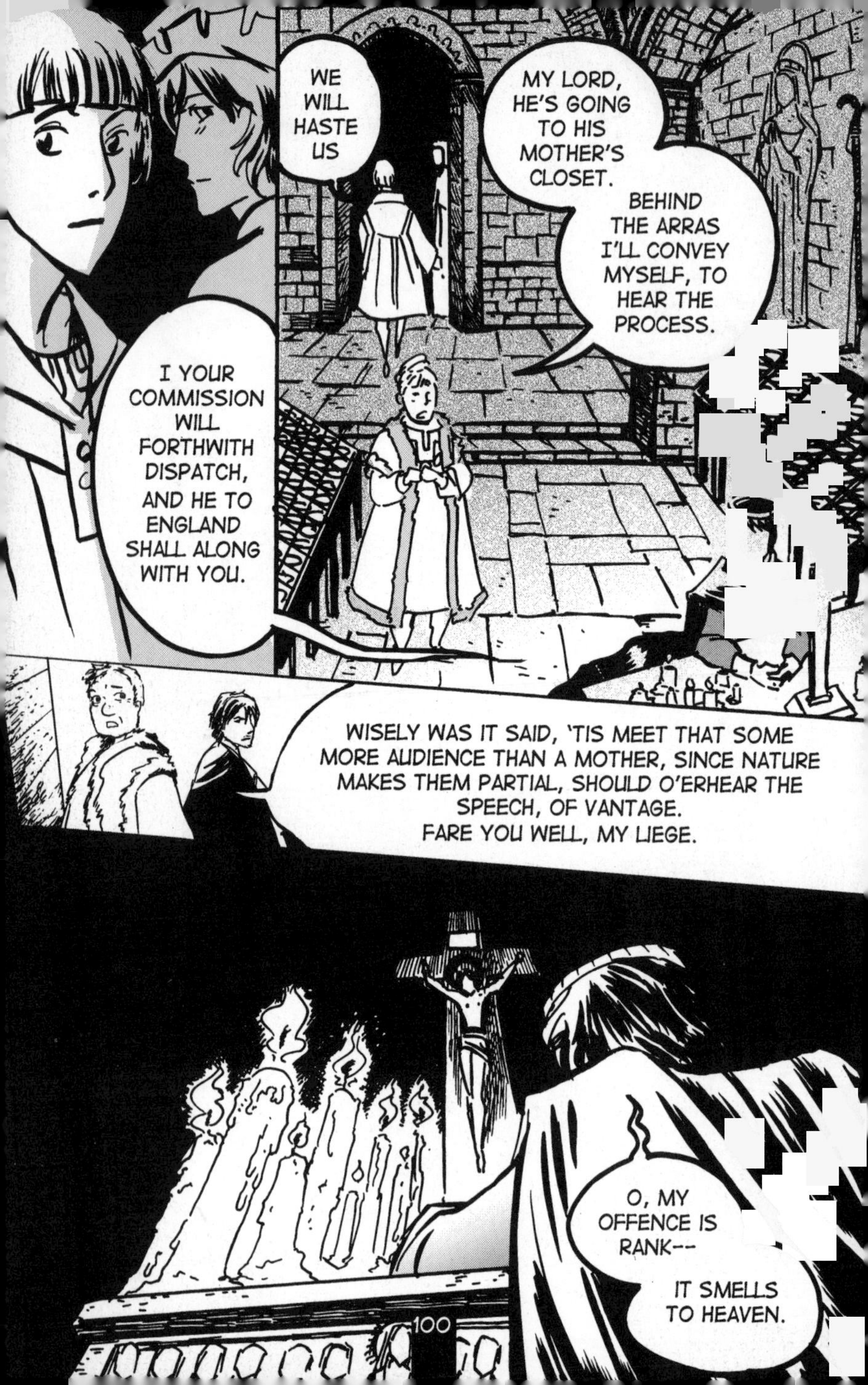
WE WILL HASTE US
MY LORD, HE'S GOING TO HIS MOTHER'S CLOSET.
BEHIND THE ARRAS I'LL CONVEY MYSELF, TO HEAR THE PROCESS.
I YOUR COMMISSION WILL FORTHWITH DISPATCH, AND HE TO ENGLAND SHALL ALONG WITH YOU.
WISELY WAS IT SAID, 'TIS MEET THAT SOME MORE AUDIENCE THAN A MOTHER, SINCE NATURE MAKES THEM PARTIAL, SHOULD O'ERHEAR THE SPEECH, OF VANTAGE.
FARE YOU WELL, MY LIEGE.
O, MY OFFENCE IS RANK--
IT SMELLS TO HEAVEN.

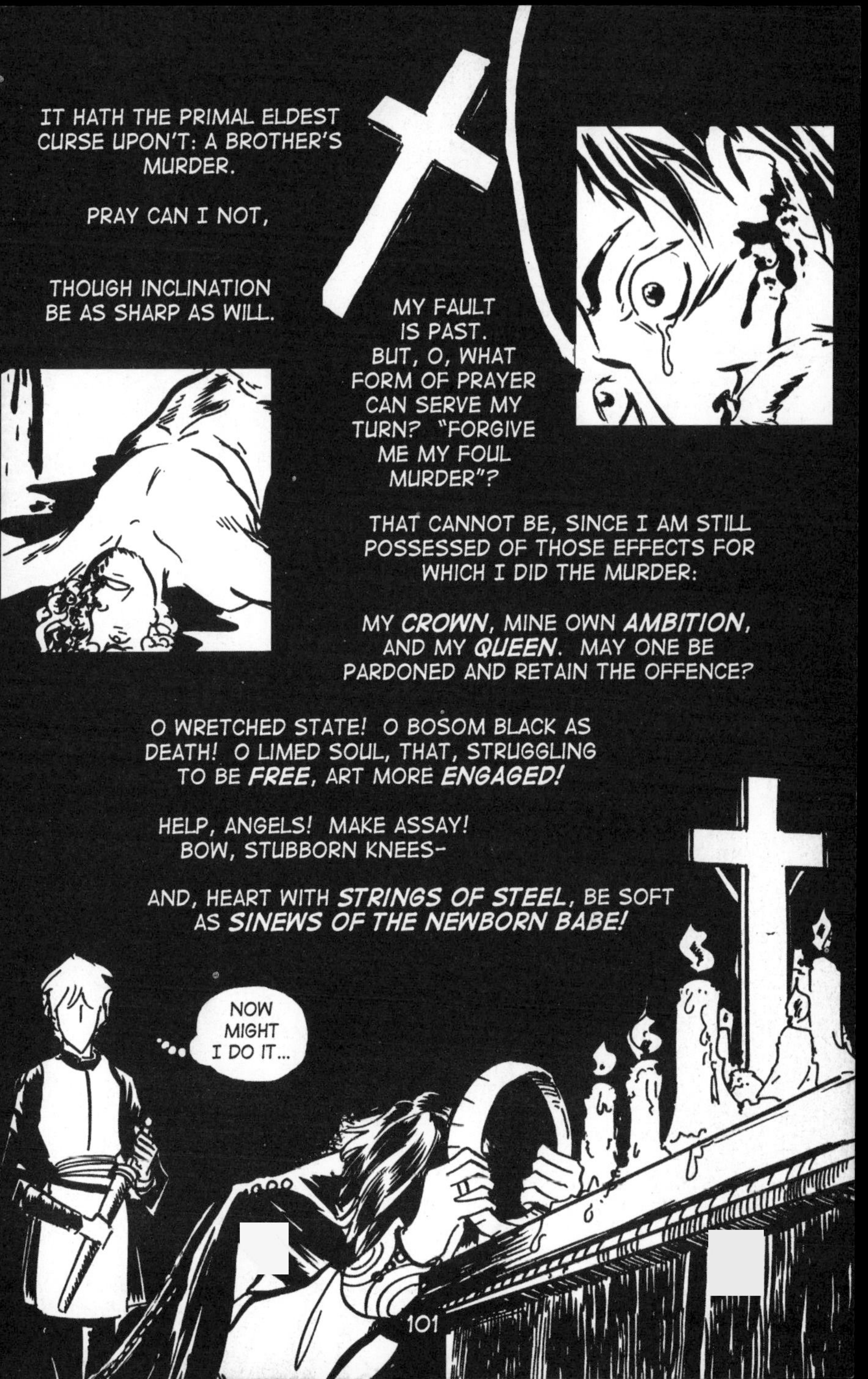
IT HATH THE PRIMAL ELDEST CURSE UPON'T: A BROTHER'S MURDER.
PRAY CAN I NOT,
THOUGH INCLINATION BE AS SHARP AS WILL.
MY FAULT IS PAST. BUT, O, WHAT FORM OF PRAYER CAN SERVE MY TURN? "FORGIVE ME MY FOUL MURDER"?
THAT CANNOT BE, SINCE I AM STILL POSSESSED OF THOSE EFFECTS FOR WHICH I DID THE MURDER:
MY *CROWN*, MINE OWN *AMBITION*, AND MY *QUEEN*. MAY ONE BE PARDONED AND RETAIN THE OFFENCE?
O WRETCHED STATE! O BOSOM BLACK AS DEATH! O LIMED SOUL, THAT, STRUGGLING TO BE *FREE*, ART MORE *ENGAGED!*
HELP, ANGELS! MAKE ASSAY! BOW, STUBBORN KNEES-
AND, HEART WITH *STRINGS OF STEEL*, BE SOFT AS *SINEWS OF THE NEWBORN BABE!*
NOW MIGHT I DO IT...

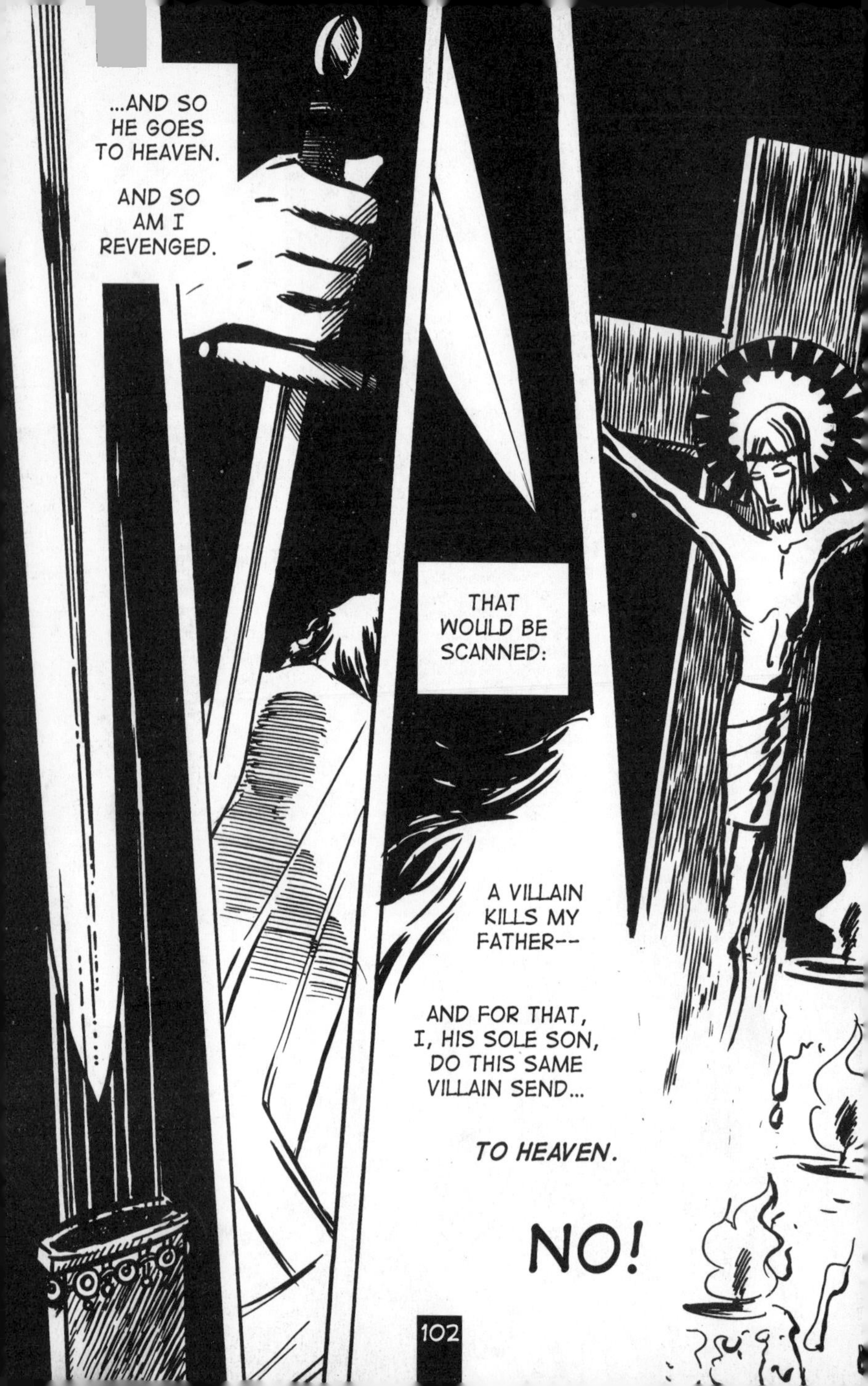
...AND SO
HE GOES
TO HEAVEN.
AND SO
AM I
REVENGED.
THAT
WOULD BE
SCANNED:
A VILLAIN
KILLS MY
FATHER--
AND FOR THAT,
I, HIS SOLE SON,
DO THIS SAME
VILLAIN SEND...
TO HEAVEN.
NO!

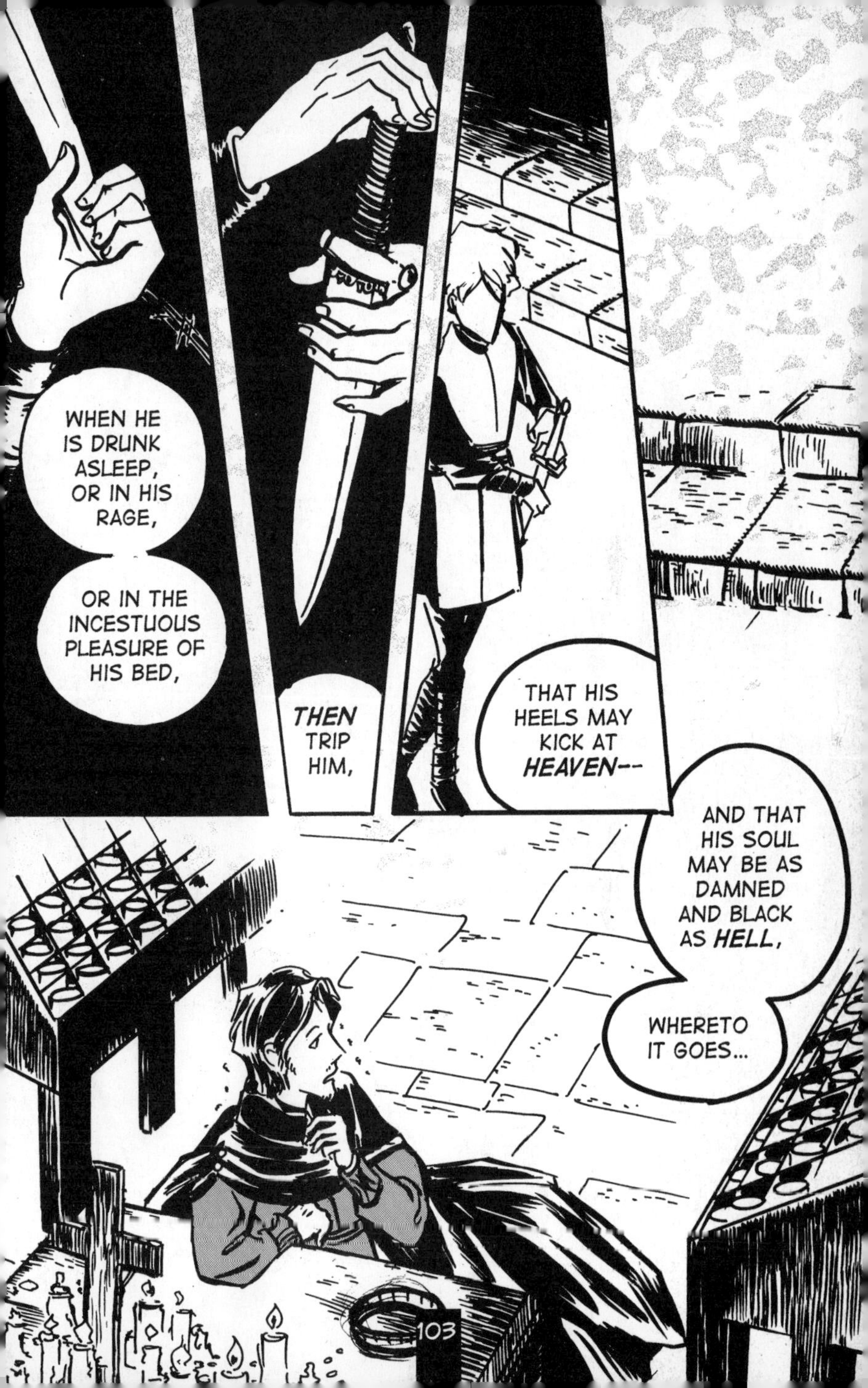

WHEN HE IS DRUNK ASLEEP, OR IN HIS RAGE,
OR IN THE INCESTUOUS PLEASURE OF HIS BED,
THEN TRIP HIM,
THAT HIS HEELS MAY KICK AT *HEAVEN*--
AND THAT HIS SOUL MAY BE AS DAMNED AND BLACK AS *HELL*,
WHERETO IT GOES...

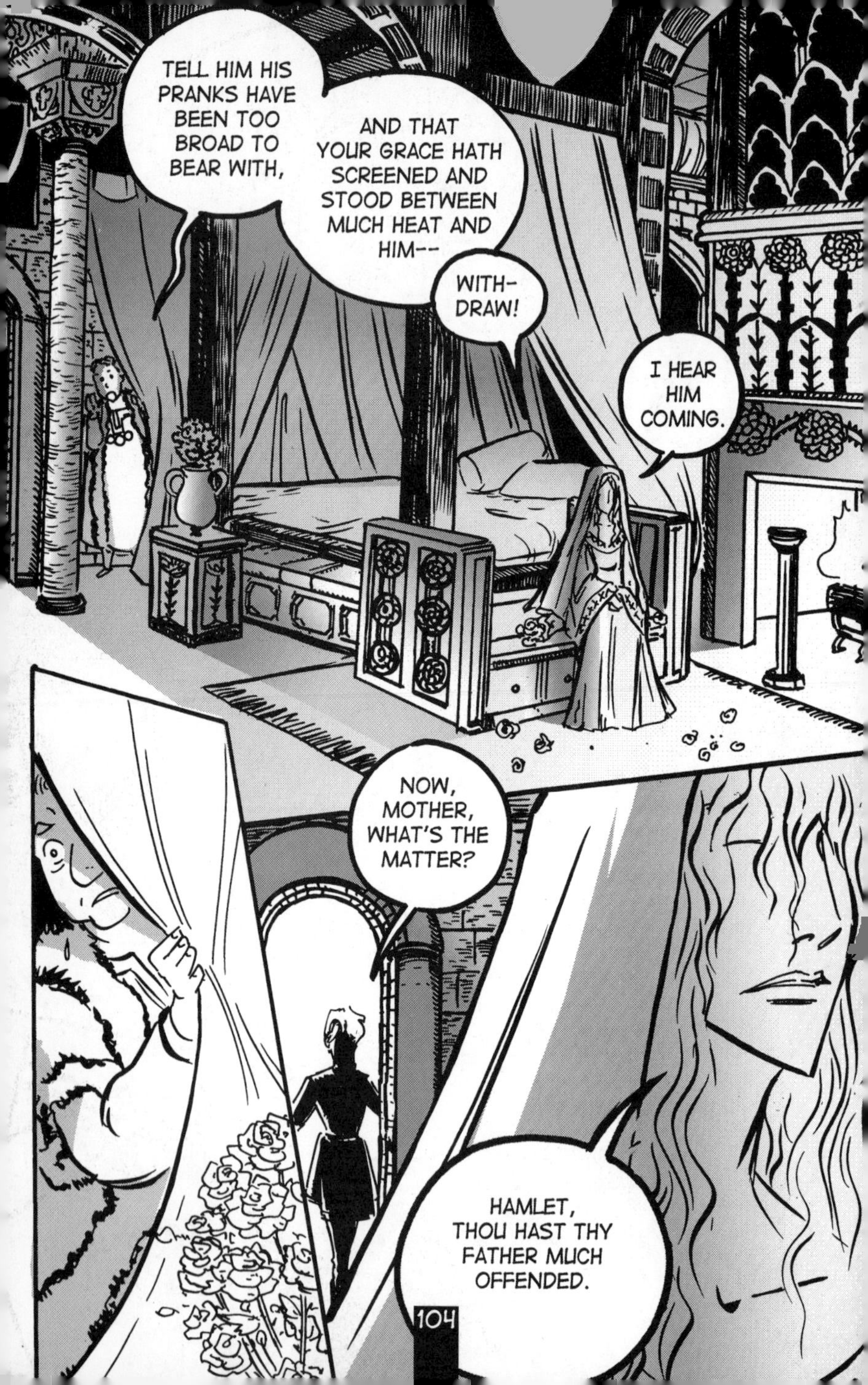
TELL HIM HIS PRANKS HAVE BEEN TOO BROAD TO BEAR WITH,
AND THAT YOUR GRACE HATH SCREENED AND STOOD BETWEEN MUCH HEAT AND HIM--
WITH-DRAW!
I HEAR HIM COMING.
NOW, MOTHER, WHAT'S THE MATTER?
HAMLET, THOU HAST THY FATHER MUCH OFFENDED.

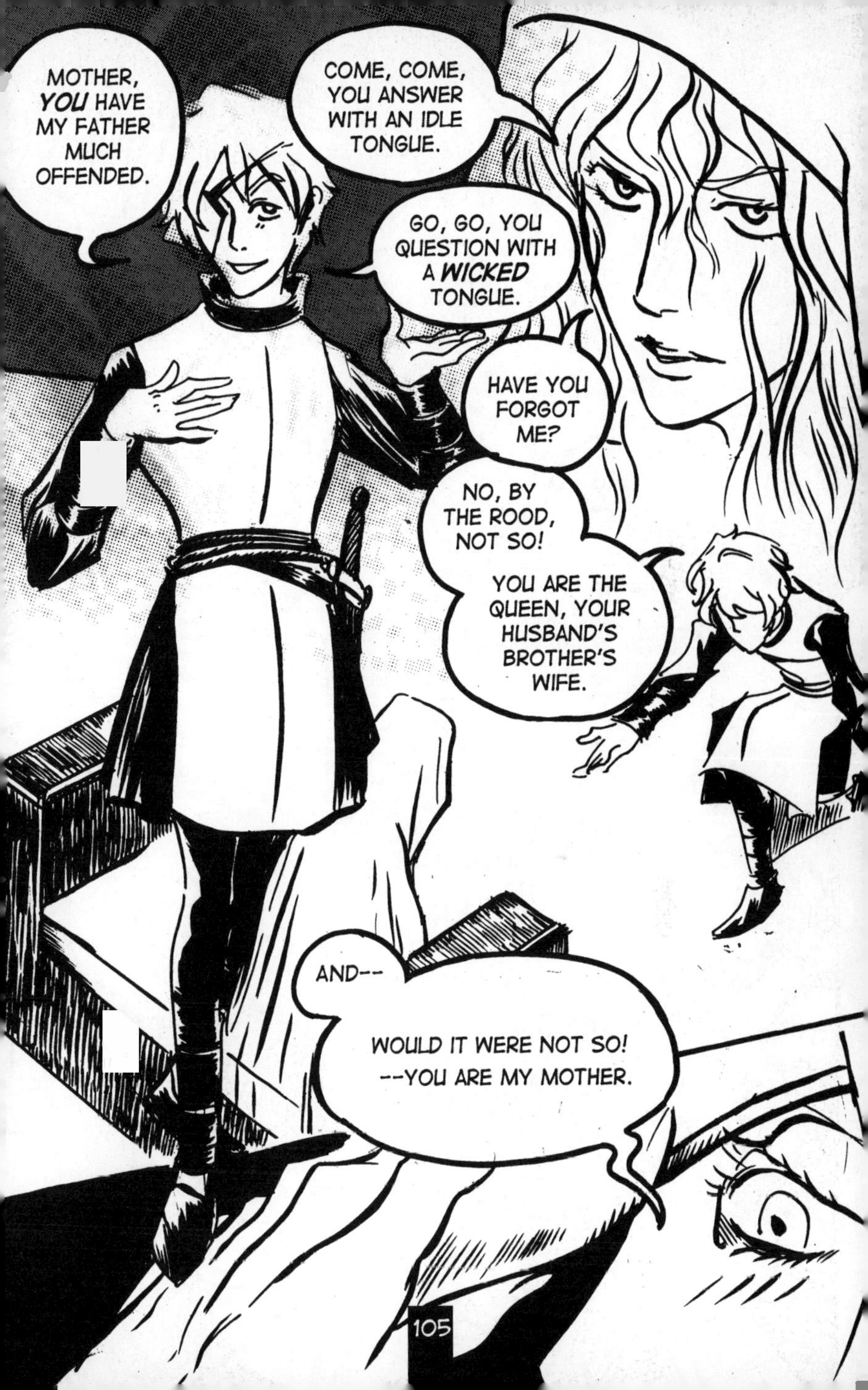
MOTHER, *YOU* HAVE MY FATHER MUCH OFFENDED.
COME, COME, YOU ANSWER WITH AN IDLE TONGUE.
GO, GO, YOU QUESTION WITH A *WICKED* TONGUE.
HAVE YOU FORGOT ME?
NO, BY THE ROOD, NOT SO!
YOU ARE THE QUEEN, YOUR HUSBAND'S BROTHER'S WIFE.
AND--
WOULD IT WERE NOT SO!
--YOU ARE MY MOTHER.

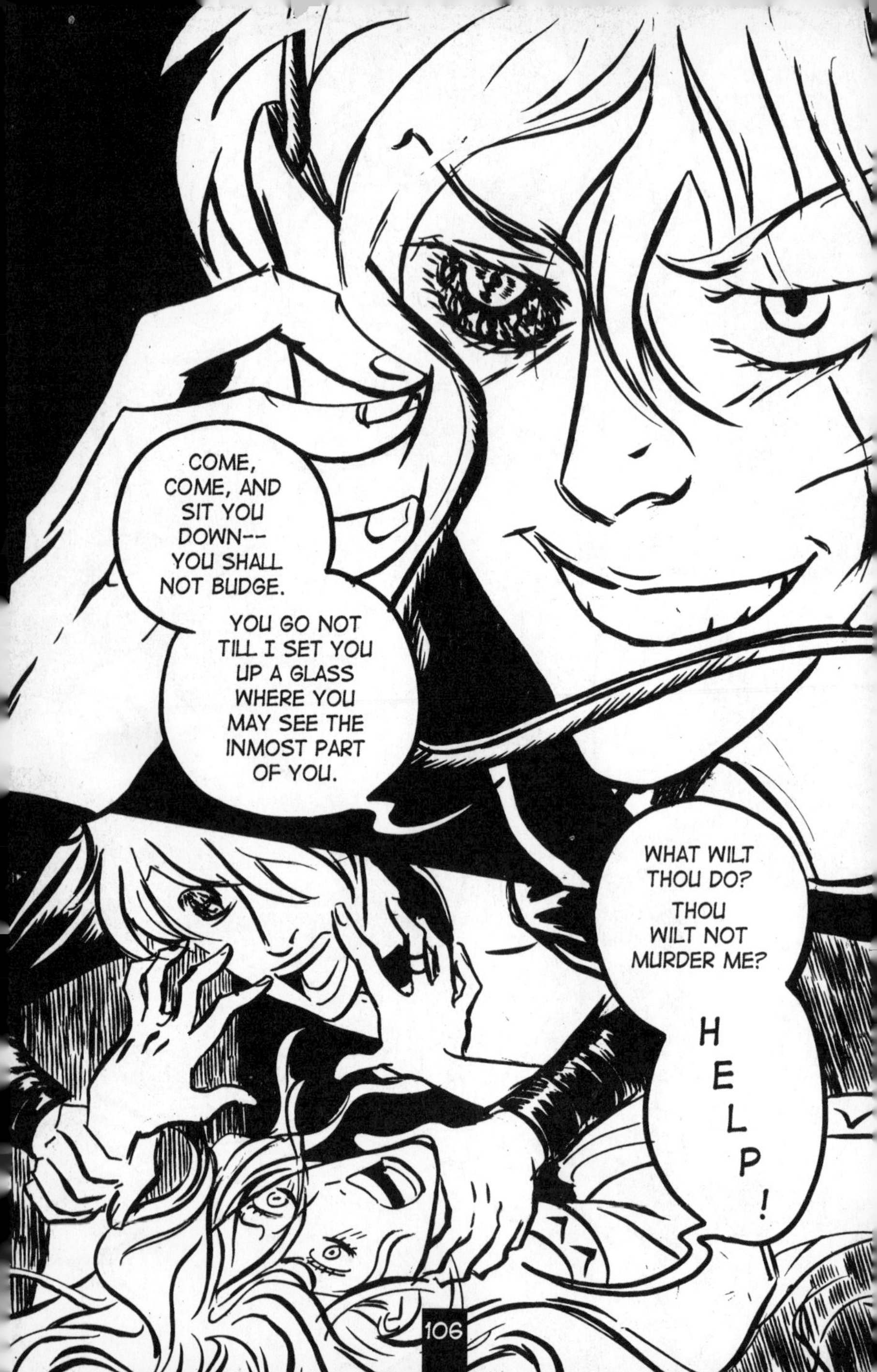
COME, COME, AND SIT YOU DOWN-- YOU SHALL NOT BUDGE.
YOU GO NOT TILL I SET YOU UP A GLASS WHERE YOU MAY SEE THE INMOST PART OF YOU.
WHAT WILT THOU DO?
THOU WILT NOT MURDER ME?
HELP!

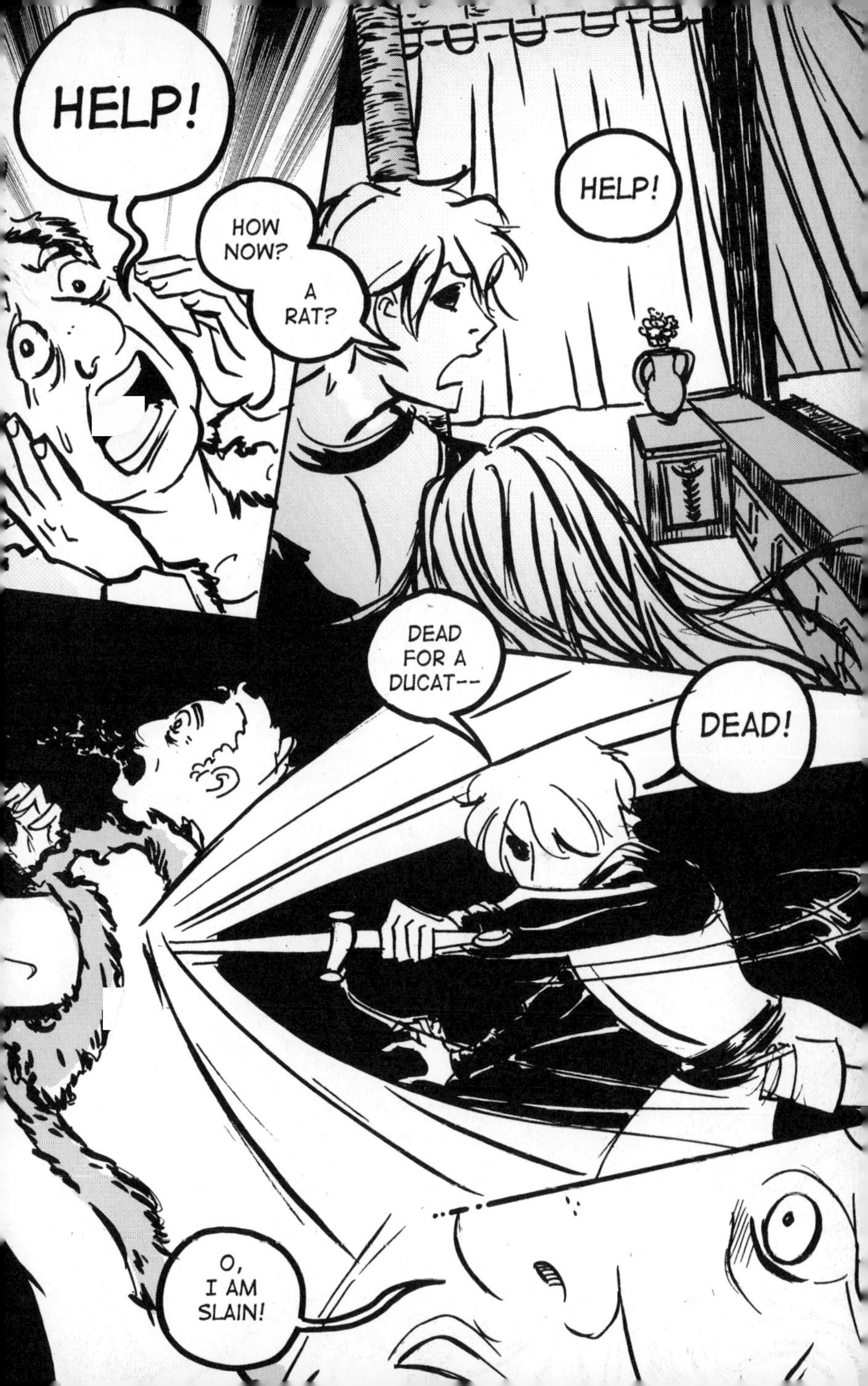
HELP!
HOW NOW? A RAT?
HELP!
DEAD FOR A DUCAT--
DEAD!
O, I AM SLAIN!

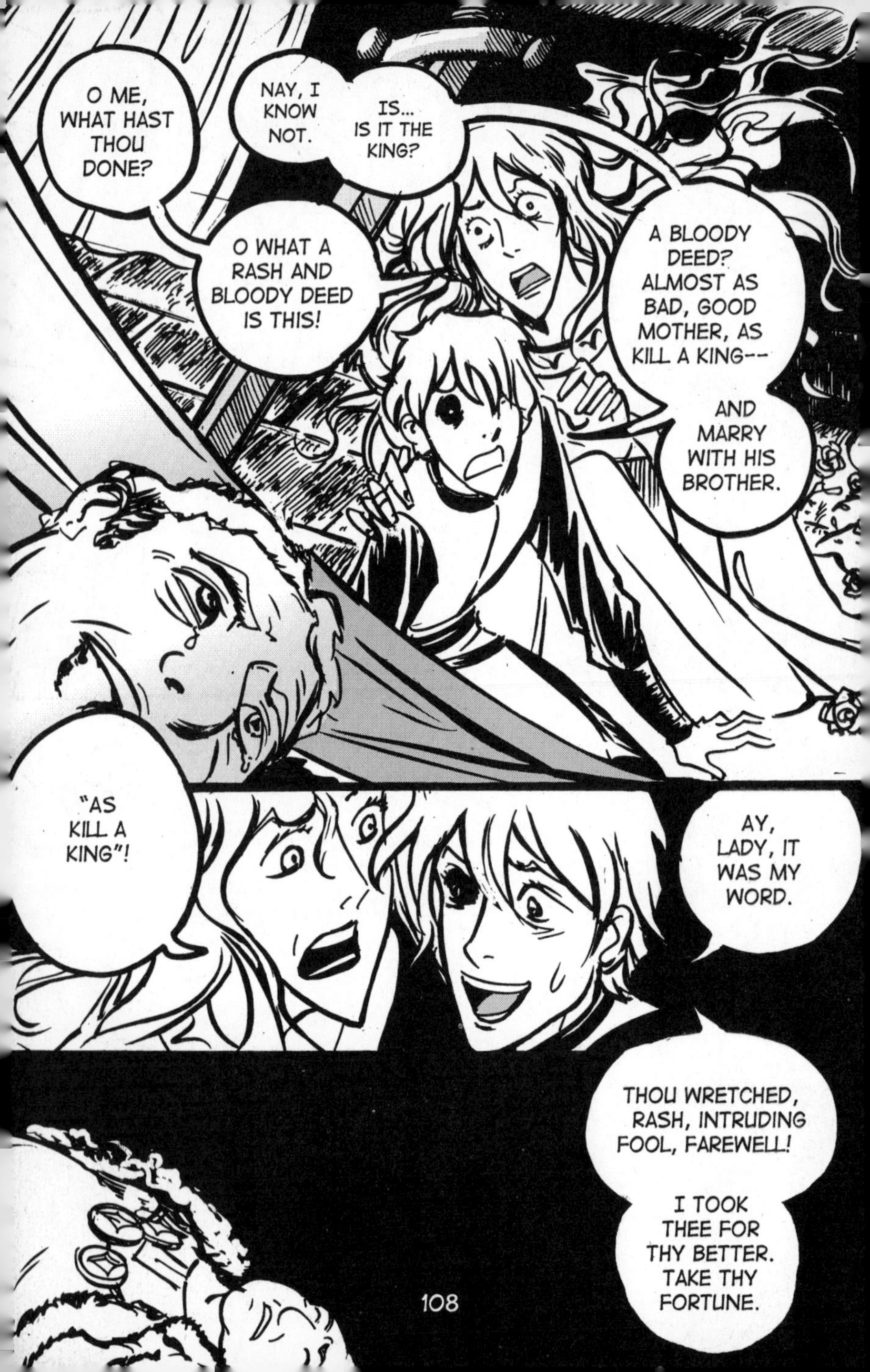
O ME, WHAT HAST THOU DONE?
NAY, I KNOW NOT.
IS... IS IT THE KING?
O WHAT A RASH AND BLOODY DEED IS THIS!
A BLOODY DEED? ALMOST AS BAD, GOOD MOTHER, AS KILL A KING--
AND MARRY WITH HIS BROTHER.
"AS KILL A KING"!
AY, LADY, IT WAS MY WORD.
THOU WRETCHED, RASH, INTRUDING FOOL, FAREWELL!
I TOOK THEE FOR THY BETTER. TAKE THY FORTUNE.

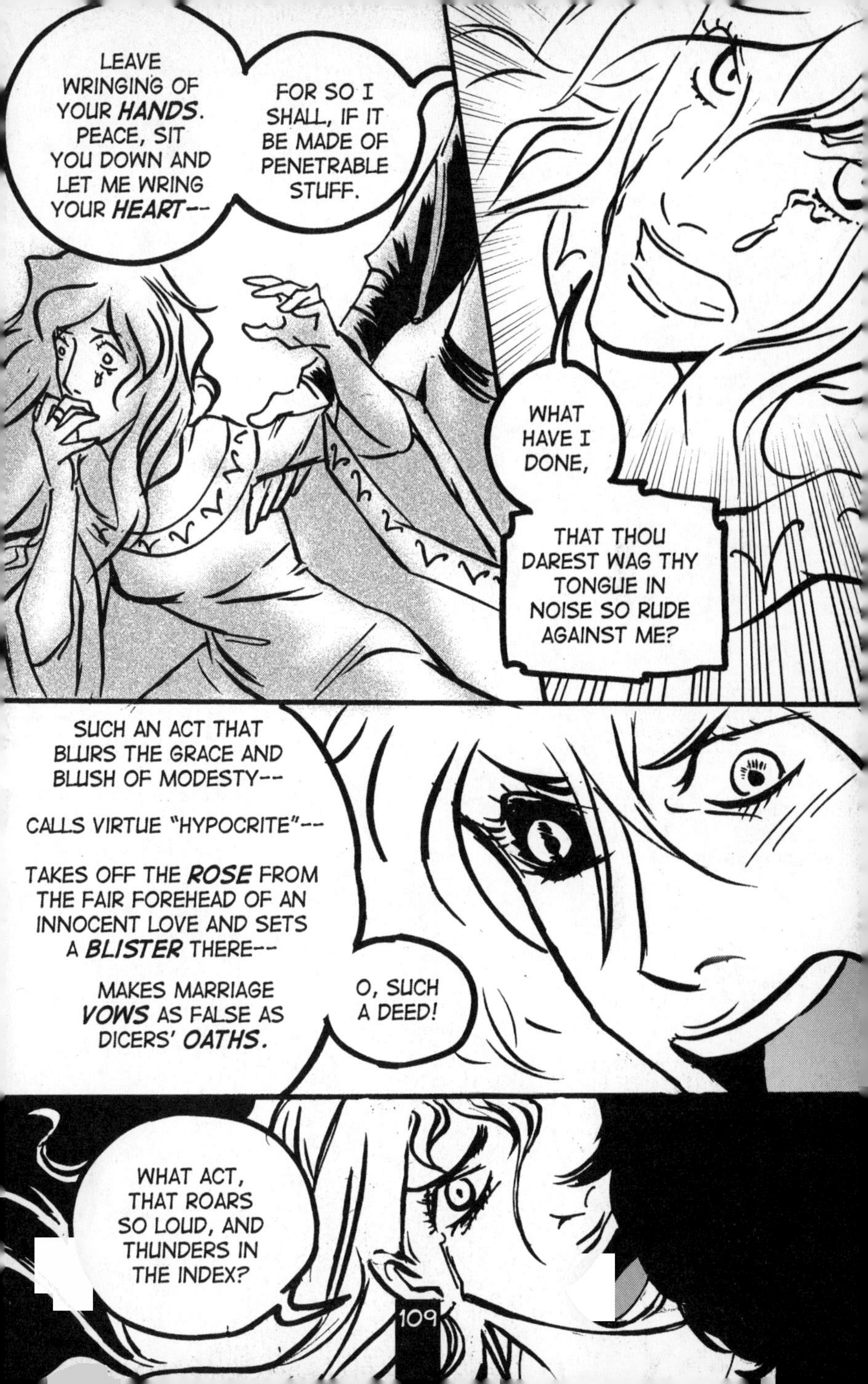
LEAVE WRINGING OF YOUR HANDS. PEACE, SIT YOU DOWN AND LET ME WRING YOUR HEART--
FOR SO I SHALL, IF IT BE MADE OF PENETRABLE STUFF.
WHAT HAVE I DONE,
THAT THOU DAREST WAG THY TONGUE IN NOISE SO RUDE AGAINST ME?
SUCH AN ACT THAT BLURS THE GRACE AND BLUSH OF MODESTY--
CALLS VIRTUE "HYPOCRITE"--
TAKES OFF THE ROSE FROM THE FAIR FOREHEAD OF AN INNOCENT LOVE AND SETS A BLISTER THERE--
MAKES MARRIAGE VOWS AS FALSE AS DICERS' OATHS.
O, SUCH A DEED!
WHAT ACT, THAT ROARS SO LOUD, AND THUNDERS IN THE INDEX?

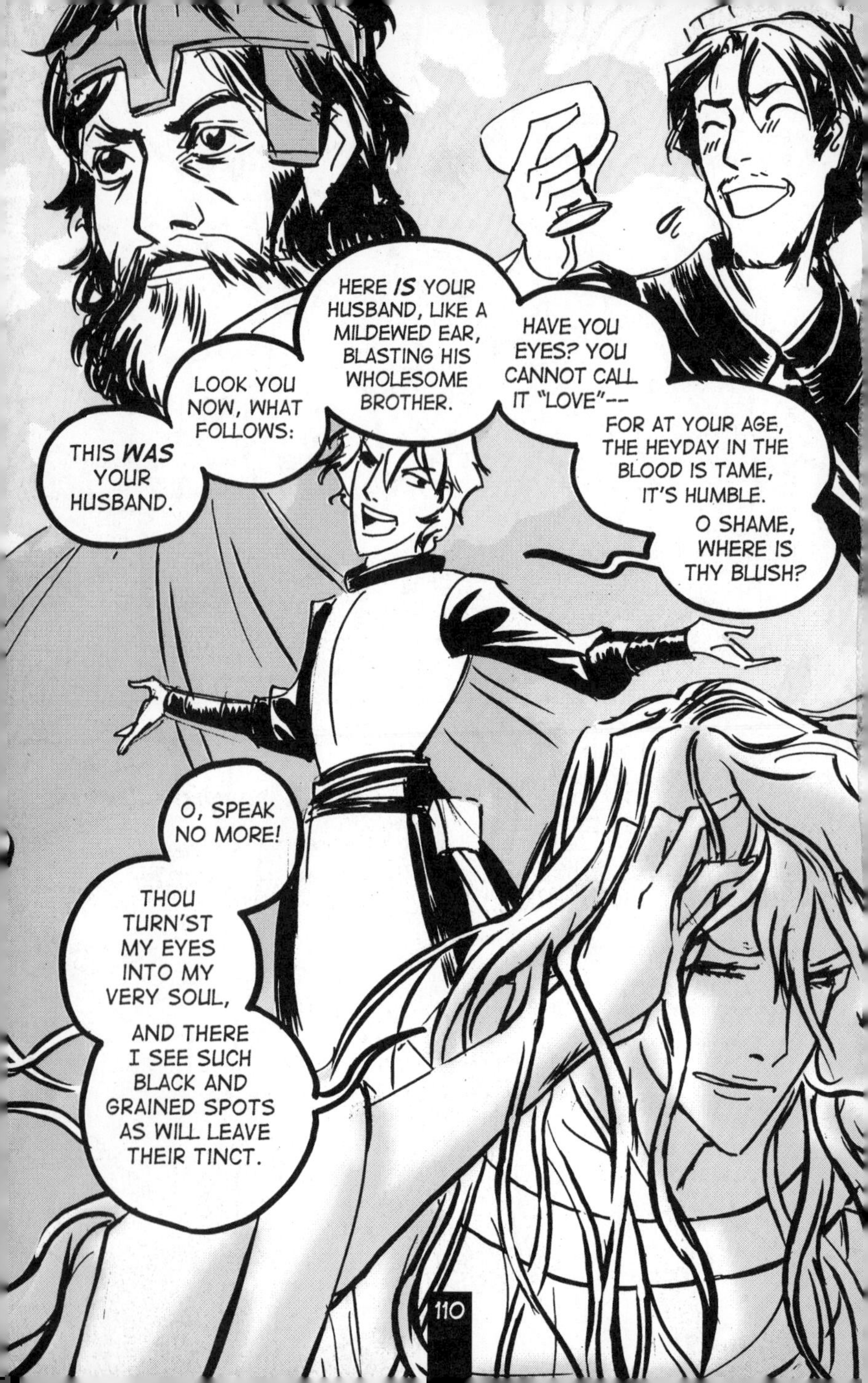
THIS WAS YOUR HUSBAND.
LOOK YOU NOW, WHAT FOLLOWS:
HERE IS YOUR HUSBAND, LIKE A MILDEWED EAR, BLASTING HIS WHOLESOME BROTHER.
HAVE YOU EYES? YOU CANNOT CALL IT "LOVE"--
FOR AT YOUR AGE, THE HEYDAY IN THE BLOOD IS TAME, IT'S HUMBLE.
O SHAME, WHERE IS THY BLUSH?
O, SPEAK NO MORE!
THOU TURN'ST MY EYES INTO MY VERY SOUL,
AND THERE I SEE SUCH BLACK AND GRAINED SPOTS AS WILL LEAVE THEIR TINCT.

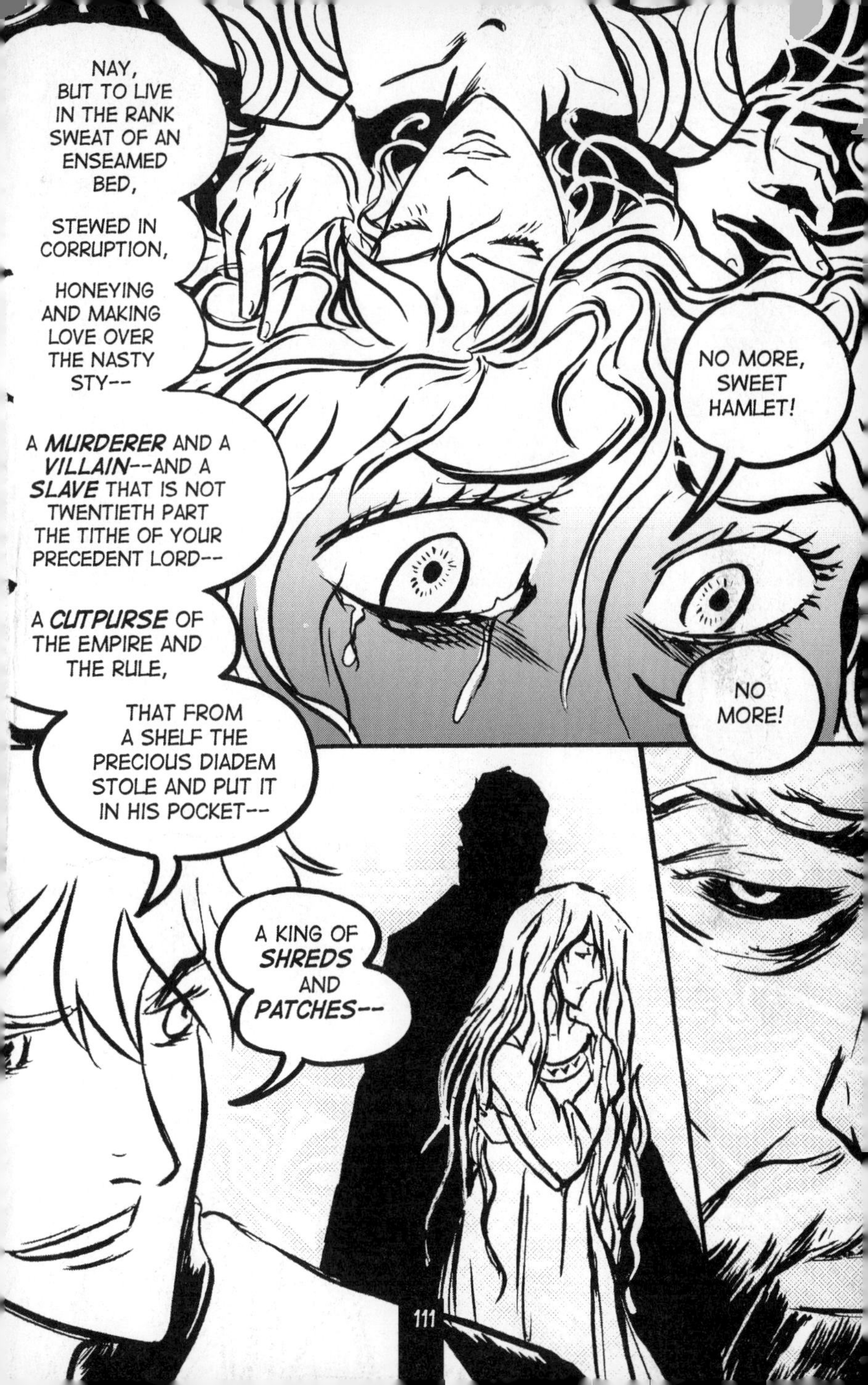
NAY, BUT TO LIVE IN THE RANK SWEAT OF AN ENSEAMED BED,
STEWED IN CORRUPTION,
HONEYING AND MAKING LOVE OVER THE NASTY STY--
NO MORE, SWEET HAMLET!
A *MURDERER* AND A *VILLAIN*--AND A *SLAVE* THAT IS NOT TWENTIETH PART THE TITHE OF YOUR PRECEDENT LORD--
A *CUTPURSE* OF THE EMPIRE AND THE RULE,
NO MORE!
THAT FROM A SHELF THE PRECIOUS DIADEM STOLE AND PUT IT IN HIS POCKET--
A KING OF *SHREDS* AND *PATCHES*--

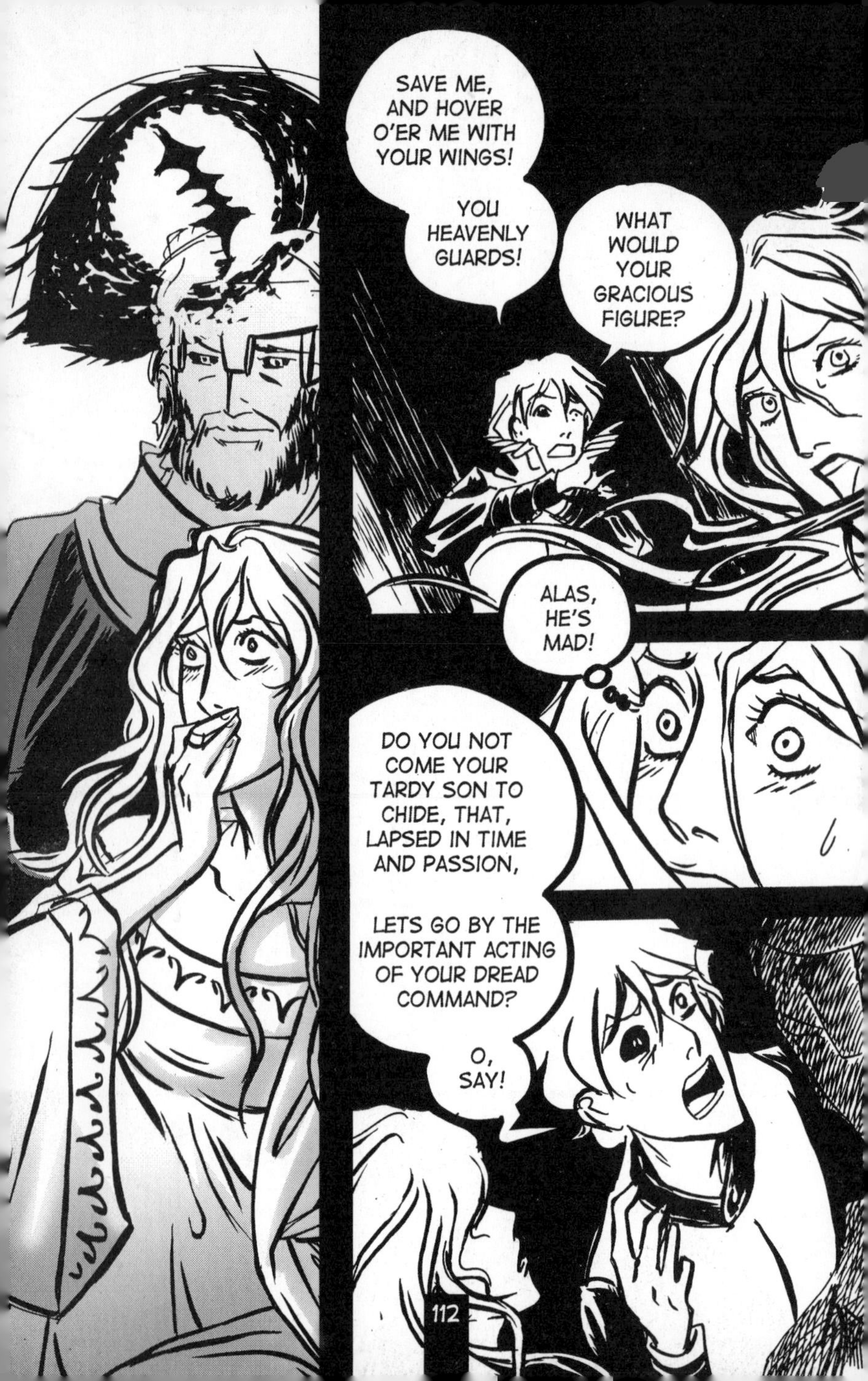
SAVE ME, AND HOVER O'ER ME WITH YOUR WINGS!
YOU HEAVENLY GUARDS!
WHAT WOULD YOUR GRACIOUS FIGURE?
ALAS, HE'S MAD!
DO YOU NOT COME YOUR TARDY SON TO CHIDE, THAT, LAPSED IN TIME AND PASSION,
LETS GO BY THE IMPORTANT ACTING OF YOUR DREAD COMMAND?
O, SAY!

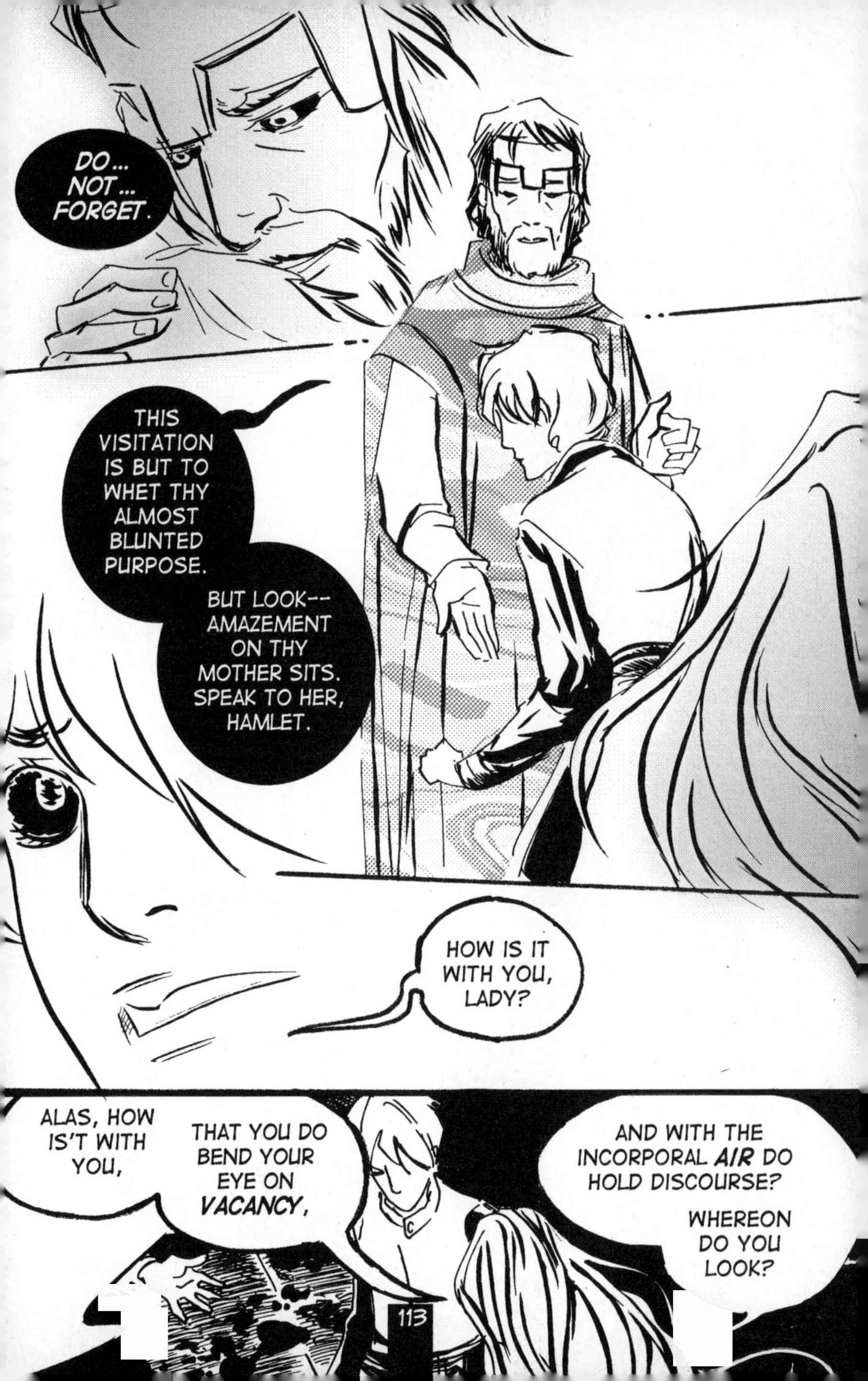
DO... NOT... FORGET.
THIS VISITATION IS BUT TO WHET THY ALMOST BLUNTED PURPOSE.
BUT LOOK-- AMAZEMENT ON THY MOTHER SITS. SPEAK TO HER, HAMLET.
HOW IS IT WITH YOU, LADY?
ALAS, HOW IS'T WITH YOU,
THAT YOU DO BEND YOUR EYE ON VACANCY,
AND WITH THE INCORPORAL AIR DO HOLD DISCOURSE?
WHEREON DO YOU LOOK?

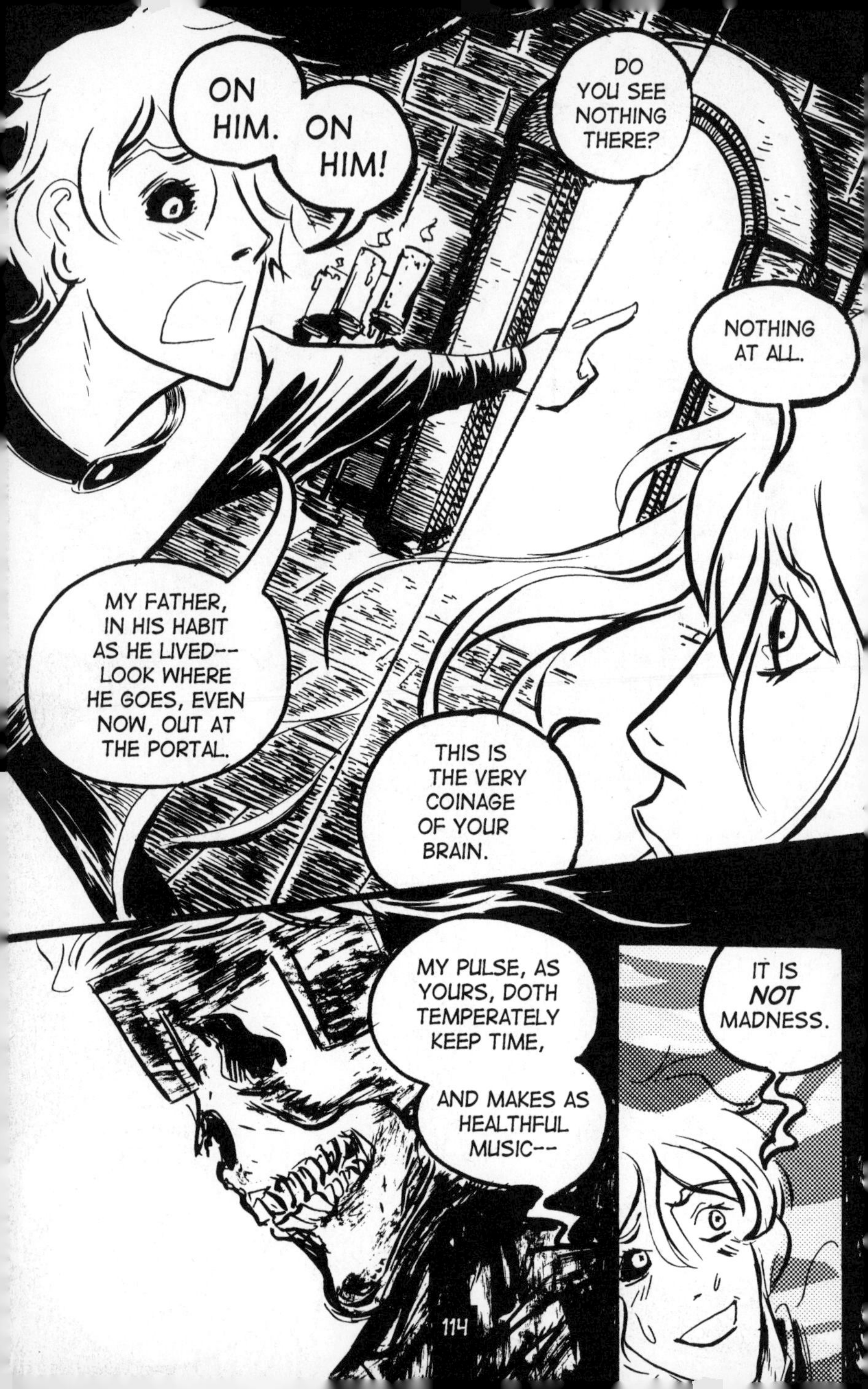
ON HIM. ON HIM!
DO YOU SEE NOTHING THERE?
NOTHING AT ALL.
MY FATHER, IN HIS HABIT AS HE LIVED-- LOOK WHERE HE GOES, EVEN NOW, OUT AT THE PORTAL.
THIS IS THE VERY COINAGE OF YOUR BRAIN.
MY PULSE, AS YOURS, DOTH TEMPERATELY KEEP TIME,
AND MAKES AS HEALTHFUL MUSIC--
IT IS *NOT* MADNESS.

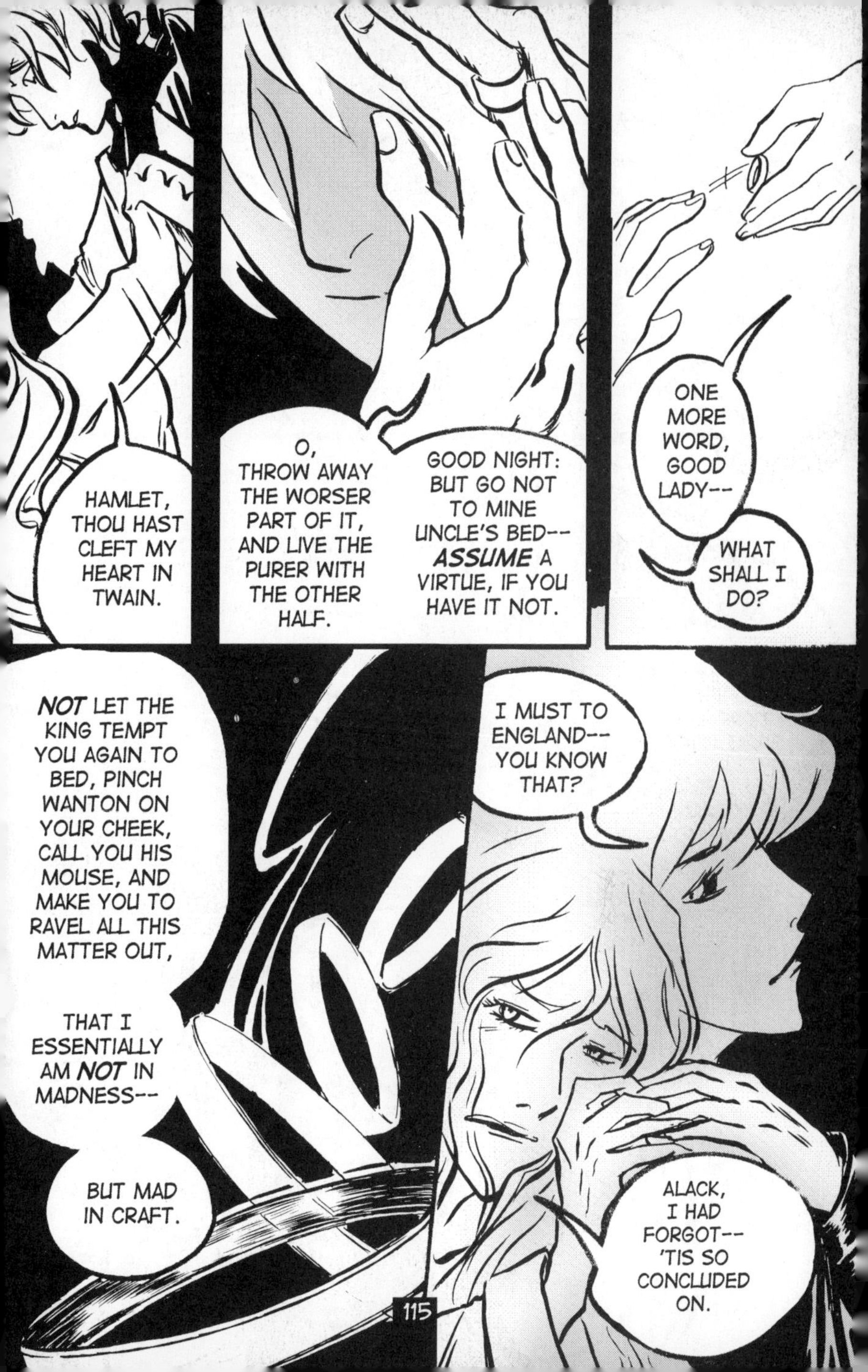
HAMLET, THOU HAST CLEFT MY HEART IN TWAIN.
O, THROW AWAY THE WORSER PART OF IT, AND LIVE THE PURER WITH THE OTHER HALF.
GOOD NIGHT: BUT GO NOT TO MINE UNCLE'S BED-- ASSUME A VIRTUE, IF YOU HAVE IT NOT.
ONE MORE WORD, GOOD LADY--
WHAT SHALL I DO?
NOT LET THE KING TEMPT YOU AGAIN TO BED, PINCH WANTON ON YOUR CHEEK, CALL YOU HIS MOUSE, AND MAKE YOU TO RAVEL ALL THIS MATTER OUT,
THAT I ESSENTIALLY AM NOT IN MADNESS--
BUT MAD IN CRAFT.
I MUST TO ENGLAND-- YOU KNOW THAT?
ALACK, I HAD FORGOT-- 'TIS SO CONCLUDED ON.

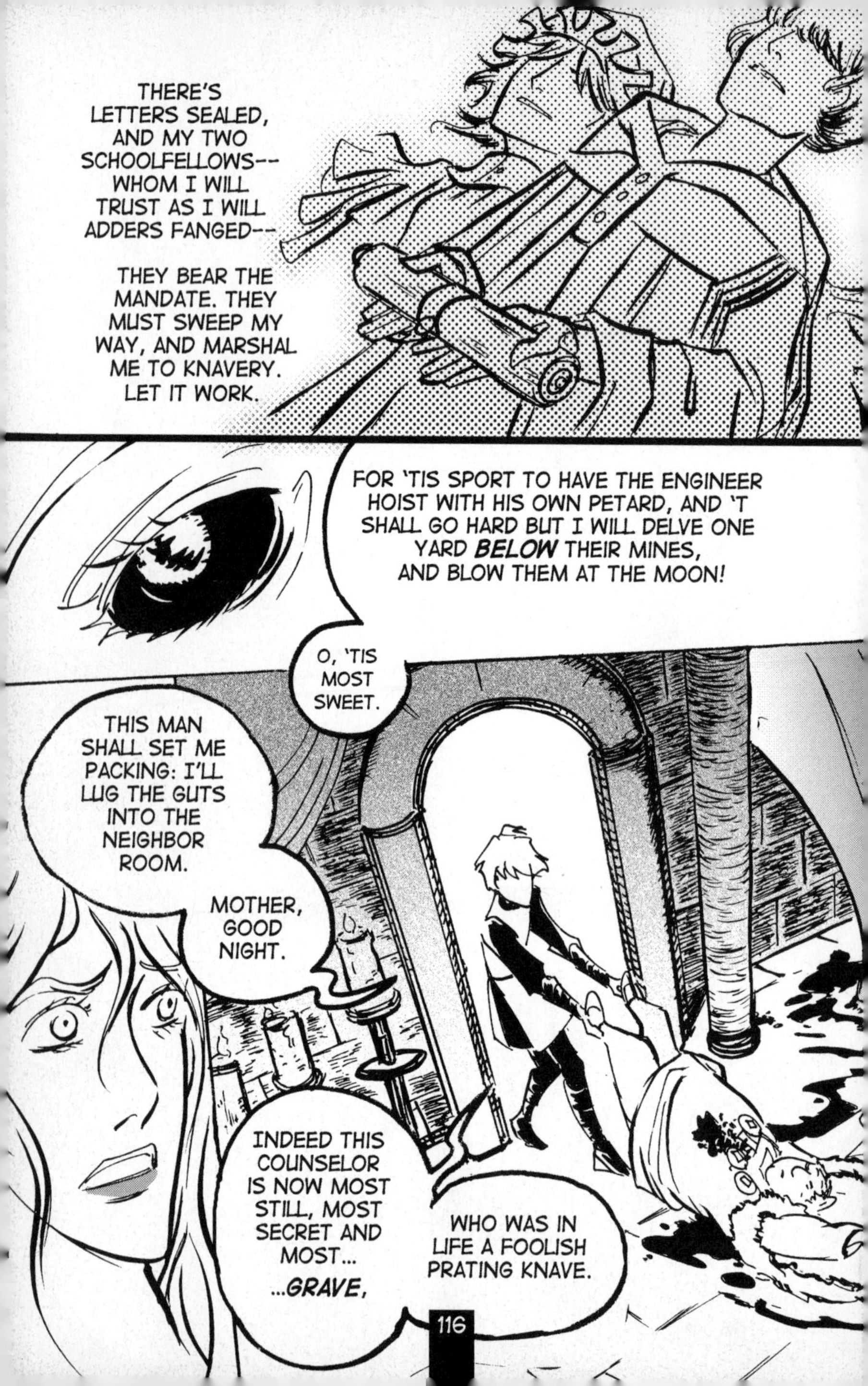
THERE'S LETTERS SEALED, AND MY TWO SCHOOLFELLOWS-- WHOM I WILL TRUST AS I WILL ADDERS FANGED--
THEY BEAR THE MANDATE. THEY MUST SWEEP MY WAY, AND MARSHAL ME TO KNAVERY. LET IT WORK.
FOR 'TIS SPORT TO HAVE THE ENGINEER HOIST WITH HIS OWN PETARD, AND 'T SHALL GO HARD BUT I WILL DELVE ONE YARD ***BELOW*** THEIR MINES, AND BLOW THEM AT THE MOON!
O, 'TIS MOST SWEET.
THIS MAN SHALL SET ME PACKING: I'LL LUG THE GUTS INTO THE NEIGHBOR ROOM.
MOTHER, GOOD NIGHT.
INDEED THIS COUNSELOR IS NOW MOST STILL, MOST SECRET AND MOST...
...***GRAVE***,
WHO WAS IN LIFE A FOOLISH PRATING KNAVE.

ACT IV

TO CUT HIS THROAT I' THE CHURCH.

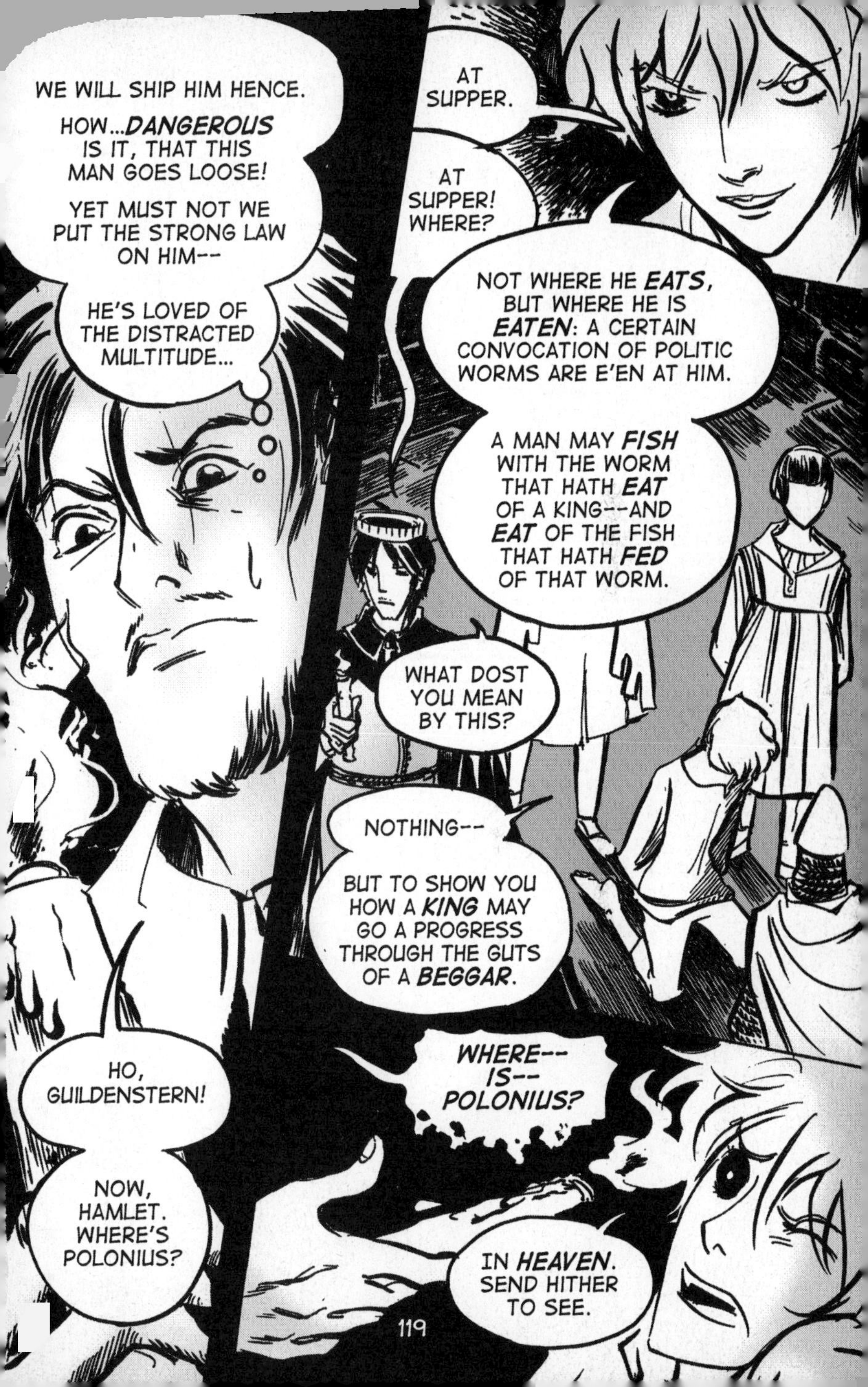
WE WILL SHIP HIM HENCE.
HOW...DANGEROUS IS IT, THAT THIS MAN GOES LOOSE!
YET MUST NOT WE PUT THE STRONG LAW ON HIM--
HE'S LOVED OF THE DISTRACTED MULTITUDE...
HO, GUILDENSTERN!
NOW, HAMLET. WHERE'S POLONIUS?
AT SUPPER.
AT SUPPER! WHERE?
NOT WHERE HE EATS, BUT WHERE HE IS EATEN: A CERTAIN CONVOCATION OF POLITIC WORMS ARE E'EN AT HIM.
A MAN MAY FISH WITH THE WORM THAT HATH EAT OF A KING--AND EAT OF THE FISH THAT HATH FED OF THAT WORM.
WHAT DOST YOU MEAN BY THIS?
NOTHING--
BUT TO SHOW YOU HOW A KING MAY GO A PROGRESS THROUGH THE GUTS OF A BEGGAR.
WHERE-- IS-- POLONIUS?
IN HEAVEN. SEND HITHER TO SEE.

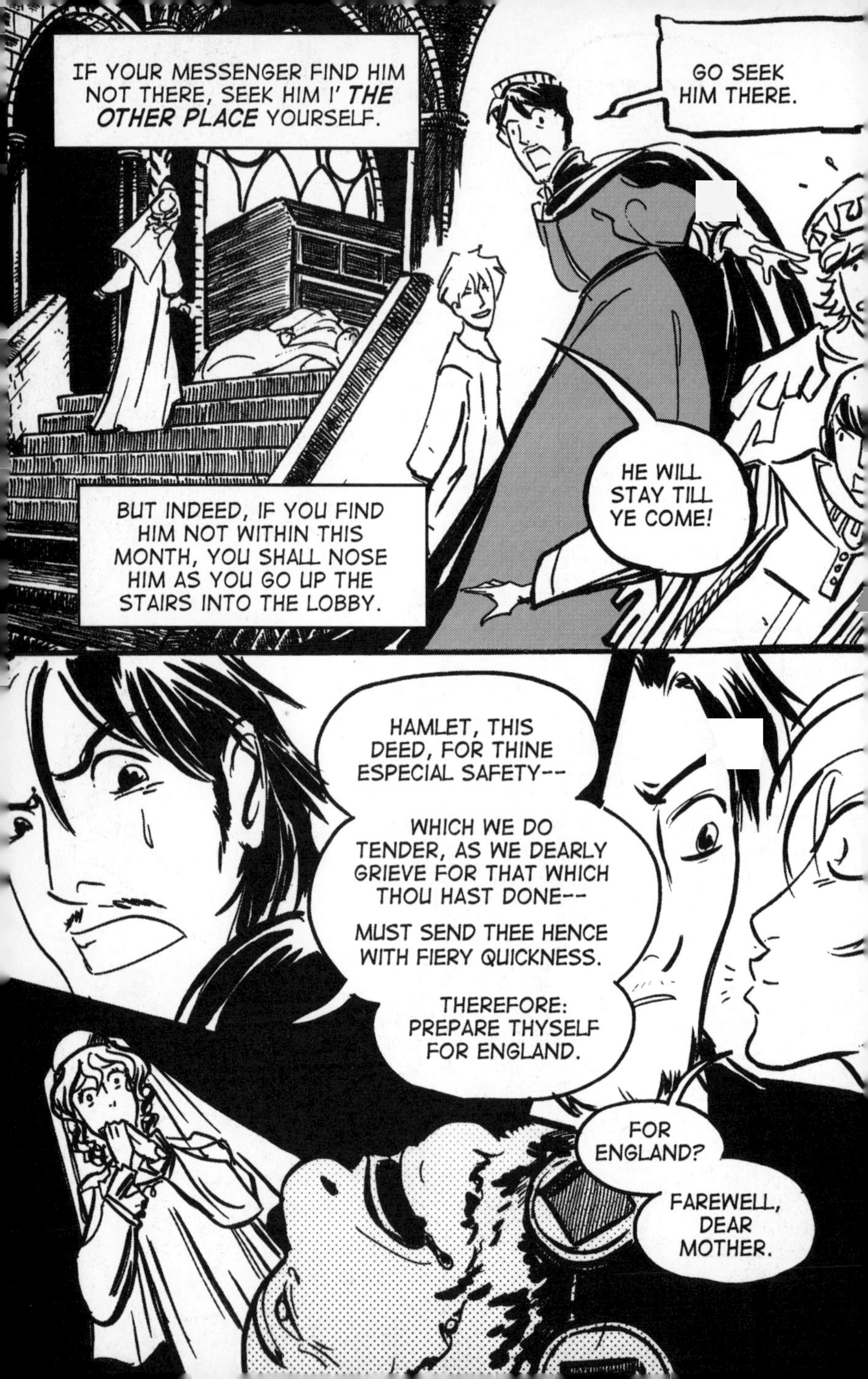
IF YOUR MESSENGER FIND HIM NOT THERE, SEEK HIM I' *THE OTHER PLACE* YOURSELF.
GO SEEK HIM THERE.
BUT INDEED, IF YOU FIND HIM NOT WITHIN THIS MONTH, YOU SHALL NOSE HIM AS YOU GO UP THE STAIRS INTO THE LOBBY.
HE WILL STAY TILL YE COME!
HAMLET, THIS DEED, FOR THINE ESPECIAL SAFETY--
WHICH WE DO TENDER, AS WE DEARLY GRIEVE FOR THAT WHICH THOU HAST DONE--
MUST SEND THEE HENCE WITH FIERY QUICKNESS.
THEREFORE: PREPARE THYSELF FOR ENGLAND.
FOR ENGLAND?
FAREWELL, DEAR MOTHER.

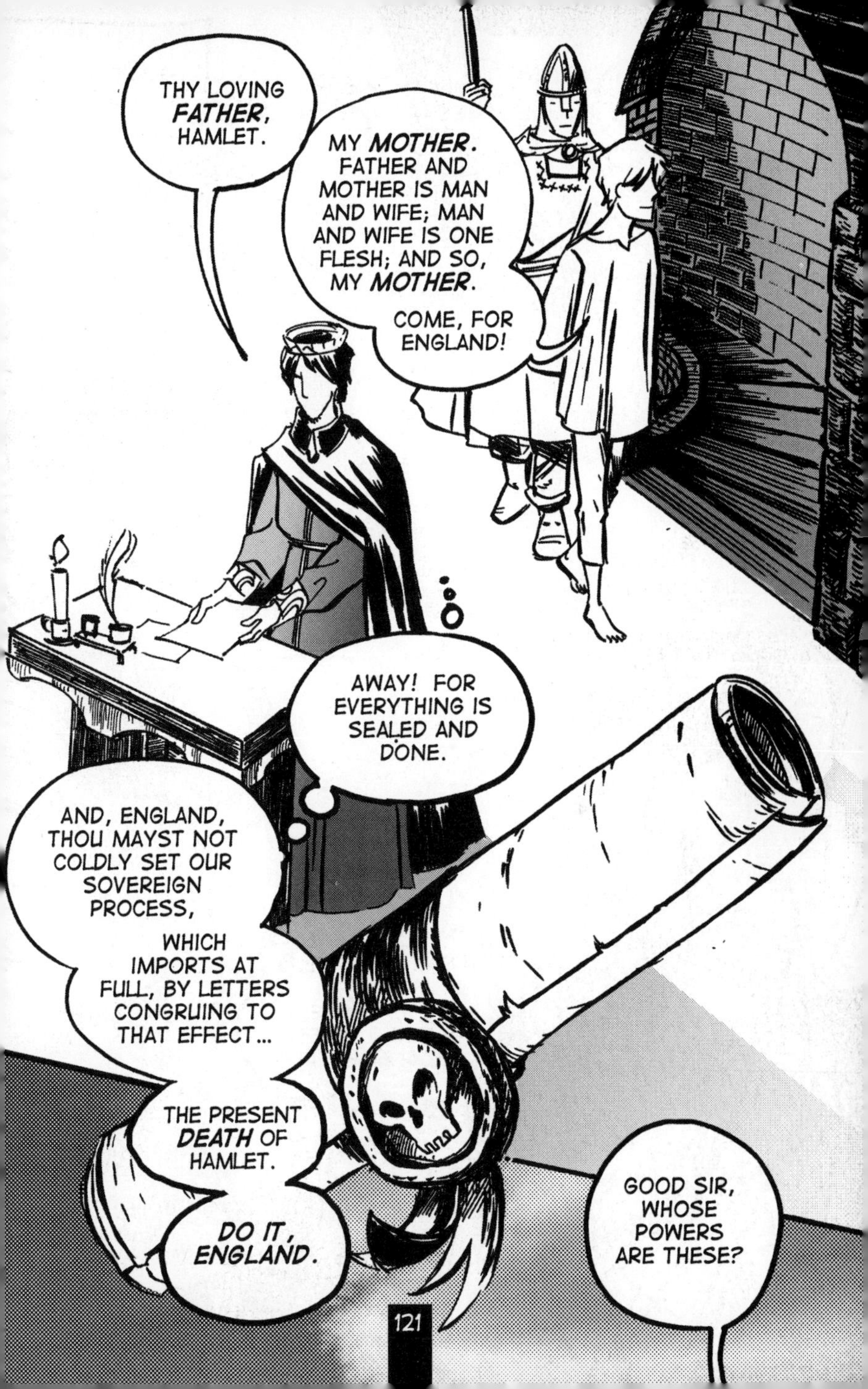

THY LOVING *FATHER*, HAMLET.
MY *MOTHER*. FATHER AND MOTHER IS MAN AND WIFE; MAN AND WIFE IS ONE FLESH; AND SO, MY *MOTHER*.
COME, FOR ENGLAND!
AWAY! FOR EVERYTHING IS SEALED AND DONE.
AND, ENGLAND, THOU MAYST NOT COLDLY SET OUR SOVEREIGN PROCESS,
WHICH IMPORTS AT FULL, BY LETTERS CONGRUING TO THAT EFFECT...
THE PRESENT *DEATH* OF HAMLET.
DO IT, ENGLAND.
GOOD SIR, WHOSE POWERS ARE THESE?

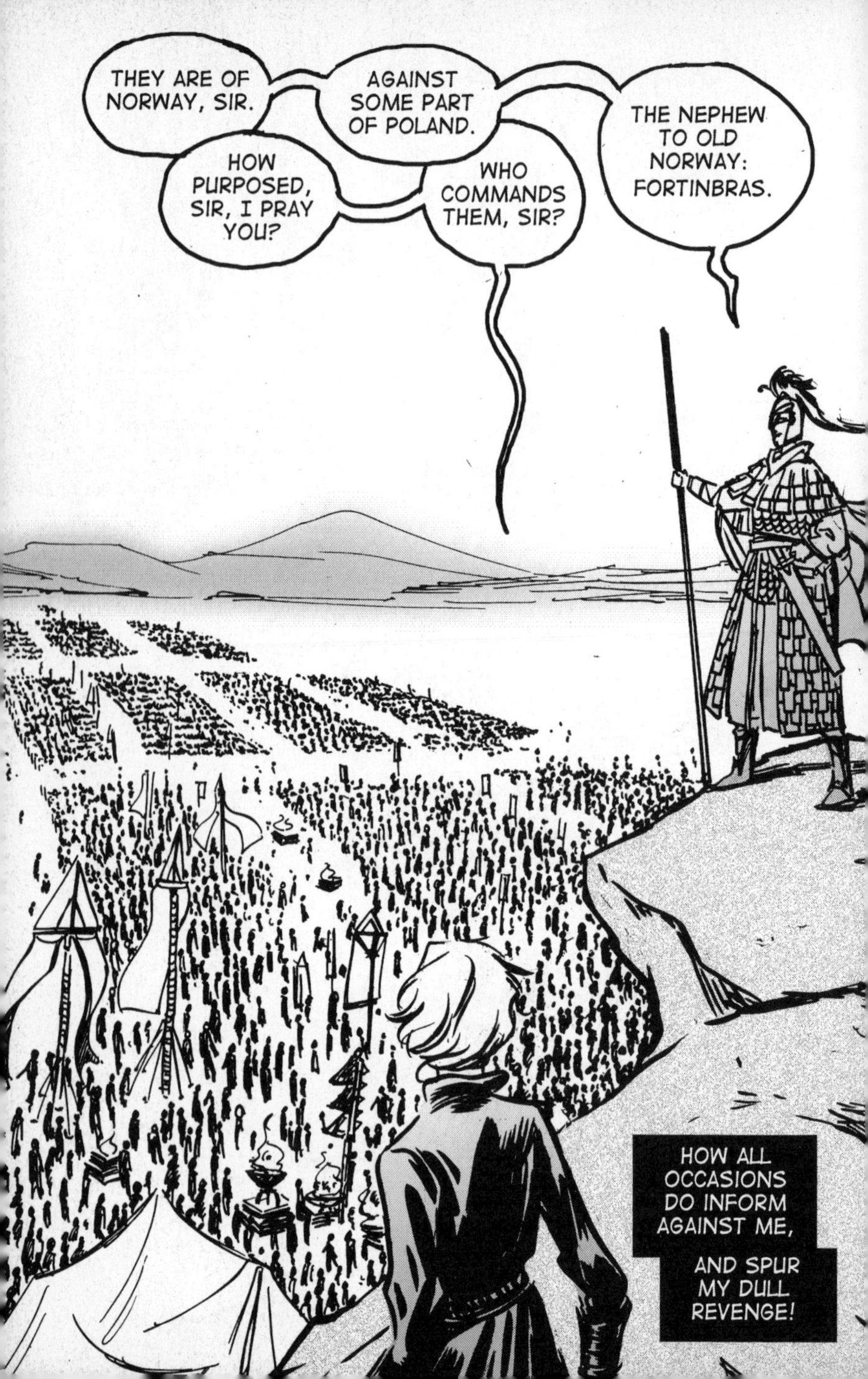
THEY ARE OF NORWAY, SIR.
HOW PURPOSED, SIR, I PRAY YOU?
AGAINST SOME PART OF POLAND.
WHO COMMANDS THEM, SIR?
THE NEPHEW TO OLD NORWAY: FORTINBRAS.
HOW ALL OCCASIONS DO INFORM AGAINST ME,
AND SPUR MY DULL REVENGE!

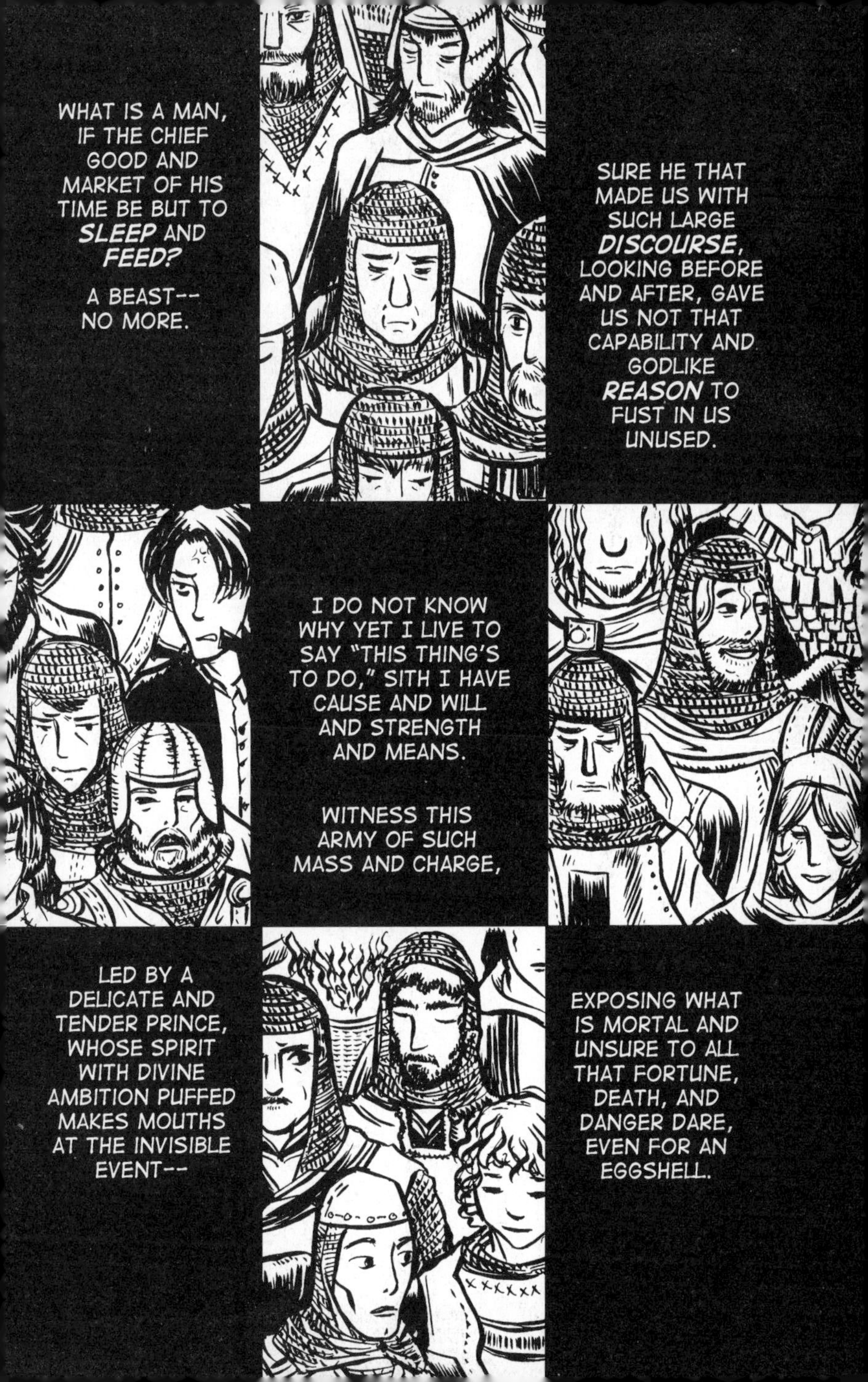
WHAT IS A MAN, IF THE CHIEF GOOD AND MARKET OF HIS TIME BE BUT TO *SLEEP* AND *FEED?*
A BEAST-- NO MORE.
SURE HE THAT MADE US WITH SUCH LARGE *DISCOURSE*, LOOKING BEFORE AND AFTER, GAVE US NOT THAT CAPABILITY AND GODLIKE *REASON* TO FUST IN US UNUSED.
I DO NOT KNOW WHY YET I LIVE TO SAY "THIS THING'S TO DO," SITH I HAVE CAUSE AND WILL AND STRENGTH AND MEANS.
WITNESS THIS ARMY OF SUCH MASS AND CHARGE,
LED BY A DELICATE AND TENDER PRINCE, WHOSE SPIRIT WITH DIVINE AMBITION PUFFED MAKES MOUTHS AT THE INVISIBLE EVENT--
EXPOSING WHAT IS MORTAL AND UNSURE TO ALL THAT FORTUNE, DEATH, AND DANGER DARE, EVEN FOR AN EGGSHELL.

HOW STAND I THEN, THAT HAVE A FATHER KILLED, A MOTHER STAINED, EXCITEMENTS OF MY REASON AND MY BLOOD, AND LET ALL SLEEP--
WHILE, TO MY SHAME, I SEE THE IMMINENT DEATH OF TWENTY THOUSAND MEN, THAT, FOR A FANTASY AND TRICK OF FAME, GO TO THEIR GRAVES LIKE BEDS?
FROM THIS TIME FORTH, MY THOUGHTS BE BLOODY...
...OR BE NOTHING WORTH!
HE IS DEAD AND GONE, LADY, HE IS DEAD AND GONE. AT HIS HEAD A GRASS-GREEN TURF, AT HIS HEELS A...STONE.
WHITE HIS SHROUD AS THE MOUNTAIN SNOW LARDED WITH SWEET FLOWERS WHICH BEWEPT TO THE GRAVE DID GO WITH TRUE-LOVE SHOWERS.

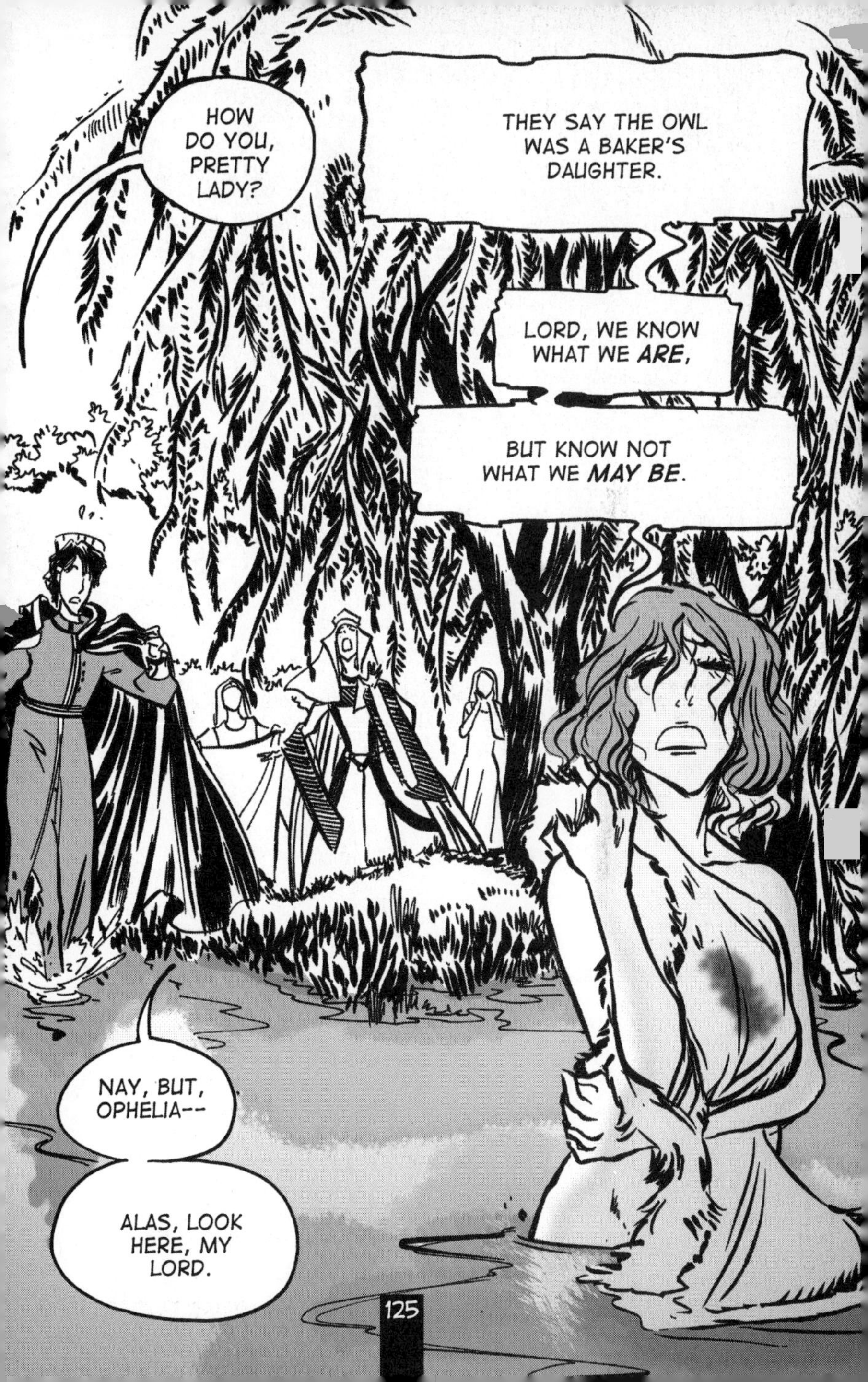
HOW DO YOU, PRETTY LADY?
THEY SAY THE OWL WAS A BAKER'S DAUGHTER.
LORD, WE KNOW WHAT WE ARE,
BUT KNOW NOT WHAT WE MAY BE.
NAY, BUT, OPHELIA--
ALAS, LOOK HERE, MY LORD.

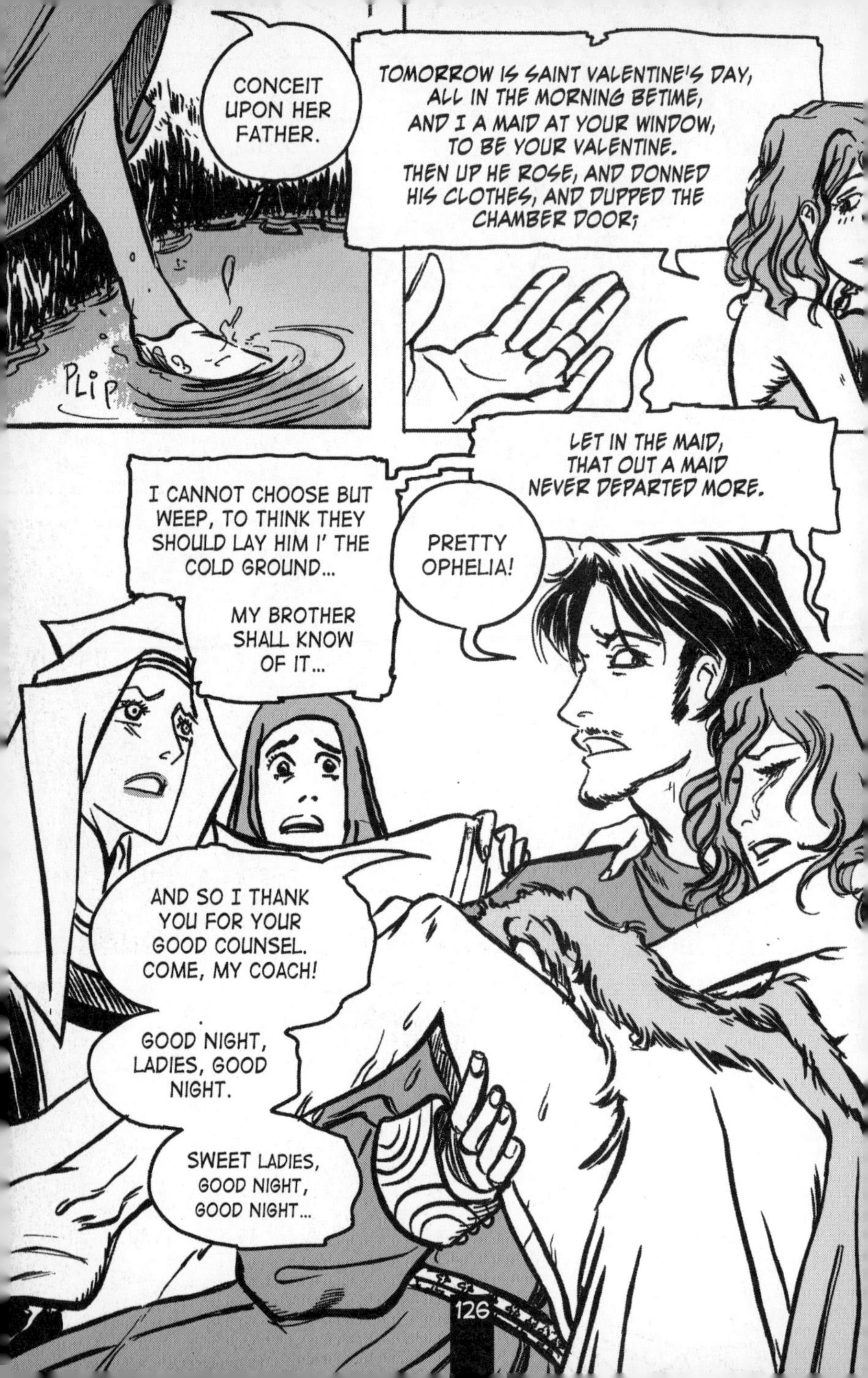

CONCEIT UPON HER FATHER.
PLIP
TOMORROW IS SAINT VALENTINE'S DAY, ALL IN THE MORNING BETIME, AND I A MAID AT YOUR WINDOW, TO BE YOUR VALENTINE. THEN UP HE ROSE, AND DONNED HIS CLOTHES, AND DUPPED THE CHAMBER DOOR;
LET IN THE MAID, THAT OUT A MAID NEVER DEPARTED MORE.
I CANNOT CHOOSE BUT WEEP, TO THINK THEY SHOULD LAY HIM I' THE COLD GROUND...
MY BROTHER SHALL KNOW OF IT...
PRETTY OPHELIA!
AND SO I THANK YOU FOR YOUR GOOD COUNSEL. COME, MY COACH!
GOOD NIGHT, LADIES, GOOD NIGHT.
SWEET LADIES, GOOD NIGHT, GOOD NIGHT...

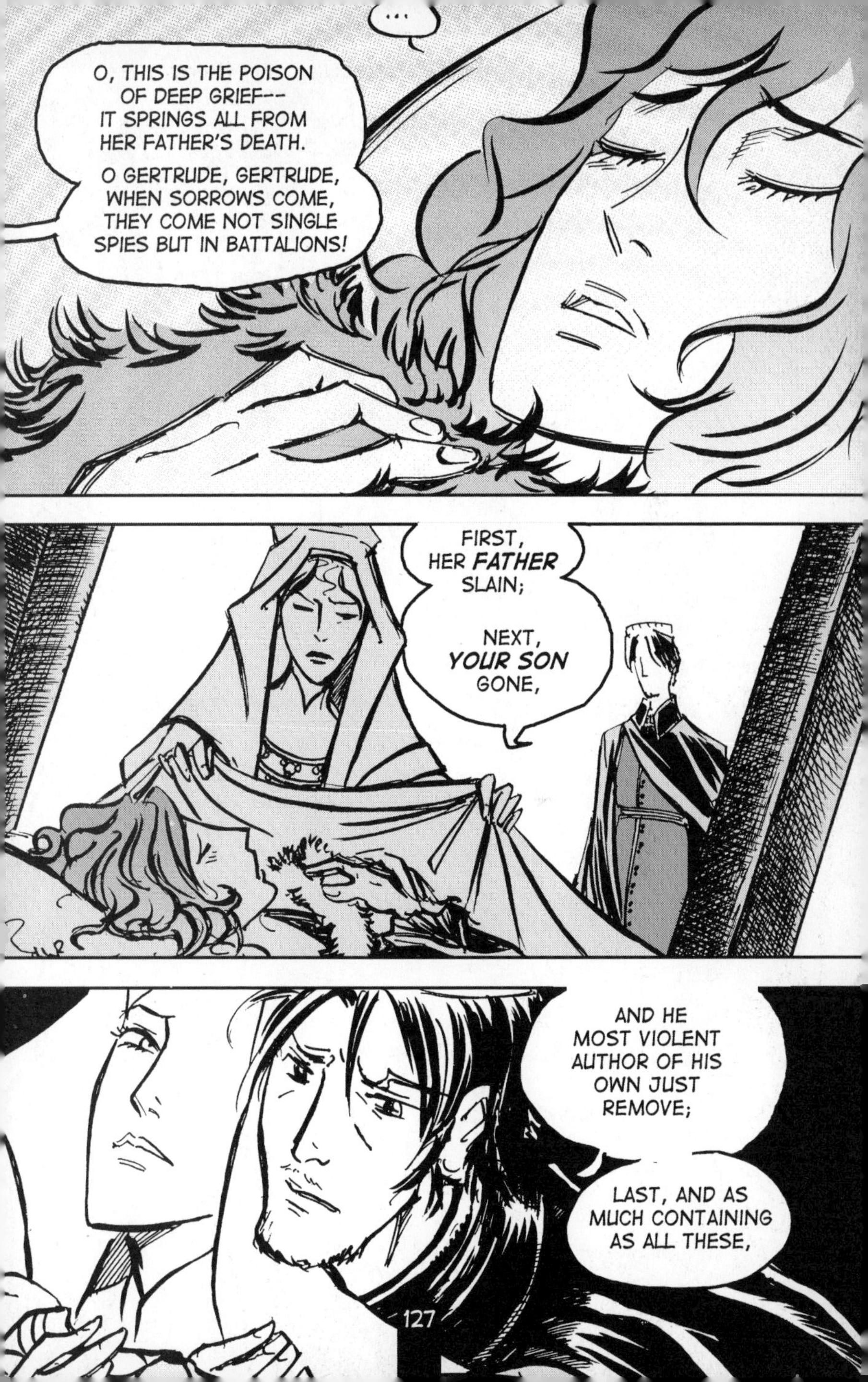
...
O, THIS IS THE POISON OF DEEP GRIEF-- IT SPRINGS ALL FROM HER FATHER'S DEATH.
O GERTRUDE, GERTRUDE, WHEN SORROWS COME, THEY COME NOT SINGLE SPIES BUT IN BATTALIONS!
FIRST, HER FATHER SLAIN;
NEXT, YOUR SON GONE,
AND HE MOST VIOLENT AUTHOR OF HIS OWN JUST REMOVE;
LAST, AND AS MUCH CONTAINING AS ALL THESE,

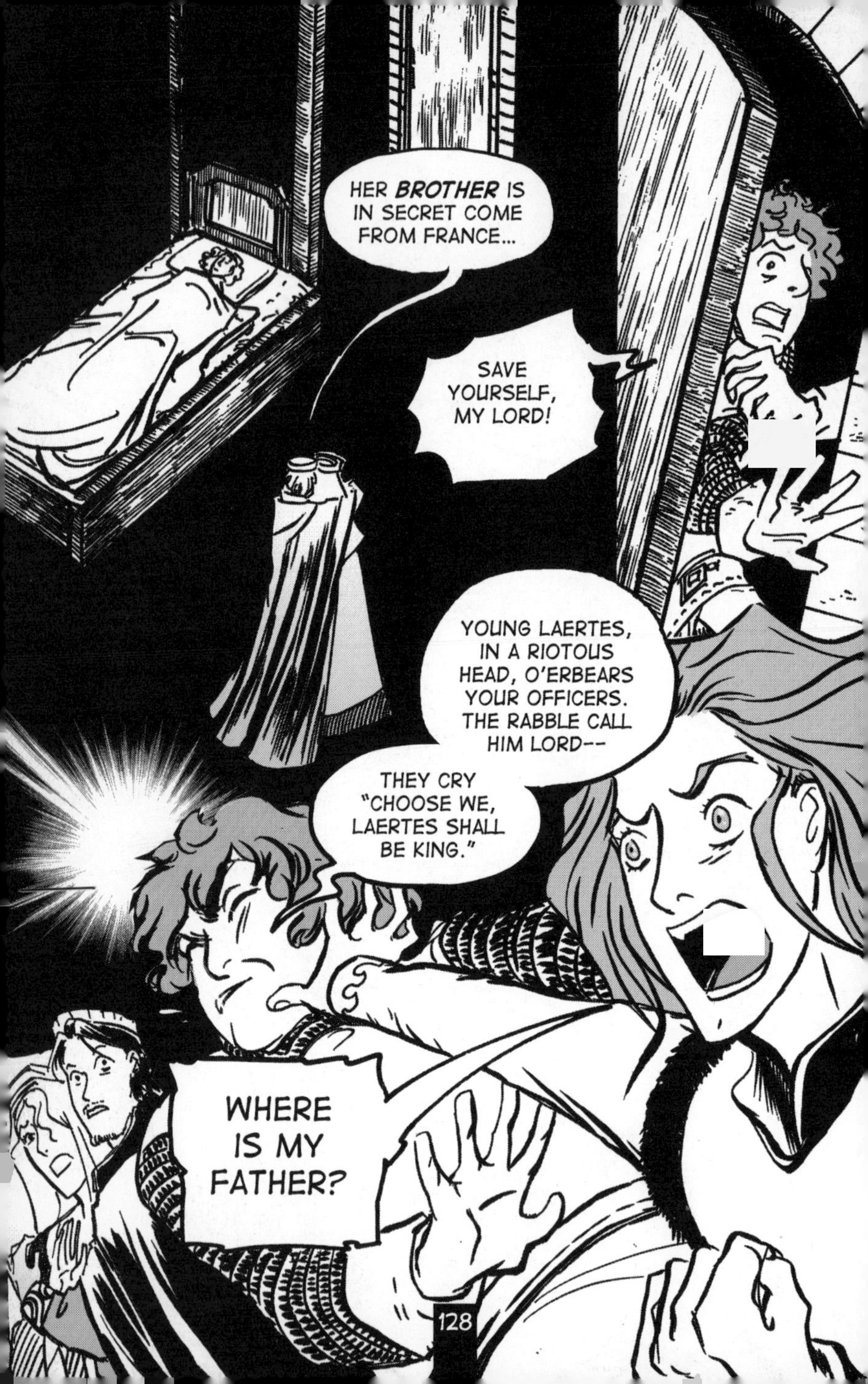
HER **BROTHER** IS IN SECRET COME FROM FRANCE...
SAVE YOURSELF, MY LORD!
YOUNG LAERTES, IN A RIOTOUS HEAD, O'ERBEARS YOUR OFFICERS. THE RABBLE CALL HIM LORD--
THEY CRY "CHOOSE WE, LAERTES SHALL BE KING."
WHERE IS MY FATHER?

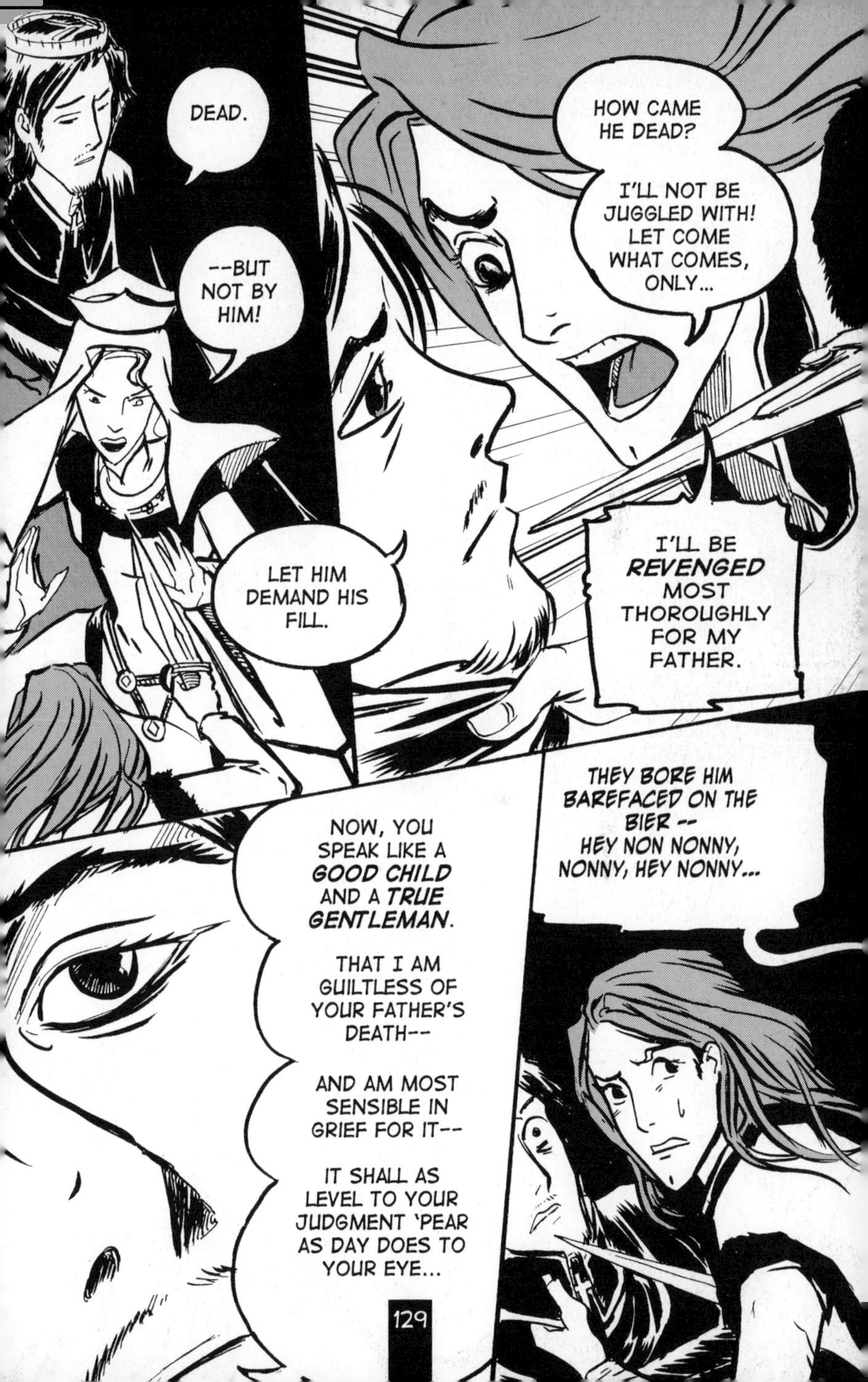
DEAD.
--BUT NOT BY HIM!
LET HIM DEMAND HIS FILL.
HOW CAME HE DEAD?
I'LL NOT BE JUGGLED WITH! LET COME WHAT COMES, ONLY...
I'LL BE *REVENGED* MOST THOROUGHLY FOR MY FATHER.
NOW, YOU SPEAK LIKE A *GOOD CHILD* AND A *TRUE GENTLEMAN*.
THAT I AM GUILTLESS OF YOUR FATHER'S DEATH--
AND AM MOST SENSIBLE IN GRIEF FOR IT--
IT SHALL AS LEVEL TO YOUR JUDGMENT 'PEAR AS DAY DOES TO YOUR EYE...
THEY BORE HIM BAREFACED ON THE BIER -- HEY NON NONNY, NONNY, HEY NONNY...

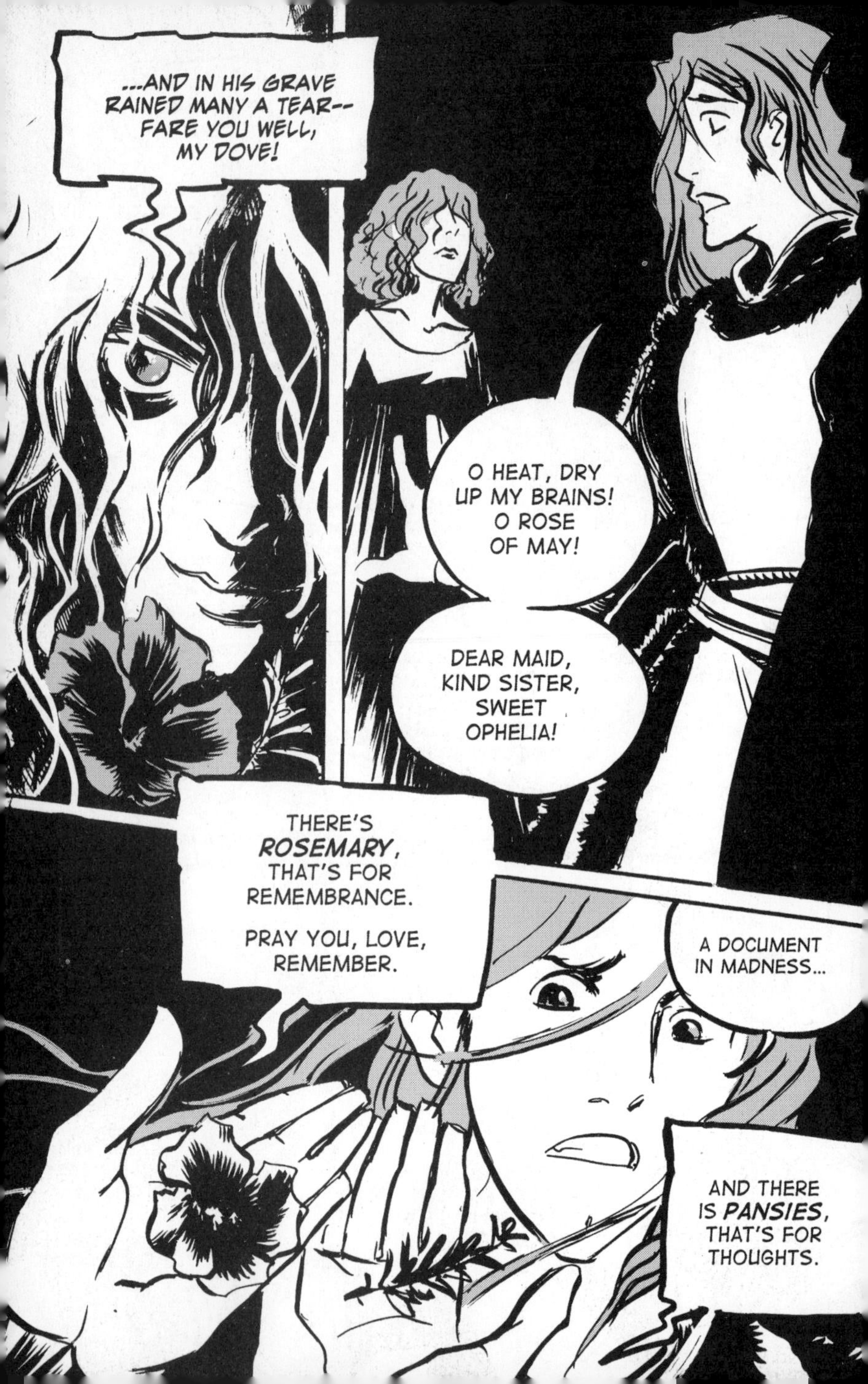
...AND IN HIS GRAVE RAINED MANY A TEAR-- FARE YOU WELL, MY DOVE!
O HEAT, DRY UP MY BRAINS! O ROSE OF MAY!
DEAR MAID, KIND SISTER, SWEET OPHELIA!
THERE'S ROSEMARY, THAT'S FOR REMEMBRANCE.
PRAY YOU, LOVE, REMEMBER.
A DOCUMENT IN MADNESS...
AND THERE IS PANSIES, THAT'S FOR THOUGHTS.

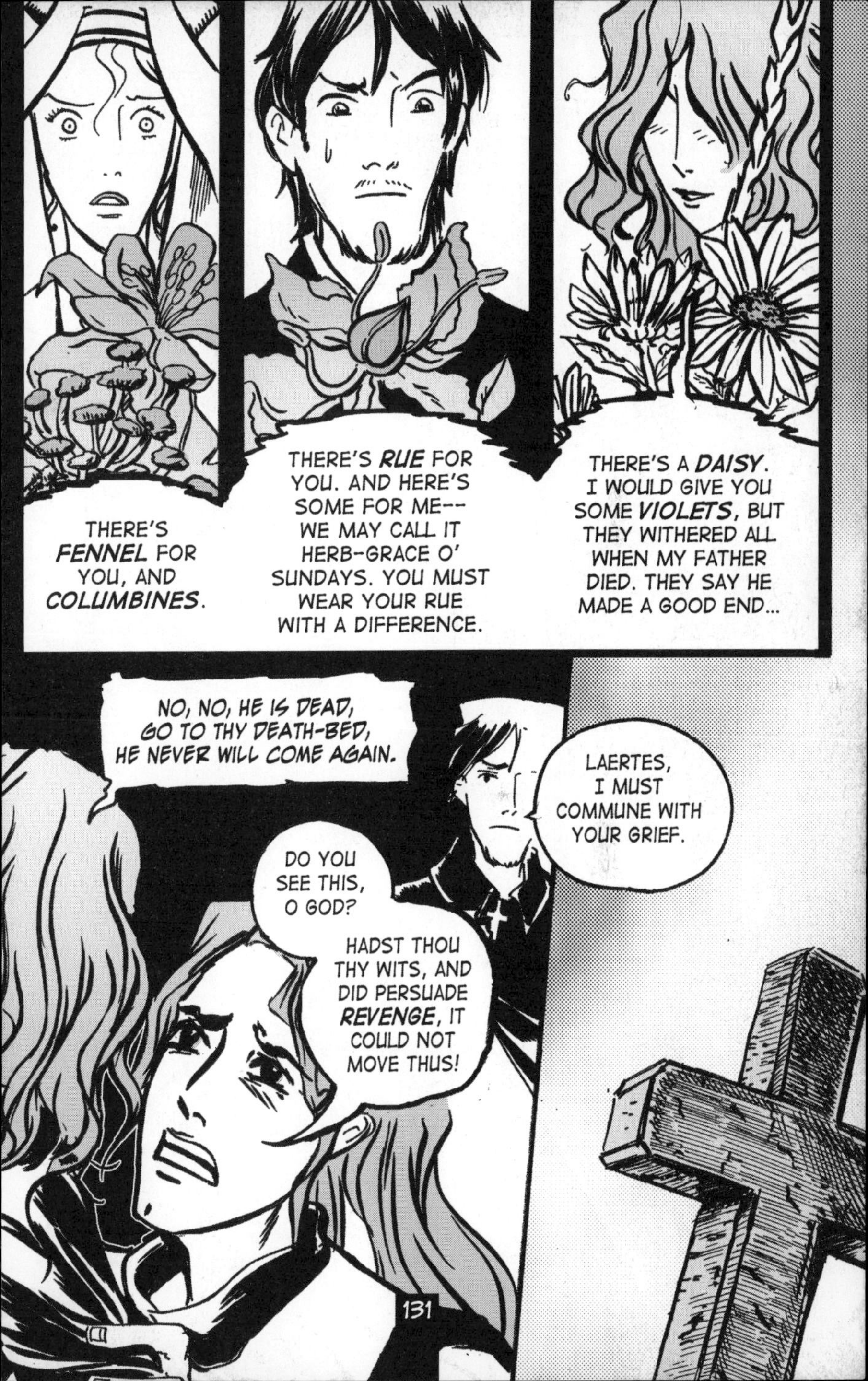

THERE'S FENNEL FOR YOU, AND COLUMBINES.
THERE'S RUE FOR YOU. AND HERE'S SOME FOR ME-- WE MAY CALL IT HERB-GRACE O' SUNDAYS. YOU MUST WEAR YOUR RUE WITH A DIFFERENCE.
THERE'S A DAISY. I WOULD GIVE YOU SOME VIOLETS, BUT THEY WITHERED ALL WHEN MY FATHER DIED. THEY SAY HE MADE A GOOD END...
NO, NO, HE IS DEAD, GO TO THY DEATH-BED, HE NEVER WILL COME AGAIN.
LAERTES, I MUST COMMUNE WITH YOUR GRIEF.
DO YOU SEE THIS, O GOD?
HADST THOU THY WITS, AND DID PERSUADE REVENGE, IT COULD NOT MOVE THUS!

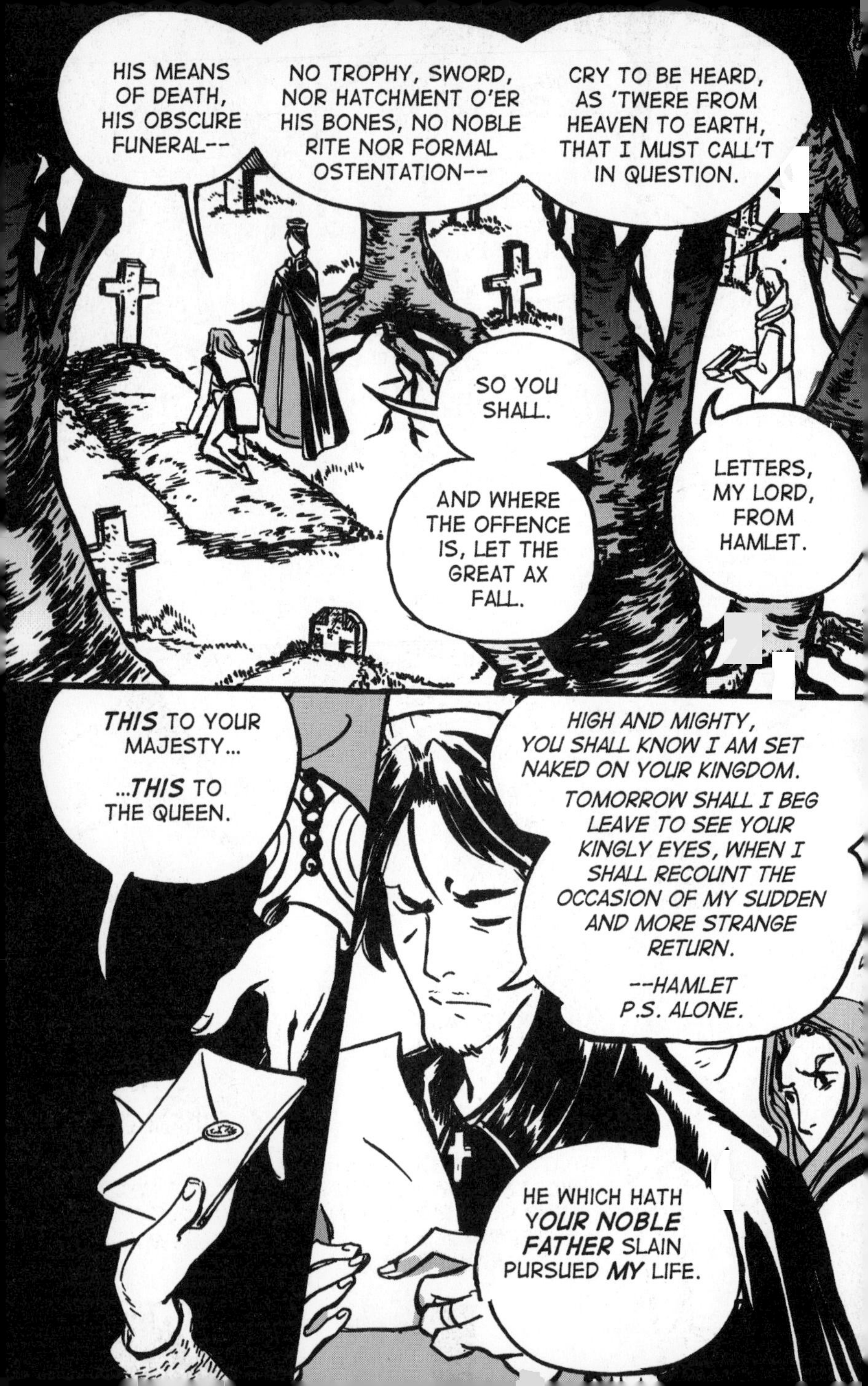
HIS MEANS OF DEATH, HIS OBSCURE FUNERAL--
NO TROPHY, SWORD, NOR HATCHMENT O'ER HIS BONES, NO NOBLE RITE NOR FORMAL OSTENTATION--
CRY TO BE HEARD, AS 'TWERE FROM HEAVEN TO EARTH, THAT I MUST CALL'T IN QUESTION.
SO YOU SHALL.
AND WHERE THE OFFENCE IS, LET THE GREAT AX FALL.
LETTERS, MY LORD, FROM HAMLET.
THIS TO YOUR MAJESTY...
...THIS TO THE QUEEN.
HIGH AND MIGHTY, YOU SHALL KNOW I AM SET NAKED ON YOUR KINGDOM.
TOMORROW SHALL I BEG LEAVE TO SEE YOUR KINGLY EYES, WHEN I SHALL RECOUNT THE OCCASION OF MY SUDDEN AND MORE STRANGE RETURN.
--HAMLET
P.S. ALONE.
HE WHICH HATH YOUR NOBLE FATHER SLAIN PURSUED MY LIFE.

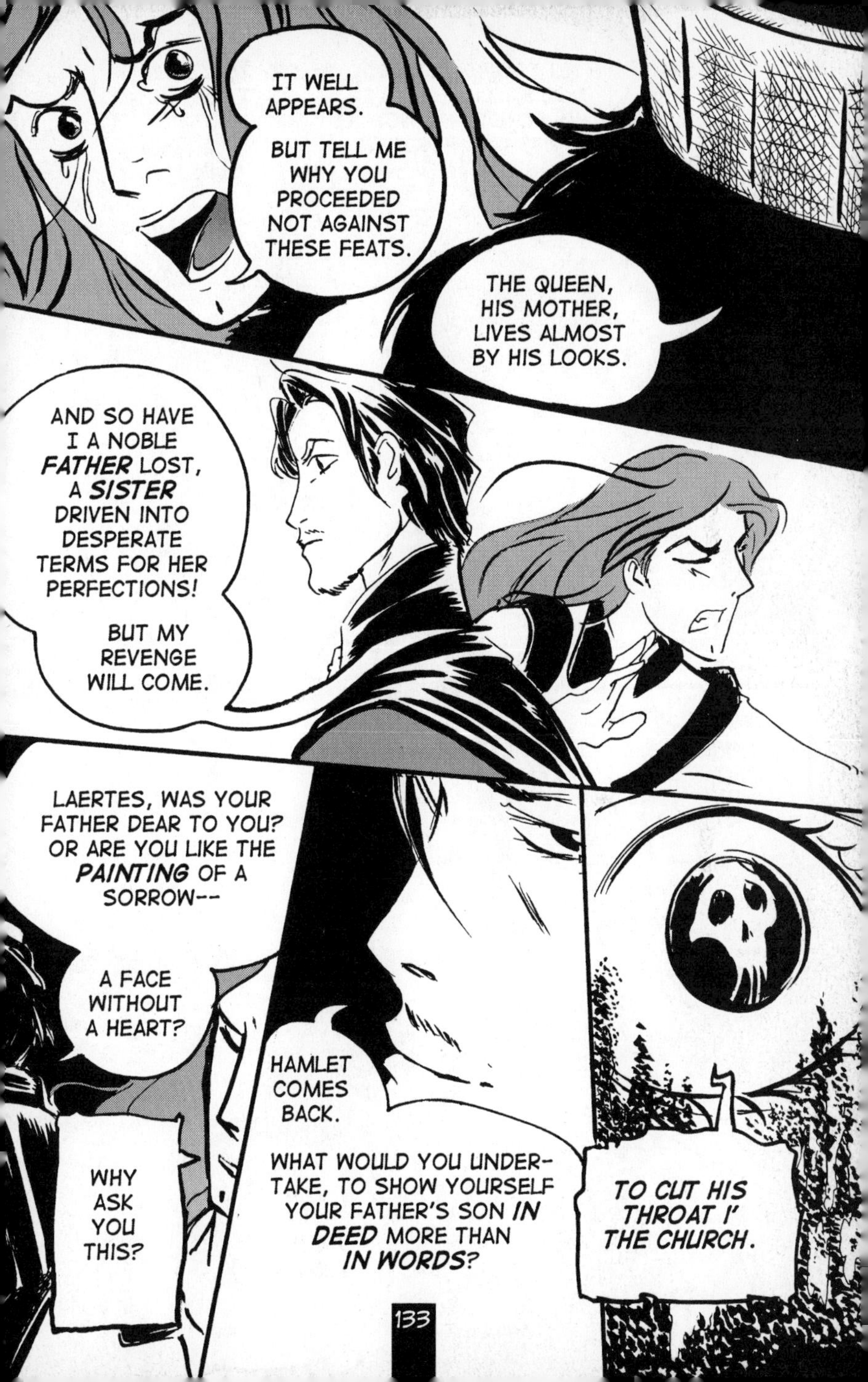
IT WELL APPEARS.
BUT TELL ME WHY YOU PROCEEDED NOT AGAINST THESE FEATS.
THE QUEEN, HIS MOTHER, LIVES ALMOST BY HIS LOOKS.
AND SO HAVE I A NOBLE *FATHER* LOST, A *SISTER* DRIVEN INTO DESPERATE TERMS FOR HER PERFECTIONS!
BUT MY REVENGE WILL COME.
LAERTES, WAS YOUR FATHER DEAR TO YOU? OR ARE YOU LIKE THE *PAINTING* OF A SORROW--
A FACE WITHOUT A HEART?
WHY ASK YOU THIS?
HAMLET COMES BACK.
WHAT WOULD YOU UNDER-TAKE, TO SHOW YOURSELF YOUR FATHER'S SON *IN DEED* MORE THAN *IN WORDS*?
TO CUT HIS THROAT I' THE CHURCH.

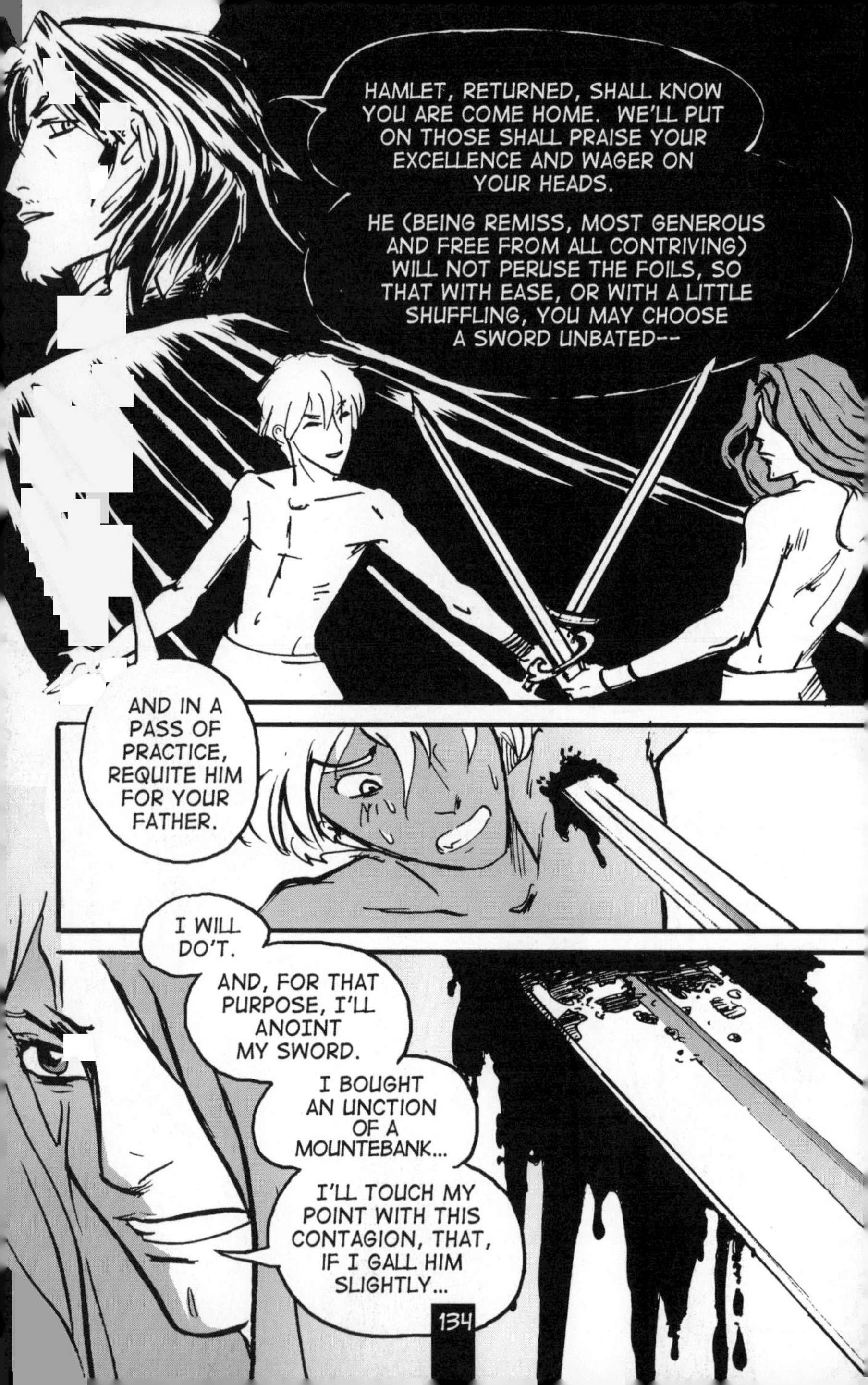
HAMLET, RETURNED, SHALL KNOW YOU ARE COME HOME. WE'LL PUT ON THOSE SHALL PRAISE YOUR EXCELLENCE AND WAGER ON YOUR HEADS.
HE (BEING REMISS, MOST GENEROUS AND FREE FROM ALL CONTRIVING) WILL NOT PERUSE THE FOILS, SO THAT WITH EASE, OR WITH A LITTLE SHUFFLING, YOU MAY CHOOSE A SWORD UNBATED--
AND IN A PASS OF PRACTICE, REQUITE HIM FOR YOUR FATHER.
I WILL DO'T.
AND, FOR THAT PURPOSE, I'LL ANOINT MY SWORD.
I BOUGHT AN UNCTION OF A MOUNTEBANK...
I'LL TOUCH MY POINT WITH THIS CONTAGION, THAT, IF I GALL HIM SLIGHTLY...

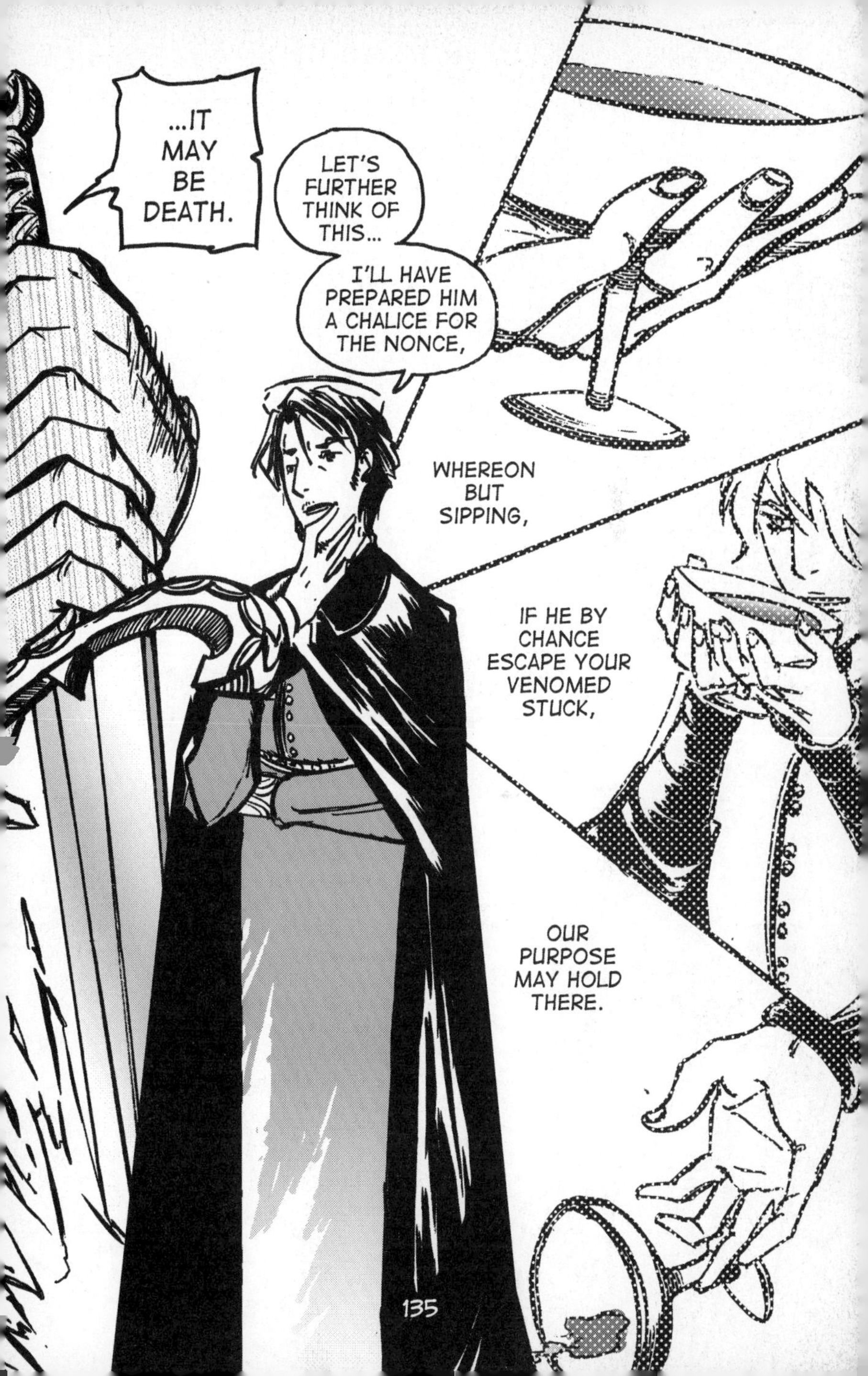
...IT MAY BE DEATH.
LET'S FURTHER THINK OF THIS...
I'LL HAVE PREPARED HIM A CHALICE FOR THE NONCE,
WHEREON BUT SIPPING,
IF HE BY CHANCE ESCAPE YOUR VENOMED STUCK,
OUR PURPOSE MAY HOLD THERE.

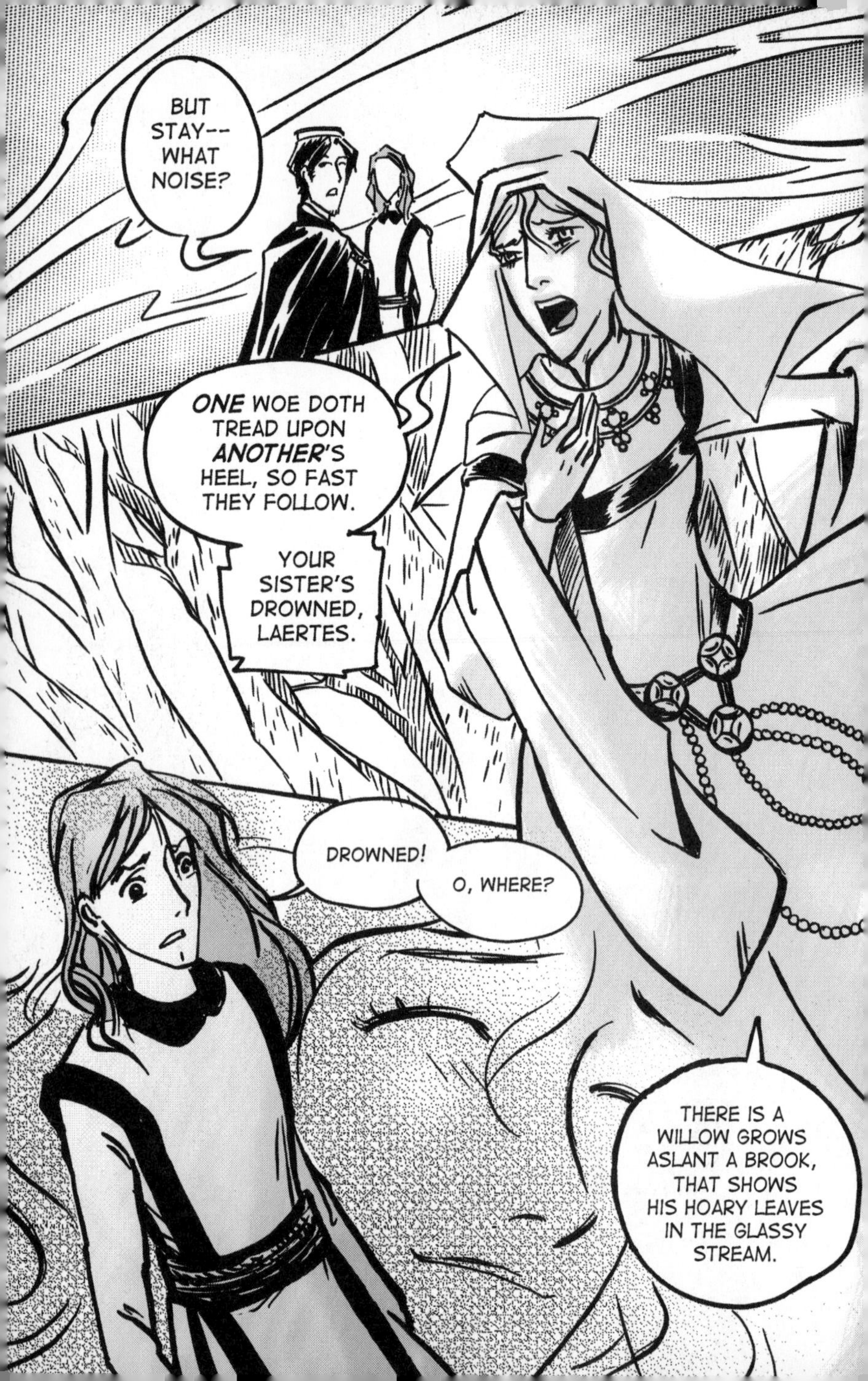
BUT STAY-- WHAT NOISE?
ONE WOE DOTH TREAD UPON ANOTHER'S HEEL, SO FAST THEY FOLLOW.
YOUR SISTER'S DROWNED, LAERTES.
DROWNED!
O, WHERE?
THERE IS A WILLOW GROWS ASLANT A BROOK, THAT SHOWS HIS HOARY LEAVES IN THE GLASSY STREAM.

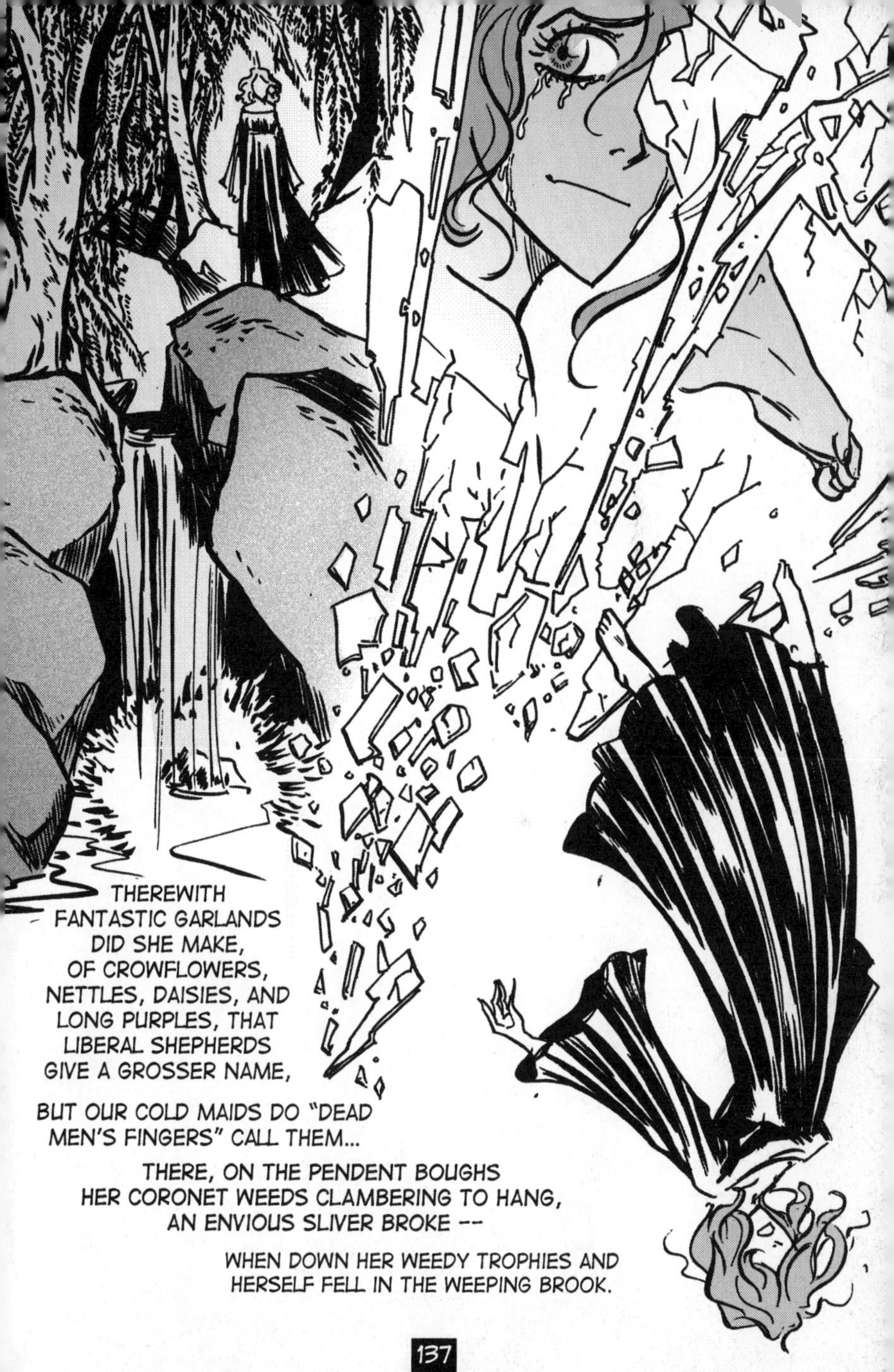
THEREWITH FANTASTIC GARLANDS DID SHE MAKE, OF CROWFLOWERS, NETTLES, DAISIES, AND LONG PURPLES, THAT LIBERAL SHEPHERDS GIVE A GROSSER NAME,
BUT OUR COLD MAIDS DO "DEAD MEN'S FINGERS" CALL THEM...
THERE, ON THE PENDENT BOUGHS HER CORONET WEEDS CLAMBERING TO HANG, AN ENVIOUS SLIVER BROKE --
WHEN DOWN HER WEEDY TROPHIES AND HERSELF FELL IN THE WEEPING BROOK.

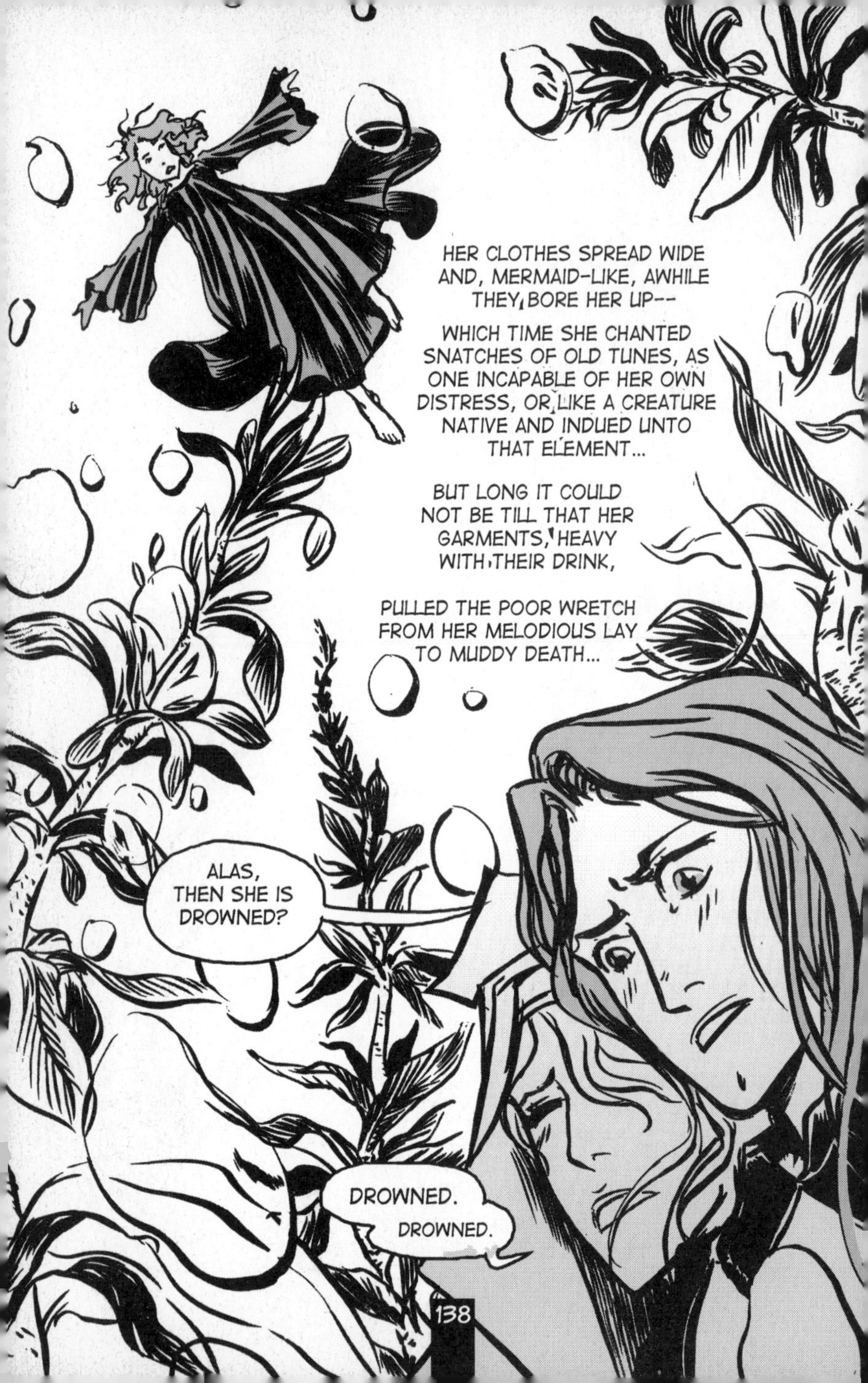
HER CLOTHES SPREAD WIDE AND, MERMAID-LIKE, AWHILE THEY BORE HER UP--
WHICH TIME SHE CHANTED SNATCHES OF OLD TUNES, AS ONE INCAPABLE OF HER OWN DISTRESS, OR LIKE A CREATURE NATIVE AND INDUED UNTO THAT ELEMENT...
BUT LONG IT COULD NOT BE TILL THAT HER GARMENTS, HEAVY WITH THEIR DRINK,
PULLED THE POOR WRETCH FROM HER MELODIOUS LAY TO MUDDY DEATH...
ALAS, THEN SHE IS DROWNED?
DROWNED.
DROWNED.

ACT V

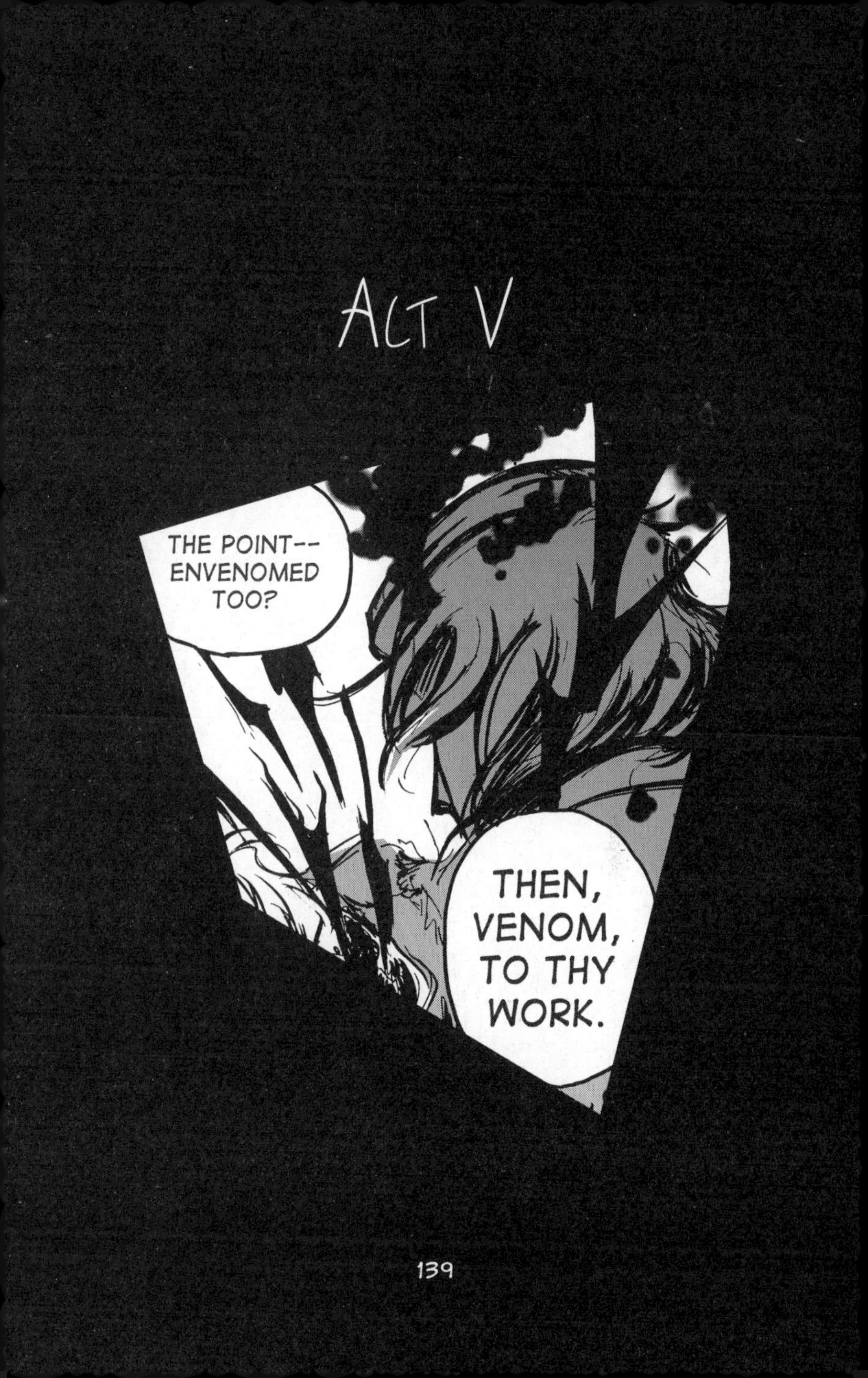
THE POINT--ENVENOMED TOO?
THEN, VENOM, TO THY WORK.

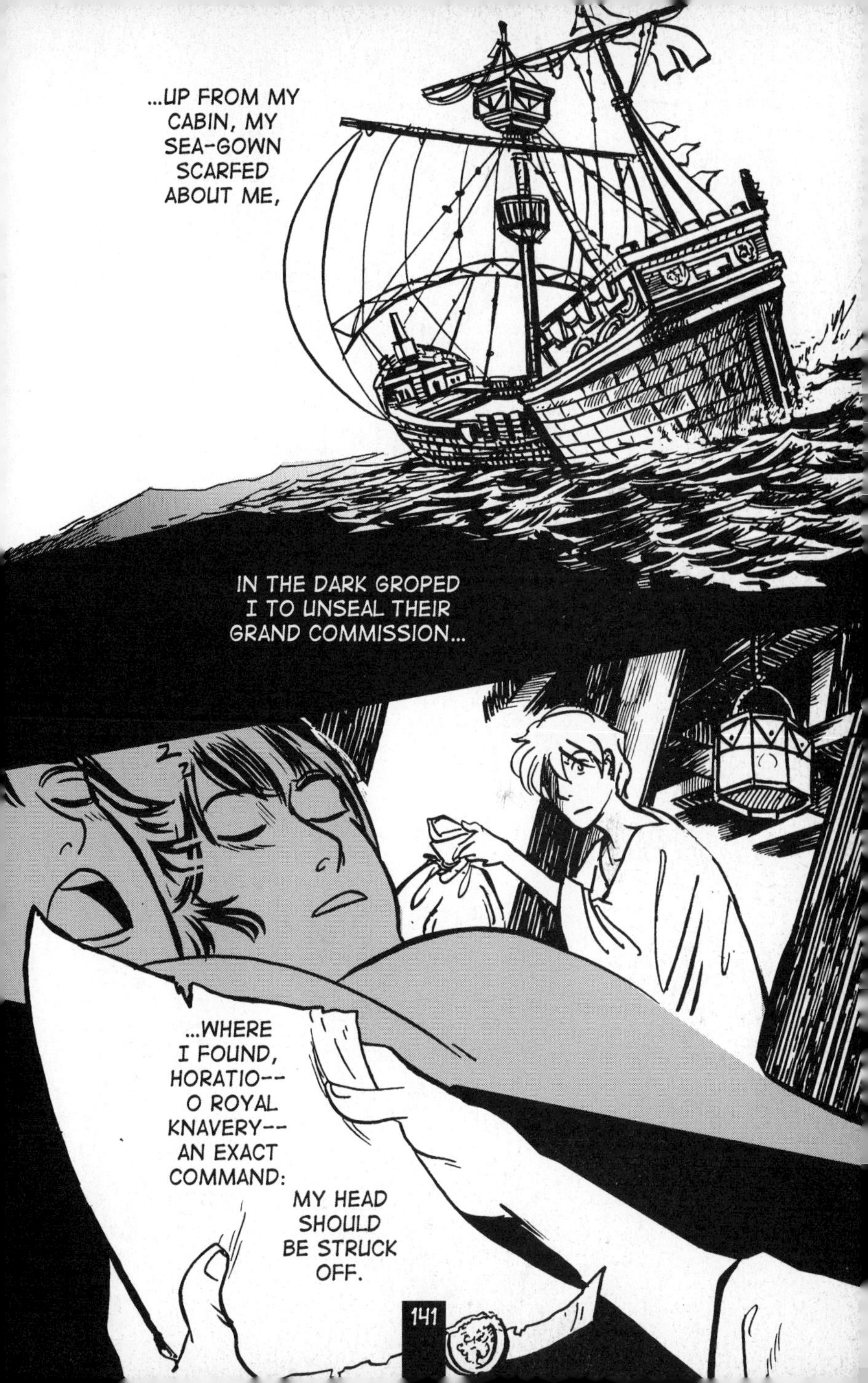

...UP FROM MY CABIN, MY SEA-GOWN SCARFED ABOUT ME,
IN THE DARK GROPED I TO UNSEAL THEIR GRAND COMMISSION...
...WHERE I FOUND, HORATIO-- O ROYAL KNAVERY-- AN EXACT COMMAND:
MY HEAD SHOULD BE STRUCK OFF.

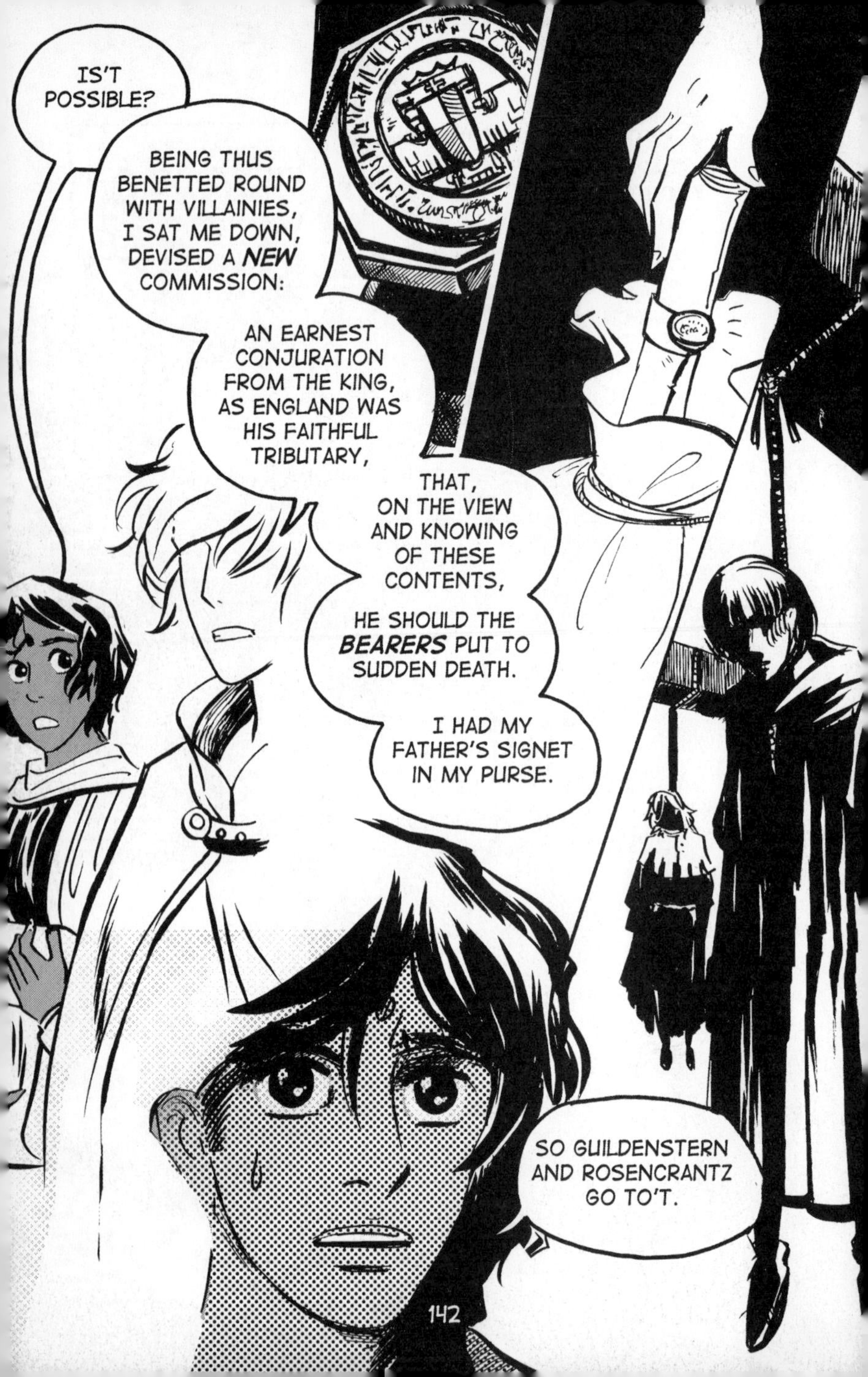
IS'T POSSIBLE?
BEING THUS BENETTED ROUND WITH VILLAINIES, I SAT ME DOWN, DEVISED A NEW COMMISSION:
AN EARNEST CONJURATION FROM THE KING, AS ENGLAND WAS HIS FAITHFUL TRIBUTARY,
THAT, ON THE VIEW AND KNOWING OF THESE CONTENTS,
HE SHOULD THE BEARERS PUT TO SUDDEN DEATH.
I HAD MY FATHER'S SIGNET IN MY PURSE.
SO GUILDENSTERN AND ROSENCRANTZ GO TO'T.

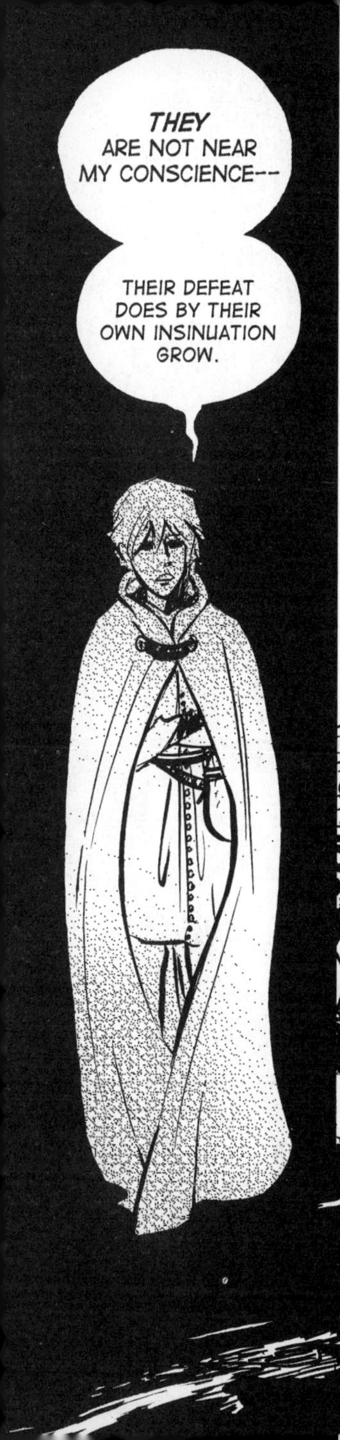
THEY ARE NOT NEAR MY CONSCIENCE--
THEIR DEFEAT DOES BY THEIR OWN INSINUATION GROW.
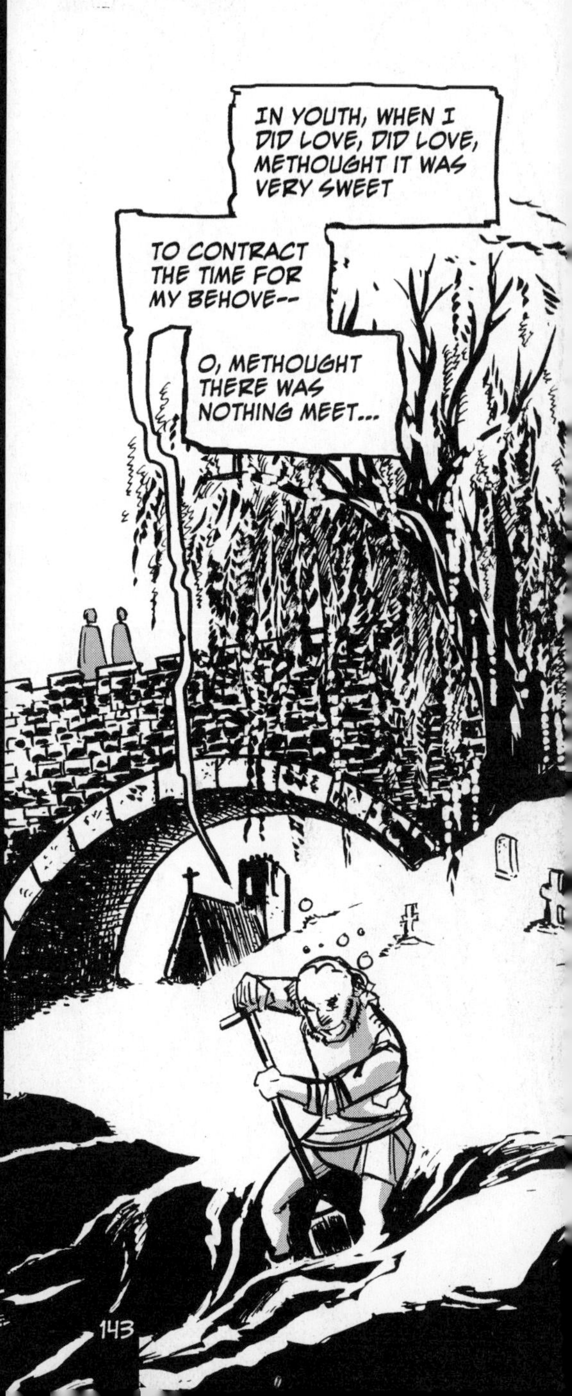
IN YOUTH, WHEN I DID LOVE, DID LOVE, METHOUGHT IT WAS VERY SWEET
TO CONTRACT THE TIME FOR MY BEHOVE--
O, METHOUGHT THERE WAS NOTHING MEET...

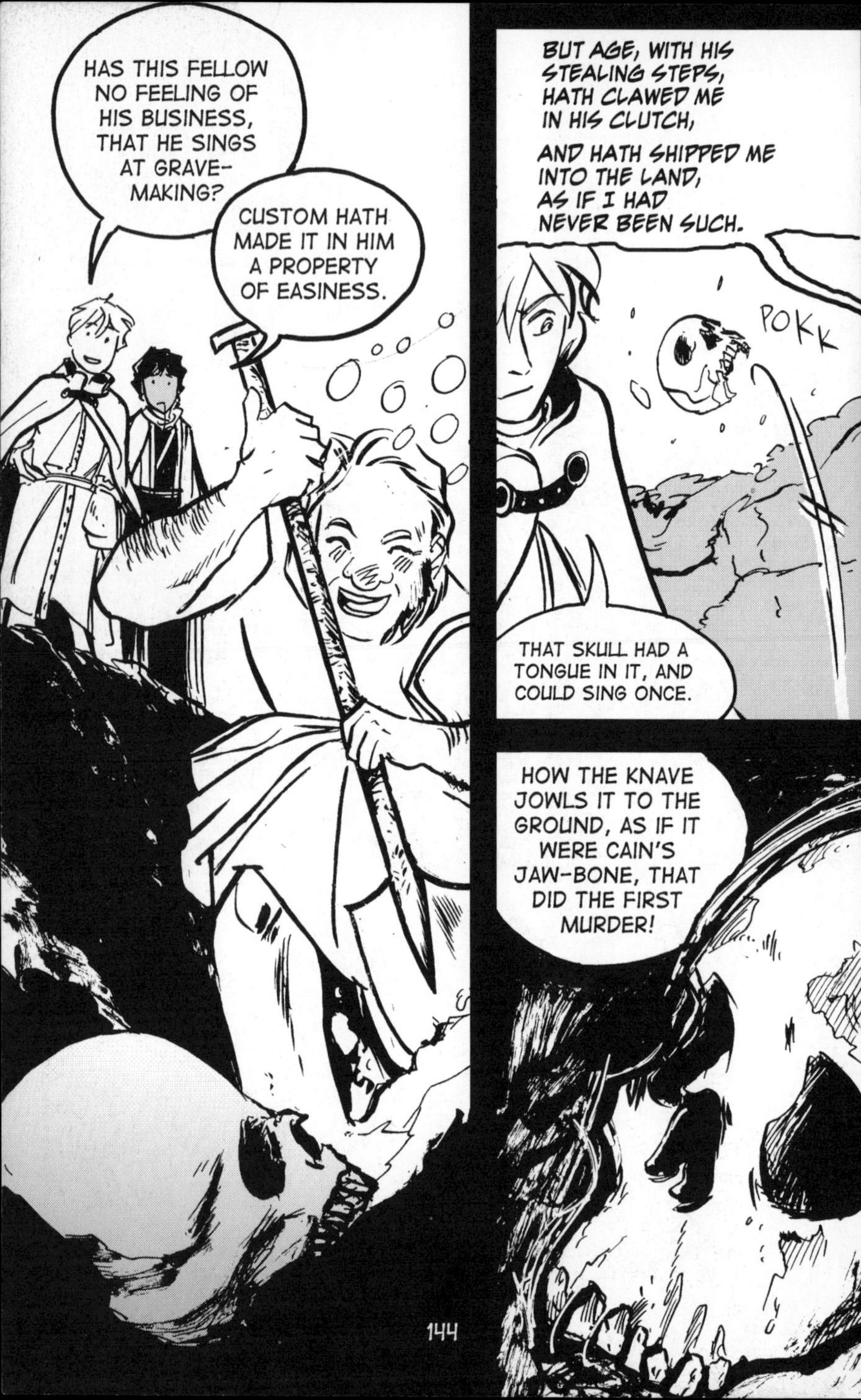
HAS THIS FELLOW NO FEELING OF HIS BUSINESS, THAT HE SINGS AT GRAVE-MAKING?
CUSTOM HATH MADE IT IN HIM A PROPERTY OF EASINESS.
BUT AGE, WITH HIS STEALING STEPS, HATH CLAWED ME IN HIS CLUTCH,
AND HATH SHIPPED ME INTO THE LAND, AS IF I HAD NEVER BEEN SUCH.
POKK
THAT SKULL HAD A TONGUE IN IT, AND COULD SING ONCE.
HOW THE KNAVE JOWLS IT TO THE GROUND, AS IF IT WERE CAIN'S JAW-BONE, THAT DID THE FIRST MURDER!

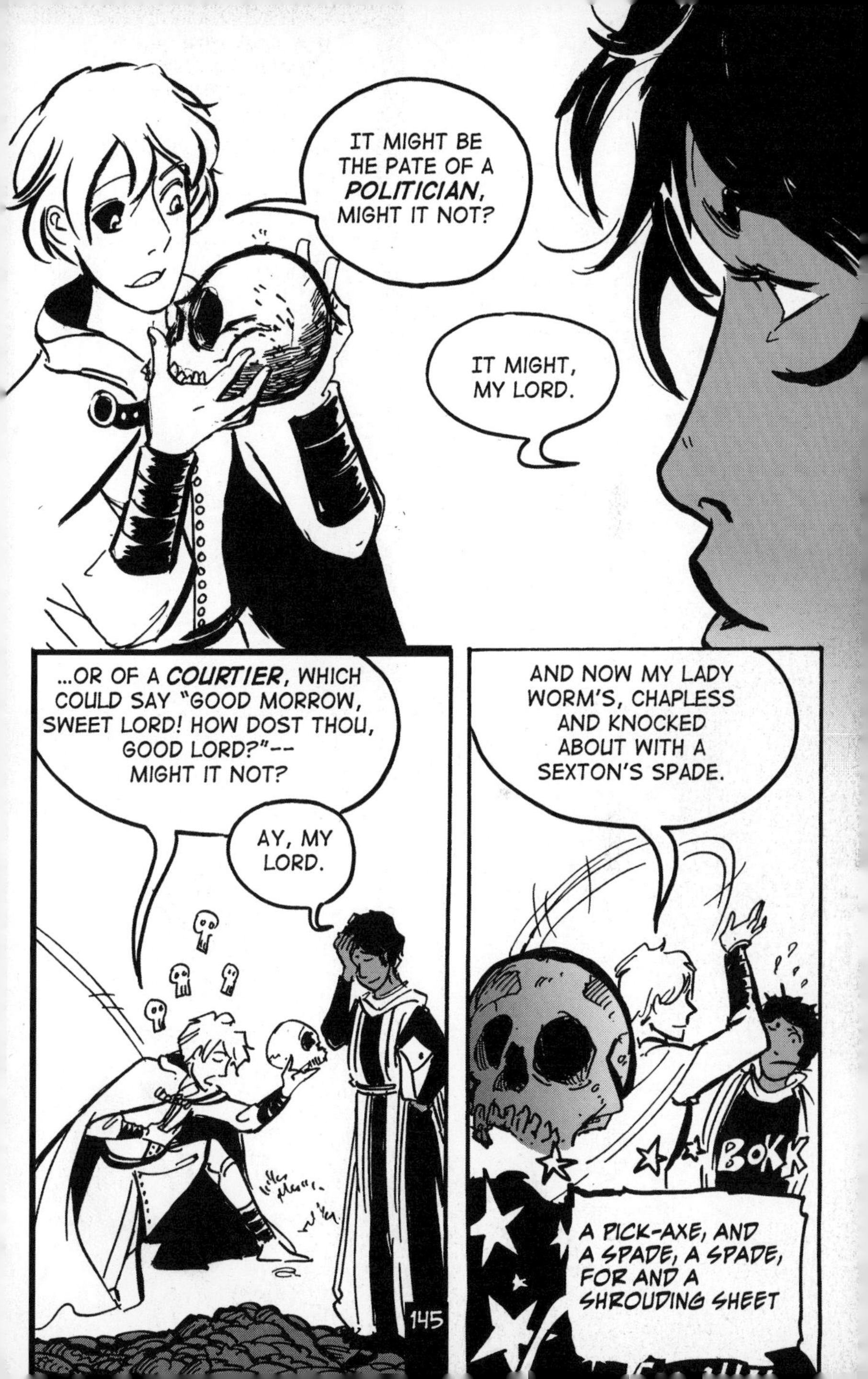
IT MIGHT BE THE PATE OF A *POLITICIAN*, MIGHT IT NOT?
IT MIGHT, MY LORD.
...OR OF A *COURTIER*, WHICH COULD SAY "GOOD MORROW, SWEET LORD! HOW DOST THOU, GOOD LORD?"-- MIGHT IT NOT?
AY, MY LORD.
AND NOW MY LADY WORM'S, CHAPLESS AND KNOCKED ABOUT WITH A SEXTON'S SPADE.
BOKK
A PICK-AXE, AND A SPADE, A SPADE, FOR AND A SHROUDING SHEET

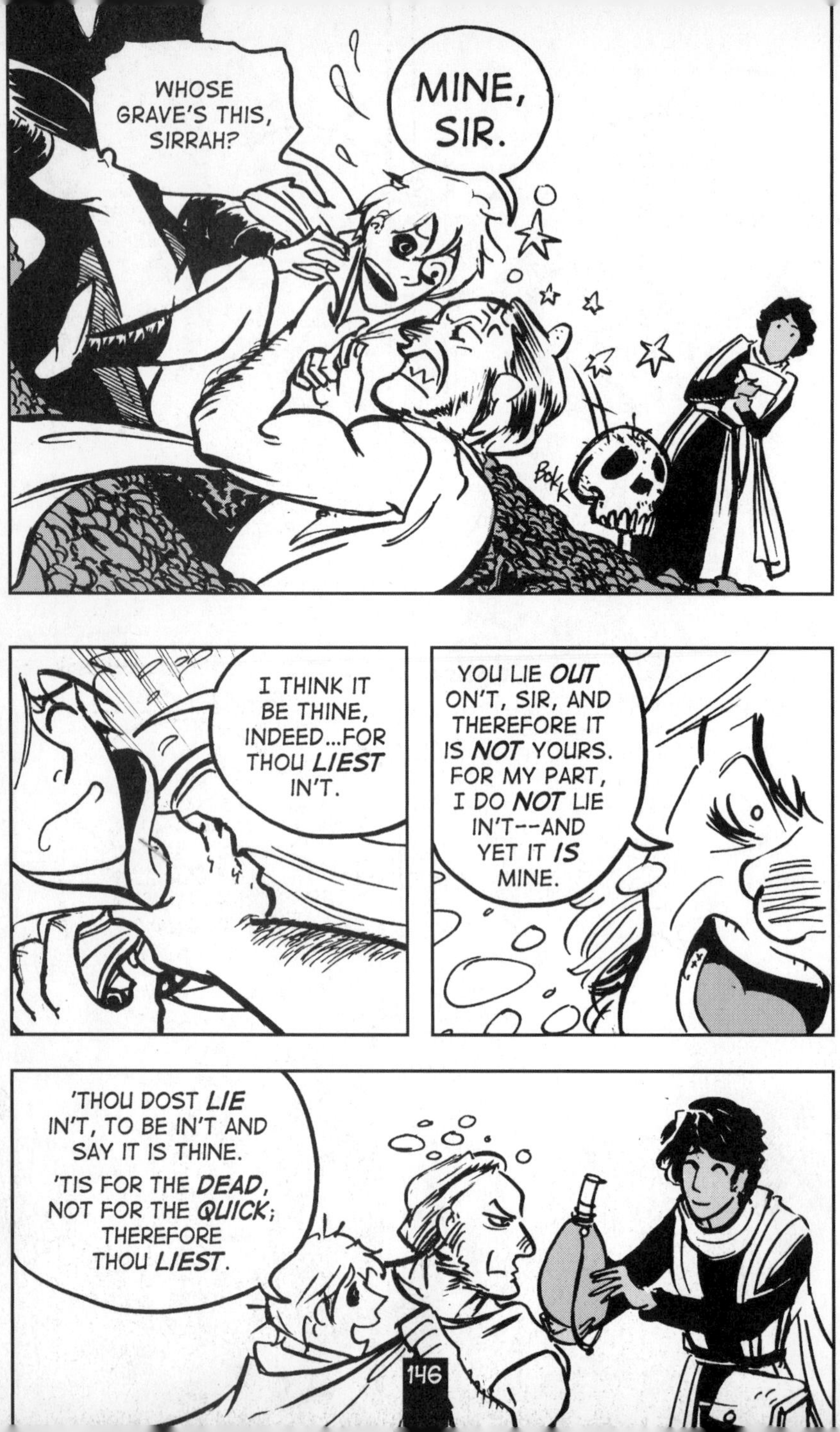
WHOSE GRAVE'S THIS, SIRRAH?
MINE, SIR.
BOKK
I THINK IT BE THINE, INDEED...FOR THOU *LIEST* IN'T.
YOU LIE *OUT* ON'T, SIR, AND THEREFORE IT IS *NOT* YOURS. FOR MY PART, I DO *NOT* LIE IN'T--AND YET IT *IS* MINE.
'THOU DOST *LIE* IN'T, TO BE IN'T AND SAY IT IS THINE.
'TIS FOR THE *DEAD*, NOT FOR THE *QUICK*; THEREFORE THOU *LIEST*.

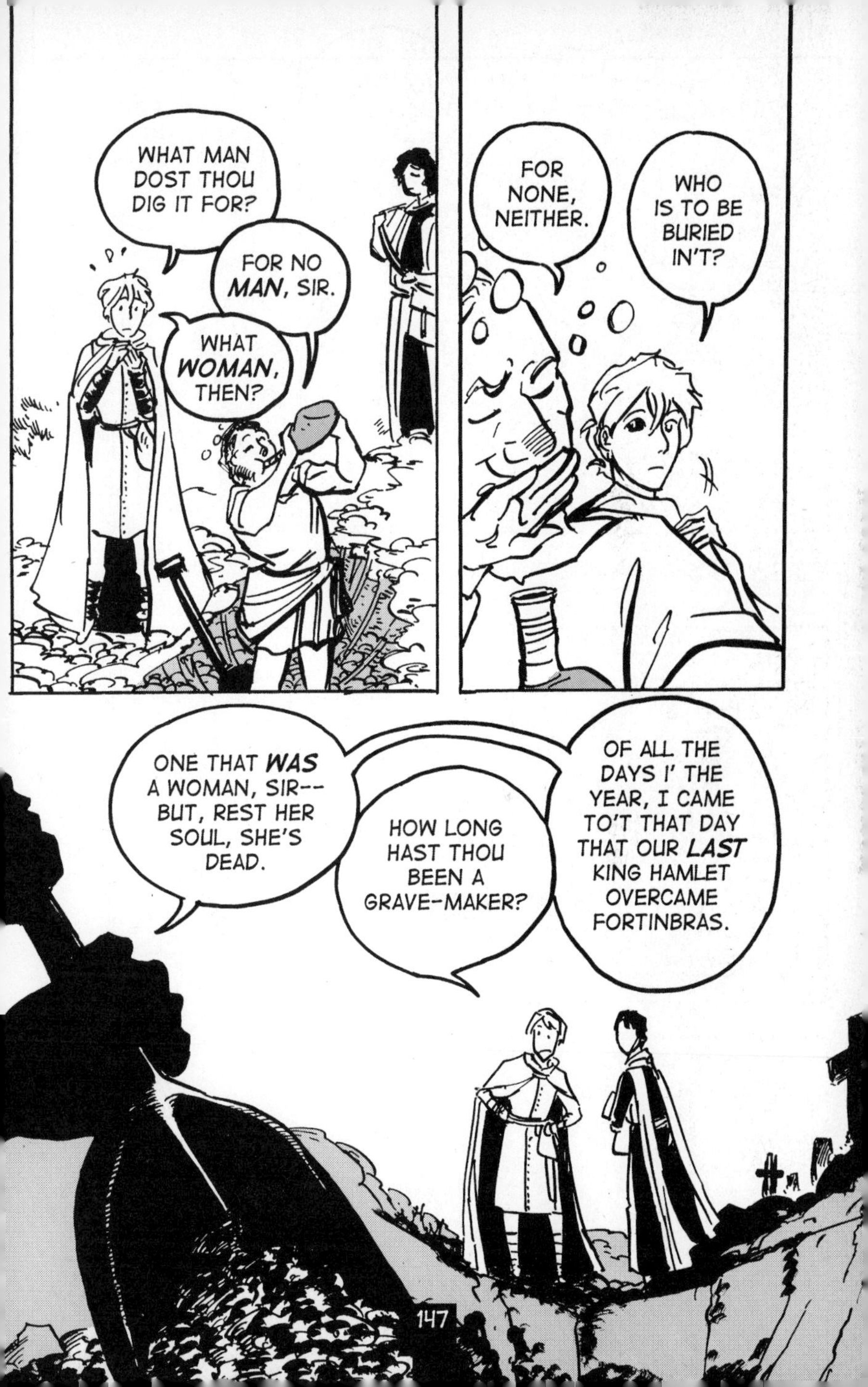
WHAT MAN DOST THOU DIG IT FOR?
FOR NO MAN, SIR.
WHAT WOMAN, THEN?
FOR NONE, NEITHER.
WHO IS TO BE BURIED IN'T?
ONE THAT WAS A WOMAN, SIR-- BUT, REST HER SOUL, SHE'S DEAD.
HOW LONG HAST THOU BEEN A GRAVE-MAKER?
OF ALL THE DAYS I' THE YEAR, I CAME TO'T THAT DAY THAT OUR LAST KING HAMLET OVERCAME FORTINBRAS.

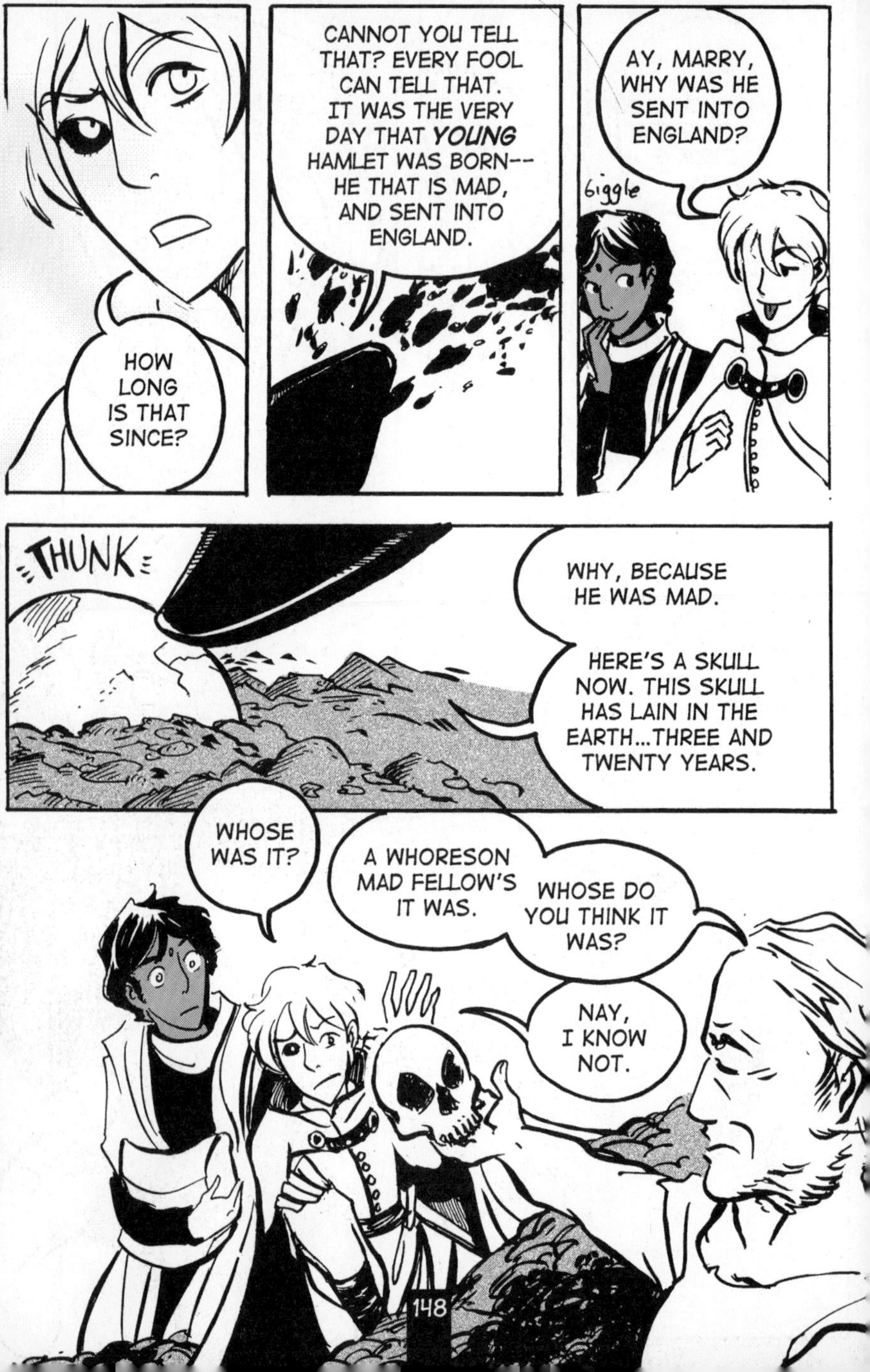
HOW LONG IS THAT SINCE?
CANNOT YOU TELL THAT? EVERY FOOL CAN TELL THAT. IT WAS THE VERY DAY THAT *YOUNG* HAMLET WAS BORN-- HE THAT IS MAD, AND SENT INTO ENGLAND.
giggle
AY, MARRY, WHY WAS HE SENT INTO ENGLAND?
THUNK
WHY, BECAUSE HE WAS MAD.
HERE'S A SKULL NOW. THIS SKULL HAS LAIN IN THE EARTH...THREE AND TWENTY YEARS.
WHOSE WAS IT?
A WHORESON MAD FELLOW'S IT WAS.
WHOSE DO YOU THINK IT WAS?
NAY, I KNOW NOT.

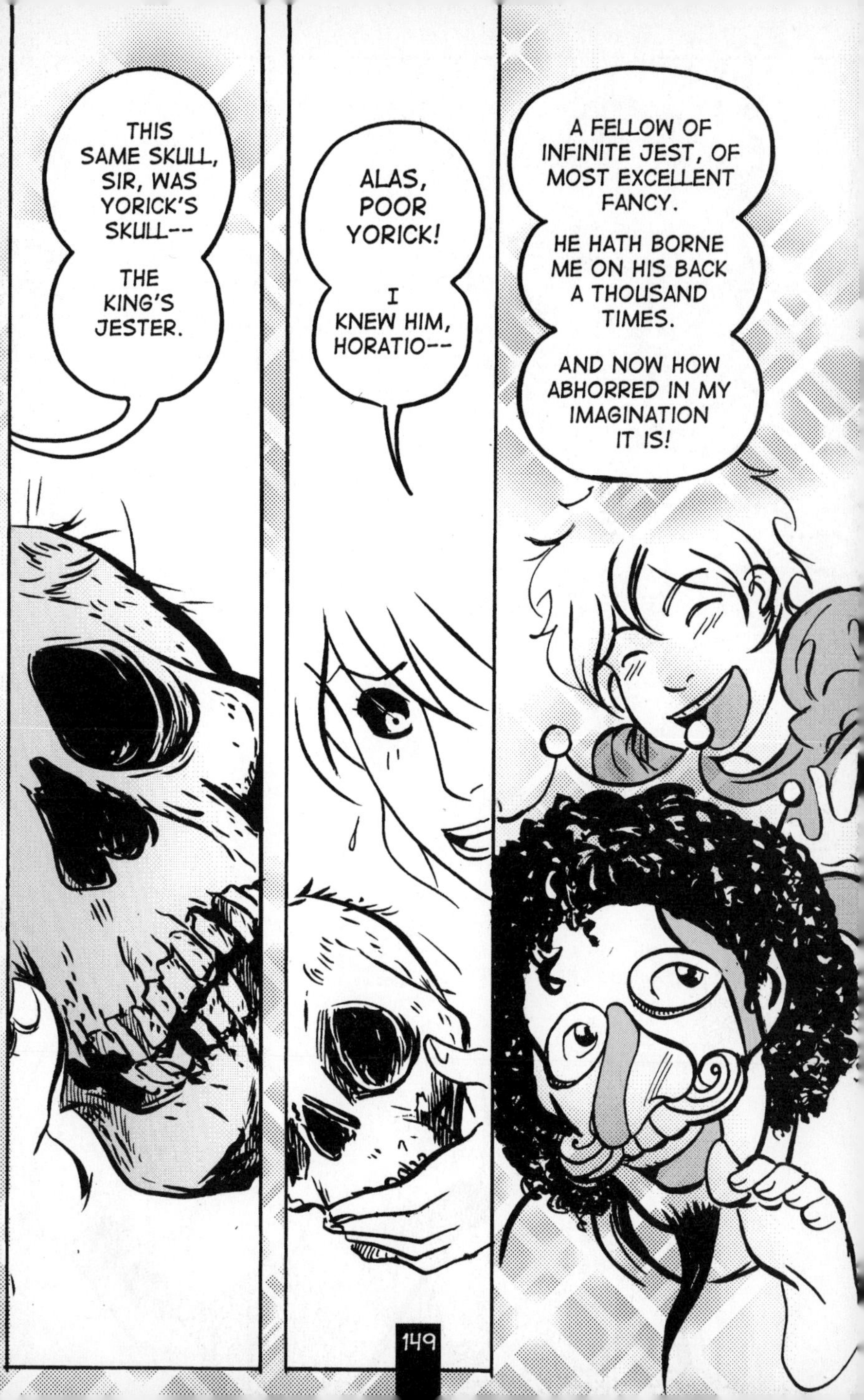
THIS SAME SKULL, SIR, WAS YORICK'S SKULL--
THE KING'S JESTER.
ALAS, POOR YORICK!
I KNEW HIM, HORATIO--
A FELLOW OF INFINITE JEST, OF MOST EXCELLENT FANCY.
HE HATH BORNE ME ON HIS BACK A THOUSAND TIMES.
AND NOW HOW ABHORRED IN MY IMAGINATION IT IS!

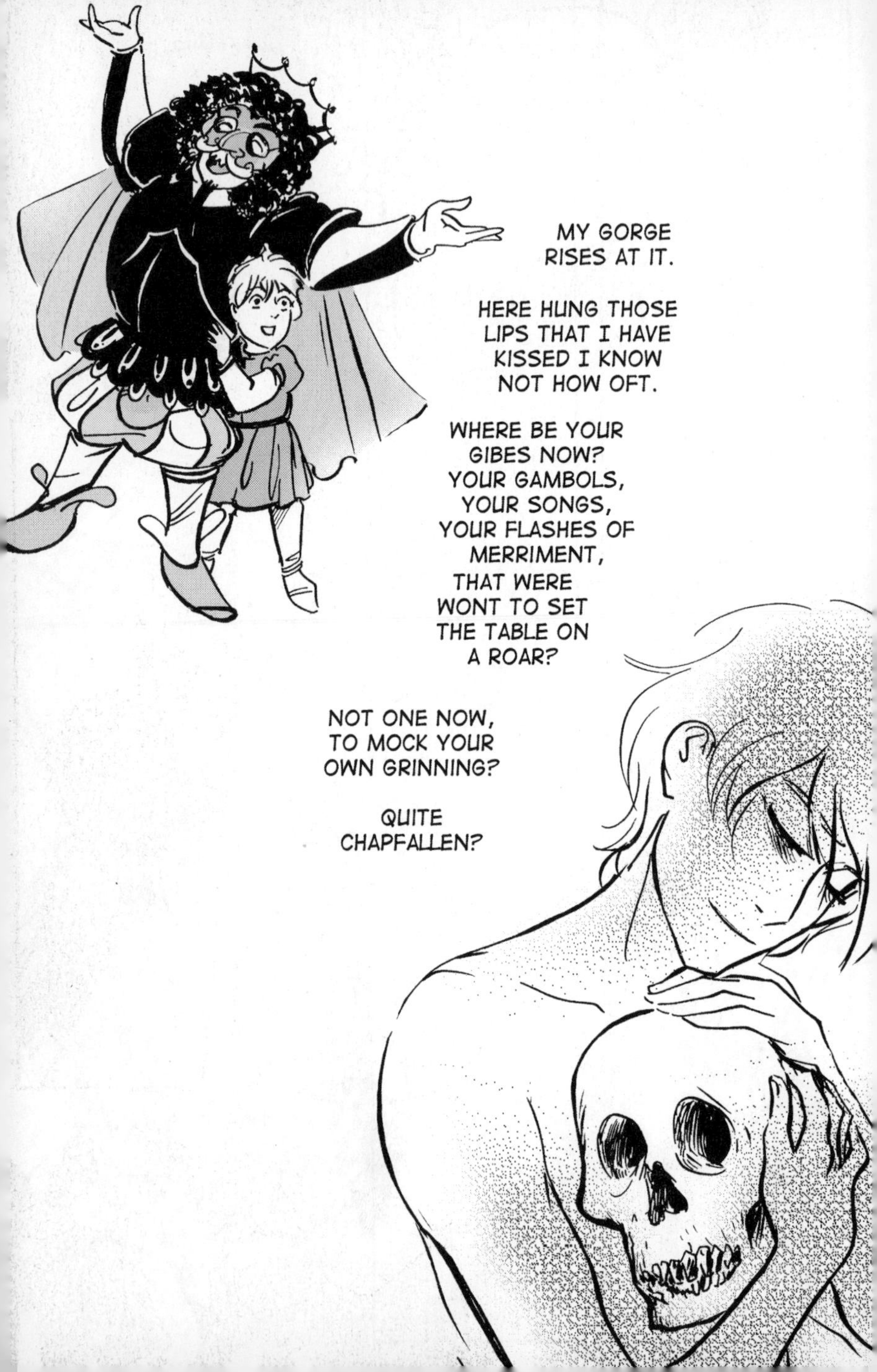
MY GORGE RISES AT IT.
HERE HUNG THOSE LIPS THAT I HAVE KISSED I KNOW NOT HOW OFT.
WHERE BE YOUR GIBES NOW? YOUR GAMBOLS, YOUR SONGS, YOUR FLASHES OF MERRIMENT, THAT WERE WONT TO SET THE TABLE ON A ROAR?
NOT ONE NOW, TO MOCK YOUR OWN GRINNING?
QUITE CHAPFALLEN?

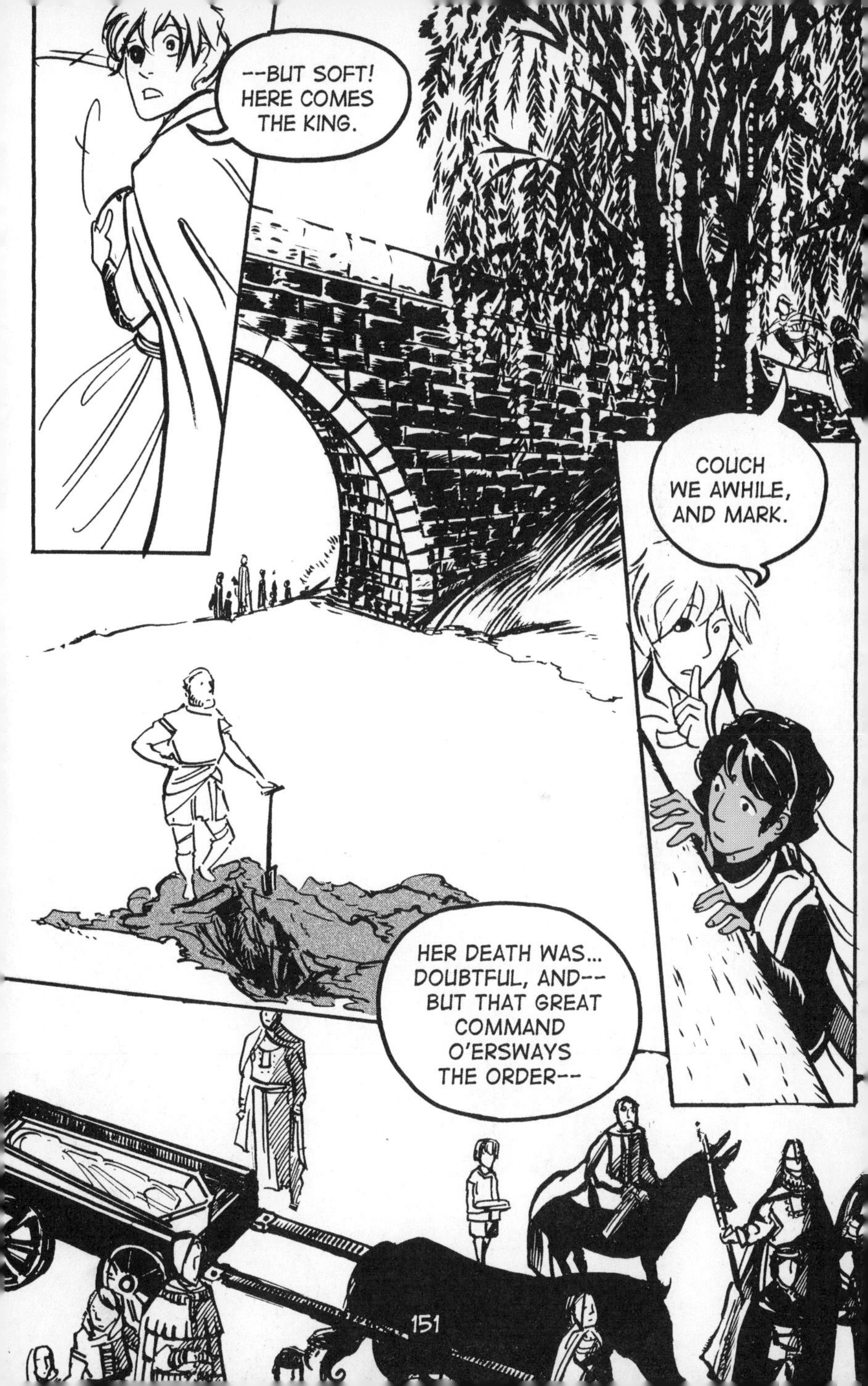
--BUT SOFT! HERE COMES THE KING.
COUCH WE AWHILE, AND MARK.
HER DEATH WAS... DOUBTFUL, AND-- BUT THAT GREAT COMMAND O'ERSWAYS THE ORDER--

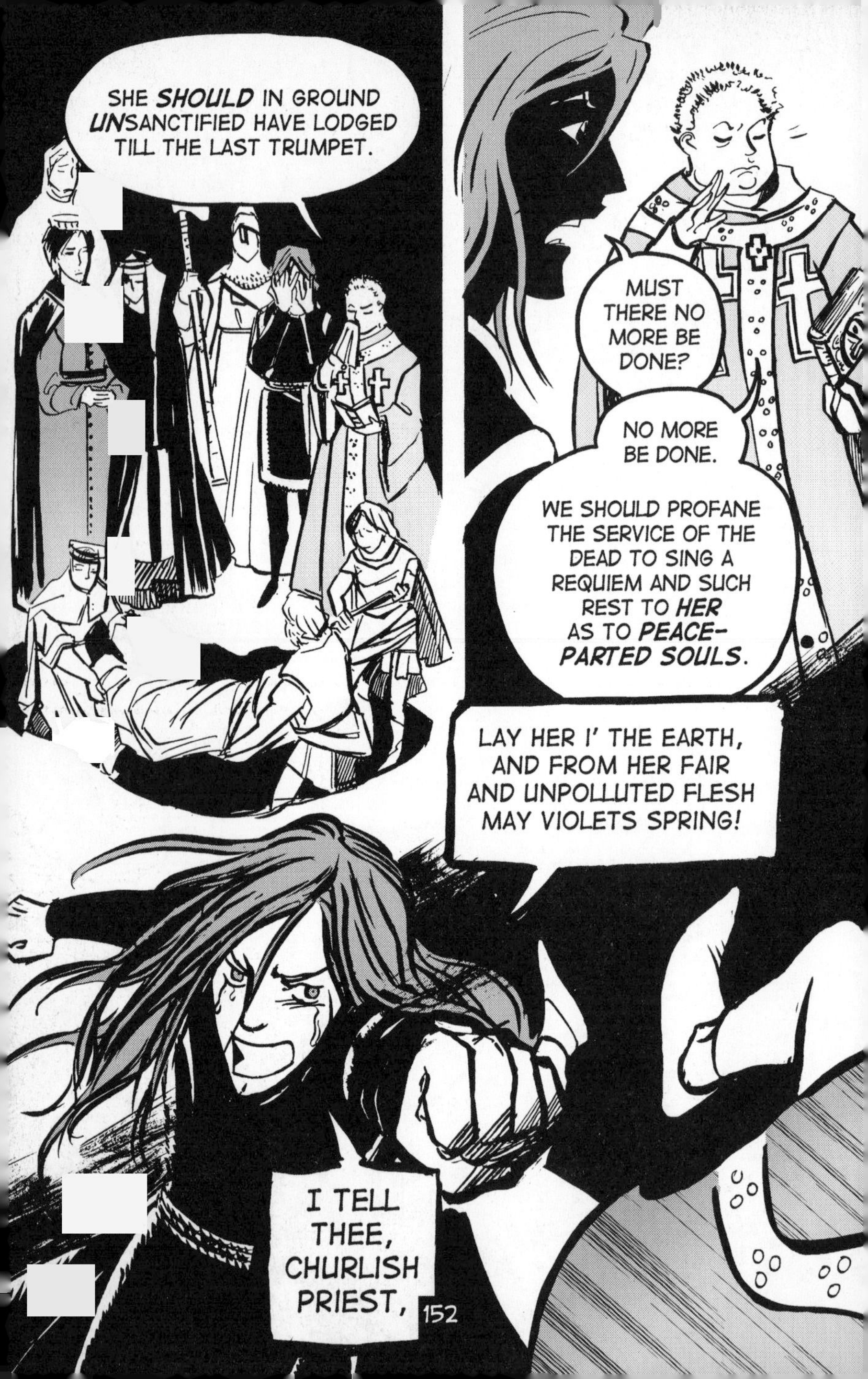
SHE SHOULD IN GROUND UNSANCTIFIED HAVE LODGED TILL THE LAST TRUMPET.
MUST THERE NO MORE BE DONE?
NO MORE BE DONE.
WE SHOULD PROFANE THE SERVICE OF THE DEAD TO SING A REQUIEM AND SUCH REST TO HER AS TO PEACE-PARTED SOULS.
LAY HER I' THE EARTH, AND FROM HER FAIR AND UNPOLLUTED FLESH MAY VIOLETS SPRING!
I TELL THEE, CHURLISH PRIEST,

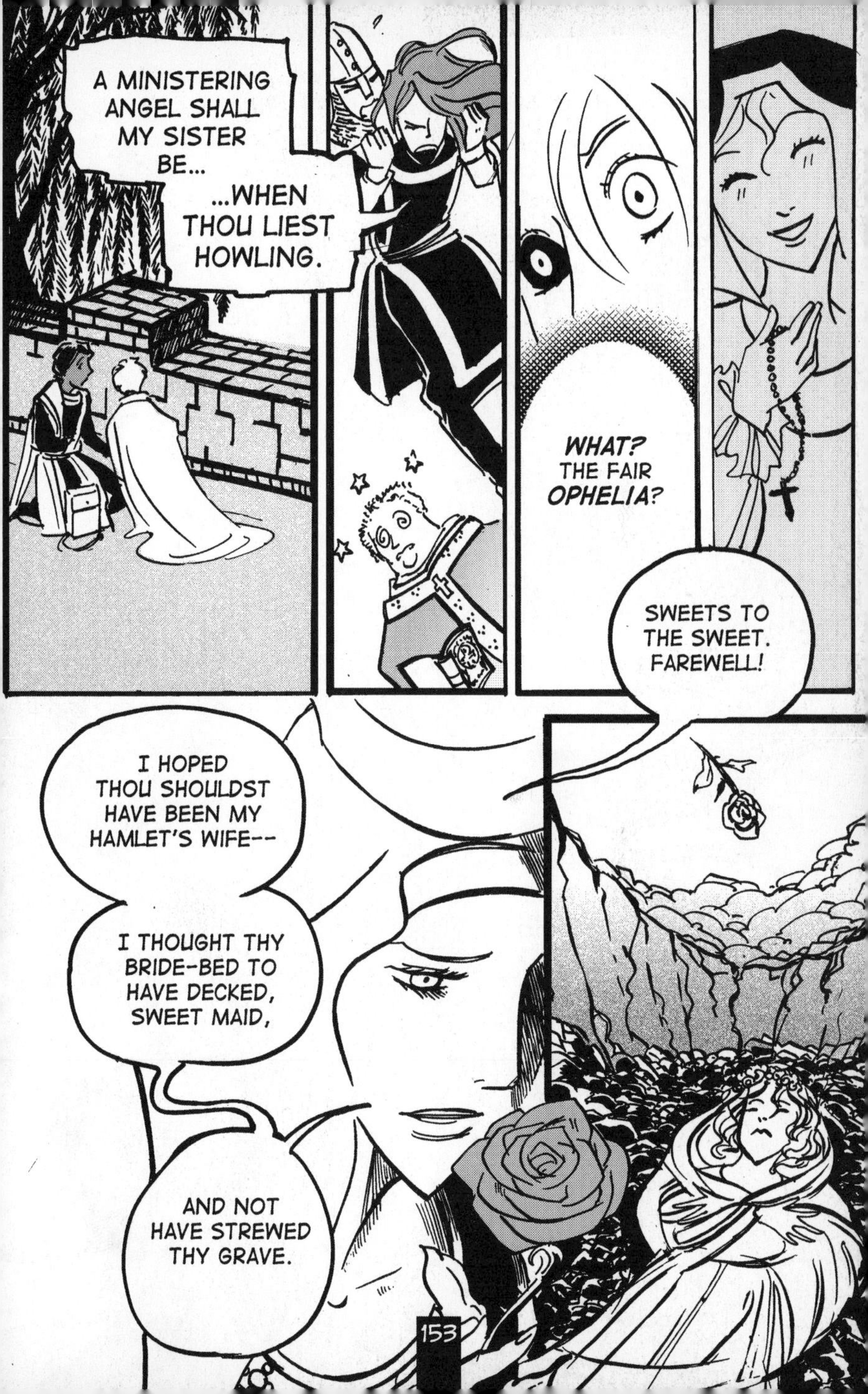
A MINISTERING ANGEL SHALL MY SISTER BE...
...WHEN THOU LIEST HOWLING.
WHAT? THE FAIR *OPHELIA?*
SWEETS TO THE SWEET. FAREWELL!
I HOPED THOU SHOULDST HAVE BEEN MY HAMLET'S WIFE--
I THOUGHT THY BRIDE-BED TO HAVE DECKED, SWEET MAID,
AND NOT HAVE STREWED THY GRAVE.

O, TREBLE WOE FALL TEN TIMES TREBLE ON THAT CURSED HEAD, WHOSE WICKED DEED THY MOST INGENIOUS SENSE DEPRIVED THEE OF!
HOLD OFF THE EARTH AWHILE, TILL I HAVE CAUGHT HER ONCE MORE IN MINE ARMS.
NOW PILE YOUR DUST UPON THE QUICK AND DEAD, TILL OF THIS *FLAT* A *MOUNTAIN* YOU HAVE MADE!
THIS IS I,

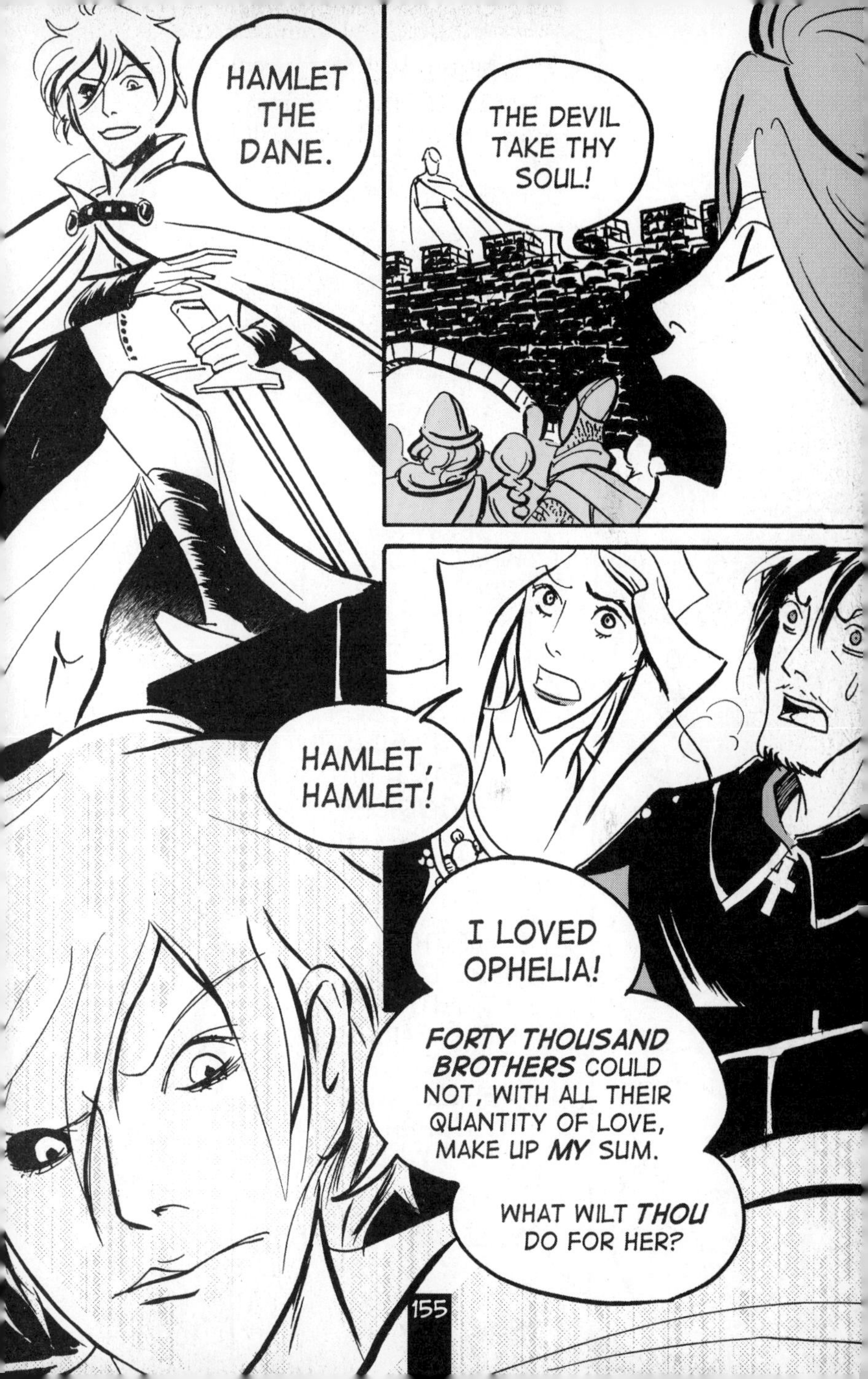
HAMLET THE DANE.
THE DEVIL TAKE THY SOUL!
HAMLET, HAMLET!
I LOVED OPHELIA!
FORTY THOUSAND BROTHERS COULD NOT, WITH ALL THEIR QUANTITY OF LOVE, MAKE UP MY SUM.
WHAT WILT THOU DO FOR HER?

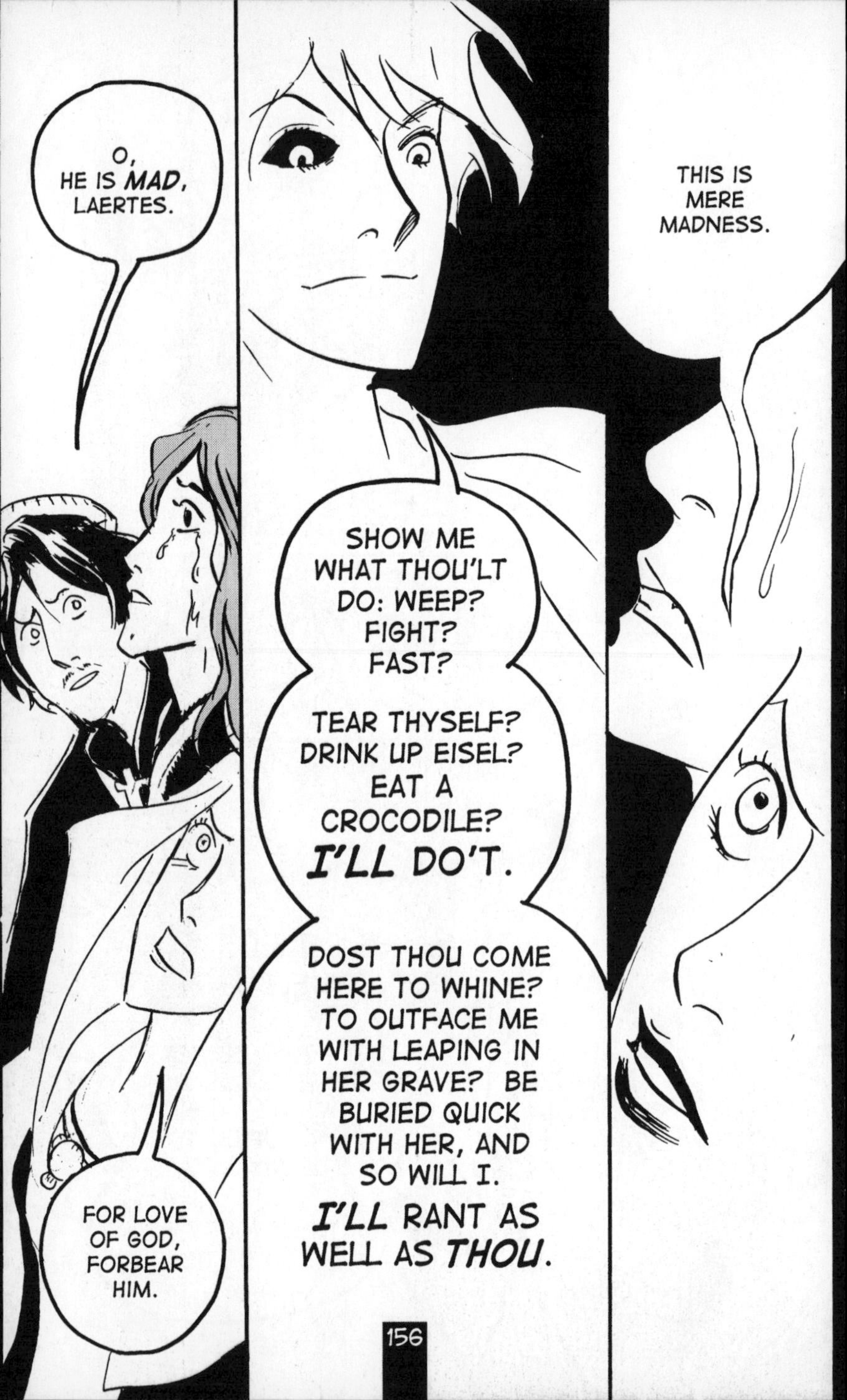

O, HE IS ***MAD***, LAERTES.
FOR LOVE OF GOD, FORBEAR HIM.
SHOW ME WHAT THOU'LT DO: WEEP? FIGHT? FAST?
TEAR THYSELF? DRINK UP EISEL? EAT A CROCODILE? ***I'LL*** DO'T.
DOST THOU COME HERE TO WHINE? TO OUTFACE ME WITH LEAPING IN HER GRAVE? BE BURIED QUICK WITH HER, AND SO WILL I.
I'LL RANT AS WELL AS ***THOU***.
THIS IS MERE MADNESS.

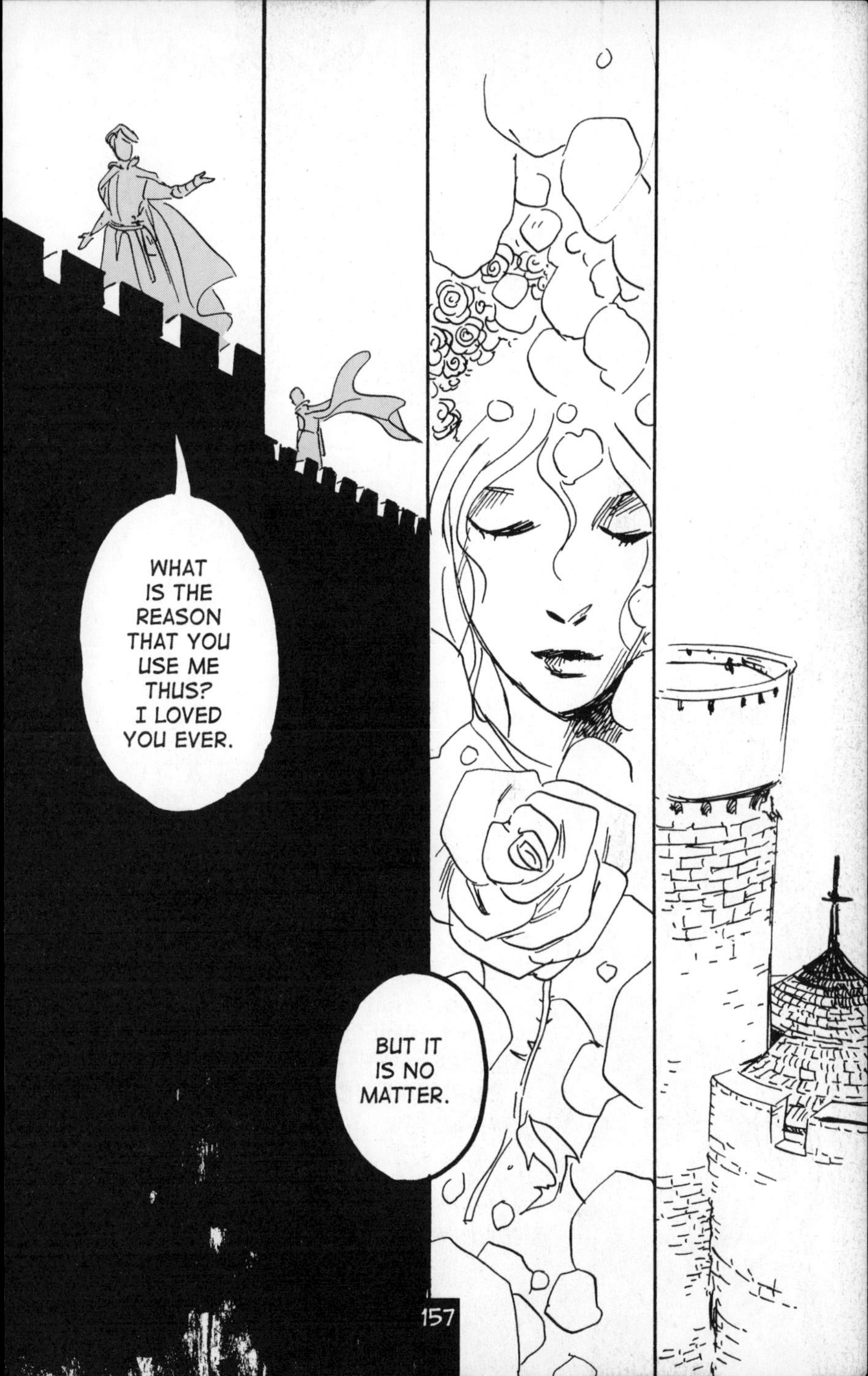
WHAT IS THE REASON THAT YOU USE ME THUS? I LOVED YOU EVER.
BUT IT IS NO MATTER.

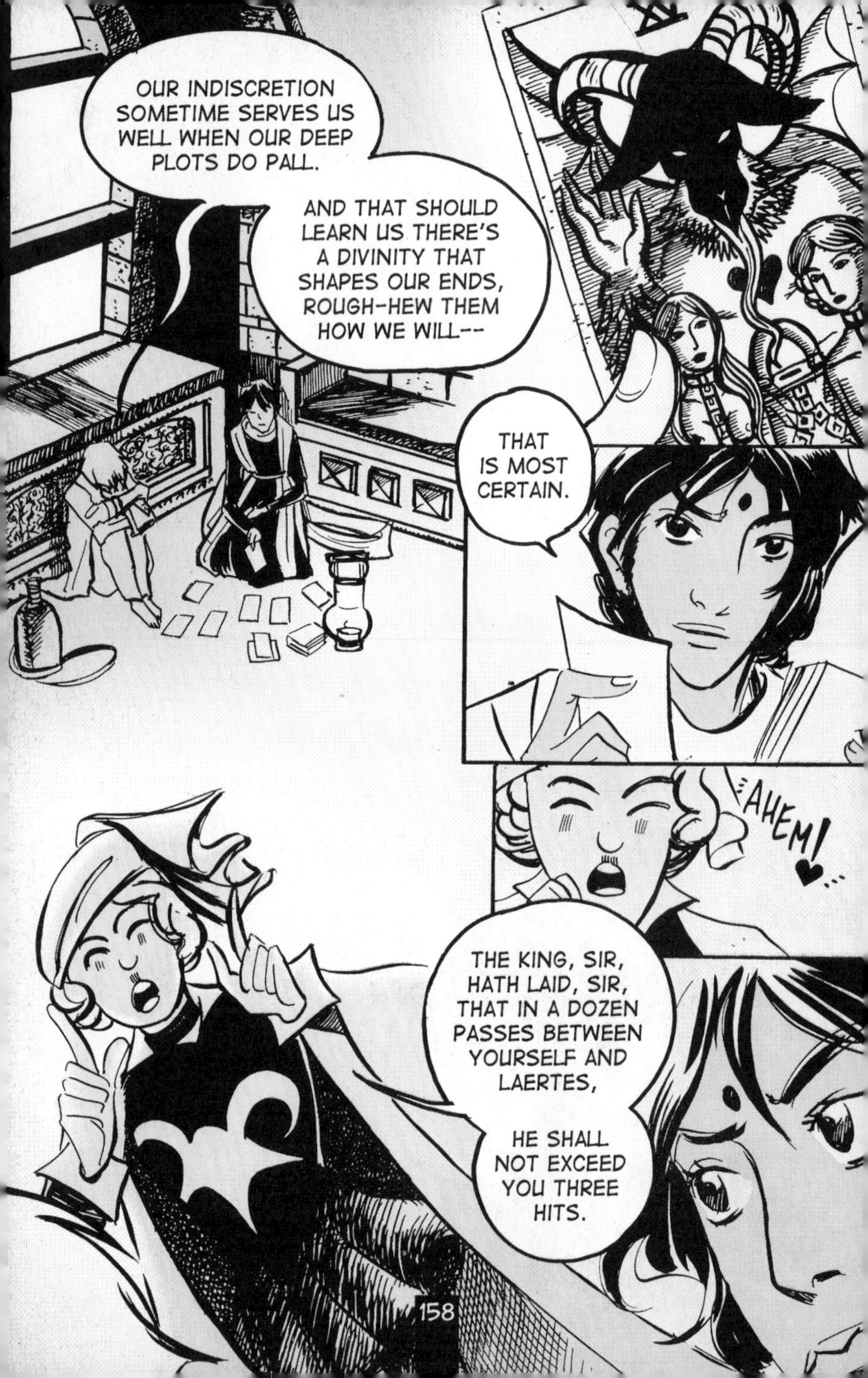
OUR INDISCRETION SOMETIME SERVES US WELL WHEN OUR DEEP PLOTS DO PALL.
AND THAT SHOULD LEARN US THERE'S A DIVINITY THAT SHAPES OUR ENDS, ROUGH-HEW THEM HOW WE WILL--
THAT IS MOST CERTAIN.
AHEM!
THE KING, SIR, HATH LAID, SIR, THAT IN A DOZEN PASSES BETWEEN YOURSELF AND LAERTES,
HE SHALL NOT EXCEED YOU THREE HITS.

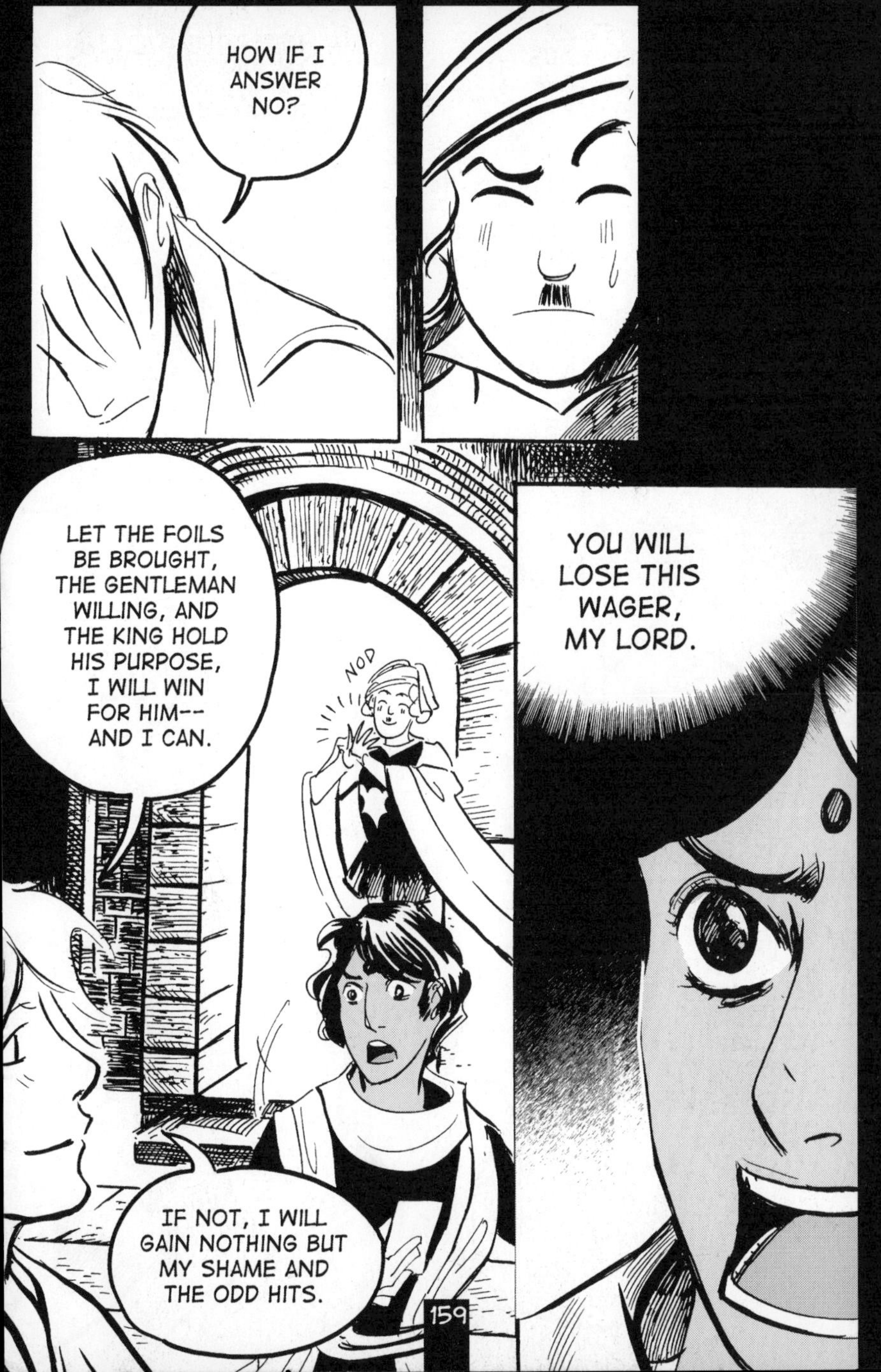
HOW IF I ANSWER NO?
LET THE FOILS BE BROUGHT, THE GENTLEMAN WILLING, AND THE KING HOLD HIS PURPOSE, I WILL WIN FOR HIM-- AND I CAN.
NOD
IF NOT, I WILL GAIN NOTHING BUT MY SHAME AND THE ODD HITS.
YOU WILL LOSE THIS WAGER, MY LORD.

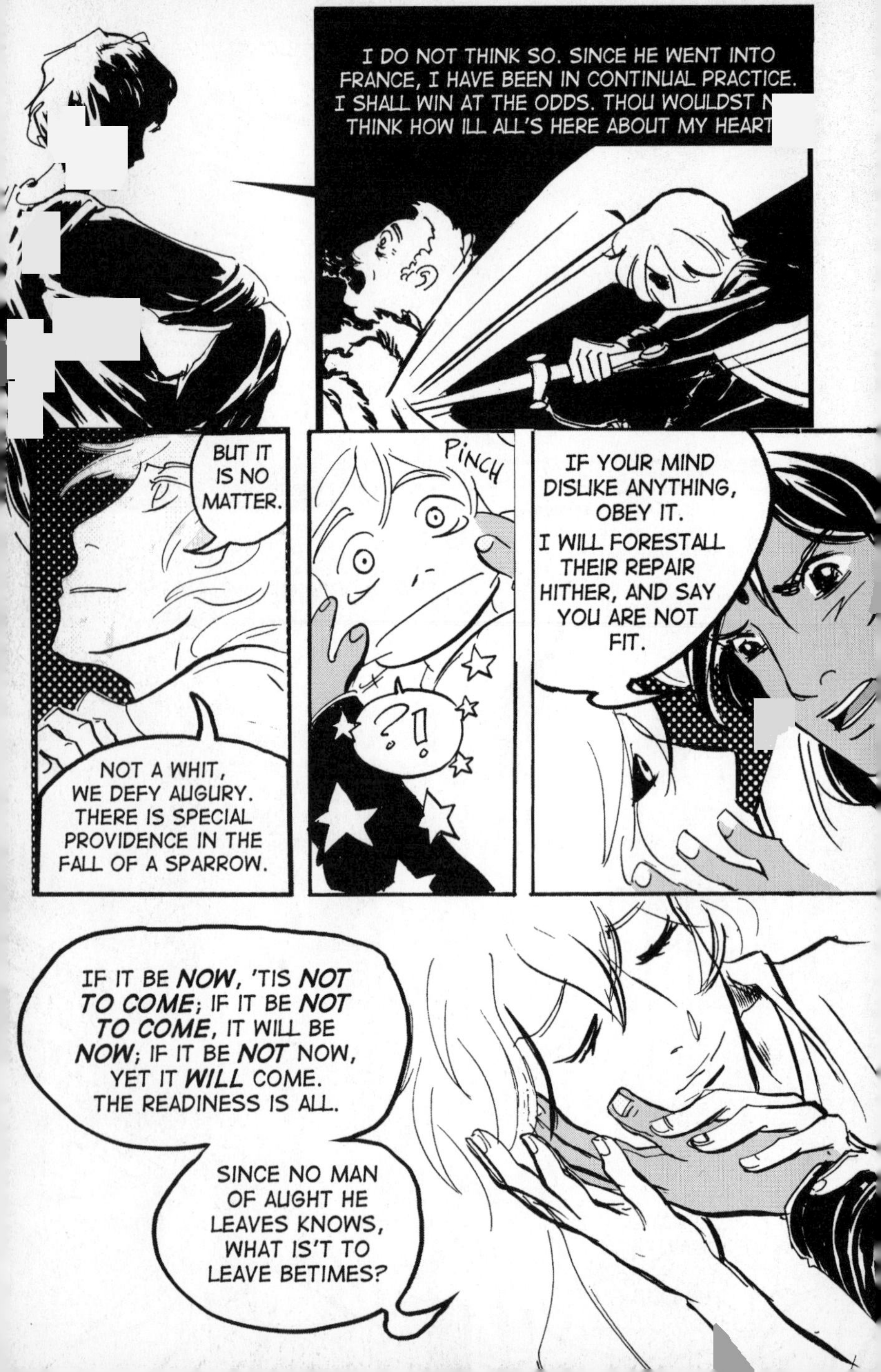
I DO NOT THINK SO. SINCE HE WENT INTO FRANCE, I HAVE BEEN IN CONTINUAL PRACTICE. I SHALL WIN AT THE ODDS. THOU WOULDST N THINK HOW ILL ALL'S HERE ABOUT MY HEART
BUT IT IS NO MATTER.
NOT A WHIT, WE DEFY AUGURY. THERE IS SPECIAL PROVIDENCE IN THE FALL OF A SPARROW.
PINCH
?!
IF YOUR MIND DISLIKE ANYTHING, OBEY IT.
I WILL FORESTALL THEIR REPAIR HITHER, AND SAY YOU ARE NOT FIT.
IF IT BE **NOW**, 'TIS **NOT TO COME**; IF IT BE **NOT TO COME**, IT WILL BE **NOW**; IF IT BE **NOT** NOW, YET IT **WILL** COME. THE READINESS IS ALL.
SINCE NO MAN OF AUGHT HE LEAVES KNOWS, WHAT IS'T TO LEAVE BETIMES?

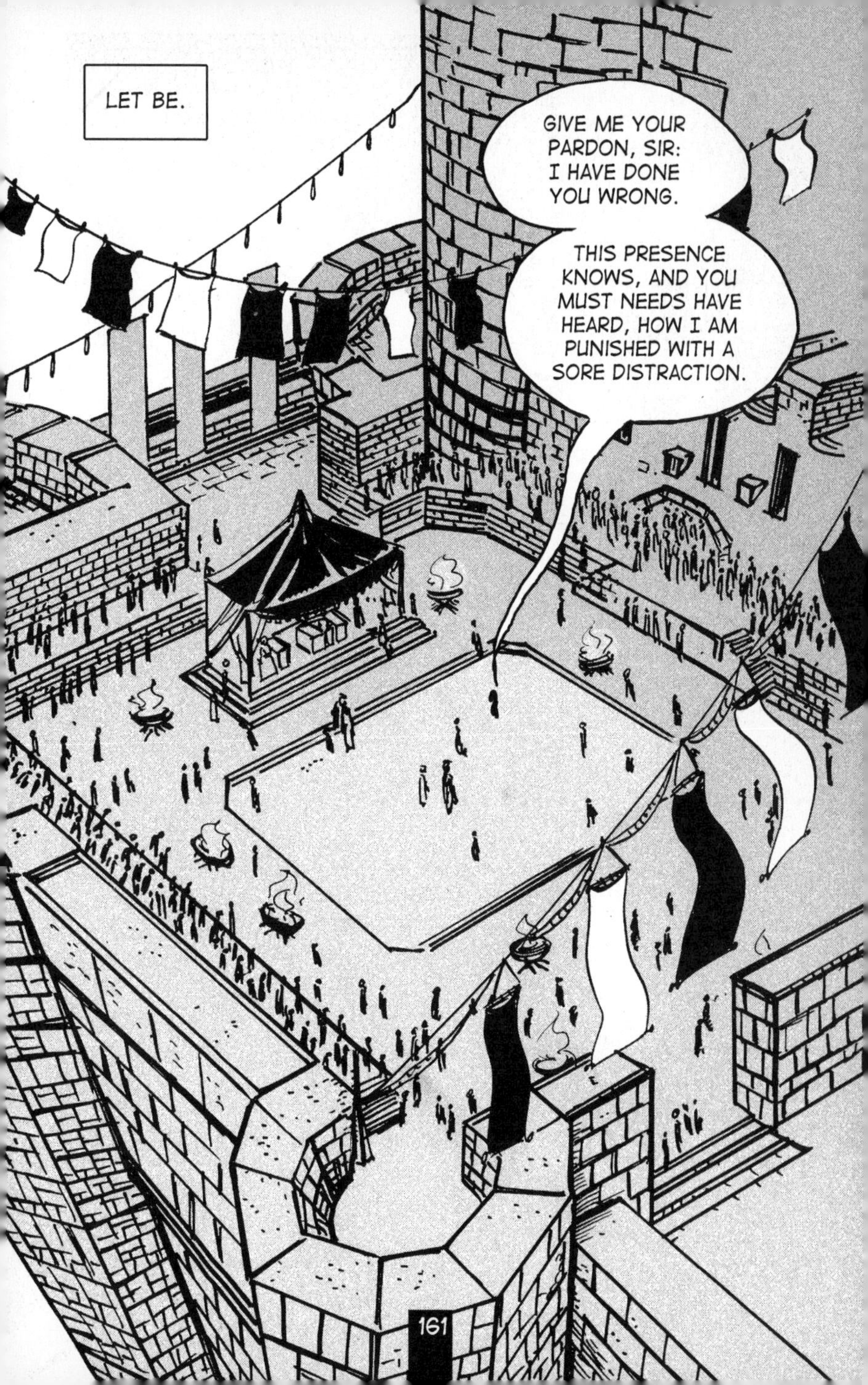
LET BE.
GIVE ME YOUR PARDON, SIR: I HAVE DONE YOU WRONG.
THIS PRESENCE KNOWS, AND YOU MUST NEEDS HAVE HEARD, HOW I AM PUNISHED WITH A SORE DISTRACTION.

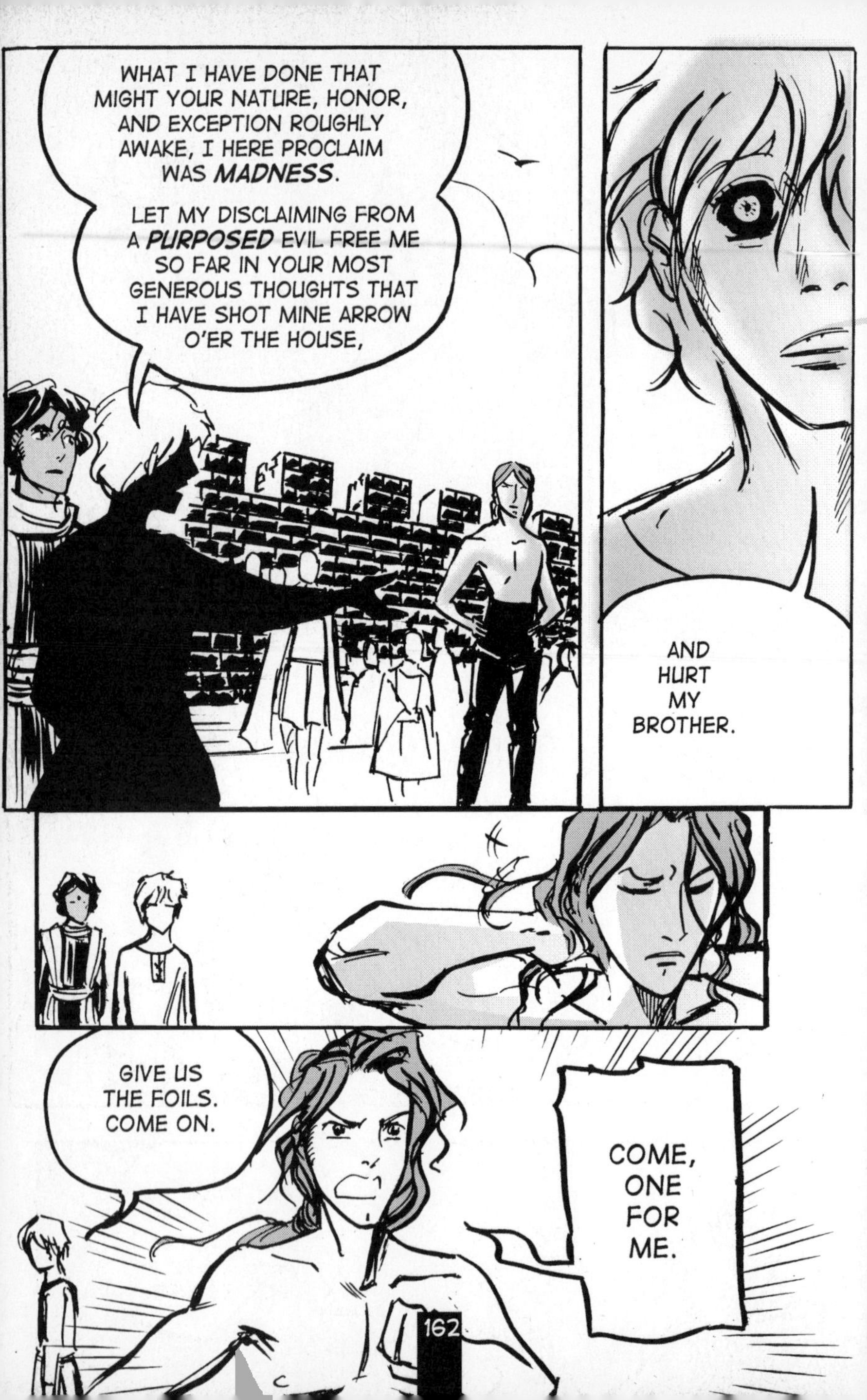
WHAT I HAVE DONE THAT MIGHT YOUR NATURE, HONOR, AND EXCEPTION ROUGHLY AWAKE, I HERE PROCLAIM WAS MADNESS.
LET MY DISCLAIMING FROM A PURPOSED EVIL FREE ME SO FAR IN YOUR MOST GENEROUS THOUGHTS THAT I HAVE SHOT MINE ARROW O'ER THE HOUSE,
AND HURT MY BROTHER.
GIVE US THE FOILS. COME ON.
COME, ONE FOR ME.

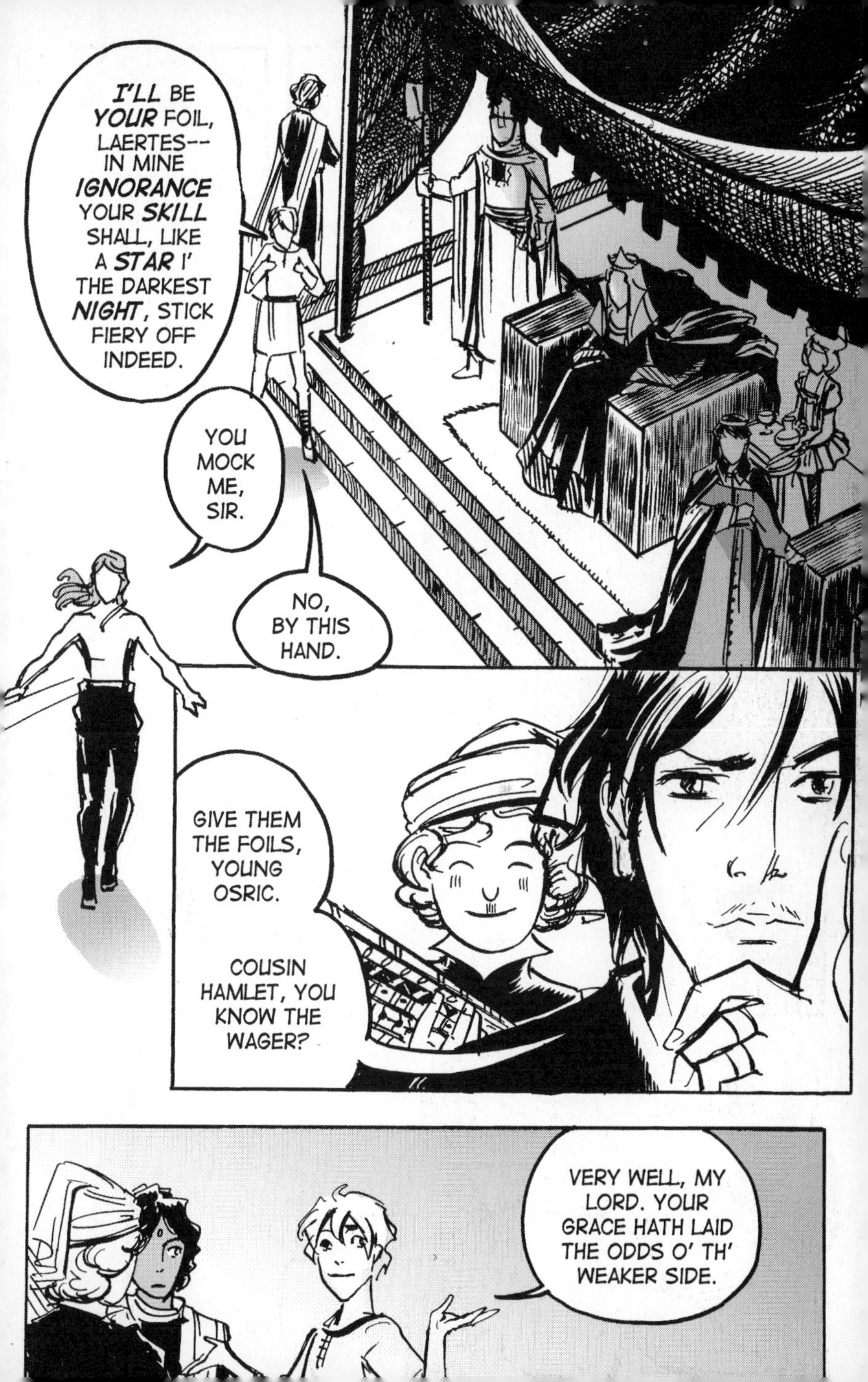
I'LL BE YOUR FOIL, LAERTES-- IN MINE IGNORANCE YOUR SKILL SHALL, LIKE A STAR I' THE DARKEST NIGHT, STICK FIERY OFF INDEED.
YOU MOCK ME, SIR.
NO, BY THIS HAND.
GIVE THEM THE FOILS, YOUNG OSRIC.
COUSIN HAMLET, YOU KNOW THE WAGER?
VERY WELL, MY LORD. YOUR GRACE HATH LAID THE ODDS O' TH' WEAKER SIDE.

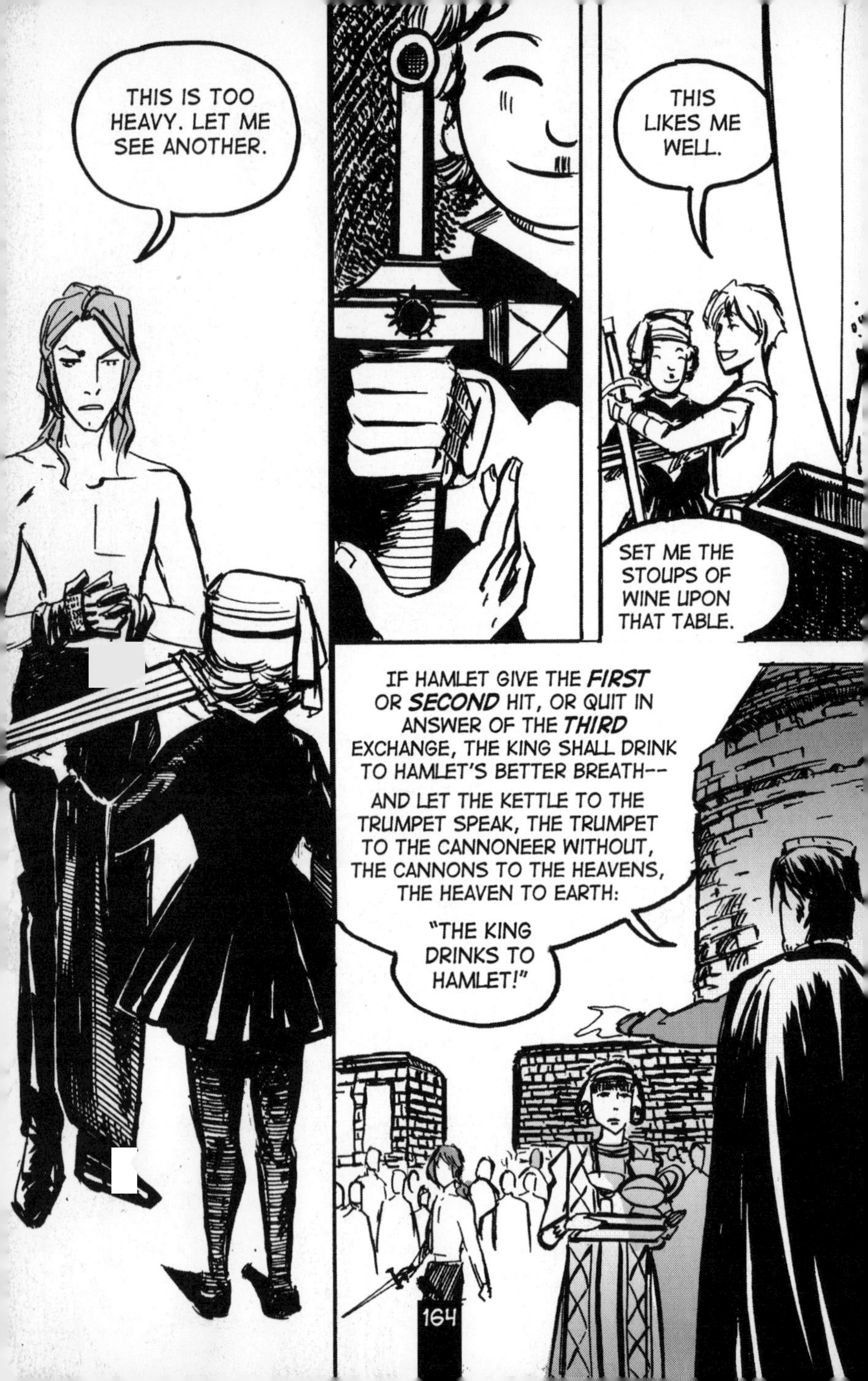
THIS IS TOO HEAVY. LET ME SEE ANOTHER.
THIS LIKES ME WELL.
SET ME THE STOUPS OF WINE UPON THAT TABLE.
IF HAMLET GIVE THE *FIRST* OR *SECOND* HIT, OR QUIT IN ANSWER OF THE *THIRD* EXCHANGE, THE KING SHALL DRINK TO HAMLET'S BETTER BREATH--
AND LET THE KETTLE TO THE TRUMPET SPEAK, THE TRUMPET TO THE CANNONEER WITHOUT, THE CANNONS TO THE HEAVENS, THE HEAVEN TO EARTH:
"THE KING DRINKS TO HAMLET!"

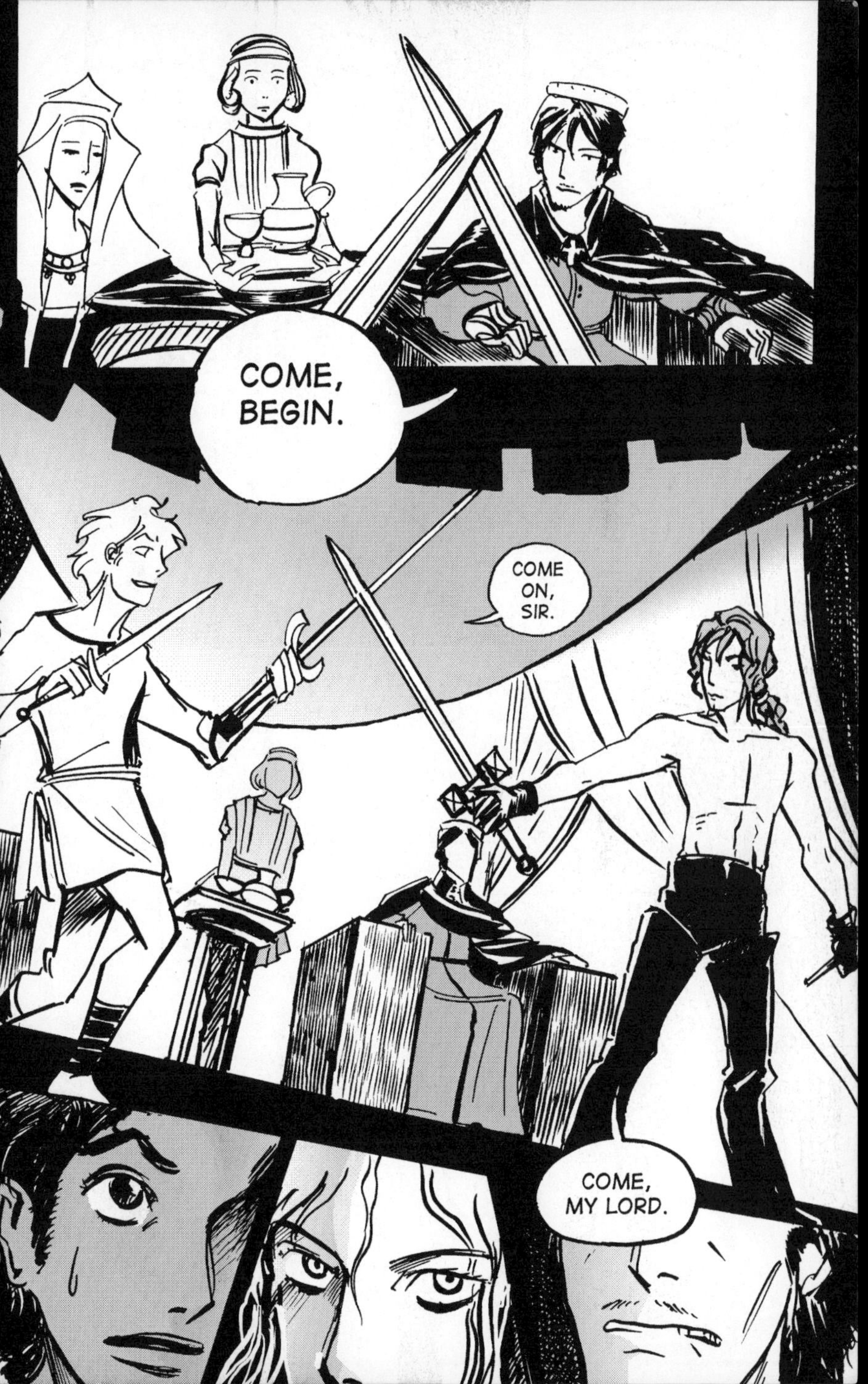
COME, BEGIN.
COME ON, SIR.
COME, MY LORD.

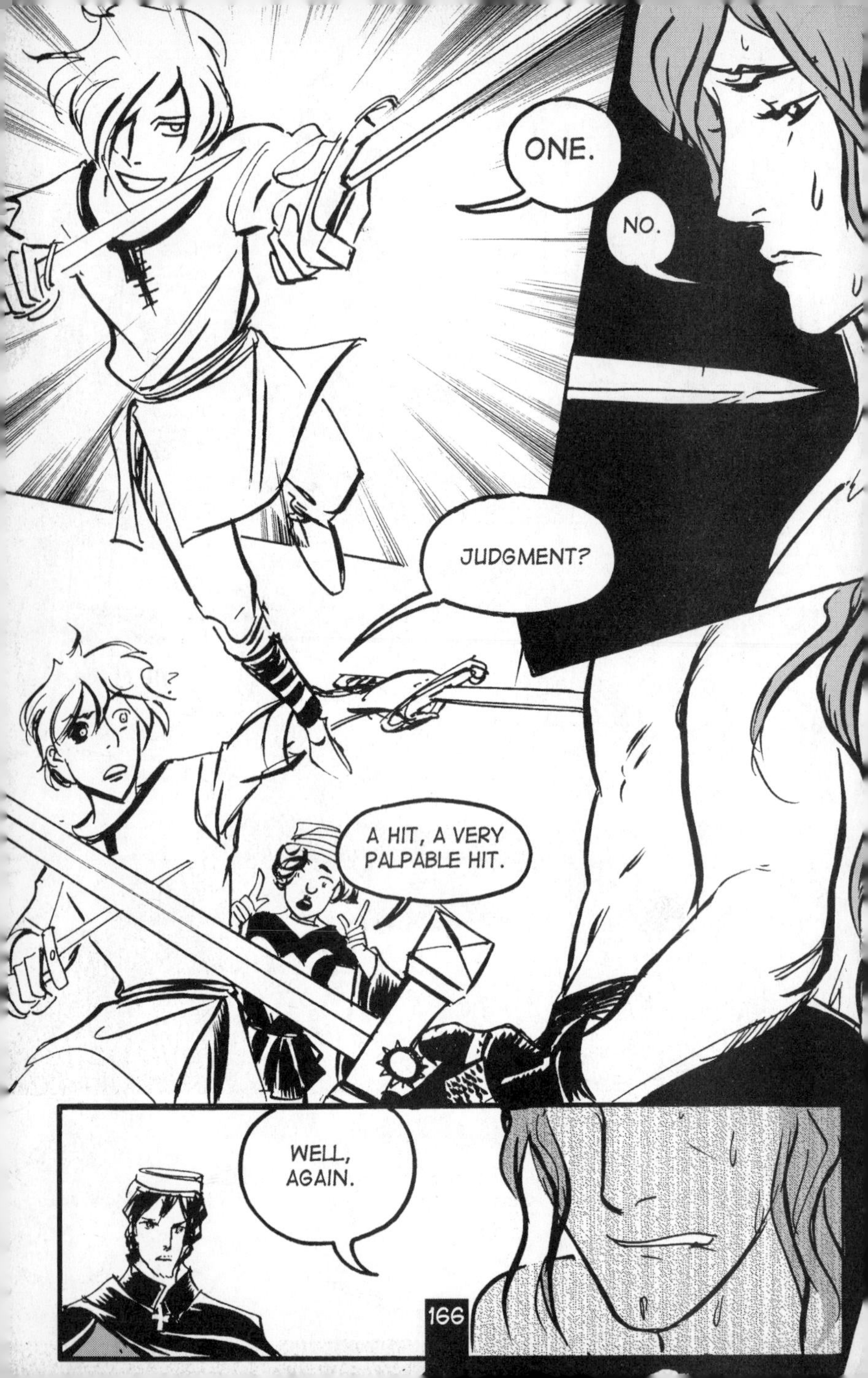
ONE.
NO.
JUDGMENT?
A HIT, A VERY PALPABLE HIT.
WELL, AGAIN.

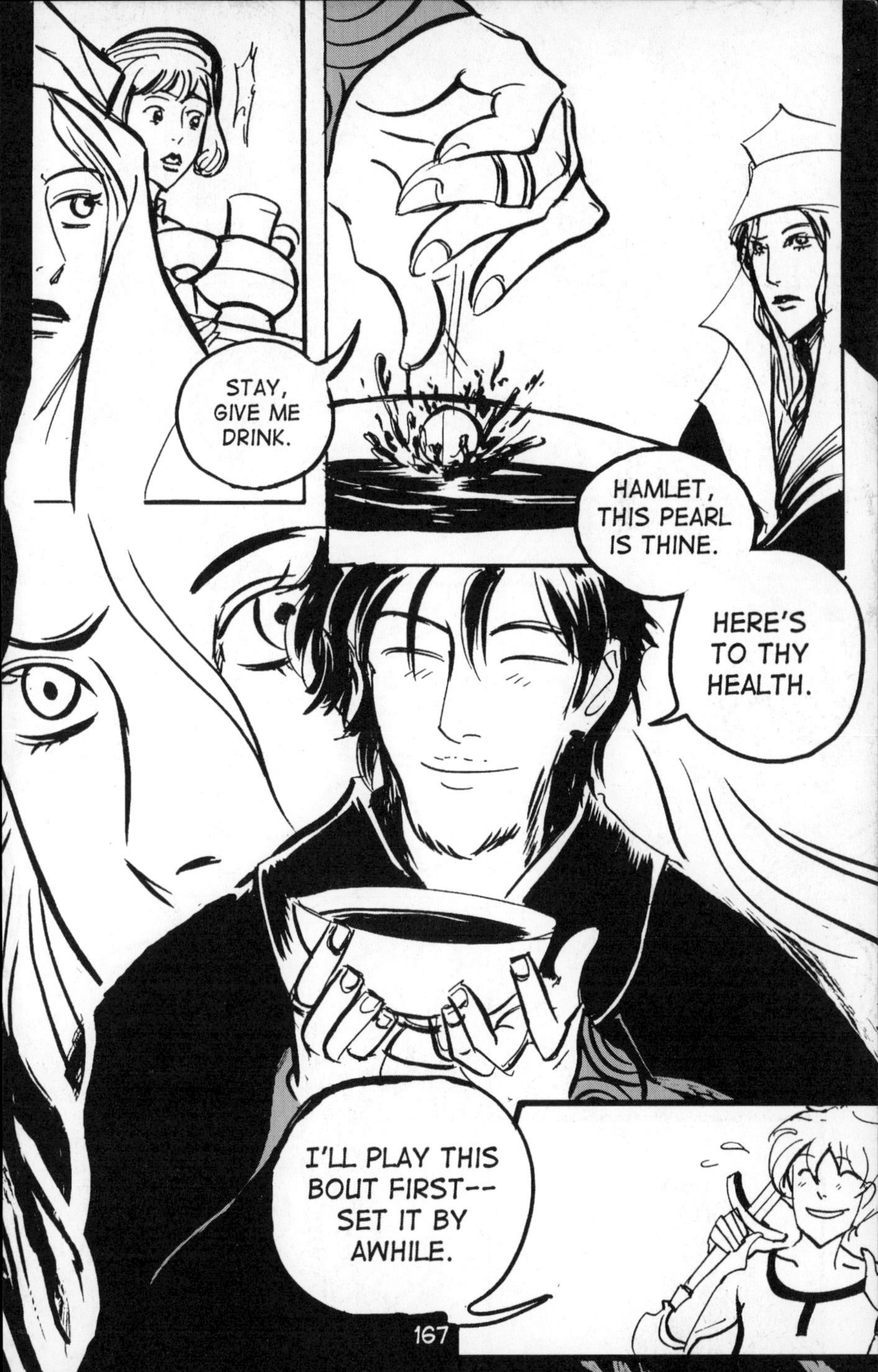
STAY, GIVE ME DRINK.
HAMLET, THIS PEARL IS THINE.
HERE'S TO THY HEALTH.
I'LL PLAY THIS BOUT FIRST-- SET IT BY AWHILE.

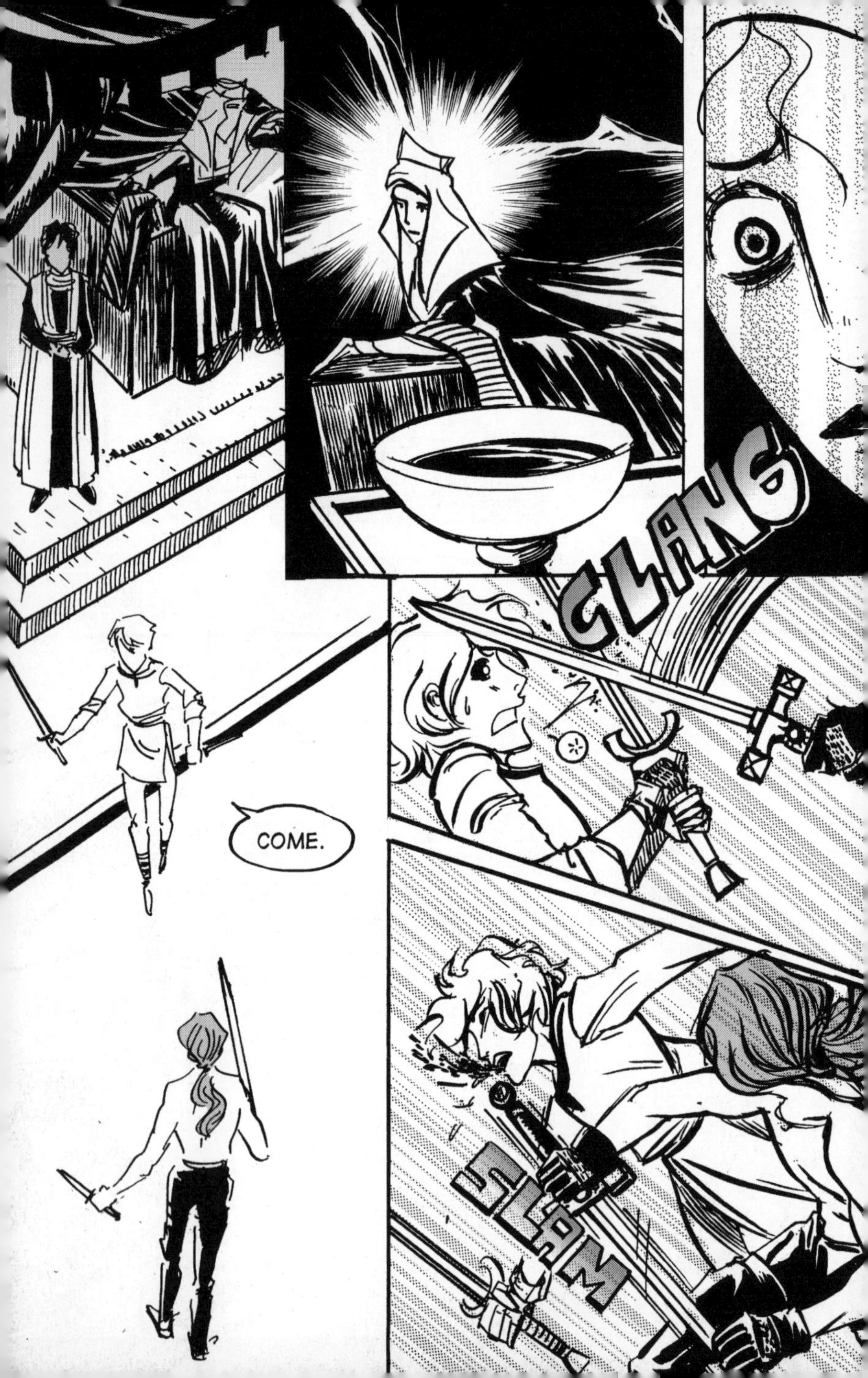
CLANG
COME.
SLAM

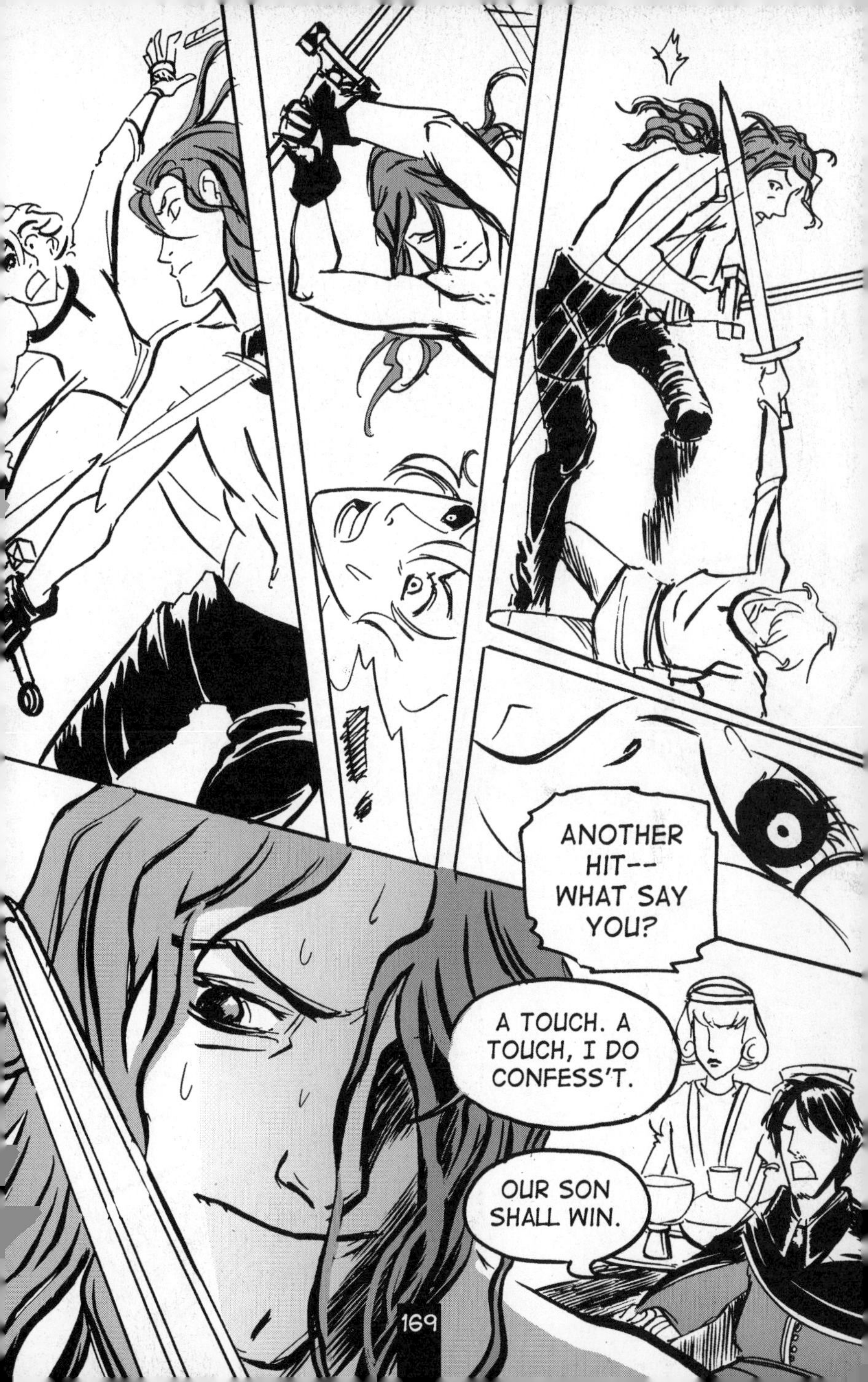
ANOTHER HIT-- WHAT SAY YOU?
A TOUCH. A TOUCH, I DO CONFESS'T.
OUR SON SHALL WIN.

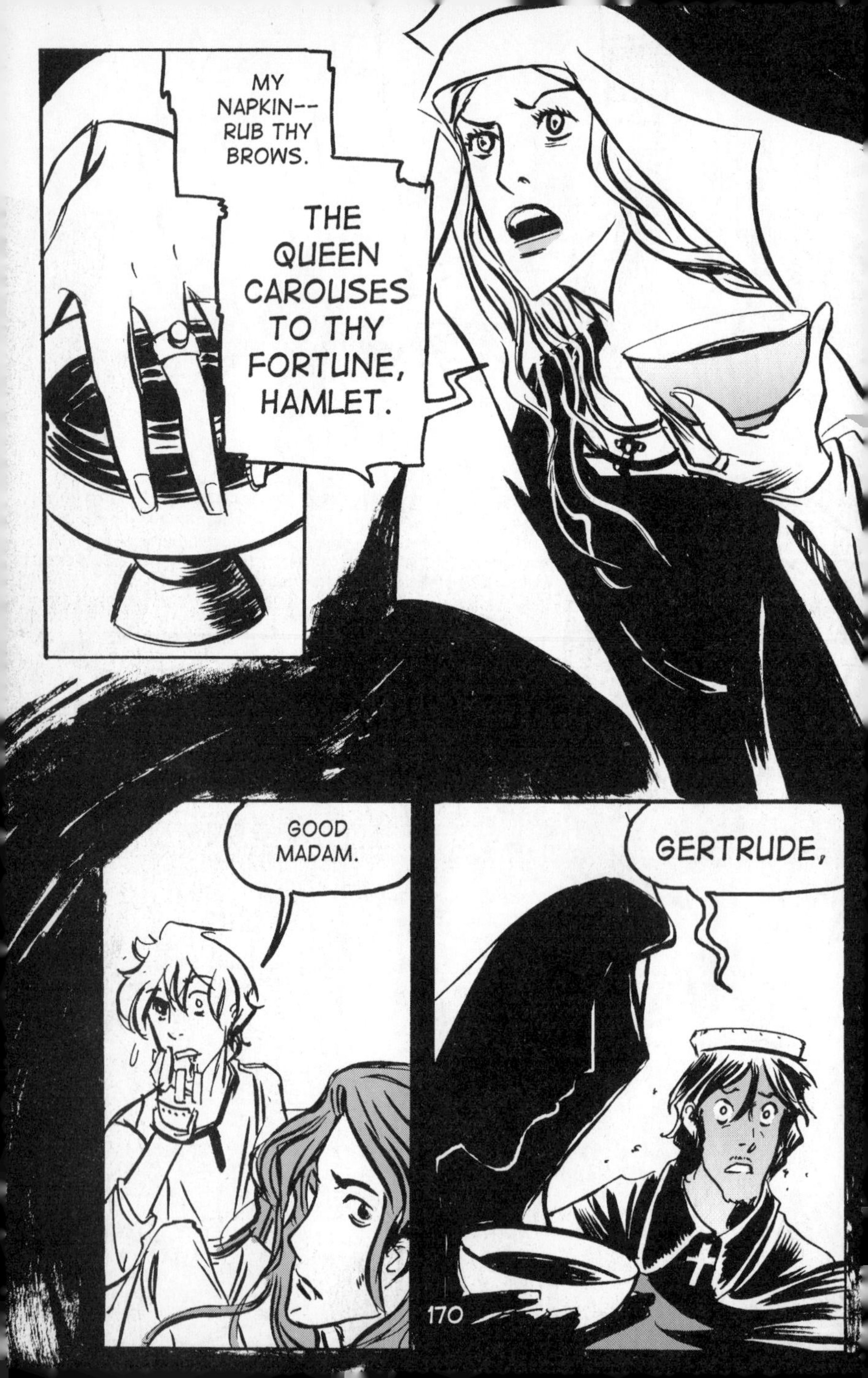
MY NAPKIN-- RUB THY BROWS.
THE QUEEN CAROUSES TO THY FORTUNE, HAMLET.
GOOD MADAM.
GERTRUDE,

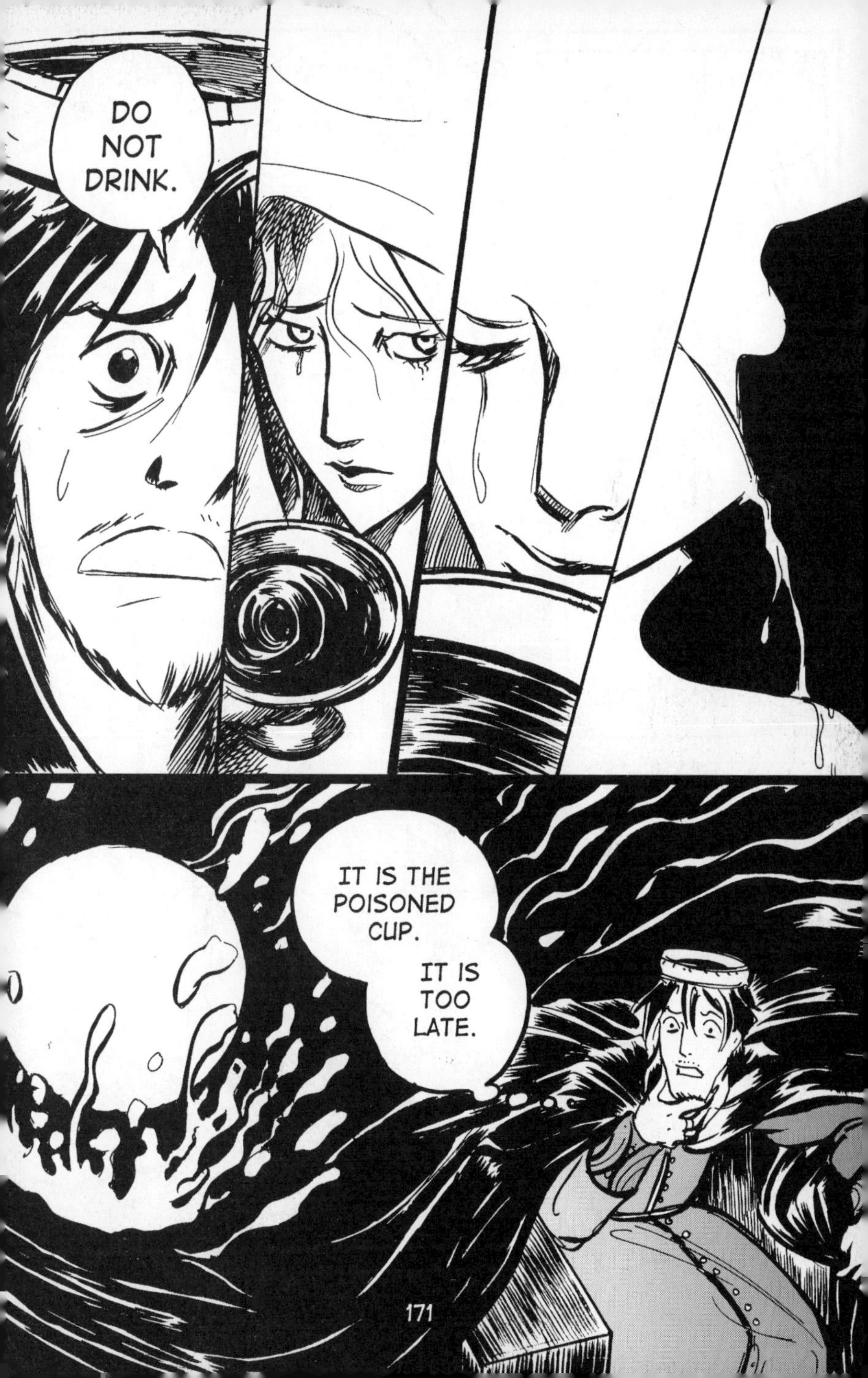
DO NOT DRINK.
IT IS THE POISONED CUP.
IT IS TOO LATE.

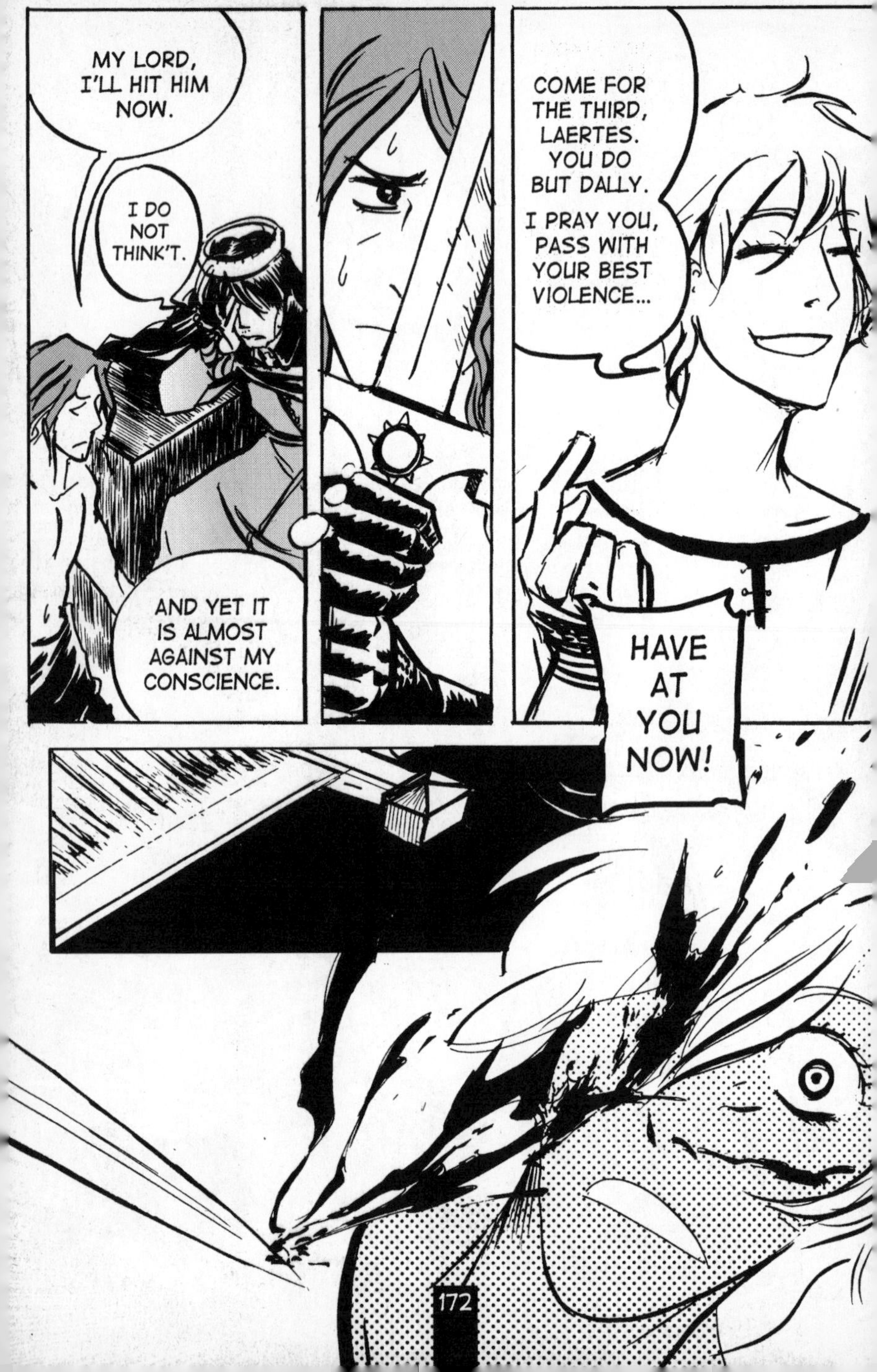
MY LORD, I'LL HIT HIM NOW.
I DO NOT THINK'T.
AND YET IT IS ALMOST AGAINST MY CONSCIENCE.
COME FOR THE THIRD, LAERTES. YOU DO BUT DALLY.
I PRAY YOU, PASS WITH YOUR BEST VIOLENCE...
HAVE AT YOU NOW!

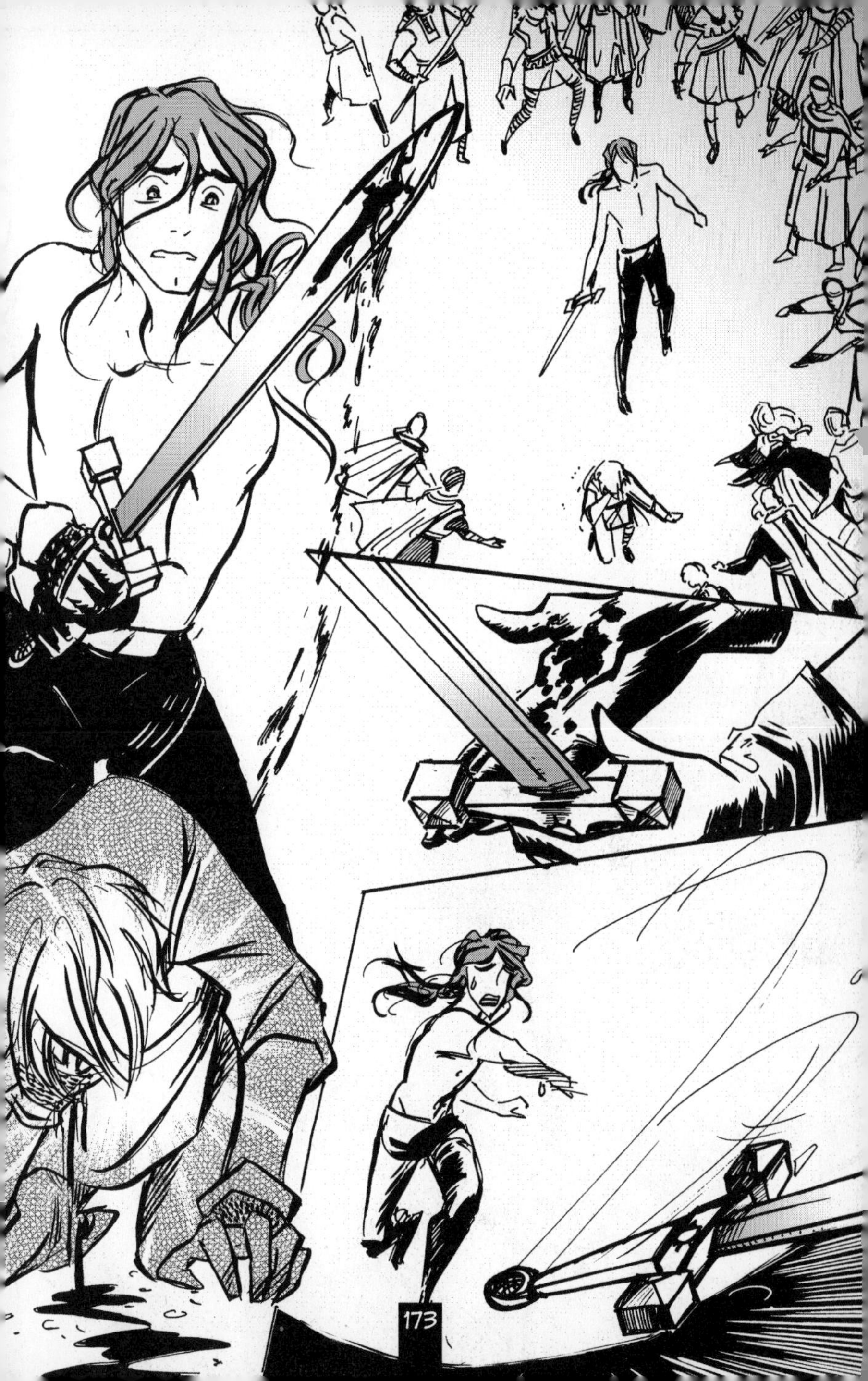

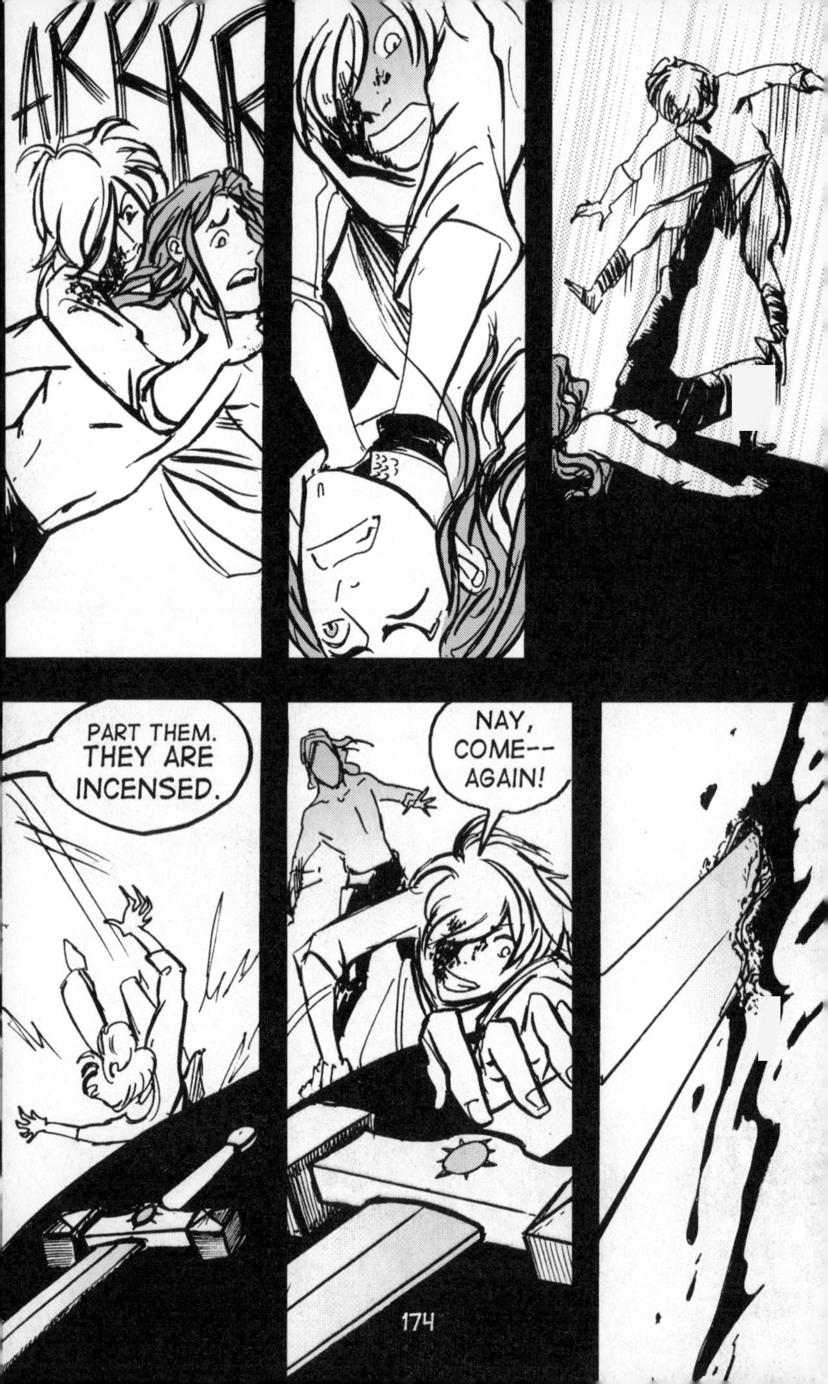
ARRRR
PART THEM. THEY ARE INCENSED.
NAY, COME-- AGAIN!

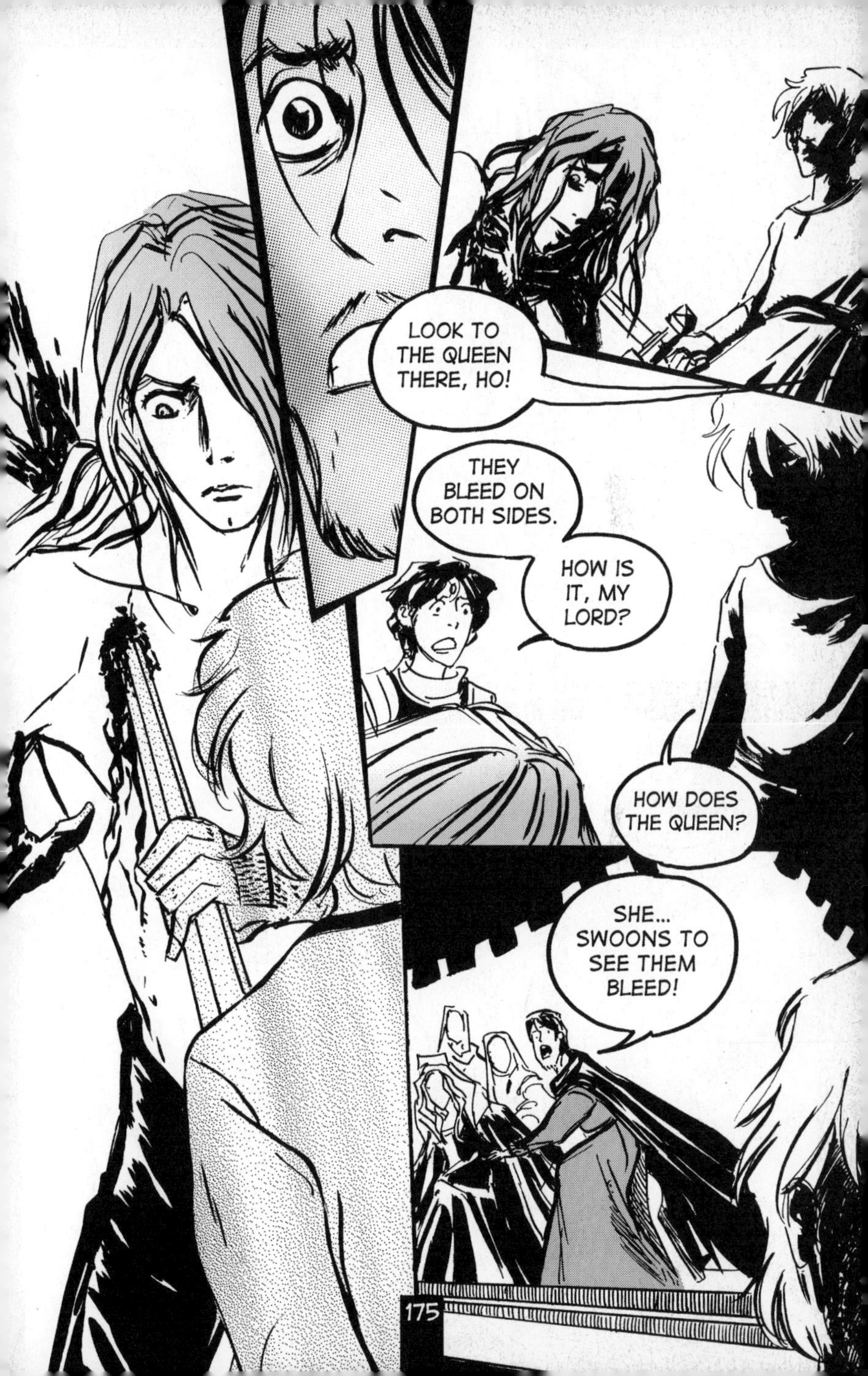
LOOK TO THE QUEEN THERE, HO!
THEY BLEED ON BOTH SIDES.
HOW IS IT, MY LORD?
HOW DOES THE QUEEN?
SHE... SWOONS TO SEE THEM BLEED!

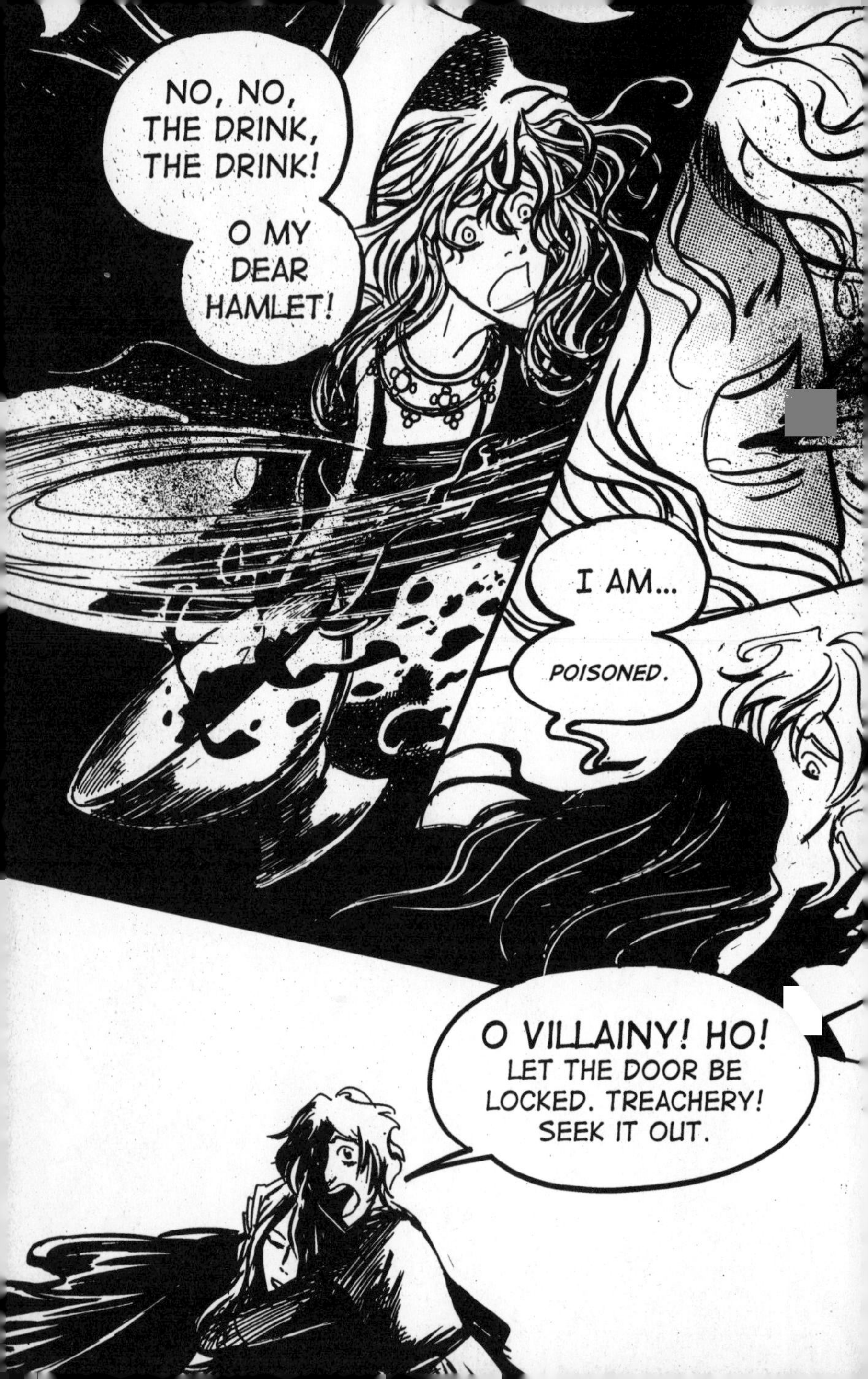
NO, NO, THE DRINK, THE DRINK!
O MY DEAR HAMLET!
I AM...
POISONED.
O VILLAINY! HO! LET THE DOOR BE LOCKED. TREACHERY! SEEK IT OUT.

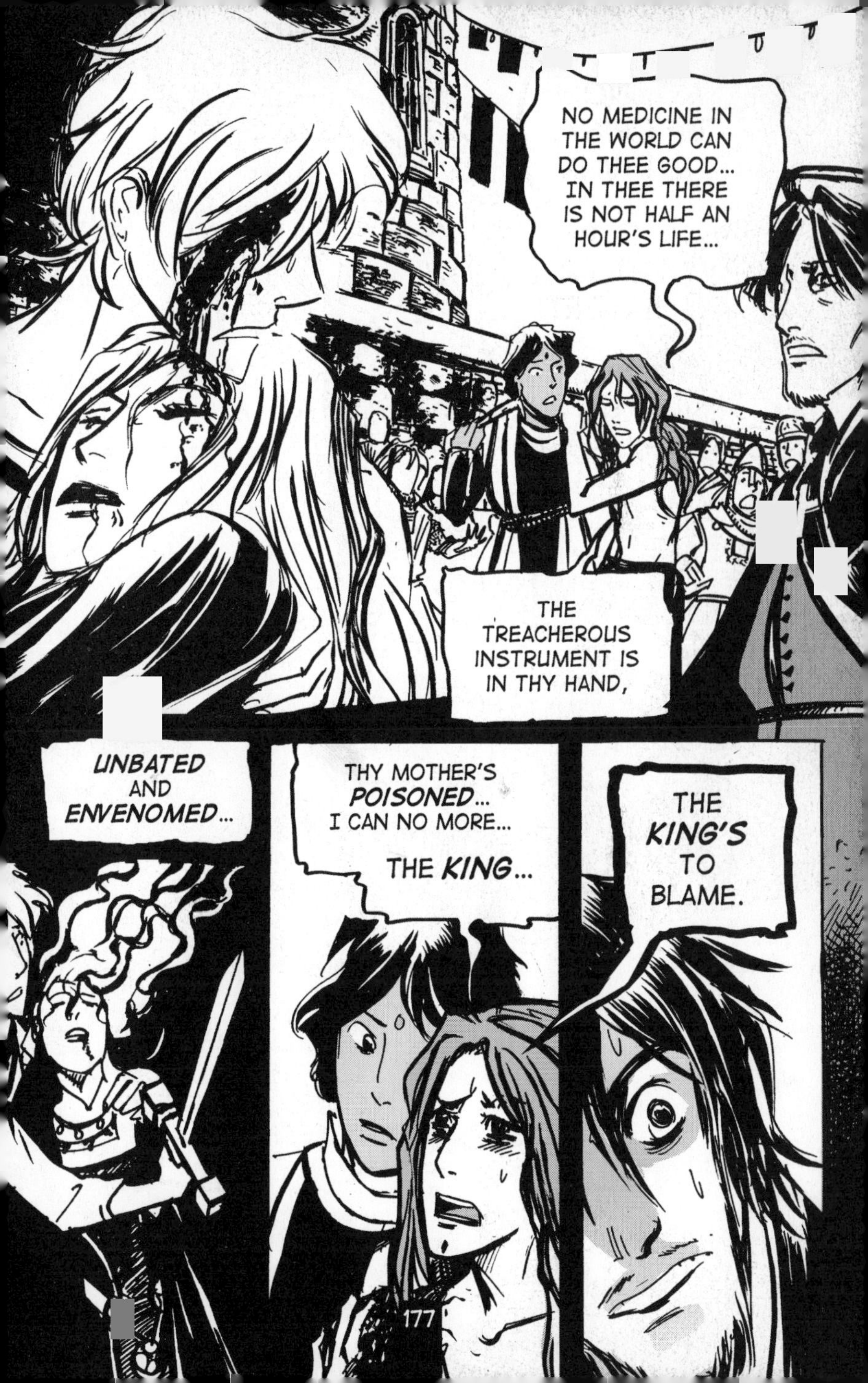
NO MEDICINE IN THE WORLD CAN DO THEE GOOD... IN THEE THERE IS NOT HALF AN HOUR'S LIFE...
THE TREACHEROUS INSTRUMENT IS IN THY HAND,
UNBATED AND ENVENOMED...
THY MOTHER'S POISONED... I CAN NO MORE...
THE KING...
THE KING'S TO BLAME.

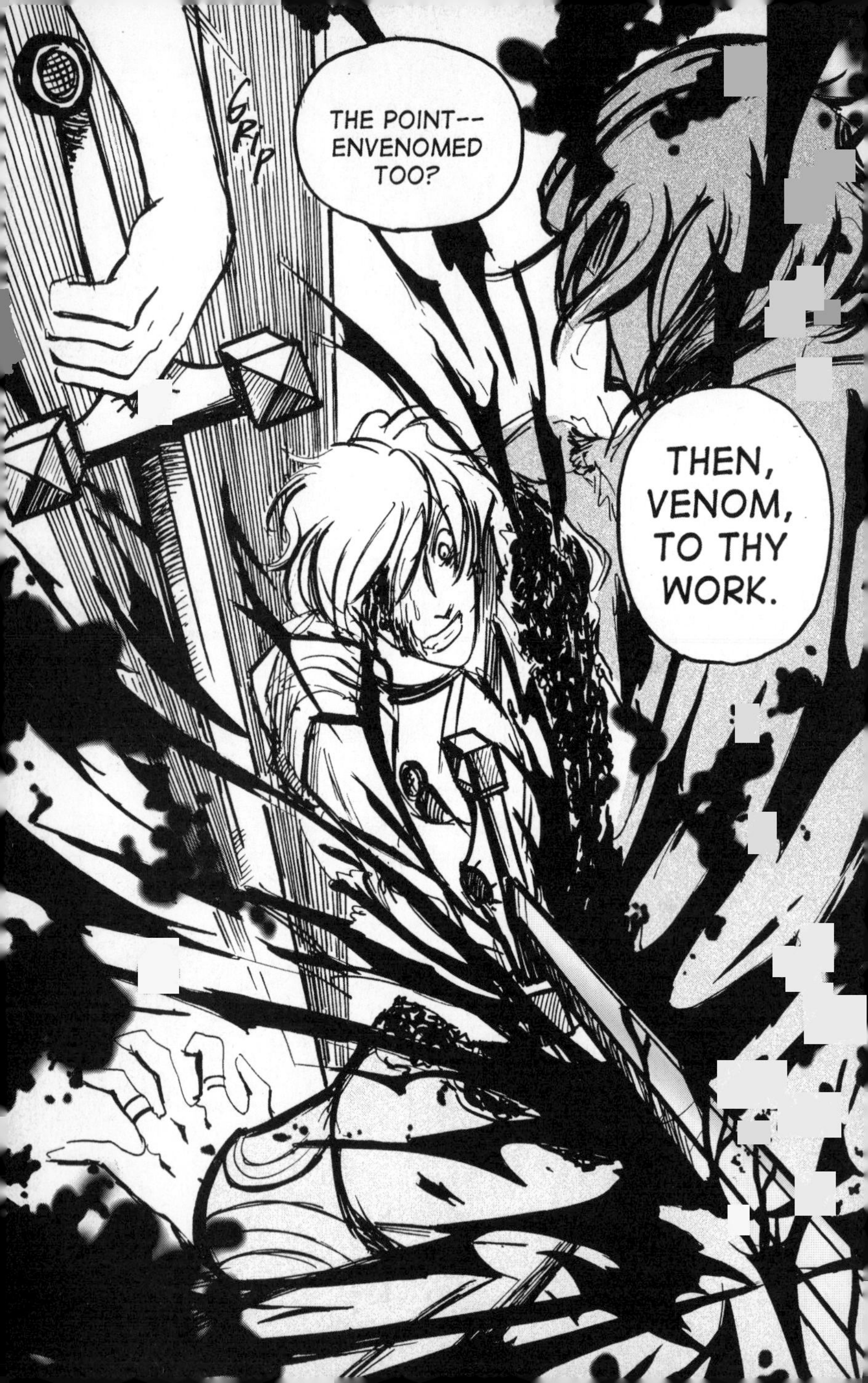
GRIP
THE POINT-- ENVENOMED TOO?
THEN, VENOM, TO THY WORK.

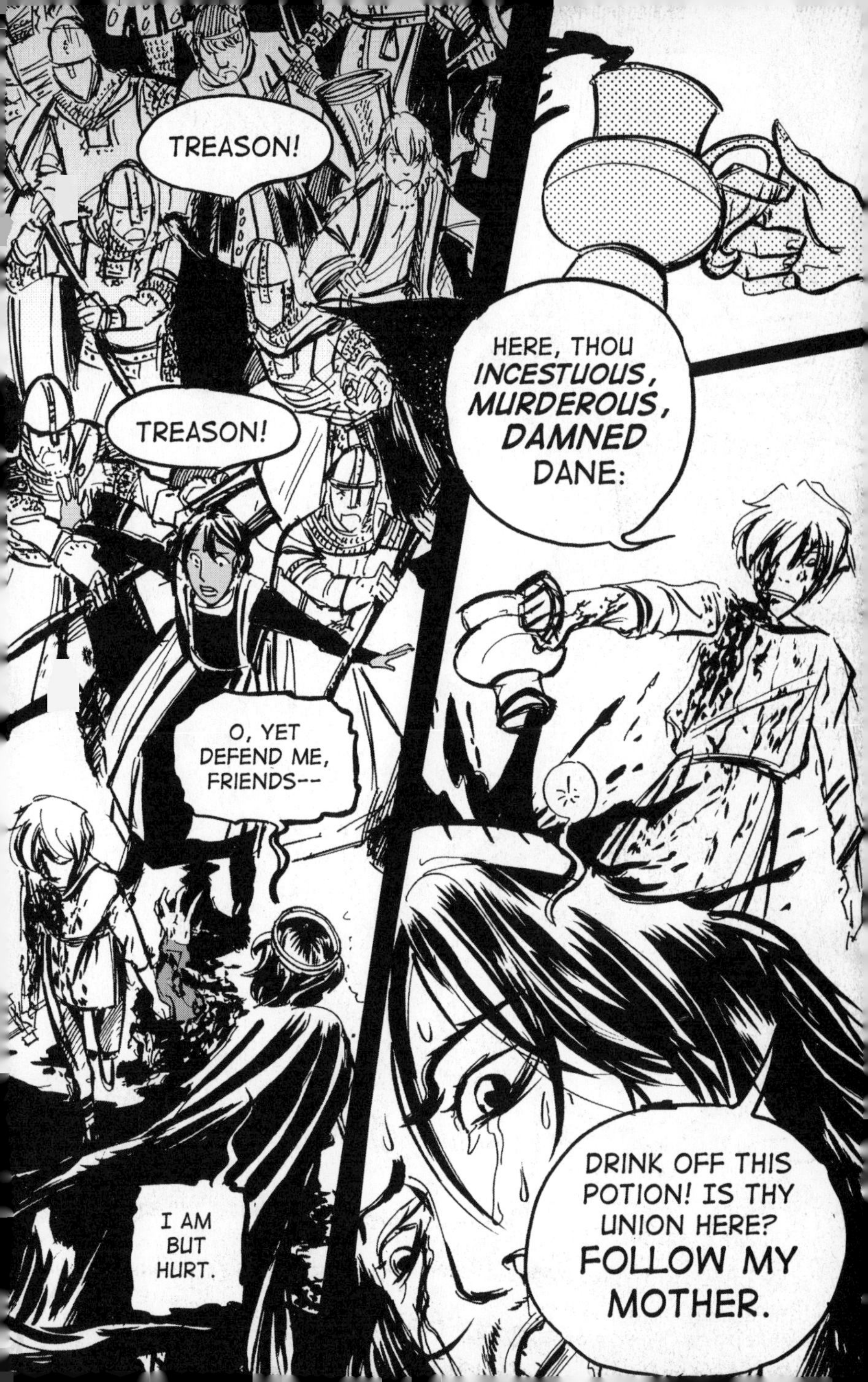
TREASON!
TREASON!
O, YET DEFEND ME, FRIENDS--
I AM BUT HURT.
HERE, THOU INCESTUOUS, MURDEROUS, DAMNED DANE:
DRINK OFF THIS POTION! IS THY UNION HERE? FOLLOW MY MOTHER.

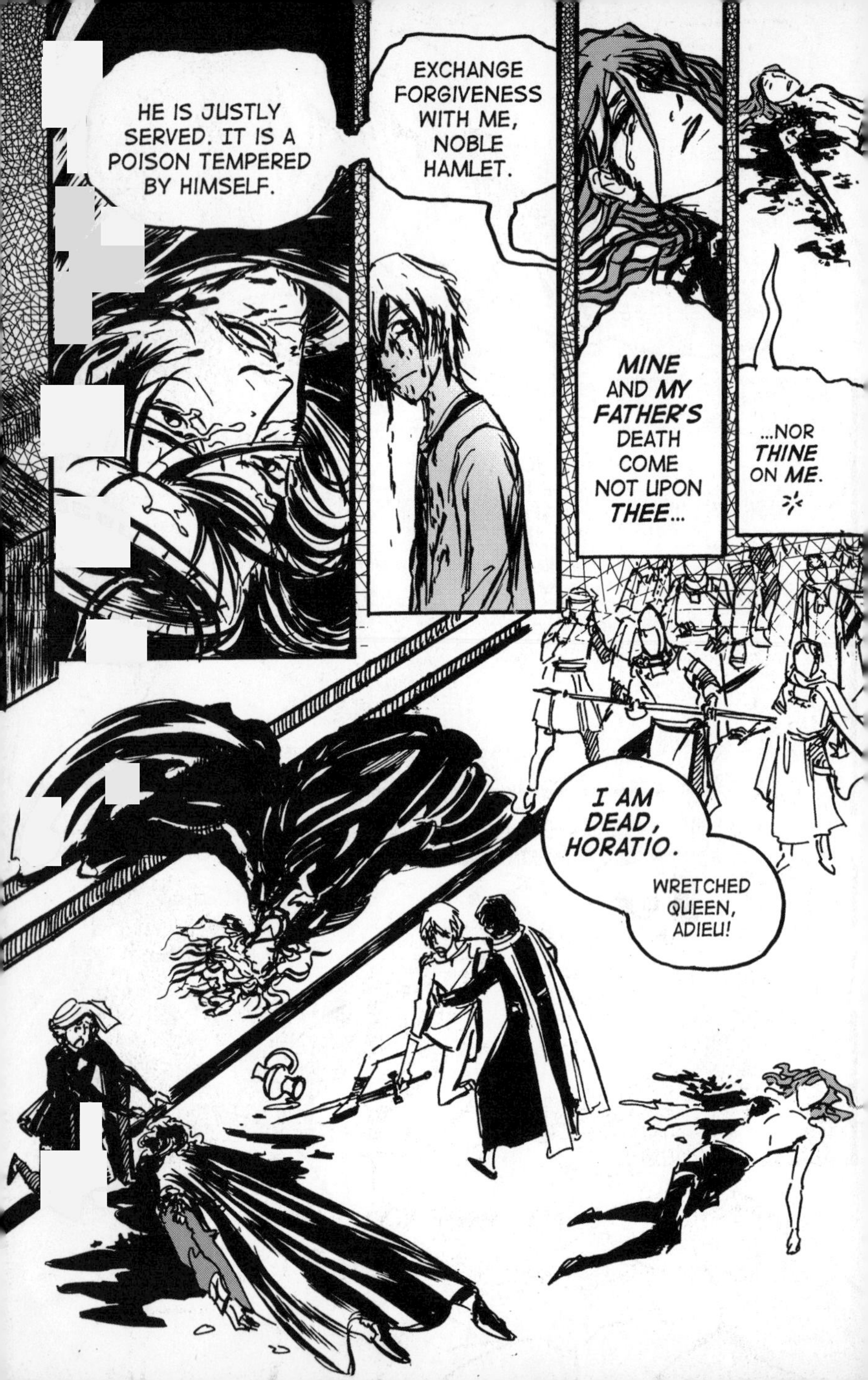
HE IS JUSTLY SERVED. IT IS A POISON TEMPERED BY HIMSELF.
EXCHANGE FORGIVENESS WITH ME, NOBLE HAMLET.
MINE AND MY FATHER'S DEATH COME NOT UPON THEE...
...NOR THINE ON ME.
I AM DEAD, HORATIO.
WRETCHED QUEEN, ADIEU!

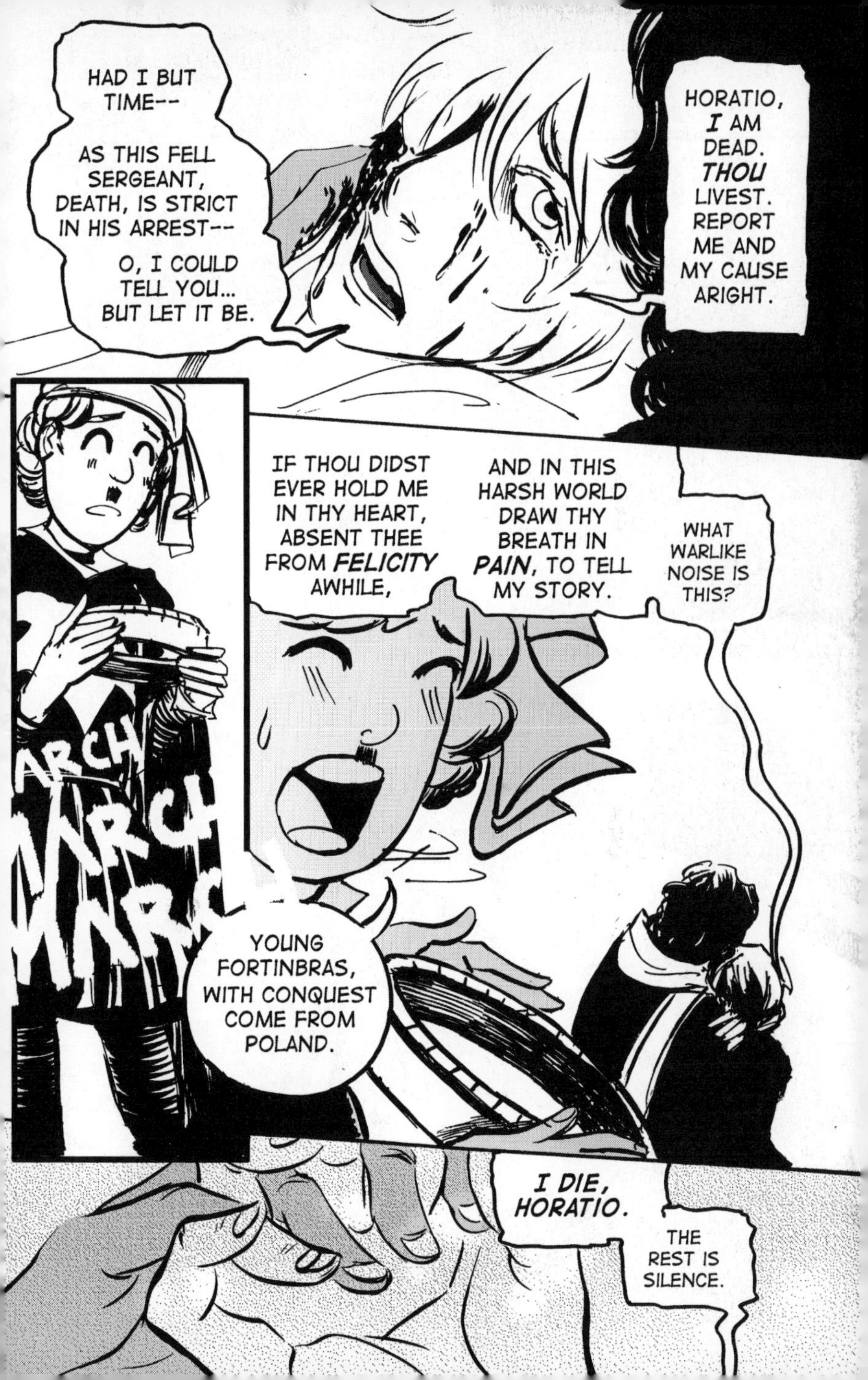
HAD I BUT TIME--
AS THIS FELL SERGEANT, DEATH, IS STRICT IN HIS ARREST--
O, I COULD TELL YOU... BUT LET IT BE.
HORATIO, I AM DEAD. THOU LIVEST. REPORT ME AND MY CAUSE ARIGHT.
IF THOU DIDST EVER HOLD ME IN THY HEART, ABSENT THEE FROM FELICITY AWHILE,
AND IN THIS HARSH WORLD DRAW THY BREATH IN PAIN, TO TELL MY STORY.
WHAT WARLIKE NOISE IS THIS?
YOUNG FORTINBRAS, WITH CONQUEST COME FROM POLAND.
I DIE, HORATIO.
THE REST IS SILENCE.

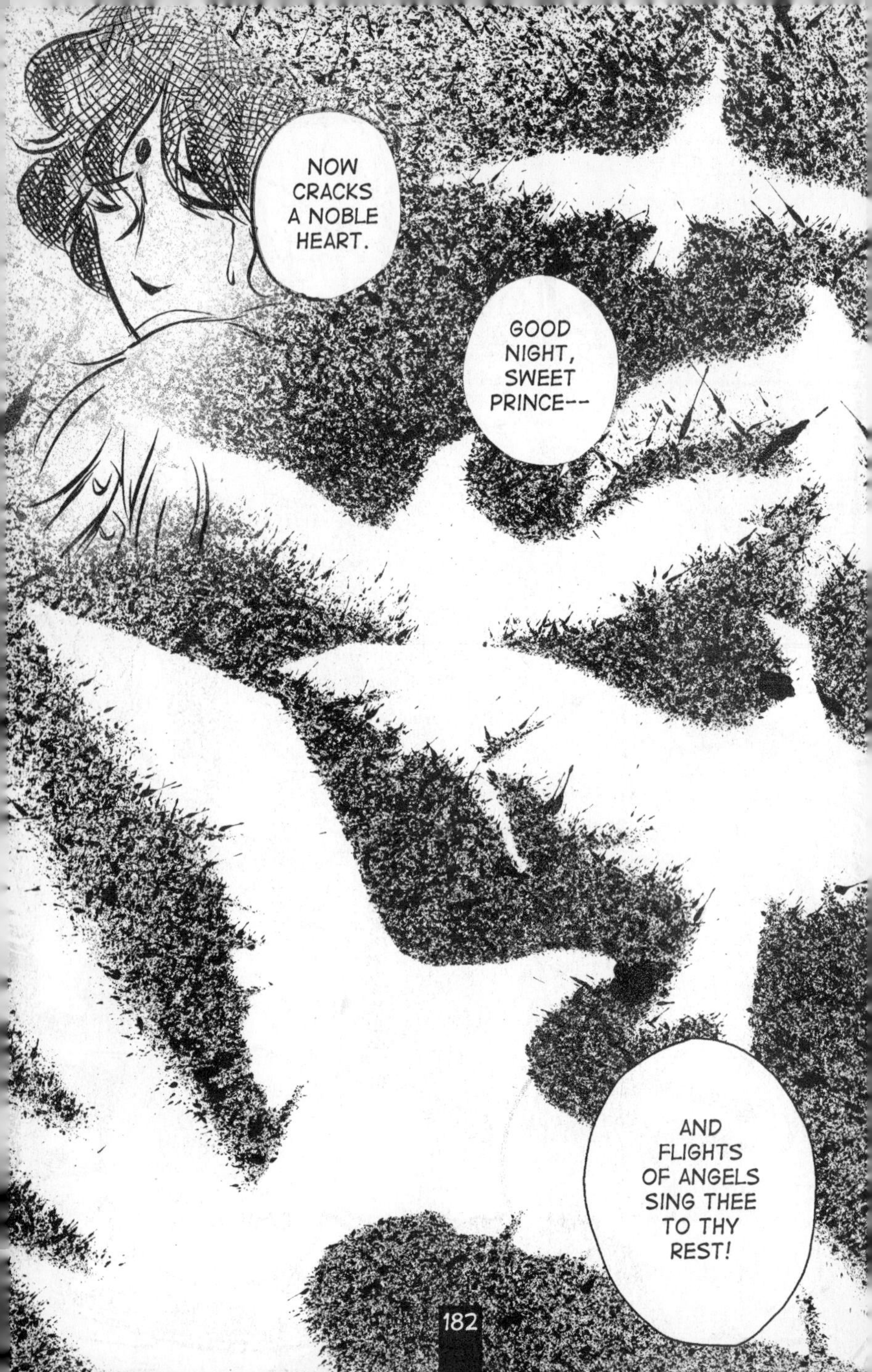
NOW CRACKS A NOBLE HEART.
GOOD NIGHT, SWEET PRINCE--
AND FLIGHTS OF ANGELS SING THEE TO THY REST!

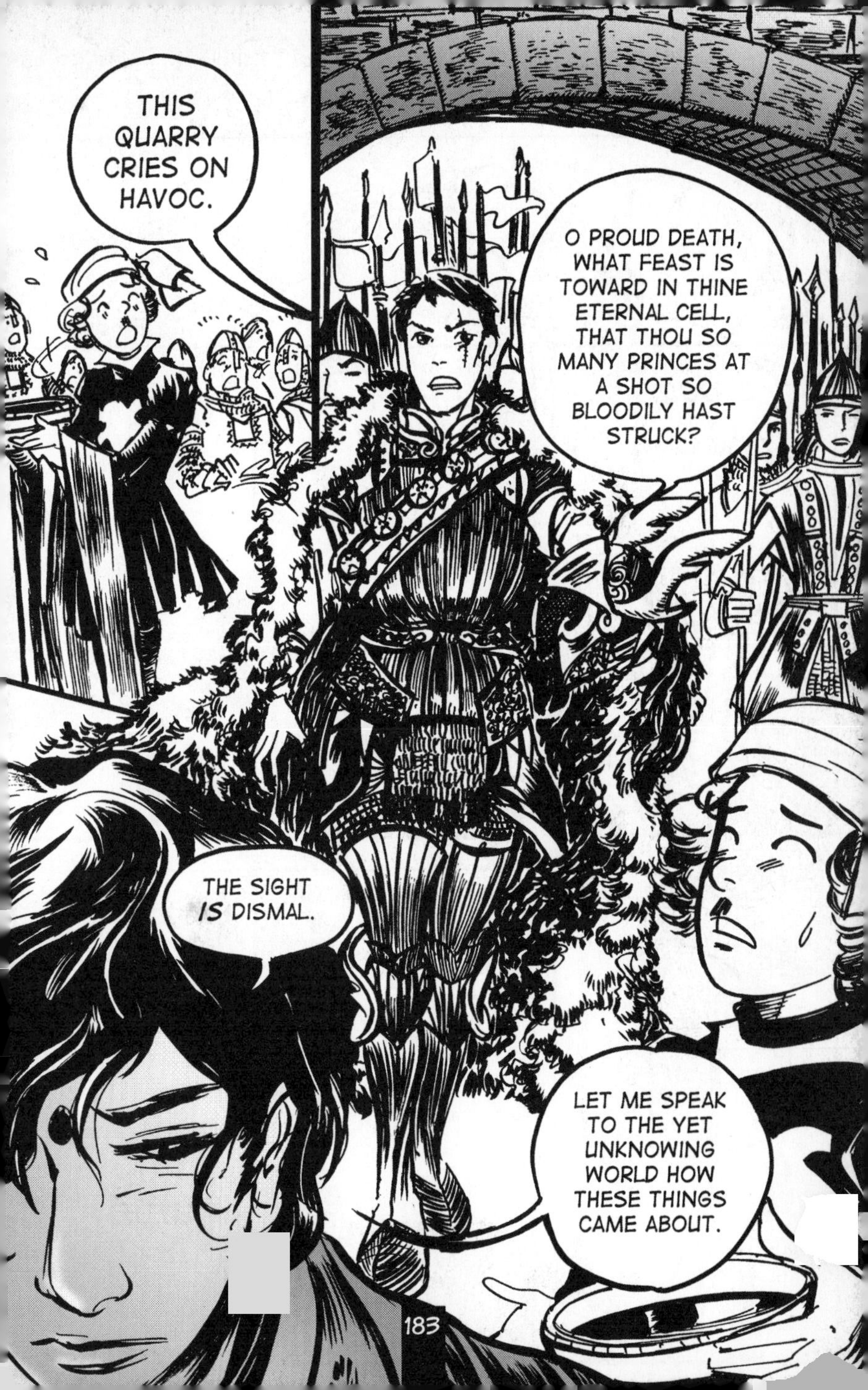
THIS QUARRY CRIES ON HAVOC.
O PROUD DEATH, WHAT FEAST IS TOWARD IN THINE ETERNAL CELL, THAT THOU SO MANY PRINCES AT A SHOT SO BLOODILY HAST STRUCK?
THE SIGHT *IS* DISMAL.
LET ME SPEAK TO THE YET UNKNOWING WORLD HOW THESE THINGS CAME ABOUT.

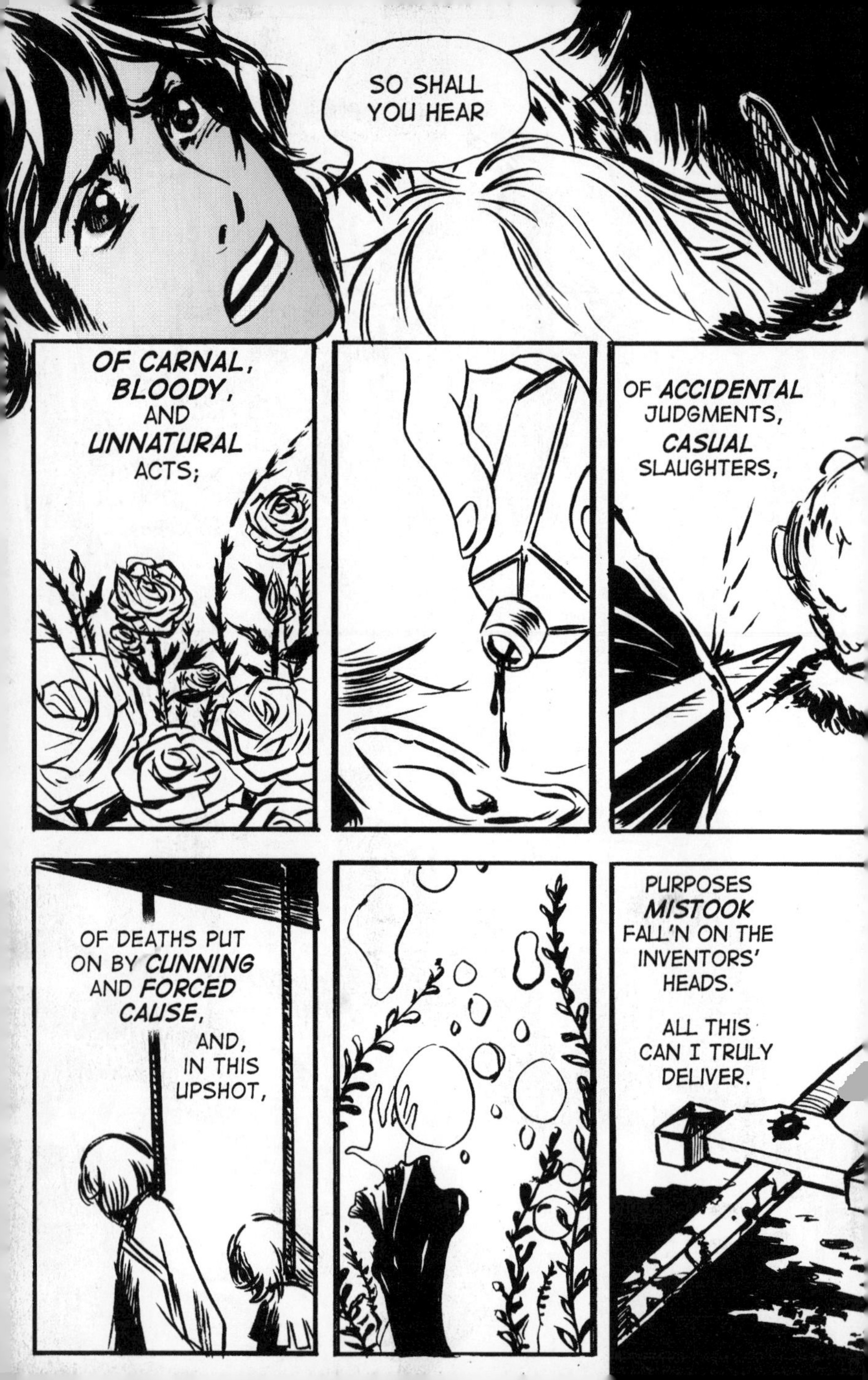
SO SHALL YOU HEAR
OF CARNAL, BLOODY, AND UNNATURAL ACTS;
OF ACCIDENTAL JUDGMENTS, CASUAL SLAUGHTERS,
OF DEATHS PUT ON BY CUNNING AND FORCED CAUSE,
AND, IN THIS UPSHOT,
PURPOSES MISTOOK FALL'N ON THE INVENTORS' HEADS.
ALL THIS CAN I TRULY DELIVER.

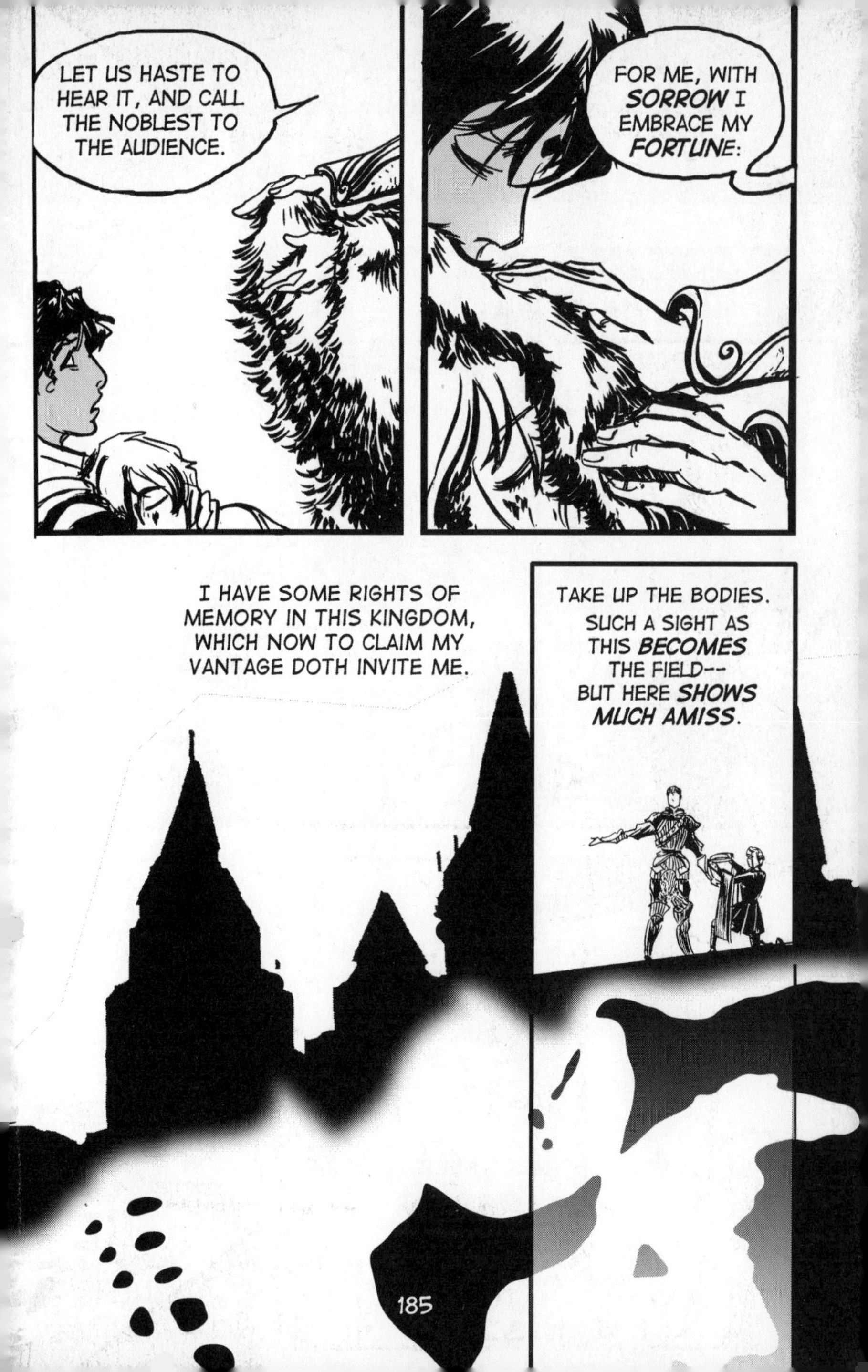
LET US HASTE TO HEAR IT, AND CALL THE NOBLEST TO THE AUDIENCE.
FOR ME, WITH SORROW I EMBRACE MY FORTUNE:
I HAVE SOME RIGHTS OF MEMORY IN THIS KINGDOM, WHICH NOW TO CLAIM MY VANTAGE DOTH INVITE ME.
TAKE UP THE BODIES. SUCH A SIGHT AS THIS BECOMES THE FIELD-- BUT HERE SHOWS MUCH AMISS.

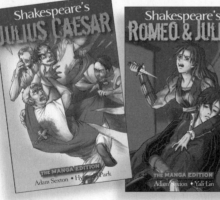